MOZART

Studies of
the Autograph Scores

MOZART

Studies of the Autograph Scores

ALAN TYSON

HARVARD UNIVERSITY PRESS
CAMBRIDGE, MASSACHUSETTS
AND LONDON, ENGLAND
1987

Publication of this book has been aided by a subvention from
the American Musicological Society

This book is printed on acid-free paper, and its binding materials
have been chosen for strength and durability.

Designed by Marianne Perlak and set in Linotron Sabon

Library of Congress Cataloging-in-Publication Data
Tyson, Alan.
Mozart: studies of the autograph scores.
Includes index.
1. Mozart, Wolfgang Amadeus, 1756–1791—
Manuscripts. 2. Music—Manuscripts. I. Title.
ML 410.M9T95   1987   780'.92'4   86-33487
ISBN 0-674-58830-4

Preface

THIS BOOK consists of articles (and, in two cases, talks) on aspects of Mozart and his autographs; they were written and for the most part published in journals or in celebratory volumes such as *Festschriften* between 1975 and 1986. (The original publications are listed on pages 361–362.)

Revised versions of the two talks, given in 1981 and 1983, form the first two chapters. They are placed at the beginning because of the introductory nature of their contents. The first provides a detailed survey of the background to two very helpful methodologies that can be used in examining an eighteenth-century composer's scores: a careful scrutiny of the watermarks in the paper, and a study of the way that the staves were ruled on it. The combination of such data, if evaluated with care, can often supply useful information as to the chronology of the music that the paper carries.

Such evidence is all the more welcome, because quite a large number of Mozart's autograph scores are inexactly or uncertainly dated; this applies in particular to his uncompleted ones ("fragments") and to those that form parts of larger compositions, such as the individual numbers that make up an opera. In such cases we probably have a precise date only for the finished work.

Revisions to the traditional datings of a variety of Mozart's autographs are not without implications for our estimates of his stylistic development in several genres, or even for certain aspects of his personality and biography, such as his compositional practices. These consequences were the subject of the 1983 talk, a summary of which constitutes the second chapter.

The published articles are reproduced here, with only minor

changes, in the approximate order in which they were written or first appeared in print. They too have been slightly revised, in part to bring them up to date and in part to expand certain matters in the light of more recently available information. In particular, about a hundred and twenty Mozart autographs, until World War II in the Berlin Staatsbibliothek and then outhoused in Silesia for security, disappeared in 1945 and came to light again only in 1977, having been deposited in the Biblioteka Jagiellońska in Kraków; they have been accessible to inspection and study there since 1980. The availability of such a large collection of very important Mozart scores (it includes, for instance, the first half of *Così fan tutte,* the second half of *Figaro,* and two of the three acts of *Idomeneo* and *Die Entführung,* as well as many important concertos and chamber-music works) has inevitably led to many fresh insights into the composer's working methods and the chronology of his output.

The penultimate chapter is an essay published here for the first time: it concerns the true version of Mozart's Rondo in A Major, K.386, for piano and orchestra. As is the case in all the other chapters, it attempts to take advantage of the methodology of paper-studies in arriving at useful conclusions. It is my hope that readers will be convinced by the practical utility of the techniques presented in this volume and will welcome the clues that they offer concerning aspects of Mozart's creativity.

A. T.

All Souls College, Oxford

Contents

MOZART

*Studies of
the Autograph Scores*

ABBREVIATIONS

AMA W. A. Mozart, *Kritisch durchgesehene Gesamtausgabe,* or *Alte Mozart-Ausgabe* (Leipzig, 1877–1905).

Anderson *The Letters of Mozart and His Family,* trans. and ed. Emily Anderson, 3d ed. (London, 1985).

Bauer-Deutsch; Eibl *Mozart: Briefe und Aufzeichnungen.* Gesamtausgabe, issued by the Internationale Stiftung Mozarteum, Salzburg. Bauer-Deutsch, I–IV: 4 vols., collected (and elucidated) by Wilhelm A. Bauer and Otto Erich Deutsch (Kassel, 1962–63). Eibl, V, VI: 2 vols. of commentary by Joseph Heinz Eibl (Kassel, 1971). Eibl, VII: index vol. compiled by Joseph Heinz Eibl (Kassel, 1975).

Köchel¹–Köchel⁶ Ludwig von Köchel, *Chronologisch-thematisches Verzeichnis(s) sämtlicher Tonwerke Wolfgang Amadé Mozarts.* Köchel¹: 1st ed. (Leipzig, 1862). Köchel²: 2d ed., ed. Paul Graf von Waldersee (Leipzig, 1905). Köchel³: 3d ed., ed. Alfred Einstein (Leipzig, 1937). Köchel³ᵃ: reprint of 3d ed., with supplement by Alfred Einstein (Ann Arbor, 1947). Köchel⁶: 6th ed., ed. Franz Giegling, Alexander Weinmann, and Gerd Sievers (Wiesbaden, 1964).

NMA W. A. Mozart, *Neue Ausgabe sämtlicher Werke,* or *Neue Mozart-Ausgabe* (Kassel, 1955–   ).

Plath, "Schriftchronologie" Wolfgang Plath, "Beiträge zur Mozart-Autographie II: Schriftchronologie 1770–1780," *Mozart-Jahrbuch 1976/77* (Kassel, 1978), pp. 131–173.

Verzeichnüss "Verzeichnüss aller meiner Werke vom Monath Febrario 1784 bis Monath . . . 1 . . ." Mozart's autograph catalogue of his compositions from 1784 to 1791, in the British Library, London (Stefan Zweig Collection). There are many editions of this catalogue, including facsimiles; one was edited by O. E. Deutsch (Vienna, 1938), and reissued in English (New York, 1956).

1

New Dating Methods:
Watermarks and Paper-Studies

THIS SURVEY of a new field of Mozart scholarship is divided
into three parts. In the first part, I describe how mold-made paper
(in German, *Büttenpapier*) is produced, and how watermarks are
formed in it. I also briefly review the methods and techniques for describing and reproducing watermarks. In the second part, I give a
historical account of Mozart's use of different kinds of paper, empha-
sizing those aspects that are of particular concern to musicologists.
And in the third part, I raise a number of more speculative issues, in
part chronological, which may provide a link with the work of other
Mozart specialists.[1]

I

TO GRASP how watermarks are formed, one must have a clear
understanding of how sheets of paper were made in Europe before the
invention of the papermaking machine at the beginning of the nineteenth century. This method has remained more or less unchanged for
some six hundred years. The paper was made by two men working as
a team, but with distinct roles; they were known as the vatman (in
German, *Schöpfer*) and the coucher (*Gautscher*). Their most important piece of equipment was a rectangular sieve called a mold (spelled
in Britain, "mould"; German, *Schöpfform*). They always worked with
a pair of molds. Those from which most of the sheets of paper used by
Mozart were made would have measured roughly 40–50 cm. by
60–70 cm.

The method is as follows: The vatman begins by dipping one of his
molds into a vat filled with paper "stuff"—that is, a white liquid prepared from broken-down linen rags. Holding the mold level above the

vat, and shaking it gently, he allows the excess water to drain through the wire mesh which forms the bottom of the mold. A more or less even film of the paper stuff settles on this mesh. The vatman then hands the mold to the coucher, who turns it over and presses it down onto a layer of damp felt. The paper stuff adheres to the felt by capillary pressure, so that when the coucher lifts the mold the paper remains on the felt, where it forms a thin layer. The coucher then hands the mold back to the vatman, in exchange for the other mold which the vatman is holding; and he will then take this second mold from the vatman and turn it over and press out another layer of paper— though before he does so he must interpose another layer of felt. By the time he has pressed out the paper layer from the second mold he will find that the vatman has refilled the first mold. And so on. The two molds are used in alternation, and beside the coucher there grows up an enormous "sandwich" of felt-paper-felt-paper-felt, known as a post.

From time to time the post is removed and squeezed in a press, to remove some of the water. Later the layers are separated; the paper stuff, now dry, is in the form of sheets of paper ("waterleaf"). Finally, the waterleaf is sized (to make it less absorbent), dried, and pressed.

It is clear that the two molds reflect the fact that there are two papermakers; this is a way of speeding up the work. And because the two molds were used in alternation, every second sheet came from a different mold. Furthermore, each sheet of paper produced by this method has two distinctive surfaces, the "mold side" (*Siebseite*), which originally lay against the mold's wires as it was being formed and therefore bears the impression of those wires, and the "felt side" (*Filzseite*), which was uppermost in the mold, but was then pressed out on to the mat of felt, and is smoother. With a bit of practice it is usually possible to distinguish these two surfaces in a piece of mold-made paper.

If one looks at a mold, one sees that it consists of a rectangular frame, strengthened by a number of wooden ribs or cross-struts (*Holzstege*) across its width. It is transformed from a frame into a sieve by the wire mesh which forms its bottom. The mesh has two kinds of wires. There are hundreds of thin wires running parallel to the long axis of the mold, very close together, called laid wires (*Rippen*); and there are several thicker wires, usually about 25–30 mm. apart, running at right angles to the laid wires and called chain wires (*Stege*). These chain wires are usually positioned above each rib.

As already stated, the wires of the mold produced an impression on the surface of the paper stuff that rested against them. But they also produced something more: a localized thinning of the finished paper, visible when the paper is held to the light. This thinning is, of course, a *watermark*. The marks produced by the laid wires are known as laid lines, and those produced by the chain wires are known as chain lines. But it is best to withhold the term "watermark" from the thinning of the paper produced by these purely structural wires (that can be called a moldmark), and to reserve it instead for the thinning produced by additional, ornamental wires sewn onto the surface of the mold (that is, attached to the laid wires and the chain wires). The purpose of these ornamental wires is to produce a distinctive mark in the paper, one that serves to identify its maker, or to indicate either its size or its quality—or a combination of any of these. For instance, the sheet-size of paper most commonly used by Mozart was the "royal" size, and the word "REAL" is very often found as part of a watermark. Probably the quality of the paper is what is indicated by the very common device of three crescent moons—"tre lune" paper.

I shall use the term "sheet-watermark" to describe the sum of the watermark elements found in a single sheet of paper. In Mozart's time, a typical sheet-watermark might show in the middle of one half of the sheet some letters indicating the paper mill or manufacturer (the letters GF or AM, for instance) with a device above them (a crown, perhaps, or a crossbow), and in the middle of the other half of the sheet three moons, with or without the word REAL under them. (See Figure 1.1.)

Since there were always two molds used in alternation in the paper-making, it is reasonable to ask if the watermark wires in each mold, and therefore the watermarks produced by each mold, were the same. The answer is, yes and no. From the papermaker's point of view, it would be sensible for all the sheets from the same batch to carry the same or similar watermarks. But the fact that almost every watermark occurs in two very similar forms was discovered, or perhaps rediscovered, as recently as 1951 by the late A. H. Stevenson and described in his classic paper, "Watermarks Are Twins."[2] These "twins" may be "identical" or "fraternal" twins. Since the watermark wires were sewn into each mold by hand, the sheet-watermarks produced by a pair of molds are never completely the same; it is always possible to find at least small differences between them—for example, in their positions in relation to the chain lines—and in Mozart's papers by far the commonest relationship is for one sheet-watermark to be the mirror image of the other.

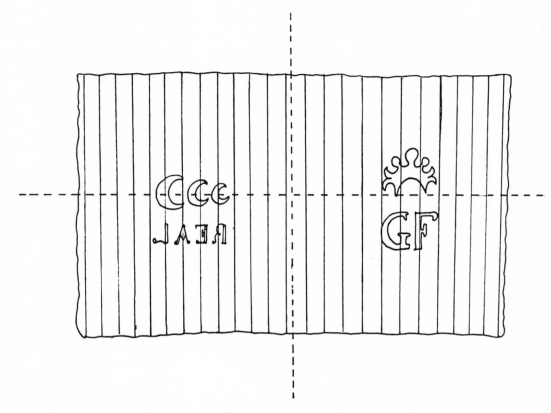

FIGURE 1.1. Sheet-watermark and its four quadrants.

But, it may be asked, how does one know that these are two different twin watermarks, and not merely the same watermark seen from
the other side of the paper? That is where the distinction between the
two sides of the paper, the mold side and the felt side, becomes useful.
It is necessary to standardize one's method, and to view *every* watermark either from the mold side, or else from the felt side, of the paper.
I have (arbitrarily) opted for a convention of viewing, tracing, and
photographing watermarks as they appear when seen from the *mold
side* of the paper. And if one does this consistently, one will find that
almost all Mozart watermarks are in mirror-image pairs. One consequence is that if parts of the watermark, such as letters, look "correct"
in paper from one mold, they will be back to front in paper from the
other mold. It is important to reproduce this feature accurately and
not to "correct" it. (And one frequently finds that the letters of the

word REAL are to be read in the opposite way to the other letters.)

The twin watermarks are distinguished as (the products of) Mold A and Mold B (see Figure 1.2).

WE ARE EVIDENTLY already passing from the subject of how watermarks are produced in paper to the subject of how watermarks should be copied and recorded. No reminder is required that this last is not an easy task. But if we understand the difficulties, perhaps we can overcome them.

In order to gain mastery of a watermark, we need to reconstruct the sheet-watermark of both the twin forms, that of Mold A and that of Mold B. But Mozart normally wrote on bifolia (*Doppelblätter*), and each bifolium can be shown to be the top half or the bottom half of a sheet. Thus a bifolium will have only half the sheet-watermark, and a leaf will have only a quarter of the sheet-watermark. The portion of the sheet-watermark that is on a single leaf is therefore described as a quadrant. In order to reconstruct the sheet-watermark, therefore, it is necessary to join the four quadrants, which will have been divided among four leaves (or between two bifolia). In doing so, we must be careful that the four quadrants which we are joining are all from the same mold—either Mold A or Mold B. We must avoid reconstructing "hybrid" forms, in which some Mold A quadrants are joined to other Mold B quadrants.

As is well known, it is not always easy to copy watermarks so accurately that the minor variations in them can be identified and compared. The traditional method has been to trace them. But anyone who has tried to trace watermarks on a light-box, or by means of a wedge-shaped light-source that can be slipped under a page, is likely to know that this is not a very accurate method—although it is of course the easiest and the cheapest. Some libraries in any case do not permit tracing. Photographing the leaf illuminated from behind has more to offer, even if the watermark is often obscured by the surface ink on both sides of the paper. The new technique of beta-radiography gives the best results. A radioactive source is placed on one side of the leaf with the watermark, and a piece of X-ray film on the other; a contact negative is then made in total darkness, the radiation from the source penetrating wherever the paper is thinner. Surface markings such as ink are not recorded, so that one gets a very clear picture of the watermark (see Figure 1.3). This technique, however, is available in only a few libraries, and it is expensive.

Nevertheless, it is possible to make much progress even by tracing

Type I

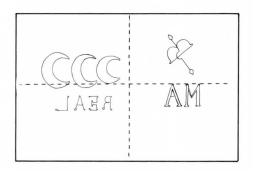

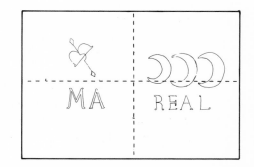

Mold A: selenometry = 86/14

Mold B: selenometry = 84/15

Type II

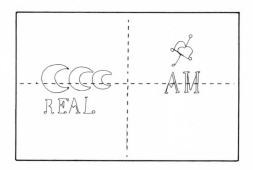

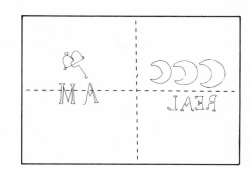

Mold A: selenometry = 80/18

Mold B: selenometry = 84/18

Type III

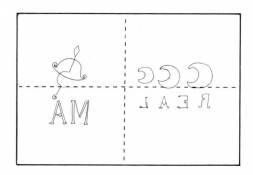

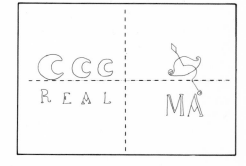

Mold A: selenometry = 86/17

Mold B: selenometry = 88/17

FIGURE 1.2. Twin watermarks.

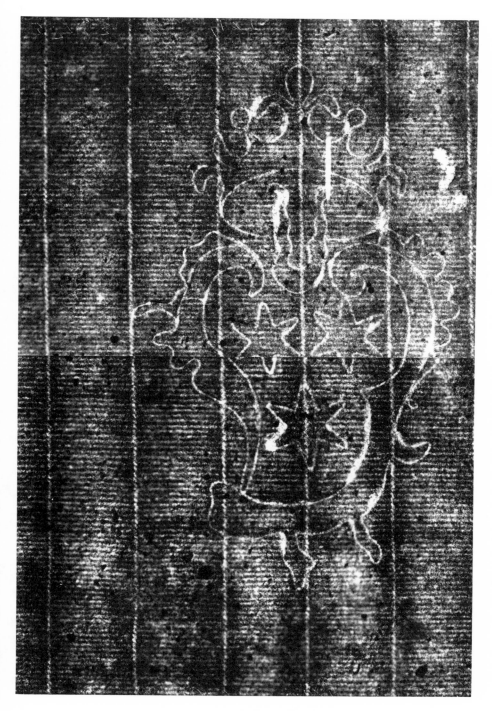

FIGURE 1.3. Beta-radiograph.

or by making simple measurements. Let me give an example. Almost all the papers used by Mozart include the three moons as part of the sheet-watermark. But the moons are far from identical; they are of varying sizes, and are variously placed. So I invented a technique that I have called (not wholly seriously) "selenometry." The two measurements that I have recorded in each case are shown in Figure 1.4. It is possible to note the selenometry in each of the two molds of a great number of watermarks, and when one finds a leaf which has the watermark of three moons only, one can often identify the paper-type from the selenometry alone.

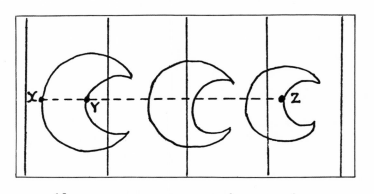

Mold A

x − y = 15 mm.
x − z = 85 mm.

selenometry of
Mold A = 85/15

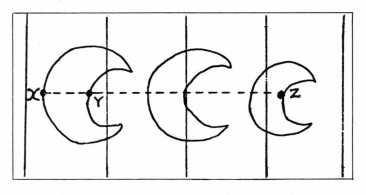

Mold B

x − y = 16 mm.
x − z = 83 mm.

selenometry of
Mold B = 83/16

FIGURE 1.4. Selenometry.

Let me sum up the more important points of this survey so far:

1. Since the unit of paper manufacture is the sheet and not the single leaf, watermarks should be described and reproduced in terms of the sheet and not in terms of what is on an individual leaf. (In any case, the watermark on a single leaf, being only a fragment of the whole, is often unintelligible by itself.)

2. In order to standardize one's method, it is best to describe watermarks as they appear when seen from the mold side, not from the felt side, of the paper.

3. The twin forms of each sheet-watermark need to be identified and carefully distinguished. Only when that has been done, and not before, can the watermark be said to have been thoroughly understood and mastered.

I have listed elsewhere some further conventions for analyzing and recording watermarks and for numbering the quadrants of each mold.[3]

I I

W E   A R E   N O W in a position to return to Mozart. In the past few years it has been my aim to inspect a great many of Mozart's autograph scores, and to examine, record, and compare the watermarks found in their leaves. Thus it has been possible to classify the autographs by the paper-types on which they were written. And when one has done that, one can begin to think about dating each of the paper-types. While examining an autograph score, I have found it essential to look at two other features besides the watermark.

The first of these is the "make-up" (*Lagen*) of the manuscript, for it is useful to see which leaves are single leaves (these are uncommon), and which are still halves of bifolia. It is important, too, to see which bifolia are gathered. (In a Mozart score, where two bifolia are gathered, they are usually the top and bottom halves of the same sheet, so that one can then reconstruct the original sheet and read the complete sheet-watermark.)

The second feature that I examine at the same time as the watermark is the rastrology or staff-ruling (*Rastrierung*). This is important enough to merit a short discussion by itself, especially since it can lead to some chronological conclusions.

How, and where, did Mozart's music paper receive its staff-ruling? Neither question can be completely answered at present. In regard to *how*, it is at least clear that some of it was ruled by hand and some by a machine. In some papers, we can see, the staves were drawn singly.

They are not parallel and no doubt were ruled by hand. But in other papers with ten or twelve staves we can see that all the staves are parallel and that the lines are straight. The distance from the top line of the top staff to the bottom line of the bottom staff, measured vertically, is constant. (I call this measurement the total span, or TS, and always make a record of it in millimeters.) Such regular staves were clearly all drawn at the same time, and not by hand but by a machine. These staff-ruling machines cannot have been uncommon, but it appears that we do not have a picture of one, or a detailed description of one, dating from the late eighteenth century.

The question of *where* Mozart's music paper was ruled has also not been fully answered yet. The obvious possibilities are these: at the place where the paper was made (usually a paper mill in North Italy), at the music shops in Vienna (where Mozart probably bought most of his paper), or in Mozart's home. For a number of reasons I believe that the paper was most commonly ruled at the music shops, at any rate in Vienna (and perhaps in Salzburg).

The possibilities for staff-ruling by machine seem to have been different in different cities, and because in Mozart's life geography can sometimes be a key to chronology, a word about this is appropriate here. The earliest paper that Mozart used in Salzburg was ruled by hand,[4] by means of a five-nibbed pen known as a rastrum (from the Latin for "rake"). Indeed it was not till about 1771 that the paper he bought and used in Salzburg was machine-ruled; from that time on, almost all the oblong (*Querformat*) paper that he used in Salzburg was machine-ruled, although some "upright-format" (*Hochformat*) paper bought in Salzburg about 1775–1777 was ruled by hand.

In Italy, in Paris, and in Vienna he seems always to have used machine-ruled paper. But in Munich and Prague he often had recourse to paper ruled several times with a 2-staff rastrum (to make twelve or fourteen staves).[5] No doubt this was hand-ruled; and the same is surely true of some paper ruled twice with a 5-staff rastrum (to make ten staves), paper that he acquired at some point during his travels in 1789.[6] (In all these cases the unusual rastrology is accompanied by unusual watermarks.)

It will probably not have escaped attention that as a general rule Mozart used 10-staff paper in Salzburg and 12-staff paper during the Vienna years.[7] I think I have discovered an explanation for this: it appears that Mozart could not buy 12-staff machine-ruled paper in Salzburg. So he was forced for the most part to make use of 10-staff paper there. Occasionally he returned from a visit to Vienna or a trip to Milan with some 12-staff paper, which he then saved for Salzburg compositions that required a lot of staves, as, for example, the *Regina Coeli,* K.108(74d), of May 1771, which is on Viennese paper,[8] or the *Litaniae de venerabili altaris sacramento,* K.125, of March 1772, on paper from the second Italian journey.[9] But he did not have any left for the Concerto for Three Pianos, K.242; so he took 10-staff machine-ruled paper, and drew by hand two extra staves, one at the top and one at the bottom of each page.[10]

It would be convenient if it could be demonstrated that Mozart never used 10-staff paper after he had moved to Vienna in March 1781. But that cannot be done: he did very occasionally use it. It is significant that several of the examples of 10-staff paper from after March 1781 are found in scores dating from the second half of 1783, when Mozart was once again living for a few months in Salzburg—and apparently once again unable to purchase 12-staff paper there.

Although 16-staff paper was readily available in Vienna—it was used sometimes by Mozart's pupil Thomas Attwood, and almost exclusively by Beethoven after his arrival there at the end of 1792—Mozart himself seems always to have preferred 12-staff paper. He used it even in a score like the *Requiem,* with four vocal parts (eight, if we distinguish soloists and chorus), and an orchestra of strings, basset-horns, bassoons, trumpets, trombones, timpani, and organ.[11] In fact, one finds 16-staff paper in only one large-scale mature score, that of the C-Minor Piano Concerto, K.491.[12]

THIS IS NOT the place for a chronological review of all the different paper-types that Mozart employed, and their watermarks. I shall mention only a few points about them.

The earliest paper-type used by Mozart in Salzburg—it is the paper of Nannerl's Notenbuch, and he continued to use the type till about 1771—has a *wilder Mann* watermark (see Figure 1.5). It was made at the Lengfelden Mill in Salzburg, and the letters ISH stand for Johann Sigismund Hofmann, at one time the owner of the mill. From about 1772 one finds a new set of initials in the paper used by Mozart: AFH, standing for Anton Fidelis Hofmann.

From the long journey of 1763–1766, which took the Mozart family to Paris, London, The Hague, Amsterdam, Paris again, Lyons, Geneva, Munich, and elsewhere, we have three scores on paper bought in England: the symphony K.16; a second symphony once listed as K.18

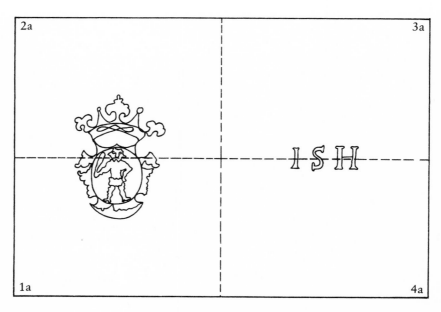

Mold A

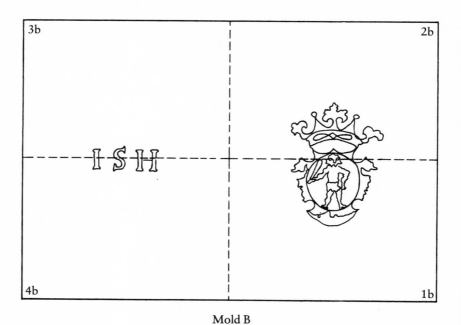

Mold B

FIGURE 1.5. *Wilder Mann.*

(but now known to be a copy made by Mozart of a symphony by Carl Friedrich Abel, so today listed as A 51 in Anhang A of Köchel[6]); and the motet "God Is Our Refuge," K.20. Another group of scores and orchestral parts (usually copied by Mozart's father, Leopold) has the monogram of Pieter van der Ley, a well-known Dutch firm of paper-makers. It appears to include K.19, 21(19c), 22, 23, 32, 78(73b), and 79(73d)—works composed in London (K.19 and 21) as well as at The Hague (K.22, 23, 32, and probably K.78 and 79). Did Leopold there-fore buy the paper at The Hague and use it to copy out works written earlier in London?

There is not much evidence of French paper in these years, except for the set of parts (in Leopold's hand) of the newly recovered sym-phony K.19a (Anh. 223), and another score of K.21(19c), both on paper with the watermark of "G Malmenaide," a firm in the Auvergne. Was this paper purchased in France *before* the Mozart family went to London? Or after their return to France in 1766? Or was it perhaps obtainable at places other than in France? From the very end of the years of travel we find in the recitative and aria K.36(33i), known as "Licenza," paper from another French firm, "M Johannot" of Annonay. The aria was performed, it seems, only three weeks after the Mozarts returned to Salzburg at the end of 1766; the preceding recitative, like the compositions of 1767, is on *wilder Mann* paper.

New papers were introduced with the 1767 trip to Vienna. I believe that the very coarse paper used for the symphony K.45, dated 16 Janu-ary 1768, may have come from Olmütz.

Figures 1.6 and 1.7 are rough drawings of the watermarks in the papers that Mozart used on his first, second, and third Italian jour-neys, as well as in a paper that I formerly suspected he acquired when he visited Munich at the end of 1774 for the performance of *La finta giardiniera*, K.196, in January 1775. It is found in the surviving auto-graph scores of Acts II and III of that opera. And I now think that perhaps he was already using it in Salzburg while preparing the opera, before leaving for Munich on 6 December 1774.

Immediately after his return to Salzburg from his third and last Ital-ian journey in March 1773, Mozart began regularly to use paper of a size that he had scarcely ever employed before. This is the size that Köchel calls *Klein-Querformat* (small oblong format). At least five types can be identified—three very common and two very rare (see Figure 1.8). Mozart must have liked this small paper, for he continued to use it in the next six years, even taking some of it with him on the

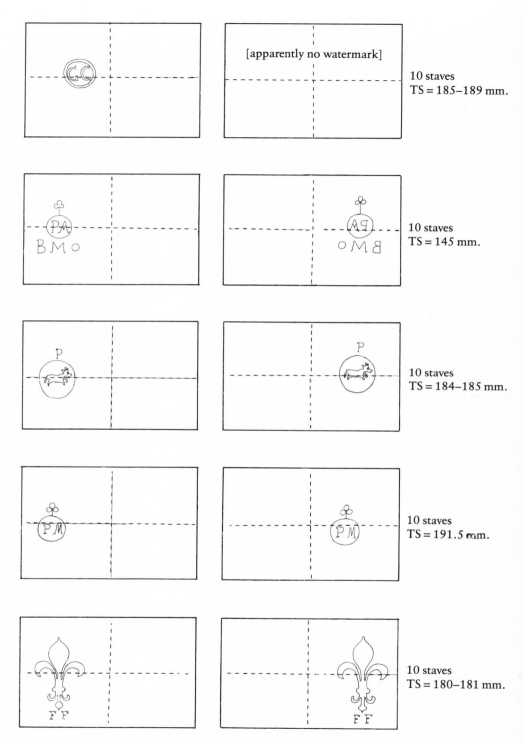

[apparently no watermark]

10 staves
TS = 185–189 mm.

10 staves
TS = 145 mm.

10 staves
TS = 184–185 mm.

10 staves
TS = 191.5 mm.

10 staves
TS = 180–181 mm.

FIGURE 1.6. First Italian journey: end of 1769 to early 1771.

Second Italian journey: 1771

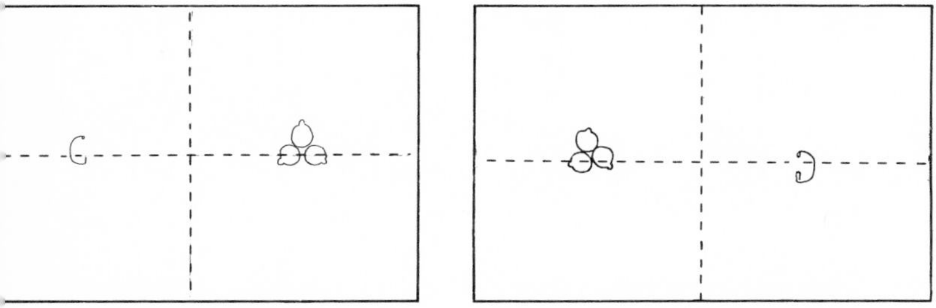

10 staves
TS = 184.5–185 mm.
and 188–188.5 mm.

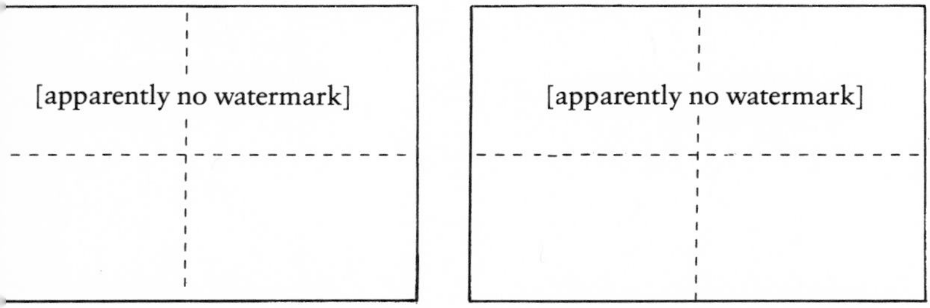

[apparently no watermark] [apparently no watermark]

12 staves
TS = 193 mm.

Third Italian journey: 1772–1773

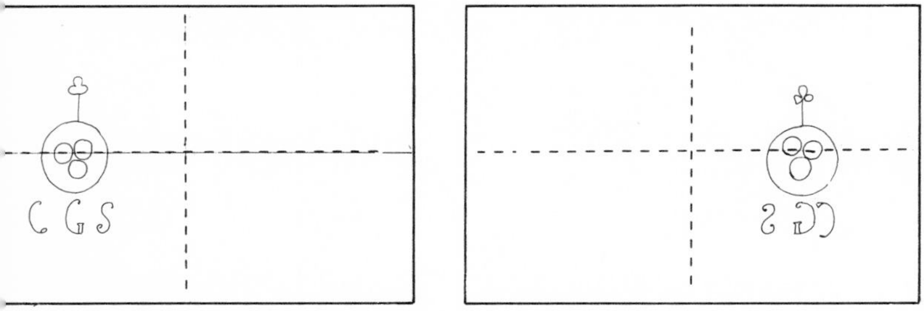

10 staves
TS = 203 mm.

Salzburg/Munich: ca. December 1774–January 1775

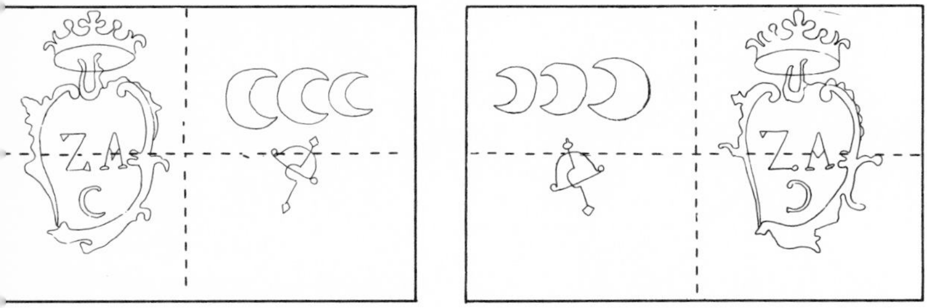

10 staves
TS = 189 mm.

nometry — 74/15   selenometry — 81/20

FIGURE 1.7. Some of the watermarks from 1771 to 1775.

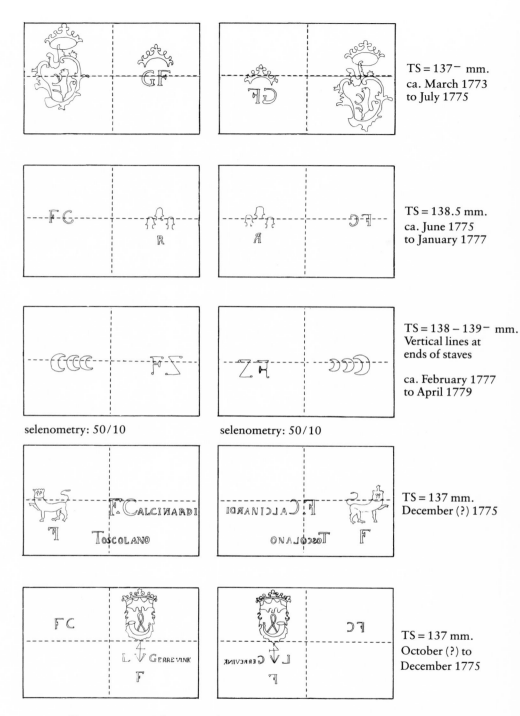

selenometry: 50/10   selenometry: 50/10

FIGURE 1.8. *Klein-Querformat* Papers: 1773–1779 (all with ten staves).

grand voyage to Munich, Mannheim, and Paris in 1777–1779. It has seemed to me to be especially important to determine exactly the periods within which each of these small-oblong-format papers was used, because the dates on so many of the scores from these years have been altered or crossed out. Luckily there are several that have not been tampered with; I have used these as my guide (see Chapter 12).

The last small-oblong paper seems to have been used about April 1779. After that, Mozart reverted to larger 10-staff paper—until the move to Vienna in March 1781, when he changed to 12-staff paper, as we have already seen.

One aspect of the change in the number of staves at this point I found instructive; it was not accompanied by a change in the paper-type. K.369, a soprano aria, is on 10-staff paper, and is dated: "Monaco [= Munich] li 8 di marzo 1781." And K.371, a rondo for horn, is on paper with the *same* watermark, but with twelve staves; it is dated: "Vienne ce 21 de mars 1781"—only thirteen days later. Did Mozart therefore sometimes carry unruled paper around with him, and have it ruled locally?

I I I

BEFORE WE TURN to look at a few interesting chronological problems, I should briefly state the simple principle that underlies the application of paper-types to chronological matters. It is the assumption that as a general rule compositions on the same paper-type are likely to have been written—or at any rate to have been begun—within the same period of time.

Perhaps this is clearest when we consider Mozart's very late papers. One paper-type is found in only six datable works, all from the last nine months of his life: K.612, 614, 616, 620, 623, and 626. Thus it seems reasonable to assign four undated autographs on the same paper-type to the same period. These are, it proves, four fragments: K.615a is a fragment in F for a mechanical clock (as is the completed Andante, K.616, dated 4 May 1791), with several sketches on the same leaf for *Die Zauberflöte;* K.515a (Anh. 87) is a fragment of an Andante in F for string quintet; and K.515c (Anh. 79) a much longer fragment (presumably of an Allegro) in A minor, also for string quintet. Should we suppose these to be two fragments of an unfinished string quintet in A minor? Mozart had already finished a string quintet in D, K.593, in December 1790; and he completed a second quintet in E-flat, K.614, on 12 April 1791. Was an A-minor quintet started as a companion piece to those other two—or was it perhaps overtaken and replaced by K.614?

The fourth fragment on this paper-type is part of K.412(386b) + 514, the horn concerto in D: fols. 5—6 of the first movement, containing a series of substitute passages and additions to what had been written on the first four leaves. But should one describe the D-major horn concerto as a "fragment"? Paper-studies indicate that the completion of the first movement and the fragmentary score of the rondo (there is no slow movement) both date from 1791. It is clear that the concerto remained unfinished at Mozart's death; I read the date at the end of Süssmayr's somewhat idiosyncratic completion of it as "Vienna Venerdì Santo li 6 Aprile $\overline{792}$."[13]

One objection to dating scores by their paper-types will no doubt always be made: "But surely Mozart could have been using *old* paper?" Certainly he did so from time to time—but not, in my experience, often—and then in most cases he used only single leaves (not normally bifolia). For instance, the song "Gesellenreise," K.468, is dated "Vienna, 26 March 1785"; but it is on the upright-format 14-staff paper of French origin that Mozart had employed seven years earlier in Paris for the first two movements of the A-Minor Piano Sonata, K.310(300d). It is of significance, however, that the autograph of the song consists of a single leaf. (Did Mozart sometimes, desperate for paper, search through old autograph scores for a blank leaf that he could remove?)

It appears to be the case that Mozart bought paper in comparatively small quantities and used it up before buying more. And perhaps the next batch of paper, even if bought at the same shop, might have a different watermark—or the same watermark but a different TS, the staves having been ruled on a different occasion. This is the justification for making a record of the TS at the same time as the watermark is noted; it may enable further chronological discriminations to be made.

Sometimes, too, when Mozart appears to have been using old paper, that turns out not to have been the case. For the true situation in some instances is that Mozart took a long time to complete a work—or, to put it another way, the work remained for a long time, perhaps for a year or even two years, in the form of a "fragment." Thus the date on which he completed the work (the date that he would write on the first page of the autograph, or enter in his Verzeichnüss— the little work-catalogue that he started to keep in February 1784) applies to the last part of the score but not the first part; and the paper on which he finished the work is later than the paper on which he began it. But that does not make it "old paper," for when he wrote down the first measures it was "new paper." A few examples may make this clearer:

1. The Piano Concerto in C, K.503, was entered in the Verzeichnüss on 4 December 1786. But the paper of what was originally the first six leaves (they are now fols. 1–5 and 7) comes from the winter season of two years earlier, the period from about November 1784 to about March 1785. So the beginning probably remained a fragment for two years.

2. The Piano Concerto in A, K.488, was entered in the Verzeichnüss on 2 March 1786. But its first eight leaves seem to have come from a time between about March 1784 and February 1785—from one season, or possibly two seasons, earlier. Here then is another fragment that Mozart later completed. In doing so he found himself in a season when his orchestra had clarinets; so the original oboes were changed to clarinets, as one can see in the autograph.

3. The first work in the Verzeichnüss, the E-flat Concerto K.449, was entered there under the date of "9 February 1784." But it seems that the opening tutti and solo exposition were written down in 1782, at the time of the three concertos K.413(387a), 414(385p), and 415(387b). Then Mozart abandoned the score, scribbled in the margins, and sketched an aria on a blank side. Much later—perhaps over a year later, at the beginning of 1784—he resumed work on the concerto, deleted the aria sketch, and completed the score. Thus the first 170 measures of K.449 are from 1782 and the rest of the concerto from 1784. The implications of this for style-analysis surely need to be worked out.[14]

My attention has been drawn by Wolfgang Plath to two or three scores from the early 1770s in which the handwriting of the start is of an earlier type than that of the continuation. Here are two of his examples:

4. The symphony K.129, dated "May 1772."

5. The *Missa in honorem Sanctissimae Trinitatis*, K.167, dated "June 1773."

What is interesting here is that paper-studies confirm the *Schriftchronologie*, the dating based on Mozart's handwriting. For in both these cases the paper-type at the start is of a different kind from, and older than, the rest. Thus it is tempting to seek the help of *Schriftchronologie* over other examples from the Salzburg years, such as:

6. The *Litaniae de venerabili altaris sacramento*, K.243. This work

is dated "March 1776." But its first four leaves are on the paper that
Mozart acquired at the end of 1774, either in Munich or in Salzburg
just before leaving for Munich. Did he start to write K.243 in Munich,
or very shortly after his return to Salzburg, but then abandon the attempt, returning to work only a year later? The idea seems worth
investigating.

I CLAIM—on the evidence of its paper—that the Piano Sonata in B-
flat, K.333(315c), was not written in Paris in 1778 (the traditional
view, although already challenged by Plath), but was written in or
around Linz about November 1783 (see Chapter 6). Thus the "concertante" piano-writing makes sense, because we can assume that the
sonata was completed just before Mozart plunged into a whirlpool of
activity, which included the composition of several piano concertos,
in the 1783–84 winter season in Vienna. I wish we could find an appropriate context for the three sonatas K.330–332, for clearly they
were *not* written (as the prevailing view has it) in Paris in 1778. The
autographs are on 10-staff paper; could they date from Mozart's visit
to Salzburg in the second half of 1783?

A new chronology of the piano sonatas should be combined with a
new stylistic appraisal, for several of the rather late sonata fragments
seem to have been wrongly dated. One that has proved especially
problematical is a G-minor movement, K.312. (Mozart wrote everything up to four measures before the recapitulation; the rest is by an
unknown hand.) In the first edition of Köchel's catalogue (Köchel[1]) it
was placed in 1778; in Köchel[3] Einstein moved it back to the end of
1774. But in the 1947 supplement Einstein decided that the summer
of 1790 was a better date—so it is now K.590d. The watermark of the
autograph is almost cut off (the two leaves were trimmed to fit into a
volume that Mendelssohn gave to his bride),[15] but it is nevertheless
possible to identify it. The paper-type was first used by Mozart in the
middle of his work on *Così fan tutte,* and was then available to him
up to the end of his life. So the fragment dates from 1790 or 1791;
Einstein's second thoughts were better than his first in this case.

Most dating involves assigning a date to a *complete* work, although,
as I have suggested, both paper-studies and *Schriftchronologie* can occasionally offer different dates for the beginning and for the end of a
piece.

This is of particular interest in a work like an opera. A composition
of that length usually has several paper-types, and if one is patient one

may be able to discover which parts of an opera were written first, and which were written later. In 1975 I published an article on the internal chronology of *La clemenza di Tito* (see Chapter 4). It appears that Mozart first tackled the ensembles, and perhaps the solos of Tito, before undertaking the big soprano arias. In *Die Zauberflöte* it is probably possible to distinguish by their paper those parts that were written (or perhaps rewritten) only after Mozart had returned from Prague to Vienna in September 1791.

Occasionally a piece of luck may help one to date the progress of work on an opera. Fol. 29 of the autograph of *Die Zauberflöte* is the penultimate leaf of the first number. It contains only two measures of music and is a substitute for the fifteenth leaf of that number, which must have contained a long cadenza for the Three Ladies. (The beginning and end of this cadenza, crossed out, will be found on fols. 28 and 30 of the score.)

It seems to me that this leaf originally came from the same sheet that yielded two other leaves to Mozart, on which he wrote out the motet "Ave verum corpus," K.618. The motet is dated "Baaden, li 17 di giunnio 1791." Thus it seems likely that Mozart was already revising the first number of *Die Zauberflöte* by the second half of June. On 2 July 1791 he wrote to Constanze:

Ich bitte dich sage dem Süssmayer dem Dalketen buben, er soll mir vom ersten Ackt, von der Introduction an bis zum *Finale,* meine Spart schicken, damit ich instrumentiren kann.[16]

[Please tell that idiot Süssmayr to send me my score of the first act, from the Introduction to the Finale, so that I can orchestrate it.]

Was this referring to the filling in of the inner parts, in his score that already existed as a "particella," with voice-parts and bass-line written down?

FINALLY, it must be admitted that the evidence of paper-types sometimes tempts one to speculation of a very bold sort. In 1978 Sotheby's auctioned in London an autograph clarino primo part for the "Paris" Symphony, K.297(300a). Unlike the score of the symphony, this part proved not to be on French paper, but on paper used very occasionally by Mozart in his middle Viennese years.

The other examples of this paper-type all seem to date from around December 1786—the second half of the piano concerto K.503, most of the first part of the "Prague" Symphony, K.504, and two fragments, one of which, K.504a(Anh. 105), was probably Mozart's first idea for a slow movement for the "Prague." In copying out the clarino primo part of the "Paris" Symphony about December 1786 (no doubt to replace a lost part), Mozart may have been planning to perform that work on his forthcoming trip to Prague.

The finale of the "Prague" Symphony is on a paper that Mozart had used for the most part much earlier in the year, to write the last two acts of *Figaro*. When in 1980 I saw the autograph of the symphony in Kraków, my first reaction was, "Was the finale written *before* the rest of the 'Prague' Symphony?" The writing looks rather different from that of the first two movements—although that could result merely from a difference of pens or of ink.

Then it occurred to me: "Did Mozart really plan to present *two* D-major symphonies in Prague?" According to F. X. Niemetschek, there were on this occasion performances there of a D-major and of an E-flat symphony.[17] And I began to wonder if Mozart had at first intended to give the "Paris" Symphony, and had then decided that he must write a new finale for it, and produced the movement that we now call the finale of the "Prague." (Both finales begin with a phrase that descends from the fifth of the scale.) If that is what happened, Mozart then perhaps saw the danger of putting new wine into old bottles, and wrote the first and second movements of the "Prague," so that he had a new *symphony* for Prague, and not merely an old symphony with a new *finale*. That might help to explain the absence of a minuet in so late a work as K.504.

Such speculation may at times appear somewhat too bold. Nevertheless, this is a good example of an entertaining hypothesis that finds some support from the useful and increasingly dependable discipline of paper-studies.

2

Redating Mozart: Some Stylistic and Biographical Implications

M U C H of Mozart's output certainly gives the impression of being securely dated. But the rearrangements of the work-order introduced by the 1937 and 1964 editions of Köchel's catalogue (Köchel³ and Köchel⁶) suggest that in many instances a good deal of uncertainty must remain. Köchel's, as we know, was conceived as a chronological catalogue, so that any changes in the dating of compositions have led and must lead to the Köchel numbers being changed and the works' sequence being rearranged.

Recent work on Mozart autographs—not only on completed scores, but on fragments, drafts, and sketches as well—has resulted in further redating. (The rearrangement has not yet taken place.) Two new methods have been used. One is *Schriftchronologie*, the chronology of the handwriting, described in the previous chapter. The expert here is Wolfgang Plath of Augsburg, one of the *Editionsleiter* of the *Neue Mozart-Ausgabe* (NMA). He has made a careful study of the changes from year to year in Mozart's handwriting, so that undated scores can often be assigned a fairly exact date. Plath's chief publication on this so far has been on the period 1770–1780, which began with Mozart's fourteenth birthday and ended just before his twenty-fifth (see Plath, "Schriftchronologie"). (It is not surprising, I think, that Mozart's handwriting changed quite a lot through his teens and the following years, before a more settled form was reached.) The other new method has been an investigation of the various paper-types—usually distinguished by their watermarks, or perhaps by details of the staff-ruling—that Mozart used at different times in his life. I am the chief proponent of this method. Fortunately the two methods have given results that are in the main consistent with, or supplementary to, each other.

BEFORE I turn to my main theme, the stylistic and biographical implications of the new datings, it is worth our while to examine the
relation between *Schriftchronologie* and paper-studies. I shall begin
with the most striking instance where they give *different* results. It
should be possible to reconcile the discrepancy, however, without
having to reject either of the two techniques.

The work that raises the difficulty consists of the choruses and
entr'actes that Mozart wrote for the play *Thamos, König in Aegypten,*
K.345(336a). The autograph sources are in Berlin (Staatsbibliothek
Preussischer Kulturbesitz); they consist of the entr'actes on oblong-
format paper and the choruses on upright-format paper. Most of the
entr'actes are on a paper found also in K.243, the *Litaniae de venerabili
altaris sacramento,* the autograph of which is dated "March 1776,"
and in K.102, the finale that Mozart wrote at some undetermined
time in order to make a symphony out of the overture to his April
1775 opera *Il Rè pastore,* K.208 (Köchel[6] gives this the number
K.213c and offers a tentative dating of August 1775). Only the
entr'acte No. 7a is on a different paper: this is found elsewhere,
folded differently to produce an upright-format shape, in the divertimento K.251, dated "July 1776." Thus the paper of the entr'actes is
matched in other Mozart autographs from the year 1776. Plath dates
them by the handwriting to "c. 1777";[1] there seems no doubt that
they were written before the *grand voyage* of the years 1777–1779 to
Paris and other places.

The paper of the choruses in *Thamos* can also be matched in other
dated scores from the same time. For it too is found in the divertimento K.251 of July 1776, and also in two church sonatas, K.244 and
K.245, dated "April 1776." It is found as well in several undated
scores, *all* of which have been assigned to the years 1776 or 1777.[2]
Thus it would seem plausible to assign the choruses in *Thamos* to the
same time as the surviving entr'actes—to 1776 or 1777.

But *Schriftchronologie* gives a different message: according to Plath
the surviving autograph of the choruses dates from 1779 or even
later.[3] Yet no other autograph from these years is on paper of this type,
with upright format: in the years 1779 and 1780, to judge from the
dated scores of K.317–321 and K.336–339, Mozart was using quite
different papers.

There is no doubt that Plath is right: the writing in the choruses is
different from that in the entr'actes. Perhaps the most plausible explanation is that, for an unknown reason, though possibly after some re-

vision, Mozart decided to recopy the choruses, and concluded that his task would be easier if he used paper of the same size and shape as before; so he purchased a small stock of the paper he had been using three or four years earlier. (This would not have been difficult, for the paper came from a mill in Salzburg itself.)

The problem we come up against, then, is the obscure stage-history of the play—the times that it was played at Salzburg, and its various revivals.[4] It would seem that we have entr'actes from 1776 or 1777, and choruses from 1779 or 1780. Here paper-studies can easily be reconciled with *Schriftchronologie*.

One more example of the relationship between *Schriftchronologie* and paper-studies: they can often supplement as well as reinforce each other, in that each may have "control" over a different period. Let us consider Mozart's violin concertos. There are five of these: K.207, 211, 216, 218, and 219; their autographs are all dated, and they were apparently all completed in 1775—on 14 April, 14 June, 12 September, in October, and on 20 December. But the dates on all these autographs have been tampered with, as is the case with many of the scores from the 1770s: in a number of instances the last two figures have been changed to read "1780," or at least some date in the 1780s, before being changed back again to a date—but the *right* date?—in the 1770s.

Plath's studies of the handwriting suggest that the first concerto, K.207, was written in 1773, not in 1775.[5] That is a most interesting idea. Paper-studies cannot help here, for Mozart used the same paper from 1773 to the middle of 1775, when he changed to another type. Thus paper-studies are only good at distinguishing between what belongs to the time before the middle of 1775 and what belongs after that. By this test, K.207 was written before, and K.216, 218, and 219 after; K.211 has paper of both types, which is of course quite right for a work of June 1775. Putting the two disciplines together, we find that K.207 is probably from April 1773, whereas K.211, 216, 218, and 219 are all from 1775.

THIS LEADS ME to my main theme: what are the stylistic, and what are the biographical, implications of the violin concerto in B-flat (K.207) being written two years earlier than the other four? Does it matter? In my view, it should matter a great deal. Mozart at nineteen was not the same as Mozart at seventeen, even if Salzburg was something of a backwater. In any case, he and his father had spent over two months in Vienna in the summer of 1773 and three months in Munich in the winter of 1774–75. The latter visit included the production of his opera *La finta giardiniera,* K.196; the visit to Vienna is often characterized as the occasion on which it is most likely that he first encountered the revolutionary music of Haydn, such as the Opus 20 quartets and several of the so-called *Sturm und Drang* symphonies. But perhaps none of this affected his view of what a violin concerto might be—or can we now, alerted by the revised chronology, see some differences between the first violin concerto and the other four?

It is certainly to be hoped that when we hear of probable new datings, we shall be provoked into inquiring into their implications for problems of style and for matters of biography. In order to do this, let us examine a number of different genres.

We shall begin by considering a few church works—or rather, fragmentary church works. I have in mind the Kyrie fragments K.91(186i), K.196a (Anh. 16), K.258a (Anh. 13), K.323, and K.422a (Anh. 14); the Gloria fragment K.323a (Anh. 20); and two settings of psalm texts, K.93 and K.93a (Anh. 22). As is normally the case with fragments, none of these was given a date by Mozart. And the Köchel numbers assigned to them indicate that only one, the Kyrie fragment K.422a, is believed to have been a product of Mozart's Vienna years—the ten and a half years starting in March 1781 and ending with his death there in December 1791. All the others are assigned to the Salzburg period.

That is not mere chance. It has long been considered an obvious truth that Mozart wrote no church music in his Vienna years apart from three works: the incomplete C-Minor Mass K.427 (417a), composed (in fulfillment of a vow) for performance in Salzburg during his brief return there in 1783 (and partly resurrected in Vienna in 1785 as the cantata *Davidde penitente,* K.469); and two works of the last year of his life, the little motet "Ave verum corpus," K.618, written for a friend who was choirmaster at Baden, and of course the unfinished *Requiem,* on which he was working in his last three months. It would seem that any wish to write solemn music of a devotional kind found ample expression in masonic music, written for his lodge.

It was a surprise to me, therefore, to discover that all the fragments mentioned above except one (K.258a) were on a single paper-type—a type that (to judge from many dated scores) Mozart seems never to have used before December 1787, when he had returned to Vienna from Prague after the first production of *Don Giovanni;* he continued to use it throughout 1788 and into 1789. K.258a, too, is on a paper from Mozart's last years. So did Mozart turn to church music in 1788? If so, what was in his mind?

It is relevant here to note that in 1953 it was discovered that two of the fragments, the psalm settings K.93 and 93a, were in fact copies made by Mozart of pieces by Georg Reutter the younger, the Hofkapellmeister who had died in 1772; in Köchel[6] they are listed in Anhang A as "A 22" and "A 23." And recently Monika Holl has discovered that K.91(186i) is part of a Kyrie by Reutter—so that too will one day be moved to the Anhang.[6] But if around 1788 Mozart was making transcriptions of church works by an esteemed Viennese Kapellmeister who had worked at St. Stephan, perhaps he was seeking to master the style that would land him a position as a church composer.[7] It is a fact that in May 1791 he was promised the succession to the position of Kapellmeister at St. Stephan whenever it fell vacant—but that was not to be until March 1793, too late for Mozart.

To return to 1788: on 2 August Mozart wrote to his sister—the last known letter he ever wrote to her—saying that he would like Michael Haydn in Salzburg to lend him scores of his two "tutti-masses" and also of some graduals.[8] So he apparently wished to study the church music of Michael Haydn as well as of Reutter. On 24 August 1788 a Danish visitor to Vienna entered in his diary (published in Copenhagen the following year) an account of a visit to Mozart which included the sentence: "He is now working on church music in Vienna, and since the operetta has come to an end, he has nothing more to do with the theater."[9] This was just after Mozart had completed his last three symphonies, on 26 June, 25 July, and 10 August.

In the light of all this, what are we to make of the splendid Kyrie in D minor, K.341(368a)? Its autograph disappeared in the early nineteenth century. Köchel's own number for it followed Otto Jahn, who assigned it to Mozart's stay in Munich from November 1780 to March 1781, the time of *Idomeneo*. The clarinets in the scoring obviously rule out Salzburg—but the later Viennese years had also been ruled out because it was formerly thought that Mozart had never turned toward church music at that time. We now know that view to be mistaken.

Nevertheless, most of those who listen to the D-Minor Kyrie today feel that none of it is beyond the ability, or remote from the style, of the Mozart who was writing *Idomeneo*. That is the essence of the problem: there are almost no examples on which it is possible to base an opinion of changes in the style of his church music from 1780 to 1791. And might not his style within this genre at any rate have remained a trifle static? [10]

THERE IS ANOTHER genre in which I suspect the same is true: *opera seria*. How far would we trust ourselves to date an *opera seria* aria—or a concert aria—by its style? The following example may serve as a warning.

The concert aria "Ah se in ciel, benigne stelle," K.538, has strong claims to be a late work, apparently written in 1788 for Mozart's sister-in-law Aloysia Lange, née Weber, the singer with whom he had been in love in 1778, four years before he married her younger sister, Constanze. An autograph score of the work has survived: it is on paper of the same type, used almost exclusively in 1788, as that on which he wrote those church-music fragments that have just been examined; it is inscribed "per la Sig.ʳᵃ Lange. Aria. Vienna li 4 di Marzo. 1788"; and Mozart entered the work in his Verzeichnüss under the same date.

There has also come down to us a so-called particella of the aria, consisting of the voice-part and bass-line only. In the summer of 1982 I inspected it (it is privately owned in Bavaria) and was astonished to find that it was not on Viennese paper but on paper from Kandern in the margraviate of Baden, not very far from Basel—paper that had been used by Mozart in Munich when writing *Idomeneo*.

If this was a Munich (or possibly a Mannheim) paper, when did Mozart write the particella? (There are small divergences, mainly in underlay, between it and the 1788 full score, which also has some extra measures at the end.) I began to wonder if Mozart had produced the aria at some concert in or near Munich on the way to (or back from) the coronation of the Emperor Leopold II at Frankfurt in October 1790. But *Schriftchronologie* cannot permit such a date. The particella must have been written down long before the surviving full score; and Plath and I together have reached the conclusion that K.538 was really composed in 1778, and that the particella probably was written out at the time of Mozart's visit to Munich at the end of that year, with Aloysia "Weber," not "Lange," in mind—the same voice, but ten years earlier.

Yet it would in my view be a bold person who could claim that the style of the concert aria was recognizably that of 1778, not of 1788.

Until now, indeed, it has not been suspected that K.538 is not in every aspect a late work (see Chapter 14).

B U T   W H A T E V E R may be thought of church music and *opera seria* as genres perhaps manifesting some fixity of style, we must surely feel different about Mozart's writing for the piano. Let us consider the piano sonatas, for instance. An early set, K.279–284, was assigned by Köchel to the year 1777. Plath's "Schriftchronologie" has now suggested "early 1775," the time when Mozart was in Munich for the production of *La finta giardiniera*, K.196;[11] and paper-studies also suggest that the sonatas are on paper purchased in Salzburg or in Munich around that time.

The next three sonatas, K.309–311, can probably also be dated fairly accurately. K.310, the famous A-minor sonata, is not only on French paper but was dated "Paris 1778" by Mozart. The current view is that K.309 in C and K.311 in D were both written at Mannheim early in November 1777. One of the two certainly was, for we learn from Mozart's letter of 6 December that its slow movement had been written to suit, and probably to depict, the character of Rose (Rosina) Cannabich, a young lady whom he was teaching.[12] Was this the Andante of K.309 or of K.311? To attempt to assess which movement corresponds more closely to Mlle Cannabich's character is certainly an unusual dating technique! But the autograph of K.309 has not survived; that of K.311 is on small-oblong paper carried about by Mozart in the three years 1777–1779—and since he did use it in Mannheim in December 1777 for the flute quartet K.285, he might well have written K.311 there in the preceding month. Its slow movement is marked "Andante con espressione," but it is usually K.309 that is taken to be Rose Cannabich's sonata.

We can at any rate follow the course taken by Mozart's piano writing in these nine sonatas, written almost certainly from 1775 to 1778, and we can compare it with his other compositions of those years. But now the trouble starts. The next four sonatas, K.330–332, and K.333, which Köchel had assigned to 1779, were moved back a year by Einstein (in Köchel³) to the Paris summer of 1778. There is nothing to be said for this; the autographs are not even on French paper. In 1982 I presented a case for K.333 being "the 'Linz' Sonata," written about November 1783 while Mozart was on his way back to Vienna after his visit to Salzburg that summer (see Chapter 6). It is possible to

point to the "concertante" style of certain passages, including the cadenza in the last movement, as harbingers of the big Vienna performing and teaching season of 1784.

The dates of K.330–332 are still unresolved. These sonatas are
mostly on a rare paper, matched only by that of three orchestral
minuets, K.363—which are also undated. I now think Mozart may
have written them during that Salzburg visit in the summer of 1783,
again with the teaching that lay ahead in Vienna in mind. (The right
hand is written in the soprano clef—see Figure 2.1—is that evidence
of their use as teaching material?) If then K.330–332 and K.333 are
all from the summer or fall of 1783, should it not make a difference
that these four famous sonatas were composed not in 1778 but five
years later?

Mozart's other Vienna sonatas are dated by his Verzeichnüss. But
fragments of course remain undated. There is the fragmentary movement in G minor, completed by someone else after Mozart's death,
which is to be found in some modern editions of the sonatas. Köchel
gave it the number K.312, assigning it to 1778. In 1937 Einstein re-
numbered it in Köchel[3] as K.189i, locating it at the end of 1774. But
in 1947 he changed his mind and relocated it in the summer of 1790,
with the number K.590d. And paper-studies now confirm that a date
of 1790 or 1791 is correct. Some other sonata fragments, however,
that Einstein also attached to June 1790 (K.590a, 590b, and 590c)
are on the 1788 paper-type to which I keep on returning.

I need not labor the point that until Mozart's sonatas and sonata-
fragments are arranged in the right order and are correctly dated, we
shall be in some confusion about this side of his stylistic development—and about the way he spent his time.

PERHAPS we can learn something about the way he allocated his
time from another Mozartian genre, his fragments. By his fragments I
mean those plentiful unfinished pieces, neatly written, that look very
much like autograph scores up to the point at which they break off. In
an essay on the fragments published in 1981 I suggested that a large
number of them were perhaps not rejected or abandoned pieces, but
rather that they represented "work in progress," not abandoned so
much as set aside (see Chapter 11). The analogy here might be to an
artist's studio, with a number of unfinished canvases around the walls,
on which the artist was not working at that moment but to which he
hoped to return later. This led me to the thought, "Did Mozart ever

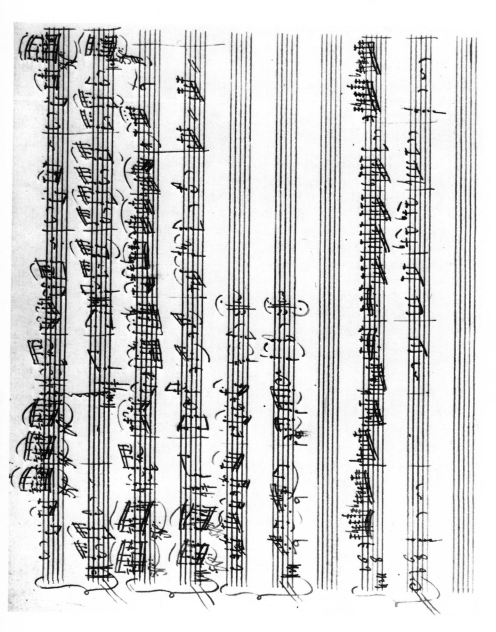

FIGURE 2.1.1. A page of the autograph of the piano sonata K.332, in the Scheide Library, Princeton.

complete such fragments, then?" and I found that there were a number
of works, including the well-known piano concertos K.449, K.488,
and K.503, the first movements of which appear to have remained as
fragments for well over a year before the movement and then the work
was completed.

This discovery of course flies in the face of some clichés about the
way that Mozart worked: conventionally he is supposed to have written everything down with great fluency, after having worked it all out
in his head. Maybe he worked like that often, but clearly not always:
some of the most admired compositions of his later years were written
in stages, over quite a long time-span. This has been known for years
about his string quartets; but did we expect it of his piano concertos?
I do not think I did. But perhaps there was not much point in completing a piano concerto if there was no opportunity to perform it;
the existence of one or two fragments might mean that Mozart had a
head start if the chance of giving a concert suddenly arose.

The notion that a number of Mozart's later works were written over
a long period gives rise to two further thoughts:

1. The dates in his Verzeichnüss tend to be the dates when pieces
were completed. If those dates come close together, we are likely
to say, "That was an intensely productive week—or month—for
Mozart." But what if this closeness merely denotes a forthcoming
concert or concert series, with a lot of fragments conceived much earlier finally being finished off? We meet a similar problem in an artist's
studio, when a forthcoming exhibition leads him to finish, to varnish,
and perhaps to date a lot of canvases that have mainly been painted
much earlier.

2. Any sharp picture of stylistic development must acknowledge
that some works were started, and in certain cases a good part of the
first movement outlined, long before their completion date in the
Verzeichnüss, which has hitherto been loosely treated as their composition date. The implications of this for style-study are obvious, and
I need not dwell on them.

MANY of the works that have been discussed are important ones.
But if we are to get a full picture of how Mozart was occupied,
we must also focus on the smaller occasional pieces that he produced.
He seems to have omitted some of them from his Verzeichnüss because of their trivial character; and scholars who did not understand
this have assumed that they were therefore works written before the

Verzeichnüss was begun in February 1784, and have dated the works accordingly.

Several of the pieces associated with his convivial friend Gottfried von Jacquin fall into this category. The comic terzetto "Das Bandel," K.441, is therefore assigned to 1783; but its 16-staff paper, most unusual in Mozart's autographs, is a leftover from the C-Minor Piano Concerto, K.491, of March 1786, suggesting that 1786 is the correct year for the terzetto. The notturni K.436–439, for two sopranos and bass with accompaniments from three clarinets or basset-horns, are also assigned to 1783; but I am sure they are no earlier than 1787, and perhaps rather later.

Other aspects of the von Jacquin relationship still await an explanation. In dating the autographs of K.516, 520, 521 (all May 1787) and K.526 (August 1787), Mozart adds the address "Landstrasse." Why? And K.520 has the additional information: "im Herrn Gottfried von Jacquins Zimmer." What is the meaning of all this?

Another light-hearted piece, a contredanse, strangely titled on the autograph "Les filles malicieuses," is entered in the Verzeichnüss under the date of "6 March 1791" and so is given the Köchel number K.610. But both *Schriftchronologie* and paper-studies show that it was written much earlier—perhaps at Salzburg in 1783. (See Figure 2.2.) What is going on? Who are "les filles malicieuses"? And why would a 1783 work be entered under a 1791 date? These are the kinds of "biographical implications" that my chapter title implies.

L E T M E in conclusion try to draw a few threads together by glancing at some of the works assigned to the last twelve months of Mozart's life, from December 1790 to December 1791.

K.593, the D-major string quintet, dated "December 1790," is apparently a late work all through. But it seems probable that much of the first, second, and fourth movements were written down before his trip to Frankfurt in the fall, and therefore remained fragments for several months.

K.595, the B-flat Piano Concerto, is dated "5 January 1791." But it is my view that much of this concerto was first written down as a fragment in 1788, a large part being on the familiar 1788 paper. The concert of the clarinettist Josef Bähr on 4 March 1791 must have given Mozart the incentive to complete it.

As for K.610, the contredanse dated "6 March 1791," I have already proposed this as a work of around 1783. K. 609, five other con-

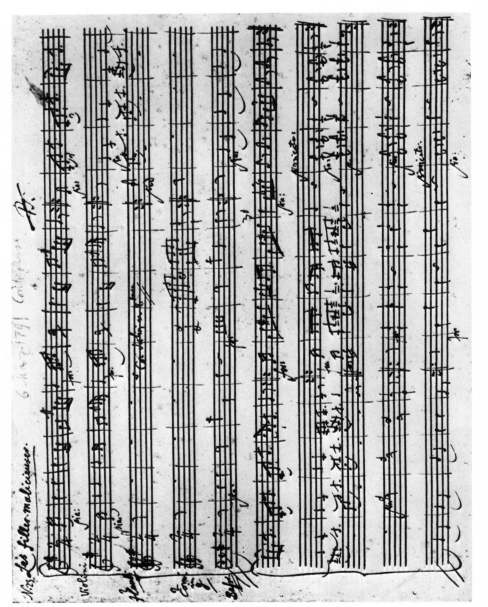

FIGURE 2.2. First page of the autograph of the contredanse K.610, "Les filles malicieuses," in the Newberry Library, Chicago.

tredanses, the last of which duplicates K.610, should also be placed earlier, probably in 1787–88.

K.622, the Clarinet Concerto, was probably completed in October. But the first 199 measures of the first movement are almost identical with a fragment of a basset-horn concerto, K.621b; this fragment was probably written down a year or two earlier, possibly even as early as 1787.

Did Mozart then write almost nothing new in 1791? Of course he did. Beyond what Köchel[6] lists for those months, there is another work not to be found there, the D-major horn concerto, K.412(386b) + 514; most of this was written in 1791, though Mozart never completed the rondo.[13] And of course there are the two last operas, *Die Zauberflöte*, K.620, and *La clemenza di Tito*, K.621.

It is well known that Mozart had virtually completed *Die Zauberflöte* by July 1791 and that he then went on to write *La clemenza di Tito*, finishing that in Prague, where it was performed on 6 September; then he returned to Vienna, wrote the overture and the Priests' March for *Die Zauberflöte* by 28 September, and conducted its premiere two days later. What paper-studies can show us is that three second-act numbers were also written—or perhaps rewritten?—after Prague: the terzetto of the three boys, "Seid uns zum zweiten Mal willkommen," Pamina's famous G-minor aria, and the B-flat terzetto "Soll ich dich, Teurer, nicht mehr sehn?" And paper-studies also indicate that none of the *Requiem* was written down before the return from Prague.

So we learn in this way quite a lot about Mozart's activities in his last twelve months. Once again the implications for style-analysis are obvious. It is important that anyone claiming to investigate Mozart's *Spätstyl* should be aware of *all* the compositions of this final year, and should not be led astray by the contemplation of works that we now know to have been wholly or at least partly written at an earlier period. A sound chronology is clearly the essential basis for assessing changes in style.

3

New Light on Mozart's "Prussian" Quartets

THE AUTOGRAPH SCORES of Mozart's last three string quartets, K.575, 589, and 590, have been in the British Library since 1907, along with the autographs of the six quartets dedicated to Haydn and the so-called "Hoffmeister" Quartet, K.499.[1] They are often known as the "Prussian" quartets, since they were evidently written with King Friedrich Wilhelm II of Prussia in mind; he was a keen cellist, and these quartets contain striking solo passages for the royal instrument. Mozart had visited the king at Potsdam at the end of April 1789 (and had played before him in Berlin on 26 May) in the course of a tour with Prince Lichnowsky that took him also to Prague, Dresden, and Leipzig. He returned to Vienna, after revisiting Prague, on 4 June, and in the thematic catalogue that he kept of his compositions (the Verzeichnüss) we find an entry for the first quartet (K.575, in D) which runs as follows: "im Junius. in Wienn. Ein Quartett für 2 violin, viola et violoncello. für Seine Mayestätt dem könig in Preussen." Apart from the further entries in this thematic catalogue, all the other references to the quartets come from Mozart's letters to his fellow mason Michael Puchberg. The clear aim of those letters was to borrow money from Puchberg (or to reassure him about the chances of repayment); this fact should be borne in mind in assessing the truth of the statements contained in them. The letter of 12–14 July 1789, for instance, after describing Mozart's financial plight and requesting a loan, enumerates his prospects: "I am composing six easy clavier sonatas for Princess Friederike [the king's eldest daughter] and six quartets for the king, all of which Kozeluch is engraving at my expense. At the same time the two dedications will bring me in something."

Again, writing probably on 29 December 1789, Mozart promised repayment to Puchberg, and added: "This summer, thanks to my work for the King of Prussia, I hope to be able to convince you completely of my honesty." Early in May of the next year he asked for a further loan: "I must have something to live on until I have arranged my subscription concerts and until the quartets on which I am working have been sent to be engraved." Later that month, on about 17 May, Mozart told Puchberg that grief and worry over his debts "had prevented me all this time from finishing my quartets"; he was proposing to perform the quartets at home the next Saturday, and invited Puchberg and his wife to come. Finally, on about 12 June 1790, Mozart wrote: "I have now been forced to give away my quartets (that exhausting labor) for a mere song, simply in order to have cash in hand to meet my present difficulties. And for the same reason I am now composing some clavier sonatas."[2] We find the B-flat quartet K.589 entered in Mozart's catalogue under the date of May 1790, and the F-major quartet K.590—the last quartet he wrote—under the date of June. Significantly, perhaps, neither entry refers to the King of Prussia. The three quartets were finally published by Artaria just after Mozart's death, in an edition that bore no dedication.

THE AIM of the present chapter, and of the following one on *La clemenza di Tito*, is to apply certain techniques of paper-analysis to major scores by Mozart, and—putting it at its tersest—to see if the method can throw some light on the way in which those works were written. Several of the physical characteristics of the autographs of the three "Prussian" quartets are summarized in a highly condensed form in Table 3.1. The first column records the present foliation of the quartets in the British Library's Add. MS 37765 (in that foliation the quartets are out of proper sequence). The next column shows the paper-type of each leaf, and the last column the watermark quadrant (a single leaf is a quarter, or "quadrant," of a complete sheet of paper); the a or b that follows the quadrant number distinguishes between the twin forms—derived from the two molds (sieves) used in papermaking—of each sheet-watermark. In Figure 3.1, which illustrates the three paper-types, the information beside the watermark drawings records the number of staves to each page and the total span (TS) in millimeters of these staves, measured from the top line of the top staff to the bottom line of the bottom staff. Whatever else may be obscure in the table, it will I hope be clear that in writing out these quartets Mozart used paper of three types, readily distinguishable from one

TABLE 3.1. The "Prussian" Quartets: contents and physical characteristics of the autograph scores.

Movement	BL's Foliation	Paper-type	Watermark quadrant
K.575 in D major ("June 1789")			
I 1r	1	I	2a
	2	I	3a
	3	I	4a
	4	I	1a
II 5r	5	I	2a
	6	I	3a
III (M) 7r	7	I	2b
	8	I	3b
IV 9v	9	I	4b
	10	I	1b
(9r, system 2 =	11	I	2b
false start)	12	I	3b
	13	I	2b
	14	I	3b
K.589 in B-flat major ("May 1790")			
I 29r	29	I	3b
	30	I	2b
	31	I	4a
	32	I	1a
II 33r	33	I	1b
	34	I	4b
	35	II	2b
III (M) 36r	36	II	3a ⎱
	37	II	2a ⎰
IV 38v	38	II	3b
(38r = false start)	39	III	3a
	40	III	2a
K.590 in F major ("June 1790")			= a sheet
I 15r	15	II	4b
	16	II	1b
	17	II	4b
	18	II	1b
II 19r	19	II	4a ⎱
	20	II	1a ⎰
	21	II	3a
III (M) 22r	22	II	2a
IV 23r	23	III	2a ⎱
	24	III	3a ⎰ =
	25	III	1a ⎱ a sheet
	26	III	4a ⎰
	27	III	3a
(28r–v: blank)	28	III	2a

Type I, Mold A (Mold B is the reverse).
10 staves: 5-staff rastrum (87.5 mm.) × 2.

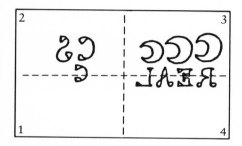

Type II, Mold A (Mold B is almost identical).
12 staves: TS = 181–182 mm.

Type III, Mold A (Mold B is partly reversed).
12 staves: TS = 187–187.5 mm.

FIGURE 3.1. Watermark drawings (somewhat schematic) of the three paper-types used in the autographs of the "Prussian" quartets.

another by their watermarks, and in the present case by the number and total spans of the staves ruled on them.

Let us see what deductions can be made from the character and distribution of these three paper-types. Two of them (Types II and III) are—like almost all Viennese music paper of this date—North Italian, and they are encountered in the autographs of other works written by Mozart about this time. As in the case of the great majority of the scores dating from Mozart's Vienna years, these two paper-types are here ruled with twelve staves. But the watermark of Type I (see Figure 3.1) is a quite unfamiliar one, the paper itself is thicker and coarser than the usual North Italian products, and (as we shall see) there are unusual features about the staff-ruling in addition to the unusual number of staves (ten) for a late Mozart work.

Alfred Einstein was the first to call attention to the singularity of this paper-type in a comment that appeared in the 1937 edition of Köchel and has been repeated unchanged in all subsequent editions: "Abert (II, 715) explains the main theme of the first movement [of the quartet in D, K.575] as being 'typical for this period.' But it is plain from the autograph—from the nature of the handwriting and from the paper—that the themes of the first and second movements derive from a much earlier date, perhaps from Mozart's time in Italy (around 1770!). It is obvious that Mozart resolved very suddenly to compose the new quartets, and reverted to old drafts or, more precisely, beginnings."[3] At that time Einstein said nothing further about the paper or the handwriting, but they were discussed in much greater detail by Alec Hyatt King in an article published in 1940:

There is no doubt that for the beginning of these works [K.575 and 589] Mozart used drafts he had made at least seventeen years before, and this furnishes further proof of the lack of impetus mentioned above. The evidence consists of three things: the type of the music paper which, for the first few pages of each work, has ten lines to a sheet [ten staves to the page] and is of a thick greyish texture, such as Mozart had not used for many years (from roughly 1778 onwards he used twelve-line paper, white in colour); the style of the writing of the opening themes and other passages, which is bold and thick and can be dated by comparison to within a few years as belonging to a period not later than 1773–74; the style of the opening melodies of each quartet, which, consisting of semibreves and minims often preceded or linked by turns or grace-notes as part of a descending theme, can be dated to the early seventies. For this type is found very largely in works written soon after his journey to Italy and Vienna of that period.

It would seem that, owing to his prevailing apathy, Mozart kept putting off the Prussian king's commission . . . and one day came upon these early drafts in his desk and was attracted by the broad singing quality of the themes.[4]

In 1945 Einstein returned to the topic: in the introduction he wrote to his edition of Mozart's "Ten Celebrated String Quartets" in score he discussed in general terms the stages in which the quartets as a whole were written, and added:

This process may be seen with special clearness in the first movement of the D maj. quartet (K.575), the first part of the initial draft of which, as has already been noted in Köchel, goes back to an earlier date, in my opinion as early as the beginning of the 70's. (The same is true of the second movement, except that here Mozart's draft, as in some other of his sketches, is of a different kind, consisting of eight bars fully worked out, which were simply retained and continued when he resumed the composition many years later.) It appears that his resolve to write a series of quartets for the King came to him very suddenly, at a moment when he was particularly overburdened or spiritually depressed, and that this is the reason for his recourse to these earlier sketches. Such a procedure may seem hard to reconcile with Mozart's fertility of invention, and to run contrary to the natural interpretation of the other sketches and beginnings of pieces that he has left us, but in this particular case the first movement to the Quartet had already been worked out to such an extent that he had little more to do than put the finishing touches to it. The early date of the opening of the Quartet is clear not merely from the character of the theme, which recalls the series of Quartets written in August/ September 1773 (cf. especially K.173), but also from the fact that Mozart still uses the alto clef for the violoncello which it was originally intended should play the entry of the theme in the ninth bar, instead of the viola.[5]

Thus both Einstein and King are in essential agreement that the paper itself and some portions at least of the first and second movements of K.575—King adds the beginning of K.589—date from a decade and a half or more earlier: from "around 1770" (Einstein) or from "not later than 1773–74" (King). In fact, the view that we are dealing here with material from an earlier period dies hard. In his introduction to his edition of the quartets in the *Neue Mozart-Ausgabe* (1961), Ludwig Finscher used some of Einstein's words in stating that Mozart "obviously began writing down the first quartet immediately after his return to Vienna (4 June) and in doing so reverted to older drafts." But Finscher added a footnote to explain that Einstein's suggested date of "around 1770" was untenable on paleographical grounds, since the handwriting of the initial measures of the first and second movements of K.575 was essentially the same as that of the rest of the quartet.[6] We might do well to take this as a hint that the whole of the quartet K.575 was written at more or less the same period, and that we should look in some other direction than backwards in time for an explanation of the peculiarities of the paper.

THE WATERMARK of Paper-type I (see Figure 3.1) has never been properly described.[7] It consists of (left) a lion rampant, crowned, with

two tails, and bearing a scepter or perhaps a sword, and (right) the
letters ES. The left-hand figure obviously represents the Bohemian
Lion, two-tailed since the year 1202 or 1203; and although it is not
easy to match the complete watermark exactly, the letters ES are
found in paper produced near the end of the eighteenth century by the
mill at Nieder-Einsiedel in Bohemia, now Dolní Poustevna in the dis-
trict of Děčín.[8] (The papermaker was Franz Anton Siebert, and the
letters probably stand for "Einsiedel Siebert.") Dolní Poustevna is
about fifty-five miles north of Prague, and even nearer to Dresden,
which lies only about twenty-five miles to the northwest; Mozart
must have passed very near to it on his journey south from Berlin to
Prague (28–31 May 1789), a route that doubtless took him through
Dresden. Could he therefore have picked up this paper in Dresden
(30 May, presumably) or in Prague (31 May–2 June) while making his
way back from Berlin to Vienna?

The notion that this was a "provincial" (non-Viennese) paper acquired by Mozart on his journey is supported not only by its inferior
quality—it is, as King says, thick and grayish—but also by details of
the staff-ruling. Paper with ten staves was not the best choice for writing out quartets, for it meant that Mozart had two useless staves on
every page (he chose to leave the fifth and tenth staves blank): one
might guess that he would not have used 10-staff paper if something
more suitable had been available. And when we examine the staff-
ruling closely, we find that the ten staves were not ruled simultaneously (as in the usual "Viennese" or North Italian 10-staff paper, and
as in the 12-staff paper used in K.589 and 590) but in two rulings
each of five staves; a 5-staff hand-rastrum with a span of 87.5 mm.
was used. Now it is just this combination of non-Italian, usually
grayish paper and staff-ruling with a small rastrum that characterizes
other autographs which we know were written out by Mozart in
Prague and certain other smaller cities. Those portions of the autograph of *Don Giovanni* (including the finale of Act II and the overture) that are known to have been composed in Prague are written out
on grayish paper ruled with a 2-staff rastrum, the span of which is
either 24 mm. or 25.5 mm.; a 25.5-mm. rastrum was used for the
autograph of K.528, the scena "Bella mia fiamma," written in Prague
on 3 November 1787; and grayish paper ruled with a 2-staff rastrum
of span 26 mm. is found in the autograph of a few numbers of *La
clemenza di Tito,* including the overture, written in Prague in the fall
of 1791. (All these papers have twelve staves to the page.) Turning to

an opera produced in Munich, we find that in *Idomeneo* much of the paper is machine-ruled 10-staff; but a few leaves have twelve or fourteen staves to the page, and these are all ruled with 2-staff rastra. No doubt this was paper that Mozart had bought in Munich. Most of the autograph of the "Paris" Symphony, K.297, is on 16-staff machine-ruled paper bought (not unexpectedly) in Paris—but the fair copy of the 6/8 slow movement is on paper from Basel (which supplied the Rhineland) and was doubtless written out by Mozart *after* he had left Paris for Nancy, Strasbourg, and Mannheim; each staff on this paper was ruled separately with a single-staff rastrum. It would be easy to multiply such examples—and to draw them from the manuscripts of other composers. It is worth recording that when, only seven years after Mozart's journey of 1789, the young Beethoven, accompanied at first by the same Prince Lichnowsky, set out on a concert tour to Prague and Berlin in 1796, he seems to have experienced the same difficulty as his predecessor in purchasing paper locally which was ruled in the way that he was used to in Vienna; in any case most of the paper that Beethoven acquired in Prague and Berlin was ruled with single-staff or 2-staff rastra.[9]

If, as I am suggesting, Mozart purchased the 10-staff paper in Dresden or Prague between 30 May and 2 June 1789, it looks as though he was impatient to start work on the commission from the king. And maybe this impatience was in part rewarded. At all events Table 3.1 shows something that one might not perhaps have guessed from the words of Einstein or King: not only is the whole of the first quartet, K.575, written on this 10-staff paper, but also the first movement and all but the last nineteen measures of the second movement of the second quartet, K.589. In view of the unsuitability of 10-staff paper for writing out quartets in score, it is quite likely that Mozart used it only on his travels, and therefore that the whole of K.575 and the substance of the first two movements of K.589 had been more or less completed by the time he reached Vienna on 4 June, or very shortly after his arrival there. Indeed, it may have been the pressures of professional and domestic life in Vienna that were to interrupt the work on the second quartet and prevent its completion at that time. (The first quartet was entered in Mozart's thematic catalogue, as we have seen, as having been finished in Vienna in June.)

The music itself perhaps presents a small piece of evidence to support the view that one-and-a-half quartets had been essentially completed by June 1789. It consists of the fact that the distribution of

prominent cello solos throughout the twelve movements of the three
quartets is by no means even. The cello is conspicuous throughout
K.575 and also in the first two movements of K.589, but for the rest of
the second quartet it plays an egalitarian role. This is true also of all
but the first movement of the last quartet, K.590. To put it another
way: except for the opening Allegro of K.590, all the passages in the
three quartets in which the cello is given conspicuous solos are on the
10-staff paper that (I am suggesting) Mozart acquired in or near
Prague. It is as if, not more than two or three weeks after he had left
Potsdam, the royal A string was still sounding vividly in his inner ear,
but after some months in Vienna it could be heard only faintly.

W E   M U S T   N O W consider Mozart's use of Paper-types II and III.
From the way in which each is distributed in K.589 and 590 it seems
probable that he used Type II first and later moved on to Type III. Type
II was available in Vienna even before Mozart's journey to Potsdam in
the spring of 1789, since paper with this watermark is the main one in
the only surviving portion (Part III) of the copyist score of K.572, the
arrangement of Handel's *Messiah* that Mozart made in March 1789.
It would be useful to establish when Mozart himself started to use this
paper; perhaps it was in the middle of composing the first act of the
work that immediately precedes the second and third quartets in
Mozart's thematic catalogue: *Così fan tutte*, K.588, completed in
January 1790. And Paper-type III is among those found in the copyist
score of K.591, Mozart's arrangement of Handel's *Alexander's Feast*
(July 1790), the work that immediately *follows* the third quartet in
the catalogue; once again it would be helpful to know when Mozart
first used it.[10]

What are the consequences of assuming that those parts of the
quartets which are on Paper-type II were written down somewhat earlier than the parts which are on Paper-type III? The clues that derive
from watermarks and from the make-up of the scores are here reinforced by inferences that can be drawn from the changes in the
color of the ink used by Mozart and in the thickness of his penpoint
(ductus). These last two aspects are discussed in the *Neue Mozart-
Ausgabe's* critical reports under each quartet separately, but it might
have been better to consider the quartets together; for it seems clear
that Mozart was working on the second and third quartets at the
same time.

It is likely that Mozart will first of all have taken up the slow move-

ment of K.589 and brought it to a conclusion: the fact that it was begun on a new bifolium of 10-staff paper suggests that the opening had
been written down before Mozart reached Vienna on 4 June 1789.
The handwriting in this movement is remarkably uniform, so that, although Mozart passes to a bifolium of a Viennese paper-type (Type II,
12-staff) at measure 71, it is not possible to detect any point at which
the work was laid aside. Perhaps we may assume therefore that the
movement begun on the journey was completed soon after his arrival
in Vienna.

It seems that he then proceeded to the leaf that at that time directly
followed fol. 35 (where the slow movement ended), namely, the other
leaf in the same bifolium, fol. 38, and that he filled most of fol. 38r
with a draft for the finale. This draft consisted of eighteen measures of
an Allegretto in 6/8 time, laid out in score but with only the first
violin part written out. It is made up of two repeated sections, an
8-measure phrase and a 10-measure phrase.[11] But Mozart decided to
delete this draft, turned the page, and without pausing (to judge from
the ink) wrote on fol. 38v the first twenty-eight measures of the
present finale: this is again in 6/8 time but is marked Allegro assai
and, like the deleted draft, is made up of two repeated sections, an
8-measure phrase and a 20-measure phrase (this last containing a partial repetition of the opening material after ten measures).

Work on this finale was then broken off, and it seems likely that
Mozart began the first movement of K.590, which was the last movement to contain those prominent cello solos. It is not possible to say
much about the sequence in which the various parts of this first movement, and of the second and third movements of this quartet were
written down; but it does not seem unlikely that he pressed on with
the later movements before the first was completed. At all events the
first movement was written in stages, since the color of the ink and the
pen's ductus vary greatly in different sections. What does seem clear is
that at this time he returned to the second quartet and completed its
minuet and trio (fols. 36–37); these were slipped into the score between fols. 35 and 38. Fols. 36–37 are a bifolium from a sheet whose
other bifolium consists of fols. 19–20, leaves that contain the beginning of the slow movement of the third quartet.

All the movements just described are on Paper-type II. Mozart may
also have made an attempt to write the finale of the third quartet on
this paper, for a single leaf of 12-staff paper with the same span and
the same watermark has been preserved in the Mozarteum, Salzburg.

This manuscript (Mozarteum No. 6) has on one side of the paper (the other is blank) the fragment K.589b (Anh. 73)—sixteen measures in 6/8 time that were obviously intended as the beginning of the finale to a string quartet in F.[12]

Subsequently, Mozart began to use Paper-type III, and he completed both quartets on this: on fols. 39–40 he continued and completed the finale of K.589 from the point at which it had been broken off (measure 29); and on fols. 23–28 he wrote down the long finale of K.590.

IN DISCUSSIONS of Mozart's compositional procedures it has become almost a cliché to assert that Mozart habitually worked with ease and speed: that each composition was conceived as a whole, and after it had been worked out in his head required little else but the time to write it down on paper. But this has never seemed credible in the case of the string quartets; the evidence is that they were composed with much effort, and that the writing was not only slow but uncertain. Mozart himself said so: he described the six "Haydn" quartets as "il frutto di una lunga, e laboriosa fatica" (the fruit of long and laborious toil); and in writing to Puchberg he referred to the "Prussian" quartets as "diese mühsame Arbeit" (that exhausting labor). Our examination of the paper-types used in these works confirms the substance of Mozart's comments. It suggests that work on the "Prussian" quartets, even though begun almost impatiently, ran into the sands after no more than one quartet had been completed. We must, I think, keep an open mind as to whether the King of Prussia had really commissioned six quartets; there is surely a tendency to take Mozart's statements in his letters too much at their face value. But he seems at one stage to have set himself a target of six quartets, and to have failed to meet that target. Within the autographs, moreover, there are signs of uncertainty: two of the three quartets he completed begin with a false start to a finale, in one case (K.575) running to eight measures, in the other (K.589) to eighteen; and if I am right about K.589b (Anh. 73) the same was true of K.590. But this uncertainty is not confined to the late quartets; there also exist drafts of movements planned (but later rejected) for the "Haydn" quartets. Paper-studies similar to those discussed here make it almost certain, for example, that the 170 measures of the A-major rondo fragment K.464a (Anh. 72) originally belonged to the A-Major Quartet K.464.[13] The many changes of paper-types within the individual quartets of the

"Haydn" set also suggest protracted labor rather than rapid composition; the comparison here is with the autographs of major works such as the C-Minor Piano Concerto, which, however complex as pieces, are nevertheless written down on paper of a single type. Thus the difficulty that Mozart experienced in completing the "Prussian" quartets need not be seen as a problem of the *Spätstyl*, as an obstacle that resulted from the stylistic changes of the last years of his life; the study of paper-types indicates that the string quartet was never an easy means of expression for the mature Mozart.

4

La clemenza di Tito
and Its Chronology

ALL RECENT DISCUSSIONS of the origins and compositional history of Mozart's last opera, *La clemenza di Tito,* first performed in Prague on 6 September 1791 as part of the celebrations surrounding the coronation there of Leopold II, have been obliged to take as their starting point an article by Tomislav Volek that appeared nearly thirty years ago in the *Mozart-Jahrbuch.*[1] For Volek produced something that was quite rare in the literature of this opera's history: a new and awkward fact that called out to be explained, or at any rate explained away. This fact is the sixth item in a Prague concert bill of 26 April 1791: "6tens. Ein Rondo von Herrn Mozart mit obligaten Bassete-Horn." The concert was given by the soprano Josepha Duschek, a friend of Mozart's in Prague for whom he had written the scena "Bella mia fiamma" (K.528) in November 1787, and another aria, K.272, ten years before that; and the program included not only vocal items but symphonic movements and a piano concerto by Mozart. The contents of the concert bill had been known for some time,[2] but it was Volek who was the first to claim that the sixth item was none other than the rondò of Vitellia, "Non più di fiori vaghe catene," from the second act of *Tito.* This aria has indeed a striking obbligato part for a basset-horn, and was certainly a particular favorite of Madame Duschek's in her concerts in the years after Mozart's death.

Volek's claim has had the effect of upsetting traditional views concerning the chronology of the opera's composition, and the confusion and interest that were created are reflected in most of the recent literature on the subject.[3] For the earliest accounts by J. F. Rochlitz and F. X. Niemetschek (both published in 1798) stress the extreme rapid-

ity with which the opera had to be completed, and even if Niemetschek's "18 days" is now regarded as an exaggeratedly low figure,
there are considerable difficulties in explaining how Mozart could
have received instructions to start on the opera before the middle of
July. Indeed it was Volek who also first published the contract between
the impresario Domenico Guardasoni and the representatives of the
Bohemian "Estates," commissioning an opera for the coronation celebrations by "un cellebre Maestro" on one of two subjects still to be
supplied—or if time proved too short, on Metastasio's *Tito;* and this
contract was signed in Prague on 8 July. Thus the performance of any
part of the opera at a concert as early as 26 April is very hard to
square with the timetable for its composition suggested either by the
early biographers or by evidence that has come to light in recent
times.

So far as I know, this chronological knot has never been untied,
though there has been more than one recent attempt to hack through
it: for instance, by denying that the concert bill refers to Vitellia's aria,
or by suggesting that Mozart had undertaken a *Tito* project (whether
under an earlier commission or on his own initiative) at a much earlier
date than had been supposed—perhaps even as far back as April or
May 1789, when he had last been in Prague. And since the whole
chronology of the opera has now been called into question, it seems to
me that a useful contribution to the discussion can be made from a
largely unexplored quarter: that of paper-analysis. A reexamination of
certain physical features of the paper on which this aria, and the rest
of *Tito,* were written may well give us new insights into the order in
which the different parts of the opera were composed. Most of the
autograph score is today in the Staatsbibliothek Preussischer Kulturbesitz, Berlin; Nos. 2, 11, and 12 are in the Biblioteka Jagiellońska,
Kraków, and No. 3 is in the British Library. Early drafts for a few
numbers have also survived and are printed in the NMA volume in
an appendix. The only missing section, apart from almost the whole
of the simple recitatives (which were probably not composed by
Mozart),[4] is the *recitativo accompagnato* No. 25. Thus we are in a
good position to start inquiring into the paper that Mozart used for
this work.

FIRST, however, it would be wise to ponder a little on the aims of
such paper-studies, and on their limitations. We would expect any
composer whose output is substantial to consume a good deal of

paper while at work, first in sketching or drafting compositions and then in writing out the completed scores. Often we know little about where such composers bought their paper. But that is not always the case; among the manuscripts of Haydn, for instance, we can distinguish between the paper made in the mills at Eszterháza, the North Italian paper that was the most readily available kind in Vienna and elsewhere, and the paper that he purchased during his two residences in England. In the same way (as explained in the preceding chapter) it is possible to a great extent to identify the papers that Mozart acquired in Paris or Mannheim or Munich,[5] and Beethoven in Prague or Berlin. The chronological and biographical implications of such paper-identifications are obvious, even though there are dangers in pressing the argument beyond a certain point (because there is always the possibility that composers may start to use, or reuse, paper bought long before).

Recent work on Beethoven has gone further in this direction, by recording changes in the types of paper bought and used by Beethoven throughout his Vienna years, and attempting to link those changes with chronology. Two features have been of most use in classifying such papers. One of these—the more important—is the watermark; refinements in our techniques for identifying, recording, and comparing watermarks now make it possible to recognize even small portions of watermarks and—no less vital—to distinguish between others that are superficially identical. The second feature used in classification has been the staff-ruling (rastrology). Normally the staves were drawn on the paper by machinery, but occasionally they were ruled by hand. Small but recurring irregularities in such staff-ruling may, when taken together with the information about the watermark, help to identify a particular batch of paper and to distinguish it from other batches; but the most useful single piece of information here, apart from the number of staves to a page, is the measurement for the "total span" (TS) of the staves—the distance in millimeters from the highest line of the first staff to the lowest line on the bottom staff.

The application of such techniques to Beethoven's papers has been surprisingly successful. For Beethoven seems to have had a rapid turnover of paper, and by calling on the evidence of watermarks alone it is often possible to suggest a very narrow time-range for a hitherto undated score. In fact it is now usually possible to date a Beethoven autograph to within about two years. Quite often the limits are still narrower, for certain watermarks are more or less diagnostic of particular years. And although one must always allow for the possibility that old paper was being used, this risk should not be exaggerated.

The question arises how far these dating skills can be applied to Mozart's autographs. At present I know of no study in print in which a particular watermark, unambiguously described, is followed through a number of scores by Mozart or other composers working in Vienna. Nor does the watermark information in several of the Kritische Berichte of the NMA that have already been published provide a very sound basis for such a study, since all too often it is fragmentary, imprecise, or frankly inaccurate. It cannot be stressed too often that descriptions of the portions of a watermark on single leaves ("watermark: three moons," or "watermark: part of an ornamental design or shield") are of little help in identifying a complete watermark; the whole sheet-watermark must be pieced together, deciphered, and described. But even that is the beginning of the story and not its end; means must be found of distinguishing a particular watermark from others, similar but not identical, that answer to the same overall description. And that requires a foreknowledge of other watermarks of the analogous type found in Mozart.

Notwithstanding this, my impression for some time now has been that the same techniques are applicable to Mozart's scores as to Beethoven's: they can be made to yield comparably illuminating results. But there is one qualification. It does appear to be the case—unless it turns out that we are failing to distinguish between similar but non-identical watermarks—that a given watermark occurs in Mozart scores extending over a somewhat wider time-span than is normally the case with Beethoven. The reason for this is not clear (it might become clearer if we knew the sources from which Mozart and Beethoven acquired their papers in Vienna). There is, however, another difference that can this time be summoned to our aid. Almost all the scores of Mozart's later Vienna years are on 12-staff paper. But whereas in Beethoven's case it is usual to find that paper with the same watermark has, for any given number of staves, the same measurement for the TS, this does not hold good for Mozart: and it is common to find that scores with the same watermark have differing TS's for the 12-staff paper. It seems that it is only when we find identity of watermark *and* of TS that we can make the same chronological claims concerning Mozart's autographs as we can in the case of Beethoven's; but where such double identity prevails the evidence is compelling. Perhaps we should call this combination a "paper-type," and use the wider term "watermark-type" where the watermark though not necessarily the TS is the same.

FIVE DISTINCT paper-types are to be found in the various parts of the *Tito* autograph (see Figure 4.1).

Type I. Watermark: in both molds, CS over C, in reverse, is on the left; three moons, over REAL in reverse, are on the right. TS = 182.5–183 mm.[6]

Type II. Watermark: in both molds, FC in reverse is on the left; three moons are on the right. TS = 186.5, 187, 187.5 mm.[7]

Type III. Watermark: in Mold A, three moons over REAL in reverse are on the left; a crossbow pointing left over AM is on the right; in Mold B, a crossbow pointing left over the letters MA is on the left; three moons over REAL are on the right (thus the two molds are neither identical nor mirror images of each other). TS = 184, 184.5, 185, 185.5 mm.[8]

Type IV. Watermark: in both molds, three moons are on the left; a crown over G over RA is on the right. TS = 188.5 mm.

Type V. Watermark: a moon with a face looking *outward* is on one side; a star with six points is on the other. There are two molds, which the symmetry of the design makes it hard to distinguish. TS = 26 mm. (2 staves) × 6.

The origin of this last paper, Type V, has been known for some time: it was obtained by Mozart in Prague. Not only is it thicker and grayer than the others, but the rastrology exhibits a typical "provincial" feature: the twelve staves have not been ruled all at once by a machine, but in pairs by means of a two-staff rastrum with a span of 26 mm., and the irregular appearance of the staves ruled on this paper can be seen in photographs (for example, p. xiii and p. xvi in the NMA). Paper of a similar quality, and similarly ruled in pairs of staves, is found in other scores written by Mozart in Prague, such as the second finale and the overture of *Don Giovanni,* and the scena for soprano K.528 mentioned earlier. The portions of *Tito* that are on Paper-type V must have been written (or, conceivably, rewritten) after Mozart's arrival in Prague on 28 August 1791, though before the 6 September premiere. These portions are the overture; the march, No. 4; Tito's aria "Ah, se fosse intorno al trono," No. 8; Tito's accom-

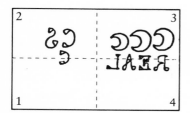

Type I, Mold A (Mold B is almost identical).
12 staves: TS = 182.5–183 mm.

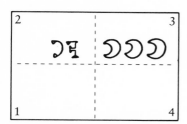

Type II, Mold A (Mold B is almost identical).
12 staves: TS = 186.5–187.5 mm.

Type III, Mold A (Mold B is partly reversed).
12 staves: TS = 184–185.5 mm.

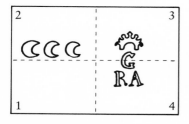

Type IV, Mold A (Mold B is almost identical).
12 staves: TS = 188.5 mm.

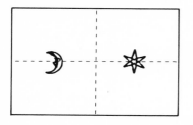

Type V, Mold A (Mold B is the reverse).
12 staves: 2-staff rastrum (26 mm.) × 6.

FIGURE 4.1. Watermark drawings (somewhat schematic) of the five
paper-types used in the autograph of *Tito*.

panied recitative "Che orror! che tradimento!," scene viii of Act II; and the last six bars of Vitellia's accompanied recitative, No. 22, before "Non più di fiori" ("si scemi" . . . "addio").

The chronological implications of Paper-type V are obvious. But with the other four paper-types, which are North Italian and thus representative of the paper bought and used by Mozart in Vienna (no doubt he took some of it with him to Prague), it may seem less easy to extract sure chronological data from the distribution of paper within the opera, which is as follows:

Type I   No. 1 duetto: Vitellia, Sesto
            No. 7 duetto: Servilia, Annio
            No. 10 terzetto: Vitellia, Annio, Publio
            No. 12 quintetto con coro, wind parts, last leaf
Type II   No. 2 aria, last four leaves: Vitellia
            No. 3 duettino: Sesto, Annio
            No. 5 chorus
            No. 6 aria: Tito
            No. 11 recitative before quintetto, last four leaves
            No. 12 quintetto con coro
            No. 12 quintetto con coro, wind parts, first two leaves
            No. 15 chorus with solo: Tito
            No. 18 terzetto: Sesto, Tito, Publio
            No. 19 rondò, up to Allegro (three leaves): Sesto
            No. 20 aria, first four leaves: Tito
            No. 24 chorus
            No. 26 sestetto, all parts except wind: all soloists, and chorus
Type III   No. 2 aria, first four leaves: Vitellia
            No. 9 aria: Sesto
            No. 11 recitative before quintetto, first four leaves
            No. 13 aria: Annio
            No. 14 terzetto: Vitellia, Sesto, Publio
            No. 16 aria: Publio
            No. 17 aria: Annio
            No. 19 rondò, from the Allegro (last six leaves): Sesto
            No. 20 aria, last four leaves: Tito
            No. 21 aria: Servilia
            No. 22 recitativo accompagnato, except last six measures: Vitellia
            No. 23 rondò, first two leaves: Vitellia
            No. 26 sestetto, wind parts
Type IV   No. 23 rondò, last eight leaves: Vitellia

Let us see, nevertheless, what this distribution suggests. In the first place, there is a lot of evidence indicating that it was Paper-type I that was nearest to hand when Mozart began work on the opera. The early drafts for Nos. 1 and 3 (Uppsala, University Library, and Coburg, Kunstsammlungen der Veste: NMA, pp. 321–323; Stockholm, Kungliga Musikaliska Akademiens Bibliotek: NMA, pp. 325–326), in which the part of Sesto is written for a tenor, are all on Paper-type I, as are the definitive versions of three Act I numbers for more than one voice: Nos. 1, 7, and 10. (Sesto, who appears in the first of these, is now a soprano.) And the same paper is also used in sketches for an Act II terzetto, No. 14 (Berlin, Deutsche Staatsbibliothek: NMA, pp. 229–230), which also shows Sesto as a soprano. The reason why these pieces—early drafts, and completed numbers for two or three voices in the first act—and *only* these (apart from a single leaf with wind parts) are on Paper-type I is surely obvious: they were written before the rest of the opera. If Mozart, badly pressed for time, decided to go ahead with some numbers before he had heard in every case who the singers were to be, it must have struck him as the least risky course to tackle a few of the duets and trios and to leave the solo arias till later.[9]

A similar line of reasoning suggests that the pieces on Paper-type II were written next, but before those on Paper-type III. It would seem that Mozart was still reluctant to commit himself to writing the solo arias; but a duettino, a terzetto, a quintetto (and preceding recitative), a sestetto, and three choruses (one of them with a solo) were duly completed. And when the problem of the arias had to be faced, there was one singer whose voice was already well known to Mozart because he had been the Ottavio in the original *Don Giovanni*. This was Antonio Baglioni, the tenor who was to sing the part of Tito. It was possible therefore for Mozart to tackle two of Tito's arias, No. 6 and No. 20;[10] and both of these as well as his number with the chorus (No. 15) are on Paper-type II.

Apart from the arias for Tito, in fact, the only solo passages that are on Paper-type II are the last four leaves of Vitellia's first aria, No. 2—perhaps a sheet of paper that turned up at a later stage?—and the Adagio section of Sesto's rondò, No. 19. And this latter aria evidently dissatisfied Mozart, for he revised it: first by inserting a 5-measure orchestral prelude (in the autograph score this is in a copyist's hand and on 10-staff, not the usual 12-staff, paper); and second by rewriting the Allegro section. (How far-reaching the latter changes were is not clear; but we know that the version that has come down to us is a revision, since six deleted measures of the earlier version—which did not at this point modulate to C major as in the later version—are still to be seen on fol. 85v of the score.) These two revisions are on Paper-type III, which is in this way shown to be later than Paper-type II. And Paper-type III supplements Type II in two other numbers: in No. 20 it supplies the last four leaves, though in this case we cannot tell if those leaves contain a replacement for a rejected earlier version of the end of this aria; and in No. 26 it provides the additional wind parts to the sestetto.

If we believe that Mozart postponed writing the solo arias and completed the rest of the opera first, we shall not be surprised to find that almost all the arias except for Tito's are on paper of Type III. There are special reasons why one concerted number, the terzetto No. 14, is also on this paper; for Robert Moberly and Christopher Raeburn have produced strong arguments to show that this was a late addition and replaced intended arias for Sesto and Vitellia.[11]

Paper-type IV is found only in the Allegro section of No. 23, "Non più di fiori." But its preceding Larghetto is on Paper-type III—and the same is true of an earlier draft of this (Coburg, Kunstsammlungen der Veste: NMA, p. 331), also in 3/8 meter and also marked Larghetto.

IF IT IS POSSIBLE to establish a plausible sequence for Mozart's use of four of these paper-types—I, II, III, V, in that order—we are bound to ask where Paper-type IV fits in. The fact that most of "Non più di fiori" is on a paper unmatched elsewhere in the opera must surely be a strong argument for its having been composed at a different time from the rest. But at what time? The most cogent evidence here would consist of the discovery of paper with exactly the same watermark and TS as Paper-type IV in other autograph scores of Mozart; but at present I know of no examples of this, though watermarks of the same overall pattern have been described in the literature on Haydn.[12] Thus we are forced to return to the autograph of No. 23; it can, I believe, be made to yield some helpful information.

This score consists of ten leaves (fols. 105–114 in the autograph of the opera). The first two leaves, as has already been pointed out, are of Paper-type III; they contain the first forty-four measures—that is, the forty-three measures of the Larghetto and the very first measure of the Allegro. The other eight leaves are of Paper-type IV. Now this distribution of paper suggests two things. First, the present Larghetto replaces something that had previously been there in the score (the first measure of the Allegro evidently needed to be replaced or at least recopied as well). Second, if any part of this aria was written at a different time from the rest of *Tito,* it was not the Larghetto. This is a somewhat unexpected notion; but if we are prepared to rely on the kinds of argument put forward here, we shall have to assume that this Larghetto, and even the rejected draft of the Larghetto (NMA, p. 331), were both written comparatively late in the work on the opera, after most of the ensembles (on Paper-types I and II) had already been completed. Since the Allegro contains a brief allusion (measures 79–86, in 4/4 meter) to the Larghetto's main theme, we must assume that Mozart decided to build in a thematic link between the two sections by expanding a short passage from the Allegro into the main content (in 3/8 meter) of the Larghetto. (The rejected draft for the Larghetto, though its opening is similarly shaped, contains no such "anticipatory" allusion.) There is in fact a small piece of evidence for this in measure 79: the singer's notes in this measure, a quarter note, a half note, and a quarter note, were originally written as $f''-d''-b'$♭, and it is possible that they were adjusted to their final form ($d''-f''-b'$♭) to match the opening of the Larghetto.

It looks as though Mozart has tacked a new Larghetto, contemporary with advanced work on the opera, onto an Allegro that comes from an earlier period—though we cannot tell how much earlier. And as Giegling points out,[13] there is a further piece of evidence to suggest that the Allegro did not originally belong to the opera of September 1791: in measure 180 there were once fermatas and the word "finis" at the first F-major chord. Thus the aria formerly ended at the first quarter note of measure 180, and the rest of that measure and the following Andante maestoso (measures 181–189) that leads to No. 24 are a later addition.

The autograph of No. 23 has been scanned for further signs that it once led an independent existence, but the evidence is untrustworthy. For instance, in the preface to his edition (NMA, p. ix) Giegling writes: "According to Wolfgang Plath's description of the manuscripts [in the still unpublished Kritischer Bericht] the outer leaves of this piece are particularly deeply yellowed [*gebräunt*] and bear more conspicuous evidence of use than do the rest of the numbers." A similar point might be made in regard to stitch-holes: No. 23 has far more of such holes in or near the fold of the paper than the other numbers do; and both these observations might be pressed in support of the notion that it had been carried around for a while on its own before being inserted into the opera. It should be noted, however, that they apply to the Larghetto as well as to the Allegro of No. 23; and so they may merely be evidence that the complete aria enjoyed a life of its own for some time *after* September 1791. This would at any rate explain why the first page of the Larghetto, fol. 105r (see the facsimile, NMA, p. xviii), became "yellowed" or brown-stained as well as fol. 114v at the end of the Allegro. The only part of No. 23 that seems to be a direct survivor from an earlier period is the portion consisting of fols. 107–114, with measures 45–180 of the Allegro.

THERE IS NOTHING inherently improbable in the notion that Mozart, commissioned in July 1791 to produce a new version of *Tito*, and extremely short of time, might at the last minute have pressed into service an impressive rondò written for an earlier occasion in Prague.[14] Unfortunately, such an explanation appears to run into difficulties almost as formidable as any that it resolves. Since these are very well discussed by Lühning (1974), I shall deal with them only briefly: they concern the context of the aria, and the question of its librettist.

To consider the former first, one might expect that an aria written for independent performance and subsequently fitted into an opera would show some sign of being a little out of place in its new context. On the contrary: "Non più di fiori," which replaces the aria that Metastasio wrote at that point ("Getta il nocchier talora"), is by universal agreement more at home in the context than the earlier words. For Vitellia, in the preceding accompanied recitative No. 22 ("Ecco il punto, o Vitellia, d'esaminar la tua costanza"), is struggling with her conscience: can she let Sesto die for a crime she has provoked, and calmly go on to marry Tito? "At his feet let me hasten to reveal everything. Let me lessen Sesto's crime, if it may not be excused. Farewell to my hopes of empire and of marriage [imenei]." In the opera the aria follows at this point, taking up this last word: "Non più di fiori vaghe catene / discenda Imene ad intrecciar . . ." (No more shall Hymen descend to weave loose chains of flowers. Bound in rough, harsh bonds I see death coming towards me. Wretch! What horror! Ah! what will be said of me? Whoever could see my suffering would yet have pity on me.) In replacing Metastasio's lyrics elsewhere in the opera, as has been pointed out, the librettist Caterino Mazzolà frequently took as his starting point some word or concept from the preceding recitative: the verses just quoted, whoever wrote them, look like another instance of the same technique. In Metastasio's original text there were three and a half further lines of recitative: to avoid being tormented in her mind, Vitellia would cast her other hopes to the wind. The following aria then took up this last concept, but in a trivial way: "The ship's captain sometimes throws to the waves even those treasures which he has carried from distant coasts and through heavy seas. Once he has reached a friendly shore, he again thanks the gods that even if he has returned a beggar, he has yet returned safely." This is rather facile; Vitellia is scarcely in a position merely to cut her losses, and in fact in any comparison of the two arias, "Non più di fiori" emerges as dramatically more appropriate and psychologically more subtle than Metastasio's original. But if it is tailor-made for its context, who did the tailoring? And when?[15]

This brings us to the second problem: the question of the aria's librettist. We are looking for an occasion earlier than 26 April 1791 on which the non-Metastasian words could have been written. Now, as Volek pointed out, from a geographical point of view it would have been possible for Guardasoni, Mozart, and Mazzolà to have undertaken to collaborate on an opera as early as April or May 1789. For on 10 April 1789 Mozart met Guardasoni in Prague, and an operatic commission was even discussed (see the letter to Constanze of that date). And two days later Mozart was in Dresden, where Mazzolà was living. But though he spent six days there (some of them in the company of Madame Duschek), there is no positive evidence that he met Mazzolà either on that occasion or on the single night (May 30?) that he appears to have spent in Dresden on his journey back to Vienna from Berlin. He could have seen Guardasoni once more in Prague between 31 May and 2 June 1789; but after that Guardasoni moved to Warsaw, remaining there from the autumn of 1789 till his return with his company to Prague on 10 June 1791.[16] Mazzolà's movements in the spring of 1791 have been elucidated by Lühning: summoned to Vienna from Dresden as court poet to succeed Da Ponte (who had fallen into disfavor), he reached Prague on 6 May and Vienna later that month, remaining there at least till the end of July, when his services were no longer required. Meanwhile Guardasoni, after concluding the contract for a coronation opera with the Bohemian Estates on 8 July, traveled south to Vienna and arrived there on 14 July. Thus a conjunction of all three men was possible only in July 1791; Mozart and Mazzolà could have met a little earlier, in May 1791, but not before that. Unless, then, one believes in a 1789 meeting, or a prodigious exchange of letters of which there is no hint, it is not easy to see how Mazzolà can have had anything to do with the text of any aria performed in Prague on 26 April 1791. And those who, with

Volek, believe that Mozart and Mazzolà agreed to collaborate on *La clemenza di Tito* in 1789 are hard put to it to explain the choice of that opera at that date, and to describe the extent of the collaboration.

THUS THE DATE of the aria and the author of its words remain for the moment open questions. What weight should we give to the fact that most of "Non più di fiori" is on paper not used elsewhere in the opera or found (up to now) in other scores of Mozart from the summer of 1791? My own inclination, it may be guessed, is to take this seriously, and (in the context of other evidence) to regard it as an indication that the Allegro section of the aria was written some considerable time before the rest of the opera (and before 26 April 1791). Whether it was even written *for* the opera—for an *Ur-Tito*, as it were—is more questionable. In spite of its aptness to the present context, and in spite of the echoing of the preceding recitative ("imenei"—"Imene"), it is possible that the aria had an origin quite independent of the opera, and that its inclusion here was an example of felicitous grafting. And if that was so, there are no special grounds for supposing that Mazzolà wrote the words.

Setting aside the problematical aria, it is clear, I think, that techniques of paper-analysis can succeed in exposing the chronological layers in a work like *Tito*. When Giegling announced that "in general the autograph gives no indication in what sequence, and at what point in time, each of the separate musical numbers came into being,"[17] he was altogether too pessimistic. Paper-studies of this nature have only fairly recently started to appear;[18] but that the conclusions derived from such techniques are more than mere paper-chains—*vaghe catene* of speculation—should be plain to anyone who takes the trouble to examine major scores of Mozart in this way.

5

A Reconstruction of
Nannerl Mozart's Music Book
(Notenbuch)

T HE LIBRARY of the Internationale Stiftung Mozarteum in Salzburg has since 1864 owned a celebrated manuscript volume usually known as Nannerl's Notenbuch.[1] This is the music book that Leopold Mozart prepared for the use of his daughter, Maria Anna (Nannerl—born in July 1751). A label on the cover of the Notenbuch, inscribed by Leopold, proclaims: "Pour le / Clavecin / ce Livre appartient á Mademoiselle / Marie Anne / Mozartin / 1759." But what has conferred especial fame on the modest volume is the fact that soon after it came into existence it was used by Nannerl's younger brother, Wolfgang. He not only studied and learned several of the pieces written in the book, some of them before his fifth birthday, but when a little later he began to compose he entered his earliest compositions there in his childish hand. Leopold also entered compositions by Wolfgang, and the dates that certain pieces had been learned or composed were added by the fond father.

Thus the Notenbuch is at once a record of part of the music that the two Mozart children studied and assimilated and a repository of Wolfgang's earliest essays in composition. Unfortunately the book is not so complete as it once was, particularly in respect of Wolfgang's compositions. Nannerl (in whose possession the book remained till her death in 1829) is known to have given away several leaves containing pieces by her brother; and although the present location of some of these leaves is known, it is clear that others have been lost. This chapter is an attempt to reconstruct the original Notenbuch, and to suggest some limit to the number of leaves that may still be missing. Some of the techniques used here, which were first developed in the process of reconstructing Beethoven's damaged sketchbooks, may also be of interest to scholars working with similar problems in incomplete manuscripts.

ANY ATTEMPT at a reconstruction must take as its starting point a careful examination of the Notenbuch's present condition. Today it consists of thirty-six oblong leaves of uniform 8-staff paper.[2] The dimensions of each page are (vertical measurement first) 209.5−210 × 295−296 mm. The eight staves have been drawn singly with a rastrum (five-nibbed pen) that has a span of exactly 10 mm. A vertical crease in the paper at the beginnings and ends of the staves was obviously used as a guide for the ruling. There are two systems of page-numbering, but since neither is satisfactory (one takes no account of blank pages, the other omits two pages after page 44), I have provided here a foliation of the leaves from 1 to 36 (see Figure 5.1).

It is obvious that there were once more leaves. In a number of places the stubs of missing leaves can still be seen; most of them have been pasted down (possibly concealing further stubs). For instance, at least three stubs and possibly a fourth can be seen after fol. 6v; there is a stub after fol. 10v; and after fol. 32v there are three, possibly four, stubs, the last of which contains a scrap of writing (the letters "de"). A reconstruction must allow for the loss of leaves at these points. Other losses are suggested by interruptions in the musical contents. But the reverse is also true: musical continuity, and even the unbroken numbering of a row of short pieces, shows that within those sections nothing can have been lost. It is possible in this way to establish that much of the Notenbuch is undamaged.

Attention also needs to be paid to the physical structure or make-up of the book, and the number and sizes of the gatherings must be noted. Here the undamaged portions will first invite scrutiny, in an attempt to discover whether or not the book consisted originally of a succession of gatherings with each containing a uniform number of leaves. If that should prove to be the case, it would be a useful guide in reconstructing the damaged parts of the Notenbuch.

The reconstruction offered here suggests that Nannerl's Notenbuch originally had forty-eight leaves (see Figure 5.1). This number is not without a special significance, but in the present case it was arrived at partly through a consideration of the probable gathering-structure and partly from the evidence of lost leaves. It is the former of these points that needs to be discussed first.

The integrity of one large section of the Notenbuch, fols. 11−32, is

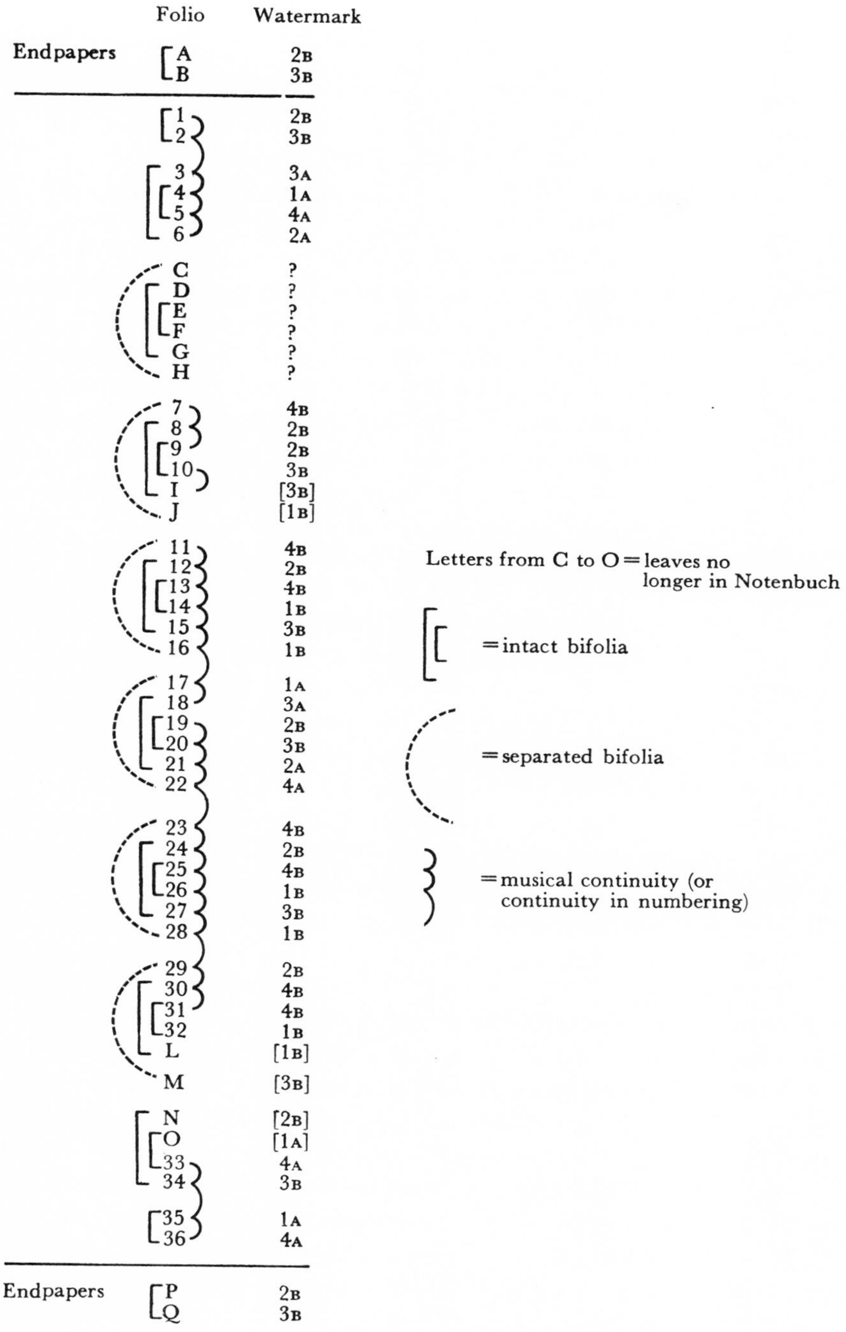

	Folio	Watermark
Endpapers	A B	2B 3B
	1 2	2B 3B
	3 4 5 6	3A 1A 4A 2A
	C D E F G H	? ? ? ? ? ?
	7 8 9 10 I J	4B 2B 2B 3B [3B] [1B]
	11 12 13 14 15 16	4B 2B 4B 1B 3B 1B
	17 18 19 20 21 22	1A 3A 2B 3B 2A 4A
	23 24 25 26 27 28	4B 2B 4B 1B 3B 1B
	29 30 31 32 L M	2B 4B 4B 1B [1B] [3B]
	N O 33 34	[2B] [1A] 4A 3B
	35 36	1A 4A
Endpapers	P Q	2B 3B

Letters from C to O = leaves no longer in Notenbuch

[= intact bifolia

= separated bifolia

} = musical continuity (or continuity in numbering)

FIGURE 5.1. Make-up of Nannerl's Notenbuch.

guaranteed by the continuity in the musical contents; no leaves can have been lost there. This section proves to have a recurring gathering-structure, the gatherings consisting of three bifolia (six leaves). A regular structure such as this suggests that we are dealing with a professionally made book. The fact that Leopold, himself the son of an Augsburg bookbinder, provided the Notenbuch for his daughter's use might lead us to suspect that this was no mere assemblage of heterogeneous papers bound up without an overall design. Moreover, the paper and the staff-ruling are uniform throughout; even the end-papers of the book are made from the same paper as the rest (these are not of course staff-ruled). All these features suggest a professionally made book.

But the Notenbuch cannot have been made up of three-bifolia gatherings throughout: the beginning and end at least must have been different. The book begins with a sequence of nineteen numbered minuets, guaranteeing the integrity of the first six leaves. In this way we can see that it starts with a single bifolium, followed by a gathering of two bifolia. It also ends with a single bifolium, in all probability preceded—though that cannot be proved—by a gathering of two bifolia. Thus it looks as if the bookbinder chose not to begin and to end with a full-sized gathering of three bifolia, but decided to break the first and last gatherings into smaller units. This was a not uncommon practice of bookbinders. For instance, the so-called Kessler Sketchbook of Beethoven, a professionally made book whose ninety-six leaves are still intact, is made up of gatherings of four bifolia, except for the first and last gathering, each of which consists of two bifolia.[3]

THE TWO DRAWINGS of Figure 5.2 show the twin forms of the watermark.[4] The letters ISH stand for Johann Sigismund Hofmann, for some time owner of the paper mill at Lengfelden near Salzburg; the *wilder Mann* (man of the woods) is a comparatively common device in watermarks.[5] It is not difficult to distinguish the quadrant and the mold of most of the leaves that are still in the Notenbuch, although leaves that have been removed may present a problem. For instance, in quadrants 3a and 4a the I of ISH is the letter that is nearest to the central fold, whereas in 3b and 4b the I is nearest to the outside of the leaf; in 3a and 3b the end of the s present on the leaf faces the H, whereas in 4a and 4b the end of the s faces the I. In 1b the club held by the *wilder Mann* is next to the central fold, but in 1a it is near to the outside of the leaf. Only 2a and 2b, both of which have a

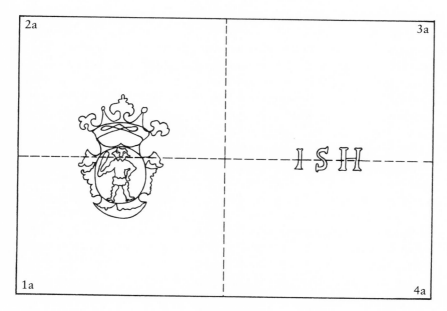

Mold A

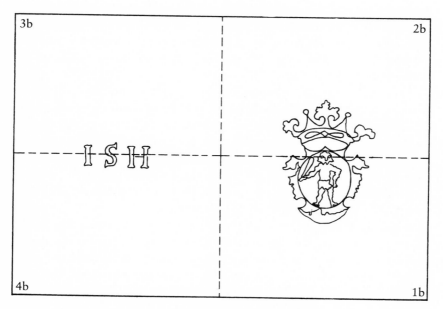

Mold B

FIGURE 5.2. Twin forms of the Notenbuch watermark.

symmetrical ornamental device (presumably a crown), are harder to distinguish.

Since each leaf in the book was once part of a bifolium, the careful identification of its quadrant and mold enables us to determine the quadrant and mold of the leaf once conjugate with it that has now left the book. In this way the quadrant and mold of about half of the missing leaves can be predicted.

My reconstruction suggests that the Notenbuch has lost twelve leaves. How many of these can be traced? Any candidate must consist of paper with the watermark just described; and ideally it will still measure about 210 by about 296 mm. and still have eight staves (ruled singly with a 10-mm. rastrum)—though if it has been trimmed it may be smaller and have fewer staves remaining. It would be reasonable, too, to expect the musical contents of such leaves to be comparable with those of the rest of the book. As it turns out, there are five leaves that possess all the required features:

1 and 2. Ms 238 in the Bibliothèque Nationale, Paris, consists of two separate but consecutive leaves. The recto of the first contains the end of a piece in F major, and the remaining three sides contain the first movement of K.8, later published as a violin sonata, in a version for piano alone. All the music is in Leopold's hand. The two leaves can be identified with certainty as I and J, between fols. 10 and 11 (where, as we have seen, there is at least one stub). The first Paris leaf completes the March in F Major in Leopold's hand started on fol. 10v. Moreover, the watermarks (3b, 1b) match exactly those predicted for I and J.

3. A leaf in the Museum Carolino Augusteum, Salzburg, contains the two minuets K.1(1e) and K.1f in Wolfgang's writing on one side; the other side is blank. The watermark is 3a. The leaf was given away by Nannerl in 1815; she added a note to say that the music had been composed by her brother "in his fifth year"—although that must surely be doubted. It is not possible to find a precise place for the leaf in the book, but it may be one of the six leaves C–H lost between fols. 6 and 7.

4 and 5. Two leaves that came to light in 1954 and are now in the Pierpont Morgan Library, New York City, are in Leopold's handwriting. The recto of the first leaf has diagrams of musical intervals (with their Latin and German descriptions). Its verso has K.1a (an Andante) and the start of K.1b (an Allegro in C). The second leaf is consecutive; its recto has the end of K.1b, and K.1c (an Allegro in F), and its verso

has K.1d (a minuet). The watermarks are 2b, 1a.[6] The leaves could possibly be identified as N and O, or they might be two of the six leaves C–H.

There is information about three further leaves, at least two of them still extant, that suggests very strongly that they too belong to the Notenbuch:

6. A leaf formerly in the Stadtbibliothek and now in the Universitätsbibliothek, Leipzig, is in Leopold's hand. Its present size is 165 × 280 mm. One side, referred to as the "recto," contains K.3 (an Allegro); the other side, called the "verso," contains four exercises in thoroughbass (the third has been crossed out). In the sixth edition of Köchel's catalogue the leaf is described as "one leaf with entries on one side, in small oblong format with six staves." That is rather misleading, for there are entries on both sides, and the "recto" has seven staves, the "verso" seven and a half. It is clear that this was originally a leaf of 8-staff paper, later trimmed at the bottom, and a likely candidate for Nannerl's Notenbuch. The watermark is 3b, and it is possible to show that the side with K.3 on it was indeed the original recto.

7. A *Salzburger Mozart-Album* published in 1871 contains the facsimile of an 8-staff page in Wolfgang's writing.[7] It shows thirty-eight measures of a piece in B-flat, ending on the dominant with repeat signs. This is now known as K.5b. The leaf—formerly in the Mozarteum, Salzburg, but evidently separated from the Notenbuch—is now lost. But further light is thrown on it by the next leaf to be considered.

8. A leaf with five measures of music in Wolfgang's hand came up for auction in Germany in 1973, and is now in a private collection.[8] I have been unable to find out the watermark. The paper has eight staves, and the five measures are clearly the beginning of the second part of K.5b. At the end of the fifth measure the music breaks off; Wolfgang apparently never finished the piece. It is likely that this side of the paper was originally the recto; the verso, which is today glued down on cardboard, is presumably blank. It follows that the page facsimilized in 1871 is a verso.

THUS EIGHT of our twelve missing leaves are accounted for. And there is a further source that helps to identify the contents of another leaf, or perhaps two more leaves. In a supplement (*Beilage*) to page 15 of his biography,[9] Nissen included a series of musical examples, together with their exact dates, first of the pieces Mozart had learned and then of the pieces he had composed in the years up to November

1763. Most of the contents of the *Beilage,* and the dates, can be shown to have been taken from Nannerl's Notenbuch. Nissen's particular contribution, evidence of an orderly if somewhat pedantic mind, was to excerpt the pieces learned and composed and then to arrange them in the chronological order of the dates—for in the Notenbuch itself the prodigy had evidently hopped around, learning pieces in no particular order and imitating his father in using whatever blank pages he could find for recording his compositions.

But there are a few pieces in the *Beilage* that are not to be found today in the Notenbuch. It is of course possible that Nissen located these dated manuscripts in some other place, and that he transcribed them there and recorded their dates. It seems much more likely, however, that at the time he made his notes the pieces were still part of the book. Thus we can probably add two minuets to it: K.2 ("composed in January 1762") and K.5 ("composed on 5 July 1762"). The piece on the Leipzig leaf, K.3, is also in Nissen's *Beilage;* no doubt that is a further argument for claiming that that leaf too comes from the Notenbuch. And the same is true of the first movement of K.8, on the two leaves now in Paris, which (as we have already seen) were certainly once in the Notenbuch.

It is worth noting the existence of dated manuscripts that Nissen did not mention: the two New York leaves with K.1a, 1b, 1c, and 1d, and the leaf in the Museum Carolino Augusteum with K.1(1e) and 1f on it. The most likely explanation of this is that by the time he inspected the Notenbuch those leaves had already been given away. (We have seen that Nannerl parted with the K.1 leaf in 1815.)

Still more hints about lost leaves and their contents are to be found in letters that Nannerl wrote to Breitkopf & Härtel in 1799 and later, though the passages themselves are less precise than one would like. Her letter of 24 November 1799 mentions that she possessed some keyboard minuets, and that of 23 March 1800 speaks of two pieces which were Wolfgang's first composition for four hands. Her letter of 1 October 1800 helps to clarify these references. The minuets were four in number; both they and the two four-handed pieces were in "a book which also contained the minuets and little pieces that my brother learned at the age of four"—this must be Nannerl's Notenbuch—and the six pieces bore inscriptions by Leopold identifying them as having been composed by Wolfgang in his fifth year.[10]

These, then, must be further lost leaves from the Notenbuch, for today there is no trace either of the two pieces—in later correspondence Nannerl calls it a single piece—for four hands or of the four minuets (Nannerl's description is surely too inaccurate to cover the Pierpont Morgan Library leaves, for only one of its four pieces is a minuet). If these leaves were removed by Nannerl in 1799 or 1800, it would probably explain why their contents are not mentioned by Nissen.

From all of this it emerges that we know something of the contents of about ten leaves which at one time were almost certainly part of the Notenbuch but which are no longer there. And since we cannot presume to be informed on all the lost leaves—a piece, for instance, that had left the book since Nissen's day would not have been recorded in his *Beilage* if it was undated, and thus some items may have slipped away silently—it is likely that the total number of leaves lost by the book is in the order of a dozen, and that its original size was accordingly about forty-eight leaves.

THIS DISCUSSION would not be complete if it did not mention four further leaves, since they are the cause of some perplexity. They have all the physical characteristics of leaves from Nannerl's Notenbuch: they are of the correct size, they have the same watermark, and each was ruled with eight staves made by a single-staff rastrum with a 10-mm. span. Yet it is hard to believe that they ever formed part of the book.

(a) Dresden, Sächsische Landesbibliothek. One leaf, 210 × 295 mm. The watermark is 1b. Contents: recto = K.73w; verso is blank.[11]

(b) New York, Pierpont Morgan Library. One leaf, 209 × 293 mm. The watermark is 3a. Contents: recto = Köchel[6], A 62; verso = A 61.

(c) Cambridge, Fitzwilliam Museum. Two leaves, 209 × 293 mm. The watermarks are 4a and 2b. Contents: fols. 1r, 1v, 2r = K.166h (Anh. 23); fol. 2v = K.375g (Anh. 41).

There is in fact a link between (a) and Nannerl, for the leaf was in her possession until 1825, when she gave it to the violinist Joseph Panny in Salzburg. There are no known links between (b) or (c) and Nannerl; those leaves were at one time with Aloys Fuchs, who authenticated Mozart's handwriting in each of the four compositions and, in two places, added the date (23 September 1847).

It is the nature of the compositions themselves, and their handwriting (Wolfgang's in every case), that appear to exclude them from the

Notenbuch. All of them fall into the category of fugal exercises, and Wolfgang Plath's recent examination of Mozart's handwriting in the years 1770–1780 has led him to conclude that none is earlier than 1772–73. This is in fact the date that he assigns to the miniature fughetti A 61 and A 62 (no doubt original pieces by Mozart, not merely transcriptions as their placement in the Anhang A of Köchel[6] implies), and also to the fugue subject K.73w.[12] The fragmentary vocal fugue "In te Domine speravi" K.166h is placed a little later by Plath, in 1774,[13] and the fragmentary keyboard fugue K.375g is dated by its handwriting to about 1776–77.[14]

It is scarcely to be believed that at the age of seventeen, and later, Mozart would have turned once more to his sister's music book in order to write down some fugal exercises, most of them incomplete and one not even for the keyboard but for voices. Yet the identity in physical characteristics (watermark and staff-ruling) between the leaves being discussed and the leaves from Nannerl's Notenbuch is disturbing, and it prompts another line of thought: was there more than one book like Nannerl's? Did Leopold perhaps have a nearly identical book made for Wolfgang?

Two other books of this kind are known. The so-called London Sketchbook, which Mozart appears to have used in London in 1764 and 1765 (see the entries from K.15a to K.15ss in Köchel[6]), must be excluded here, because its pages have only six staves on them, clearly ruled by machine, and the paper has a very different watermark. (The book itself, formerly in the Preussische Staatsbibliothek, Berlin, is today in the Biblioteka Jagiellońska, Kraków.) The other Notenbuch, mentioned several times in Constanze Mozart's correspondence with Breitkopf & Härtel and Johann Anton André between 1799 and 1802, is listed in Köchel[6] as K.32a. From letters to Breitkopf & Härtel of 13 February and 2 March 1799 we learn that it was labeled "Capricci di W. Mozart a Londra nel mese Decembre 1764," and that this title was not in Wolfgang's hand but probably in Leopold's; it is possible that the book included an aria, "Quel destrier che all' albergo è vicino," but the passage in question is somewhat ambiguous. Nothing is known of the fate of the "Capricci" after Constanze acknowledged the return of the book from André (to whom she had lent it) on 3 April 1802. All in all, it seems unlikely that the leaves under discussion came from the Notenbuch known as "Capricci." A book inscribed in London in December 1764, eighteen months after the family had left Salzburg, would be unlikely to be on paper from the

Salzburg mill, and it would be strange if Wolfgang were still using it in 1772–73. And if the book stayed with Constanze, it is not clear how Nannerl could have obtained one of its leaves by 1825. Although the widow and the sister were both living in Salzburg and could hardly have avoided meeting each other, the two were not friends.

Thus the origin of these four leaves remains for the present a mystery. The fact that they have been trimmed along the bottom and do not therefore exhibit the irregular margin of handmade paper, the so-called deckle edge—unlike most of the autograph scores listed in note 5—makes it improbable that they have come merely from loose sheets of paper. But there may have been other music books used by the Mozart family in the 1760s and 1770s of which we know nothing. Perhaps these leaves are the sole survivors of one such book.

THE ORIGINAL SIZE of the Notenbuch suggested in the present reconstruction—exactly forty-eight leaves—is not in fact an arbitrary figure but a recognized size from the point of view of the paper trade. One of its standard units consisted of twenty-five *Bogen* of ordinary paper or twenty-four *Bogen* of music paper. This unit was known as a *Buch*. The term *Bogen* is awkwardly ambiguous in German; it is sometimes used to mean a large sheet of paper, and sometimes to mean a bifolium (*Doppelblatt,* or two conjugate leaves), which in the Notenbuch's paper would be *half* a sheet. Thus we may regard the Notenbuch as being made out of a *Buch* of twenty-four bifolia (24 × 2 = the 48 leaves). Or if *Bogen* is to be understood as a sheet, making two bifolia (four leaves), then the Notenbuch is made out of half a *Buch* of paper. In either case we are dealing with a standard quantity of paper—one that was often used to make "real" books. For instance, Mozart's little thematic catalogue of his compositions from 1784 to his death in 1791—the Verzeichnüss—consists of forty-eight leaves (six gatherings of eight leaves, the first and last gatherings also providing the endpapers). Mozart's London Sketchbook too has forty-eight leaves of music paper—once again six gatherings of eight leaves. And several of Beethoven's professionally made sketchbooks seem originally to have had forty-eight leaves (for example, Grasnick 1, Grasnick 2, Grasnick 3), while others probably started with ninety-six leaves (for example, Landsberg 6, Wielhorsky, Pastoral); the undamaged Kessler Sketchbook still has ninety-six leaves today.[15]

If we now ask what results come from having determined the original structure and size of the Notenbuch, the candid answer must be, very few. Nevertheless, these pages represent the first testing-ground of genius—even if it was one that remained within the family circle. There are no earlier examples than these of Wolfgang's efforts at composition, and they are appropriately mixed with the very first pieces that he learned to play—pieces that must have served him to some extent as models for his earliest attempts to write down his own ideas. Nannerl's Notenbuch begins with nineteen minuets, and we need not be surprised that so many of his early compositions (K.1d, 1e, 1f, 2, 4, 5) also take the form of minuets. Melodic resemblances have also been noticed between Wolfgang's pieces and others in the book; this too is only to be expected.[16] Thus it seems wholly justifiable for the NMA to include an edition of the Notenbuch; only in this way are Mozart's very first compositions placed within their true and proper context.

6

The Date of Mozart's Piano Sonata in B-flat, K.333(315c): The "Linz" Sonata?

THE COMPOSITION DATE of Mozart's Sonata in B-flat, K.333, has always been in doubt. The autograph score, in the Staatsbibliothek Preussischer Kulturbesitz, Berlin, bears no date. In the first edition of his catalogue Köchel assigned it provisionally to the year 1779. For a long time that date remained unchallenged. It was not questioned by Abert, and it was even refined in 1936 by Saint-Foix, who concluded that the work had been written in Salzburg between January and March 1779.[1] But the sonata was not allowed to rest there. In the third edition of Köchel, Alfred Einstein moved the work back to the end of Mozart's stay in Paris ("Komp.* im Spätsommer 1778 in Paris"), and this date has been retained in subsequent editions. It is only recently, in fact, that it has been questioned in a somewhat startling way. In the course of his penetrating study of Mozart's handwriting during the decade 1770–1780 Wolfgang Plath concludes that the autograph was not written in Paris or even shortly after; the handwriting suggests to him a date of around 1783–84, "probably not all that long before its first publication in 1784."[2]

I believe Plath to be essentially right, and in this chapter I shall offer evidence of another kind that the sonata was written in the autumn of 1783.

LET US START by examining the autograph of the sonata. One glance at it—or at the facsimile, unfortunately much reduced in size, which was published by Ichthys Verlag of Stuttgart in 1965—is sufficient to note its untypical appearance. In the first place, unlike most Mozart scores, its shape is not oblong (*Querformat*) but upright (*Hochformat*); it consists of three leaves each measuring about 378 mm. × 233 mm. (the vertical dimensions are given first). But its most unusual feature is that every page is ruled with twenty-four staves. This ruling is regular and must have been done mechanically. On each page there is a larger interval between the twelfth and the thirteenth staff. It would be possible, therefore, to regard each page as a double one, with twelve upper and twelve lower staves—although in writing out the sonata Mozart pays no attention to the gap.

The paper itself is lighter and thinner than the kind Mozart normally used. And the thought springs to mind: was it intended to be smaller as well? For the gap in the staff-ruling suggests that the paper was meant to be folded in a different way and thus to emerge with a different format. If a bifolium of this 24-staff *Hochformat* paper is folded horizontally, the horizontal fold will fall along the gap between the two groups of twelve staves; and if the paper is then folded vertically and cut along the horizontal fold, the result is four leaves (two bifolia) of small, 12-staff, *Querformat* paper. The more that one reflects on it, in fact, the plainer it becomes that this was the format in which the paper, ruled with this gap in the staves, was meant to be used: not as 24-staff *upright* paper but as 12-staff *oblong* paper. It is true that the page size of such oblong paper would be very small, only about 189 mm. × 233 mm. That was certainly a smaller surface area than the ones to which Mozart was accustomed, and perhaps it explains why he declined to fold the paper in the way implied by the staff-ruling.

Where, then, did Mozart purchase and use this unusual paper? It is clear that if that question could be answered, the mystery of the sonata's date would be solved. But the paper's provenance does not readily betray itself. There are watermarks in it, but they are indistinct and afford no immediate clue. And the paper cannot easily be matched; at all events no other autograph of a Mozart work on 24-staff paper seems to have survived.

There is, however, another score on 24-staff paper which has come down to us in Mozart's handwriting. This is his transcription of a movement by Michael Haydn, the "Pignus futurae gloriae" from the G-Minor *Litaniae de Venerabili Sacramento*. The score, listed as Anhang A 12 in the sixth edition of Köchel, is today in the Staatsbibliothek Preussischer Kulturbesitz, Berlin. Like the autograph of K.333, it is in *upright* format, and the size of each of the six leaves which make up the score—three bifolia, not gathered—is about 380 mm. × 235 mm. The staves are machine-ruled, and there is a gap between the twelfth and the thirteenth staff on each page. The vertical span of each group of twelve staves is 158 mm. Since all these details are precisely the same as in K.333, there can be little doubt that we are dealing not merely with similar but with identical paper.

The great advantage of this manuscript is that it is possible to make out most of the watermark. This—the sheet-watermark—is in two parts. One part, which falls in the middle of fols. 1, 4, and 6, is the well-known device usually referred to as a *posthorn shield*. This consists of a shield with a crown (or occasionally a flower, such as a carnation) at the top and containing a posthorn with its sling.[3] It is a characteristic mark in thin papers designed to be used for letter writing (hence the lightness and—when folded—the small format of this particular paper). Underneath the shield there are two small letters: IK. The other part of the watermark, though less easy to read, is apparently the name STEYR; this is found in the middle of fols. 2, 3, and 5. I have been able to make out all the letters except for the tail of the Y. The sheet-watermark is represented in the manuscript by both its twin forms (see Figure 6.1). The form arbitrarily designated Mold A occurs in the first bifolium (fols. 1–2); the form designated Mold B is found in the second and third bifolia (fols. 3–6). Mozart has used each bifolium with the watermark upside down.

Furnished with this information we can make something of the otherwise obscure watermarks in the B-flat Sonata. The watermark of the third leaf can be read: it is the Mold A form of the posthorn shield. And the very indistinct traces of a watermark in the first and second leaves can be worked out: they are STEYR and the shield in the Mold B form. (These two leaves, though now separate, could once have been conjugate.) All three leaves were used by Mozart with the watermark upside down.

THE PAPER MILLS of Steyr, near Linz in Upper Austria, are discussed in some detail in Georg Eineder's comprehensive survey.[4] Of the three mills the most important was no doubt the Altmühle, which in the period with which we are concerned was owned by Johann Kienmoser. All three were within the town of Steyr itself, along the Wehrgraben.

Eineder has no illustration of any paper with a posthorn shield and the name STEYR. Nevertheless, we can scarcely doubt that the paper of

Mold A

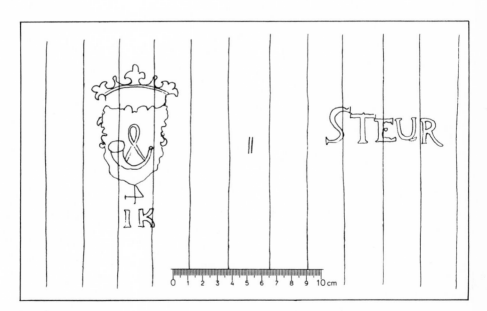

Mold B

FIGURE 6.1. Twin forms of the watermark in a paper from Steyr.

K.333 and of A 12 comes from one of the paper mills of Steyr. Thus the most likely conjecture is that Mozart bought this paper when he was himself near Steyr or Linz. This can only have been in the year 1783, either when he was on his way from Vienna to Salzburg at the end of July or when he was making his journey back at the end of October or early in November. Of the alternatives the latter, as I shall now show, is the more probable.

For there is at least one more example of this paper known to Mozart scholarship—but it is not in the 24-staff, *upright* form. Among the fragmentary material from the unfinished "dramma giocoso" *L'oca del Cairo*, K.422, that has been preserved in the Staatsbibliothek Preussischer Kulturbesitz, Berlin, there is one group of three very small, oblong sketchleaves.[5] They represent three-quarters of a large sheet, and in their present arrangement are paginated as pages 147–152. These leaves have twelve staves, and the vertical span of the staves is 158 mm., the same measurement as is found in K.333 and in A 12 for each group of twelve staves. Moreover, the watermark, though once again not easy to decipher, appears to be the same as the Mold B form of the Steyr watermark.

The contents of these three sketchleaves are significant. Page 147 has a sketch for the quartetto from near the end of the first act of *L'oca del Cairo* (NMA II/5/13, No. 5), while pages 148–149 contain sketches for the coda of the first-act finale (NMA II/5/13, No. 6). But page 150 is more complex: there is the start of a Dona nobis pacem in four parts, followed by a unilinear sketch for the first movement of the piano quintet K.452, a work not completed till March 1784. (This sketch relates to most of the development section and the first bars of the recapitulation.) The remaining leaf, pages 151–152, is blank.

Although much remains uncertain about the history of *L'oca del Cairo*, it has never been suggested that this operatic venture was put in hand before Mozart's arrival in Salzburg in the summer of 1783; it was developed in discussions which he had there with his librettist, the Abbé Varesco. What seems clear is that Varesco set to work quickly, so that Mozart could begin composing some of the first-act numbers. Thus the earliest sketches that Mozart made must date from his time in Salzburg. He too worked fast, and on 6 December 1783, hardly more than a week after he found himself back in Vienna, he could report to his father that apart from three arias the first act was complete. It seems evident that he had continued to work on the opera during his somewhat leisurely journey back to Vienna, which included a stay in Linz and a performance there of a new symphony (K.425, the "Linz" Symphony).

Were these sketches for K.422 written *in* Salzburg or *after* Salzburg? Our best clue here comes from the paper and staff-ruling of the numbers of *L'oca del Cairo* that he completed. For some of these numbers, the duet "Così si fa" (NMA II/5/13, No. 1) and the arias "Se fosse, qui nascono" and "Ogni momento" (Nos. 2 and 3), as well as a pair of sketchleaves for the same two numbers, are on 10-staff paper of a type he was using in Salzburg that summer—it is found in the supplementary wind parts for the C-Minor Mass, K.427(417a), first performed at Salzburg on 26 October 1783. (The watermark of this paper shows the letters A/HF/REAL and a crowned shield containing three stars.) No doubt, then, the three numbers from the opera were not only sketched but written out in Salzburg. The first-act finale, on the other hand, is on 12-staff paper that we do not encounter elsewhere before the piano concerto K.450, completed in March 1784; it is clear this finale was written out only after Mozart had returned to Vienna.

Two other numbers appear to have been written out somewhere between Salzburg and Vienna. These are Don Pippo's recitative "O pazzo, o pazzo" (NMA II/5/13, recitative to No. 4) and the quartetto "S'oggi, oh Dei, sperar" (No. 5). The paper has ten staves, and the striking watermark, depicted by both Eineder and Heawood, shows a key and the letters IK.[6] We have met the same letters before, but here they are far larger and clearer. Eineder is surely right in identifying the letters as the initials of Johann Kienmoser, owner of the Altmühle at Steyr. In this way both the sketch for this quartetto and the score of it are linked with the town of Steyr.

A logical picture thus emerges of the progress of Mozart's work on *L'oca del Cairo* and on the other compositions and transcriptions of these months—one that is derived from the different papers that he bought and used:

(a) Salzburg (10-staff paper, watermark A/HF/REAL and crowned shield containing three stars):
   Wind parts for the C-Minor Mass, K.427(417a).
   Sketchleaves for *L'oca del Cairo*, K.422, Nos. 2, 3, and Biondello's aria "Che parli, che dica"; also an unidentified contrapuntal piece in score (with system of eight staves).
   L'oca del Cairo, scores of Nos. 1, 2, and 3.

(b) Steyr (24-staff and 12-staff paper, watermark STEYR and posthorn shield):

Piano Sonata in B-flat, K.333(315c) (24-staff).

Transcription of Michael Haydn's "Pignus futurae gloriae," Anhang A 12 (24-staff).

Sketchleaves for *L'oca del Cairo*, Nos. 5 and 6; also for the start of a Dona nobis pacem, and for the first movement of the Piano Quintet K.452 (12-staff).

(c) Steyr (10-staff paper, watermark IK and key):

L'oca del Cairo, scores of recitative to No. 4, and No. 5.

(d) Vienna (12-staff paper, watermark FL under crown and REAL under three moons):

L'oca del Cairo, No. 6.

THE SEQUENCE of work on the opera suggested here accords well with what can be deduced from other sources, in particular Mozart's letters. In his introduction to his edition of *L'oca del Cairo* in the NMA, the late Friedrich-Heinrich Neumann called attention to one implication of the letter dated 6 December 1783 (some days after his return to Vienna): since Mozart goes out of his way to inform his father that he is *entirely satisfied* with three numbers, the aria buffa (No. 3), the quartetto (No. 5), and the first-act finale (No. 6), these must be numbers that he had not written (or had not at any rate completed) by the time he left Salzburg on 27 October.[7]

There is therefore nothing so surprising in the fact that Nos. 5 and 6 should have been sketched on paper from Steyr, and then put in score on another Steyr paper (No. 5) and a Vienna paper (No. 6). No doubt we are entitled to deduce as well that Nos. 1 and 2 were completed in Salzburg before 27 October, and that No. 3—since that too is on Salzburg paper—was at least begun there. But for our present purpose the most important conclusion is that Mozart's use of the Steyr papers postdates rather than antedates the three months that he spent in Salzburg. And this allows us to make the further claim that the Piano Sonata in B-flat was written between Salzburg and Vienna in November 1783.

The notion that the B-flat Sonata K.333 dates from November 1783 will of course come as a shock to those who are still committed to placing the sonata among the works of the Paris period five years earlier. But the scholarship of recent years has in any case considerably revised our notions of what Mozart produced in 1778 and 1779,[8] and I think that the late 1783 date for the sonata will gradually come to be recognized as a convincing one.

At the same time we are reminded of how little we know about Mozart's life and activities at periods during which the flow of family letters ceased, or has been rendered incomplete through lost correspondence. I am inclined to place the writing of the sonata in the middle of November—at any rate after the *Akademie* at Linz on 4 November, for which he had to write a new symphony, K.425, at breakneck speed ("über Hals und Kopf"). But no letters survive from the five-week period between 31 October, when Mozart wrote to his father soon after arriving at Linz, and 6 December, when he wrote from Vienna. Since he indicates on 6 December that this was his second letter from Vienna, at least one letter has been lost. This might well have alluded to the writing of the sonata and have given an account of the Linz concert (if that was not already stale news); and it must surely have related the sad tidings that awaited Mozart and his wife on their return to Vienna, namely that their infant son Raimund, left in the care of a nurse, had died during their absence on 19 August.

Thus a lacuna in the correspondence between Mozart and his father is sufficient to explain why we have no account of the writing of the sonata. Yet I believe the sonata is not wholly absent from the letters. For on 20 February 1784 Mozart wrote: "Two gentlemen, an assistant comptroller and a cook, are going to Salzburg in a few days, and I shall probably ask them to take with them a sonata, a symphony, and a new concerto." The symphony and the concerto are easily identifiable as the "Linz" Symphony, K.425, and the E-flat Concerto, K.449, which he had just written for Barbara Ployer (the autograph is dated 9 February 1784).[9] The sonata, however, has been tentatively identified as K.448(375a), the Sonata in D for Two Pianos, which he had written in Vienna about November 1781. There are at least two objections to this identification. First, Mozart always refers to that work as "die Sonate auf 2 Clavier." And second, this was a composition long known to Mozart's father and sister, since he had sent the score to Salzburg more than two years earlier, on 15 December 1781. But if the B-flat Sonata K.333 was composed in November 1783, it would make perfect sense for Mozart to take advantage of the two travelers bound for Salzburg and send along scores of the only three substantial works that he had written since he had left there on 27 October 1783.[10]

B E F O R E we leave the topic of K.333 we should spare a thought for the other music on 24-staff paper from Steyr, the "Pignus futurae gloriae" in G minor by Michael Haydn, transcribed by Mozart and listed as Anhang A 12 in the sixth edition of Köchel. One might have expected such a movement to have been copied *in* Salzburg rather than shortly after a visit to Salzburg; but if my argument is sound, the paper-type excludes that possibility. There is, however, a transcription by Mozart of *another* "Pignus" composed by Michael Haydn which is on the same 10-staff paper used by Mozart at Salzburg in 1783 that I have described above. This movement is in D minor; Mozart's transcription, listed as Anhang A 11 in the sixth edition of Köchel, is in the Bibliothèque Nationale, Paris.

Why should Mozart have copied not one "Pignus" by Michael Haydn but two, in the course of a month or two? The movements in question are fugues, and it seems likely that he was already thinking of the concerts of the Baron van Swieten which awaited him on his return to Vienna. We cannot be sure where A 12, the G-minor "Pignus," was copied: possibly at the monastery of Lambach, where Mozart spent the whole day of 29 October, possibly later. At all events it appears that Mozart was looking ahead to the winter in Vienna. His continued concern with fugues is manifest in letters of 6 and 24 December, requesting his father to send him fugues by J. S. Bach (possibly his own arrangements of them for string quartet, K.405) and C. P. E. Bach, and in an original composition of this time, the fugue in C minor for two pianos, K.426.[11]

Perhaps it is in the same light that we should see the writing of the B-flat Sonata: his mind was already on Vienna and on the material that he needed for teaching and for private concerts and soirées. These too are concerns that we encounter in the letters of the following season. For on 10 February 1784 he wrote to his father that the whole of each morning was occupied in giving lessons; he repeated this on 3 March and added that "almost every evening I have to play." The list of his engagements which he appended shows that that was indeed the case. Between its composition in November 1783 and its publication in the summer of 1784 Mozart is likely to have made much use of the Sonata in B-flat.

Mozart's "Haydn" Quartets:
The Contribution of Paper-Studies

T HE MATERIAL presented here is offered as a contribution to the chronology of Mozart's six "Haydn" quartets. It concerns the paper-types used by Mozart in writing out the six autographs, which are today in the British Library, London.

Two broad questions arise at the start which it is prudent to distinguish:

1. What contribution, if any, can an examination of Mozart's paper make towards the chronology of the six quartets?

2. What contribution, if any, can a determination of the detailed chronology of the quartets make either towards the elucidation of Mozart's working methods—and perhaps his difficulties, too—or to the understanding of his music?

My comments will be addressed largely to the first question, though it will be obvious that it is the possibility of finding answers to the second, more interesting, question which provides the fuel for investigations of the kind attempted here.

T HE WRITING of the six "Haydn" quartets was extended by Mozart over a period of more than two years. This much at least is to be derived from his own dating. The autograph of the first quartet, K.387 in G major, is dated at the beginning: "di Wolfgango Amadeo Mozart mpa li 31 di decembre 1782 in vieña." None of the other autographs bears a date. But the last three quartets fall within the period of Mozart's own catalogue of his works, the Verzeichnüss: the B-flat ("Hunt") quartet K.458 is entered under the date of 9 November 1784, the A-major K.464 under 10 January 1785, and the C-major K.465 under 14 January 1785.

The two quartets left undated by Mozart, the D-minor K.421(417b) and the E-flat K.428(421b), are provisionally assigned in the sixth edition of Köchel to "the middle of June 1783" and to "June or July 1783"—the D-minor on the strength of a statement made many years later by Constanze that this quartet was being written during her first confinement (the baby was born on 17 June 1783).

So much for the traditional dating, based on what Wolfgang wrote down and what Constanze remembered. It will be seen that the quartets fall here into two sharply separated groups, one of six or seven months from the last day of 1782 to the summer of 1783, and one of just over two months from November 1784 to January 1785. Between the first and the second group lies a gap of something like sixteen months. Perhaps in recognition of this gap, a stylistic difference between the first three and the last three quartets has sometimes been remarked on—an observation that may go back to Leopold Mozart, who wrote to Nannerl on 16 February 1785 that the last three quartets "sind zwar ein bischen leichter, aber vortrefflich componiert" (are somewhat easier, but at the same time excellent compositions).

More generally, it seems to have been assumed that each quartet was written very quickly (though not necessarily without difficulty) at around the time of its traditional date. This is an assumption that derives from a long-held view about the speed with which Mozart habitually worked and (in particular) wrote down his scores. He himself described the six quartets in his dedicatory letter to Haydn as "il frutto di una lunga, e laboriosa fatica" (the fruit of long and laborious toil). Later, in 1790, he was to refer to the three "Prussian" quartets as "diese mühsame Arbeit" (that exhausting labor).

THE SIX QUARTETS are written on paper of ten different paper-types, as distinguished by their watermarks (see Figures 7.1–7.5 at the end of this chapter). The distribution of the papers among the quartets is indicated in Table 7.1, just preceding the figures. In the table the column of figures running from 1 to 68 represents the present-day foliation of the quartets in the British Library (Add. MS 37763). (This foliation follows the order of the quartets in the first edition of 1785, where K.458 stands third and not fourth.) The other foliation column, headed WAM, shows the numbering that Mozart himself wrote on each leaf of the quartets.

At the left of the British Library's folio numbers are brackets that indicate the gathering structure. As in almost all of Mozart's scores, the commonest unit is the bifolium. Occasionally (in the first three quartets) the bifolia are gathered in pairs; these are always the two bifolia that come from the same original sheet of paper. Only very occasionally do we find a single, unpaired leaf (fols. 10, 22, 27, 38) in a quartet. (The breaks in some of the bifolia seem to have been made deliberately by the British Library in rebinding the quartets.) The column at the extreme left of the table shows the distribution of the movements within the six quartets: M = minuet.

To the right of the foliations is a column with the ten paper-types (or watermark-types). They are all quite distinct, though a careless investigator might confuse types II and V, or types III and VIII. The last column indicates the watermark-quadrant (1–4) and the mold (a or b).[1]

Furthest to the right are brackets linking the bifolia (or in a couple of cases, leaves) that came originally from the same sheet of paper. Where the bifolia are adjacent this probably has no more significance than to show that after filling up one bifolium Mozart moved on to use the next bifolium on his desk. But where the linked bifolia (or leaves) are found in two different quartets, the conclusion is more striking: it appears that Mozart was working on these parts of the two quartets at around the same time.

THE FIRST paper-type has not been found elsewhere in a Mozart autograph. Most of the other nine types are found in other Mozart autographs that date from these years, though unfortunately they cannot be pinned down to a very narrow time-span. There is one exception: Paper-type VI is not found in any important scores of Mozart's Vienna years (1781–1791) except here (at the beginning of K.458), in the horn concerto K.417 (dated "27 May 1783"), and in one place in the unfinished C-Minor Mass, K.427(417a); but it does occur in a few much earlier autographs from the years 1768–1771. I argue (see Chapter 8) that Mozart acquired this paper during his early visit to Vienna in 1768, and used it in scores written then and in the following two or three years; much later, searching for paper in the spring or summer of 1783, he found a small remnant of it that had been purchased some fifteen years earlier. Although this argument is complex, its conclusion can be simply stated: Mozart started the "Hunt" Quartet in Vienna in the spring or summer of 1783.

This conclusion has some bearing on the gap between the first three and the second three quartets. It looks as though Mozart was keen to press on but ran into difficulties, or became distracted by the pressures to teach, to compose piano works, and to perform at soirées and subscription concerts in the winter-spring of 1783–84 (see the list of engagements in his letter of 3 March 1784). Mozart had all along planned a set of six quartets, and as early as 23 April 1783 he offered six quartets to the Paris publisher Sieber; at that time he cannot have imagined that they would not be before the public for almost two and a half years (the dedicatory letter to Haydn is dated "il p.^{mo} Settembre 1785").

The distribution of papers makes it fairly clear that even if K.458 was begun in the summer of 1783, it was still the fourth quartet to be finished and is not in any way (*pace* the first edition) the third of the set. But the relative order of the D-minor and E-flat quartets is less clear. Perhaps Mozart worked on them at about the same time. It is interesting to find that fol. 38 in the E-flat quartet comes from the same original sheet as fols. 14–15 at the beginning of the D-minor. Can it be that at a time when Mozart was completing the slow movement of the E-flat he was just beginning the D-minor?

Another link between two quartets is provided by fol. 22, the last leaf of the D-minor, and fol. 10, an insertion in the last movement of K.387. These two leaves once formed a bifolium. The most likely explanation is that on finishing the D-minor in the summer of 1783 Mozart decided to revise a passage in the G-major, the "31 di decembre" date of which evidently does not extend to every measure.

After this we shall not be surprised to find linked bifolia in the last movement of K.464 and the first movement of K.465, since these quartets appear in the Verzeichnüss at almost the same time. Perhaps the new paper-type towards the end of the variation movement of K.464—fols. 51–52—is of greater interest, since it suggests that there was some change of plan. The autograph shows complex renumberings and additions of variations here too.

THE PAPER-TYPE of fols. 51–52 is found also in the 170-bar fragment K.464a (Anh. 72). This can only reinforce the view of Einstein (and of others since him) that this long A-major fragment in 6/8 meter was originally intended for K.464; Finscher identifies it as the draft for a finale—correctly, I am sure.

This brings me to my last point: the light that paper-analysis can throw on the quartet fragments, eleven of which are printed in the NMA.[2] It is my impression that most of these fragments have been

TABLE 7.1. Paper distribution in the autographs
of Mozart's "Haydn" quartets.

Movement	Foliation BL	WAM	Paper-type	Quadrant	
K.387, in G major ("31 December 1782")					
I 1r	1	1	I	3a	⎫ =
	2	2	I	4a	⎬ a sheet
	3	3	I	1a	⎪ (watermark
II (M) 4v, system 2	4	4	I	2a	⎭ at bottom)
	5	5	II	2a	⎫
III 6v	6	6	II	1a	⎬ =
	7	7	II	4a	⎪ a sheet
	8	8	II	3a	⎭
IV 9r	9	9	III	4a	
	10	10	IV	1b	⎤
	11	10	III	1a	⎦ = a bifolium
	12	11	III	1b	
	13	12	III	4b	
K.421 (417b), in D minor (June? 1783)					
1 14r	14	1	III	3b	⎱
	15	2	III	2b	⎰
II 17r	16	3	III	4a	
	17	4	III	1a	
III (M) 18v	18	5	IV	1b	⎫
IV 19v	19	6	IV	2b	⎬ =
	20	7	IV	3b	⎪ a sheet
	21	8	IV	4b	⎭
	22	9	IV	4b	
K.428 (421b), in E-flat major (June/July? 1783)					
I 34r	34	1	V	1a	⎫
	35	2	V	2a	⎬ =
II 36v, system 2	36	3	V	3a	⎪ a sheet ⎱ =
	37	4	V	4a	⎭ ⎰ ¾ sheet
	38	5	III	1b	
III (M) 39r	39	6	V	3b	
IV 40v	40	7	V	2b	
	41	8	IV	3b	⎫
	42	9	IV	4b	⎬ =
	43	10	IV	1b	⎪ a sheet
	44	11	IV	2b	⎭

TABLE 7.1. *(continued)*

Movement	Foliation BL	Foliation WAM	Paper-type	Quadrant	
K.458, in B-flat major ("9 November 1784")					
I 23r	┌ 23	1	VI	1b	
	└ 24	2	VI	4b	
	┌ 25	3	VII	3a }	
	└ 26	4	VII	2a }	] =
II (M) 27r	— 27	5	IV	1a	a sheet
III 28r	┌ 28	6	VII	4a }	]
	└ 29	7	VII	1a }	
IV 30r	┌ 30	5	VII	2b }	
	└ 31	6	VII	3b }	] =
	┌ 32	7	VII	1b }	] a sheet
	└ 33	–	VII	4b }	
K.464, in A major ("10 January 1785")					
I 45r	┌ 45	1	VII	3b }	
	└ 46	2	VII	2b }	] =
	┌ 47	3	VII	4b }	] a sheet
II (M) 48r, system 2	└ 48	4	VII	1b }	
III 49v	┌ 49	1	VII	3a	
	└ 50	2	VII	2a	
	┌ 51	3	VIII	1b	
	└ 52	4	VIII	4b	
IV 53r	┌ 53	1	IX	2a }	
	└ 54	2	IX	3a }	┐
	┌ 55	3	IX	2b	│
	└ 56	4	IX	3b	=
K.465, in C major ("14 January 1785")					a sheet
I 57r	┌ 57	1	X	3b	│
	└ 58	2	X	2b	│
	┌ 59	3	IX	1a }	┘
	└ 60	4	IX	4a }	
II 61r	┌ 61	1	X	3b }	
	└ 62	2	X	2b }	] =
III (M) 63r	┌ 63	–	X	4b }	] a sheet
	└ 64	–	X	1b }	
IV 65r	┌ 65	1	X	3b }	
	└ 66	2	X	2b }	] =
	┌ 67	3	X	4b }	] a sheet
	└ 68	4	X	1b }	

In the six quartets these pages are blank: 10v, 22v, 33r–v, 44v, 52v, 56v, 64v, 68v.

FIGURES 7.1–7.5. The drawings of watermarks presented here are schematic. For the sake of clarity, the chain lines have been omitted, and the watermarks are overly large in relation to the size of the sheet, as indicated by the frame. Scale (in millimeters): 0   50   100

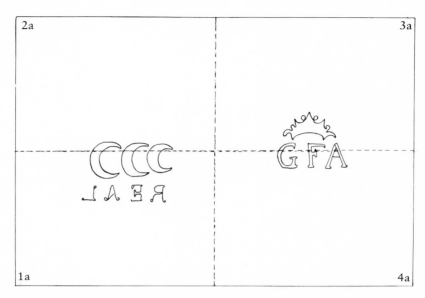

Paper-type I, watermark of Mold A (no example known of Mold B in a Mozart autograph).

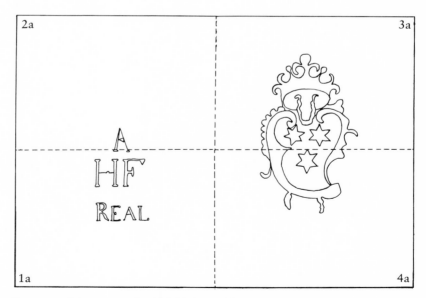

Paper-type IV, watermark of Mold A (Mold B is the reverse).

FIGURE 7.1.

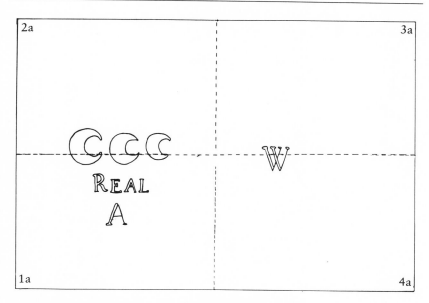

Paper-type III, watermark of Mold A (Mold B is the reverse).
Paper type VIII shows the letter W in a different relation to a
chain line in both molds (see diagrams below), but it is otherwise identical.

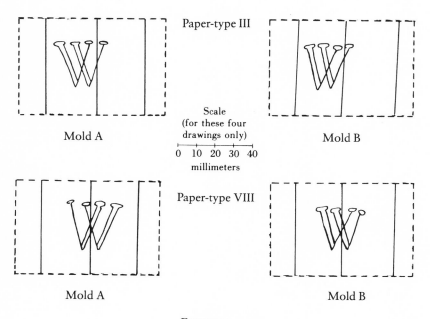

FIGURE 7.2.

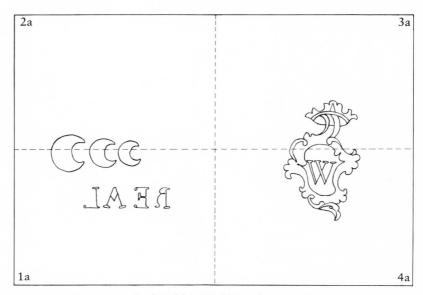

Paper-type V, watermark of Mold A (Mold B is the reverse).
Paper-type II is without the word REAL in both molds, but is
otherwise identical.

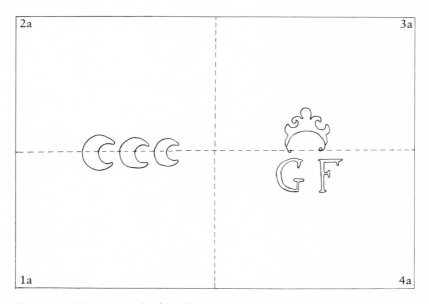

Paper-type VI, watermark of Mold A (Mold B is very similar)

FIGURE 7.3.

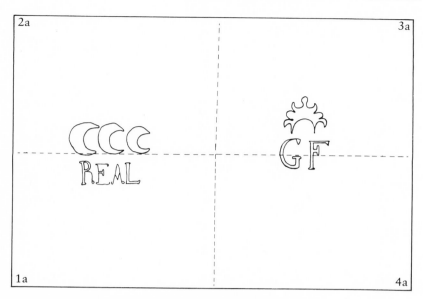

Paper-type VII, watermark of Mold A (Mold B is the reverse)

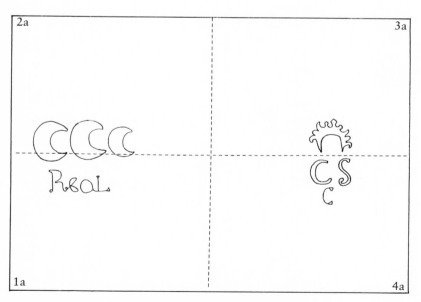

Paper-type IX, watermark of Mold A (Mold B is the reverse)

FIGURE 7.4.

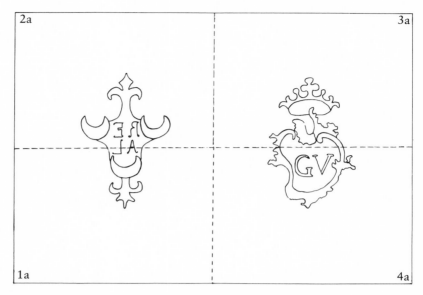

Paper-type X, watermark of Mold A (Mold B is the reverse)

FIGURE 7.5.

All the papers in the six "Haydn" quartets have twelve staves to the page, though each of the different types has a different total span (TS), as follows:

Paper-type	TS in mm.
I	183
II	189.5 – 190⁻
III	188.5 – 189.5
IV	182.5 – 183
V	186 – 186.5
VI	185 – 186⁻
VII	188.5 – 189.5
VIII	183⁻ – 183
IX	188.5 – 189⁻
X	183.5 – 184

ascribed to the wrong quartets, and to the wrong period of Mozart's life. In addition to K.464a, only one of the fragments appears to belong to the years of the "Haydn" quartets. This is K.589a (Anh. 68), an allegretto of sixty-five measures in polonaise rhythm. It has been suggested as a finale for the B-flat quartet K.589, or as a middle movement for the F-major quartet K.590. But the single leaf is of Paper-type IV, which surely marks it down as a finale for the "Hunt," K.458. This is the paper-type of K.458's minuet (as well as of a slightly earlier version of the minuet). Other quartet fragments that have been assigned on grounds of their keys to K.458 can be shown by their paper to date from the time of the "Prussian" quartets; K.458a (Anh. 75) and K.458b (Anh. 71) are no doubt to be connected with K.589. And K.417d, in E minor, probably represents an attempt to produce a minor-mode quartet for the "Prussian" set (seemingly at first planned as six).[3] Certainly an examination of Mozart's quartet fragments, after they have been placed in their correct chronological contexts, will suggest some answers to the second of the two questions that I posed at the beginning of this chapter.

8

The Origins of Mozart's "Hunt" Quartet, K.458

MOZART SPENT something like two and a half years in writing and at times rewriting the six string quartets that he dedicated to Haydn in September 1785. The long and laborious effort (as he describes it) is reflected in the number of different papers that he used in the six autographs, which have been in the British Museum (and subsequently the British Library) since 1907.

More than that: the variety of papers within the autographs is sometimes our best clue to the times at which the various parts of the autographs were written down. This is true even though for four of the quartets Mozart himself supplied a date. At the beginning of the G-major quartet K.387 he wrote, "li 31 di decembre 1782 in vieña," and he entered the last three quartets in the little catalogue of his works that runs from February 1784 up to his death: the "Hunt," K.458, with the date of 9 November 1784; the A-major, K.464, and the C-major, K.465, with the dates of 10 and 14 January 1785. But what do those dates represent? Perhaps only the dates at which those four works were for the first time ready to be copied and rehearsed—an event that did not necessarily preclude further alteration or improvement almost up to the moment of their publication in the autumn of 1785. So even in the case of these four quartets it is still worthwhile attempting to determine rather more closely the period over which each was composed. As for the two remaining quartets, the second in D minor, K.421(417b), and the third in E-flat, K.428(421b), we should be grateful for whatever clues to their dates we can obtain, since we have nothing more to go on than a story told by Constanze Mozart to Friedrich Rochlitz some time after her husband's death. According to this anecdote, the D-minor was being written during her first confinement—namely, in June 1783.[1]

In this chapter I shall try to present evidence that bears on the period during which the "Hunt" Quartet was being composed.

THE QUARTET has come down to us on three different paper-types, recognizable by their watermarks and by differences in the vertical span of the staves, which number twelve on each page. We can distinguish them as Types I, II, and III. From the table below it will be seen that Type I was used for the first two leaves of the first movement, and that the whole of the rest of the quartet is on paper of Type II, with the exception of the minuet and trio, written on a single leaf of Type III.

Movement	Foliation	Paper-type	Quadrant
I	23	I	1b
	24	I	4b
	25	II	3a
	26	II	2a
II (M)	27	III	1a = a sheet
III	28	II	4a
	29	II	1a
IV	30	II	2b
	31	II	3b = a sheet
	32	II	1b
	33	II	4b

Types II and III are familiar to students of Mozart from many of his other scores dating from this period. It is not even necessary to go outside the six "Haydn" quartets, for we encounter Type II again in the fifth quartet, K.464, and Type III is represented in all of the first three quartets, as well as here in the minuet and trio of the fourth. But for a long time Type I was a puzzle, at any rate to those few scholars who have made a study of the paper-types used by Mozart in his Vienna days. The problem was that it seemed impossible to match it elsewhere. The bifolium that is formed by the first two leaves of the "Hunt" Quartet is the lower half of a sheet, the watermarks being (fol. 1) the lower part of three moons and (fol. 2), the letters GF. On the analogy of similar watermarks (such as that of Type II here), one might expect that the watermarks in the unrepresented upper half of the sheet would consist of the remaining part of the three moons, and (over the GF) a device such as a crown. But among the Mozart autographs of the Vienna period no leaves could be found either to match fols. 1 and 2 of the "Hunt" or to complement them. One was forced to the conclusion that the paper-type found there was a unique specimen—a disappointment, since *unica* cannot contribute anything to the question of dating.

IT WAS THEREFORE with considerable surprise and interest that while working in Berlin in the summer of 1978 I came across four scores by Mozart which not only included leaves of Paper-type I but provided them in sufficient quantity for me to determine the precise form of the watermark in both its twin forms (see Figures 8.1 and 8.2). The most bewildering aspect was that three of the four scores came from more than a decade before the "Hunt" Quartet. Since then I have come across a few other instances of this paper-type. The scores are as follows:

1. K.51(46a), *La finta semplice* (opera buffa): four unnumbered leaves before fol. 219, with a new version of No. 23, Ninetta's aria "Sono in amore, voglio marito." Staatsbibliothek Preussischer Kulturbesitz, Berlin.
2. K.67(41h), 68(41i), 69(41k), 144(124a), and 145(124b), five church sonatas: four leaves. Mills College Library, Oakland, California.
3. K.108(74d), *Regina Coeli*: all twenty leaves. Deutsche Staatsbibliothek, Berlin.
4. K.139(47a), Mass in C Minor: fols. 17–46. Staatsbibliothek Preussischer Kulturbesitz, Berlin.
5. K.348(382g), canon "V'amo di core teneramente": one leaf. Biblioteka Jagiellońska, Kraków.
6. K.417, horn concerto: first four leaves. Biblioteka Jagiellońska, Kraków.
7. K.427(417a), Mass in C Minor: fols. 7–10. Deutsche Staatsbibliothek, Berlin.
8. K.560, canon "O du eselhafter Jacob" (in G major): one leaf, with top six staves only. Prof. Otto Winkler, Starnberg.
9. K.447, horn concerto: one leaf in last movement. British Library, London.

The third, sixth, and seventh of these autographs were dated by Mozart. The *Regina Coeli* is inscribed "nel mese di Maggio 1771";

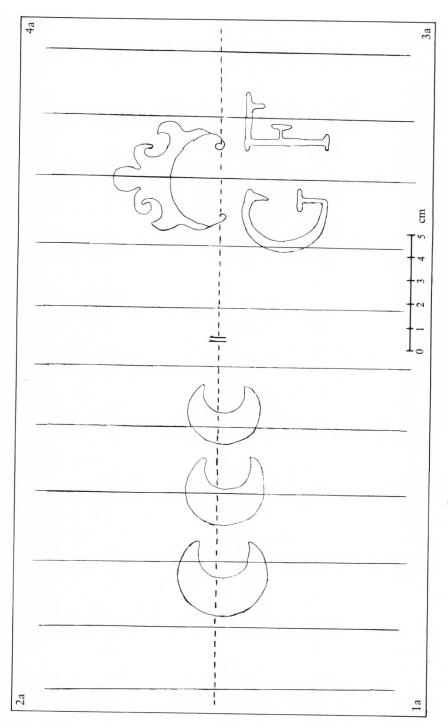

FIGURE 8.1. Watermark of Paper-type I: Mold A.

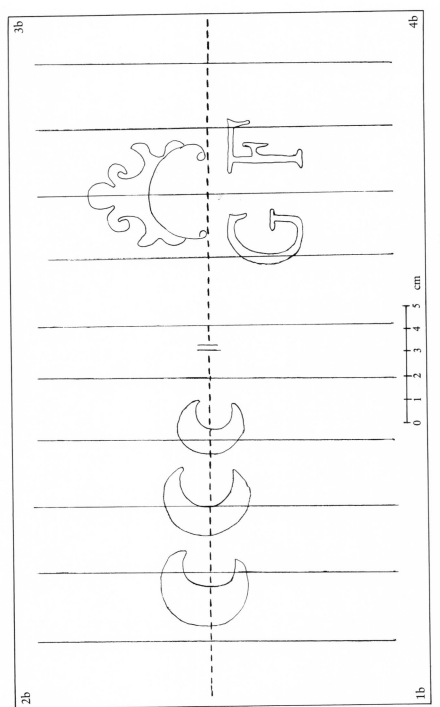

FIGURE 8.2. Watermark of Paper-type I: Mold B.

the horn concerto K.417 bears the words "Wien den 27 May 1783"; and the Kyrie of the unfinished C-Minor Mass is dated "1783." The first, second, and fourth autographs are not dated, but perhaps we shall not go far wrong if we ascribe the revised version of the aria in *La finta semplice* (written in Vienna between April and July 1768) either to 1768 or to 1769; and it seems that the early C-Minor Mass falls within the same period as well.[2] It is probable that the first three church sonatas in the manuscript that carries five of them date from about 1771 or 1772.

We appear, then, to have four examples of Paper-type I in scores dating from between 1768 and 1771 (or 1772), and (with the "Hunt") three examples in scores carrying dates of "1783" or "1784." It is natural to suspect that the watermarks are not after all identical, and that we have more than one paper-type before us. Yet tracings of the watermarks in the "early" and "late" examples match perfectly, and the vertical span of the twelve staves is exactly the same in all seven scores. And there is a further small feature that is, I believe, sufficient to confirm that we are dealing with a single batch of paper. In each of the scores one can observe the same peculiarity in the inking of the staff-ruling: the second line of the first staff, and the first and fifth lines of the second staff, are darker than the others. (This feature can be seen in the 1969 and 1985 facsimiles of K.458, and in the 1982 facsimile of K.427.)[3] I think it is safe, therefore, to assume that the paper is the same, and that Mozart acquired it in or around the year 1768, almost certainly in Vienna. What still has to be explained is his subsequent use of it in 1771 or 1772, and in 1783 or 1784.

THAT MOZART ACQUIRED the paper "almost certainly in Vienna" is an assumption that goes some way ahead of the evidence so far presented, and it needs to be justified. The paper we are considering is of the standard-size oblong format (*Querformat*), and the evenness of the staff-ruling shows that all the staves were ruled simultaneously by a machine. Since paper of this size and shape, originating for the most part from Italian paper mills, was used by Mozart not only on his Italian journeys but also in Salzburg, as well as throughout the last ten years of his life in Vienna, its physical appearance cannot be used to decide where it was purchased. But the fact that it was machine-ruled with twelve staves weighs heavily against its having been acquired in Salzburg. For music paper seems in the normal way to have been ruled not at the place of manufacture, the paper mill, but at the retail outlet;

and the evidence is stronger and stronger that Mozart could not get paper machine-ruled with twelve staves in Salzburg.

There were instead three possibilities open to him. He could rule a dozen staves singly with a rastrum (a five-nibbed pen); or he could purchase 12-staff paper elsewhere and take it back to Salzburg; or he could content himself with 10-staff paper. This last solution was much the most common. For most of his needs in Salzburg 10-staff paper was quite adequate, and he became adept at accommodating himself to it; in fact, it was usually only choral works with an orchestra that included trumpets and drums as well as strings and woodwind which called for some ingenuity. It is, however, striking that from the moment of Mozart's arrival in Vienna in March 1781 his choice fell upon paper with twelve staves. This remained his preference until his death ten years later; he very rarely returned to 10-staff paper, and even when very large forces were involved, he pointedly eschewed 16-staff paper, the kind adopted by Beethoven for most purposes from the time when he settled in Vienna in November 1792.

This is not the place to review all the instances of Mozart using machine-ruled 12-staff paper in Salzburg and to demonstrate that the paper was acquired elsewhere. But a few examples can be given. The autograph of K.125, the earlier of Mozart's two *Litaniae de venerabili altaris sacramento,* is dated "nel Mese di Marzo 1772," and although it is on 12-staff paper there is no reason to doubt that it was written in Salzburg. The source of this paper is easily explained, for it is found also in the choruses of his serenata *Ascanio in Alba,* K.111, composed in Milan some six months earlier. Several other examples that apparently show machine-ruled 12-staff paper being bought and used by Mozart in Salzburg prove on examination to be not what they seem. Some are post-1781 fragments wrongly ascribed to the Salzburg years: for example, K.196a (Anh. 16), K.323 (Anh. 15), K.323a (Anh. 20), and K.258a (Anh. 13). Others prove on examination not to have twelve staves: for example, K.166g (Anh. 19), where in any case the staves have been ruled singly with a rastrum. And the 1776 concerto for three pianos, K.242, is on 12-staff paper, but only ten of the twelve are machine-ruled, since the first and the twelfth staves have been drawn with a rastrum. Would Mozart have gone to this trouble if he had been able at that time to have twelve staves ruled by machine?

IN THE LIGHT of the foregoing we can assume, I think, that Mozart acquired his stock of Paper-type I in Vienna in the course of the year

1768 (he arrived there on 10 January and left at the end of December). We need not be surprised that he preserved a sufficient quantity of it to enable him to write out K.108(74d), the *Regina Coeli* of 1771, on it; that, after all, was a choral work with an orchestra that included oboes, horns, trumpets, and timpani. But what of the three works of his Vienna years that include this paper? I have come to the conclusion that the parts of those scores that are on Paper-type I were in fact written in Vienna in 1783, before the trip to Salzburg in the summer of that year.

The C-Minor Mass K.427(417a) was undertaken in fulfillment of a vow. From Mozart's letter of 4 January 1783 we learn that he had "promised in his heart" before he was married that if he were to bring Constanze to Salzburg as his bride, he would perform a new mass of his composition there. He claimed at that time that the score of half such a mass had been finished. Yet when the work was finally performed in Salzburg on 26 October 1783, with Constanze taking the soprano part, only four movements had been completed: the Kyrie, Gloria, Sanctus, and Benedictus. The score that has come down to us today, in the Deutsche Staatsbibliothek, Berlin, is not so complete as it once was. Some of the portions that Mozart apparently finished are no longer extant in his autograph. But the score contains a substantial portion of the unfinished Credo, down to the words "Et homo factus est."

Most of the surviving parts of the score are on 12-staff paper—as one would expect of a Mozart score written in Vienna after his arrival there in March 1781. But there are also nine leaves of 10-staff paper, now bound in at the end of the score. These contain extra wind parts for the Gloria and the Sanctus (of the Sanctus, indeed, they are all that survives in autograph). We know from other works that such wind parts were very frequently written out by Mozart after the rest of a score. When we bear in mind that Mozart and his wife arrived in Salzburg on 29 July 1783, and that the Mass, still uncompleted, was not performed there till 26 October, the very day before the couple left Salzburg for their journey back, it seems almost certain that the supplementary wind parts were written in the course of Mozart's stay in Salzburg (no doubt near the end), and that this is the reason why they are not on Viennese 12-staff but on Salzburg 10-staff paper.

There are some interesting parallels here with another work composed about this time partly in Salzburg and partly in Vienna; it too remained a fragment. This was the "dramma giocoso" *L'oca del*

Cairo, K.422.[4] Although the history of that undertaking remains in part conjectural, it was during Mozart's stay in Salzburg that the Abbé Varesco furnished him with a draft libretto of the first act. Mozart evidently set to work at once, and on 6 December 1783, only a few days after his return to Vienna, he was reporting in a letter to his father that the first act had been finished apart from three arias. Subsequent letters indicate Mozart's increasing dissatisfaction with the libretto and with his inability to extract necessary changes in it from the Abbé; by February 1784 he had suspended work on it. The portions of the score that have come down to us (Staatsbibliothek Preussischer Kulturbesitz, Berlin) are, as in the case of the C-Minor Mass, partly on 10-staff and partly on 12-staff paper; and it is precisely the earliest numbers, which we might suppose him to have tackled first while still in Salzburg, that are on 10-staff paper identical with that used for the extra wind parts in the Mass.

ALL THIS PROVIDES a useful confirmation of my claim that Mozart could not purchase 12-staff paper in Salzburg. The fact that almost all of the surviving portions of the main score are on 12-staff paper of types that Mozart was using in Vienna in 1782 and 1783 lends support to his claim in January 1783 that "the score of half a mass" had already been completed; some of it at least must have been well in hand. The four leaves of Type I come near the beginning; they are fols. 7–10. On fol. 7r is the conclusion of the Kyrie fugue. Fol. 7v is blank apart from a deleted bar containing music on the dominant of D minor. "No. 2," the start of the Gloria, begins on fol. 8r, and continues up to 10r (10v is blank). And here Type I ends. The continuation of the Gloria ("No. 3," "Laudamus te") is on a different paper, found in Vienna works of the second half of 1782. Although other explanations are possible, it strikes me as highly probable that the music on Type I represents a later rewriting of the end of the Kyrie and the beginning of the Gloria.

Since it seems unlikely that such old paper as Type I would have been purchasable in Vienna in 1783, it looks as though Mozart may have found some leaves of it while sifting through his old scores, which he was constantly requesting his father, Leopold, to send him from Salzburg. Not that he drew on much of it: four leaves (two bifolia) were sufficient to fill the gap in the Mass; four further leaves (two more bifolia) were used for the beginning of the horn concerto K.417, which bears the date "27 May 1783"; and at least two single leaves seem to have been used for writing down canons. It is a further bifolium that concerns us here: for on it he wrote a substantial part of the quartet movement in B-flat which is now the first movement of the "Hunt" Quartet.

THIS HAS BEEN a somewhat circuitous journey, but its conclusion is clear enough. Mozart began writing the "Hunt" Quartet in Vienna in the spring or early summer of 1783. Or perhaps we should say it was there and then that he began to write a first movement which satisfied him—for we do not know how many false starts he made and rejected.

How much of the first movement he wrote at that time is less certain. Examination of the ink suggests that he broke off at measure 106, after the first sixteen measures of the development. (This is the third measure on the fourth side.) And it is quite likely that, with the exception of the minuet and trio, he completed no more of the quartet for a whole year after that. This time the evidence comes not from the ink but from the paper. The rest of the first movement, the slow movement, and the finale are all on paper of a single type—Type II—that he also used for approximately the first half (opening allegro, minuet and trio, and three sides of the variation movement) of the fifth quartet, K.464, in A major—a work not entered in Mozart's Verzeichnüss till January 1785. Since the "Hunt" Quartet, as we have seen, is dated "9 November 1784" in the Verzeichnüss, it is a plausible suggestion that not only most of the "Hunt" but also about half of K.464 was finished around that time.

That still leaves the minuet and trio of K.458 unaccounted for. Its paper-type—Type III—is found in the latter parts of the two preceding quartets, K.421(417b) and K.428(421b), as well as in a single leaf inserted into the first quartet, K.387 (this is fol. 10, with a revised version of measures 125–142 of the last movement). It would certainly be convenient if Mozart's use of this paper-type (with 12-staff pages and a total staff-span of 182.5–183 mm.)[5] could be confined to the time preceding his journey to Salzburg at the end of July 1783. But that is not possible: Mozart used it again in K.426, the fugue for two pianos in C minor dated 29 December 1783, a month after his return from Salzburg to Vienna.[6] I know of no instance of this paper-type dated after the end of 1783—although a leftover single leaf might be used by Mozart after the rest of a paper supply had been exhausted. With some hesitation and qualification, then, we may ascribe the composition of the minuet and trio of the "Hunt," like the start of its first movement, to the year 1783. A fragment of the opening of the minuet, showing the first nine and a half measures in an earlier version, and preserved in the Musée Adam-Mickiewicz of the Bibliothèque Polonaise in Paris, is on the same paper.

Two other fragments for string quartet, both in B-flat, were tentatively assigned to the year 1784 by Einstein in the third edition of Köchel. There are K.458a (Anh. 75), nine measures of an Allegretto in 3/4 meter (with only the first violin and violoncello entered), and K.458b (Anh. 71), ten measures obviously of a fast tempo in 2/4 meter. Both fragments are in the Mozarteum, Salzburg, and have been published in the NMA.[7]

Paper-studies, however, indicate that the link with the "Hunt" Quartet is unacceptable, since both fragments are on paper of a type that does not appear in the surviving autographs of Mozart before the end of 1789.[8] It is the principal paper-type of the second act of *Così fan tutte*, K.588. And, more to the point, it is found in the autographs of both the second and third "Prussian" quartets, K.589 in B-flat and K.590 in F, works entered in Mozart's Verzeichnüss in May and June 1790 respectively. Given this information, we can hardly doubt that the two fragments K.458a and K.458b represent attempts to compose a minuet and a finale for the late B-flat quartet K.589.

But there is a third fragment for string quartet in the Mozarteum which is on a paper-type appropriate to the "Hunt," but which by an irony of scholarship was assigned by Einstein to K.589 and therefore given the provisional date of May 1790. This is K.589a (Anh. 68), a substantial draft for what must surely have been intended as a finale. It is in B-flat, in 3/4 meter, and has the character of a polonaise, fully scored for eight measures and with the first violin only for fifty-seven measures more. It has been published in the NMA.[9]

The paper is of Type III, like the minuet and trio of the "Hunt." And since there is (so far as I can see) nothing to connect the fragment with K.589 except its key of B-flat, it is much more plausible to link it with Mozart's earlier quartet in B-flat from the Vienna years. I conclude that K.589a is an attempt, later abandoned by Mozart, to write a finale for the "Hunt" in 1783.

WE HAVE SEEN that the first of the six "Haydn" quartets bears the date of the last day of 1782. Moreover, as early as 26 April 1783 Mozart was offering a set of six quartets to the Paris publisher Sieber.

But the dedicatory letter at the beginning of the first edition is dated "il p.ᵐᵒ Settembre 1785." Can he have foreseen that it would be almost two and a half years after the letter to Sieber before they would be ready for the public?

One is certainly left with the impression that the whole project cost Mozart much more effort than he had foreseen: the quartets seem truly to have been, as he says in the dedicatory letter, "il frutto di una lunga e laboriosa fatica." In that respect the present inquiry throws light on two points. First, the traditional division of Mozart's work on the quartets into two short bursts of activity, the first from December 1782 to about July 1783 (quartets 1–3), and the second from November 1784 to January 1785 (quartets 4–6), is blurred once we accept that some of the "Hunt"—the fourth quartet—was written and still more of it was attempted in the year 1783. And second, the claim that each quartet was conceived as a whole by Mozart in his head, and then at once written down—a notion for which there is little evidence in the sources and which is increasingly coming under challenge—must stand abashed before a demonstration that several movements were begun and then given up, and that over a year separates the earliest from the latest portions of the completed "Hunt" Quartet.

9

The Two Slow Movements of Mozart's "Paris" Symphony, K.297

THAT Mozart wrote two slow movements for his "Paris" Symphony, K.297(300a), has long been known. And there seems to be a general agreement today as to which was the original slow movement and which the movement written to replace it. The latest edition of Köchel (sixth, 1964) states the matter as though it were beyond doubt: "The Andantino is the middle movement of the original version; the middle movement (Andante) that was played on a later occasion in Paris is found only in the first edition." By the Andantino the editors of Köchel mean the movement in 6/8 meter consisting of ninety-eight measures (called Andantino in a draft but Andante in the final score); the movement found in the first edition is in 3/4 meter and consists of fifty-eight measures. I shall call them here the 6/8 movement and the 3/4 movement.

The view stated in Köchel[6] that the 3/4 movement is the later of the two has been held by several responsible Mozart scholars in recent years: for instance, by Hermann Beck, Otto Erich Deutsch, and J. H. Eibl.[1] It is also to be found in Alfred Einstein's 1947 Supplement to his third edition of Köchel, and was perhaps first voiced by Georges de Saint-Foix in 1936.[2] My own view, which I have hinted at from time to time,[3] is that it is the other way round: the 6/8 movement was written later. (This was assumed by the first two editions of Köchel, and by Einstein on publishing the third edition in 1937.) I should now like to spell out my arguments in greater detail.

But I realize from the start that I shall have little help from the man whose genius is the only excuse for inquiries such as the present one. For it seems that Mozart was not intending to clarify the true facts of the case but to obscure them; his motives for doing so become themselves part of the inquiry.

IT SOON becomes clear that for most of the information about Mozart's activities in Paris we are dependent on a single source—his letters to his father, Leopold. The first reference to the "Paris" Symphony is in a letter of 12 June 1778; he was visiting Count Sickingen and took along with him "the new symphony which I have just finished and with which the Concert Spirituel will open on Corpus Christi" (18 June). It was no doubt the serious illness of his mother, which ended with her death on 3 July, that prevented a report soon after the concert. But on that day, after warning Leopold of the gravity of his mother's illness (she had died an hour or two earlier, but he temporarily hid the fact from his father in order to break the news gently), he went on to describe the applause that had greeted the symphony—the first and last movements in particular, but "the Andante also found favour." It was only later, in his letter of 9 July, that he revealed that the original slow movement had not won total acclaim:

The Andante did not succeed in satisfying him [the impresario Legros]. He said it contained too much modulation and was too long. But that only happened because the audience forgot to make such a loud and continuous noise with their applause as they did in the first and last movements. For the Andante gave very much pleasure *to me,* to all connoisseurs, amateurs, and most of the audience. The movement is just the opposite of what Legros says—it is completely natural, and short. But to satisfy him (and according to him, several others), I have written another movement. Each is appropriate in its own way, for each has its own distinct character. But I like the later one even more. I shall send you the symphony . . . as soon as there is a good opportunity . . . On 15 August, the Feast of the Assumption, the symphony will receive its second performance, with the new Andante. The symphony is in Re and the Andante in Sol—here you mustn't say D or G.

The promise to send the symphony to Leopold as soon as a good opportunity arose was repeated in Mozart's letter of 20 July. But there is nothing more in the correspondence about any performance of the "Paris" Symphony. The letters of 27 August, 11 September, and 3 October (this last from the town of Nancy, a week after he left Paris) make no reference to the concert of 15 August, though newspaper announcements indicate that a Mozart symphony was to be played then.

Two further references to the symphony raise a separate problem—one that has been perceptively discussed by Neal Zaslaw[4]—since they make mention of *another* symphony besides the "Paris." In his letter of 11 September Mozart claimed: "I have made quite a name for myself by my two symphonies, the second of which was performed on the 8th" (according to newspaper announcements, "une nouvelle symphonie" by Mozart was to be played at the Concert Spirituel on that date). The final reference, in the 3 October letter from Nancy, seems designed to prepare Leopold for the meager harvest of works that resulted from the Paris sojourn: "I am not bringing you many new compositions, for I haven't composed very much . . . so I shall bring no finished work with me except my sonatas—for Legros purchased from me the two overtures [symphonies] and the sinfonia concertante. He thinks that he alone has them, but that is not true; they are still fresh in my mind, and as soon as I get home I shall write them down again."

That is the sum of the references to the "Paris" Symphony in Mozart's letters written at the time. And before we turn to other sources, we should ask whether any of this is evidence that the 6/8 movement is the earlier of the two.

It looks as though the proponents of that view have relied on two considerations. First, if Legros found the earlier movement too long, is not its replacement, designed to please him, likely to have been shorter? The 6/8 movement, as we have already said, has ninety-eight measures, whereas the 3/4 movement has only fifty-eight measures. But its first section is marked to be repeated, bringing it up to eighty-four measures; thus in performance there is little to choose between them.[5] Second, the version of the symphony that Mozart left with Legros appears to have been the one with the 3/4 movement, since that is what is found in the first edition, published in Paris by Sieber in the 1780s under the title "Du Repertoire Du Concert Spirituel."[6] But the question of what Mozart did and did not leave with Legros needs some further consideration.

ONE OF THE THINGS that he clearly did not leave with Legros but instead took away with him on leaving Paris was a collection of papers that amounted to a complete score of the symphony—the first of the two sources that I propose to call in evidence. This collection, which formed the basis of André's edition of 1800, and is today in the Musikabteilung of the Staatsbibliothek Preussischer Kulturbesitz in Berlin, is often referred to as "the autograph." But not all of it is in Mozart's hand, and it is perhaps better considered as four separate but related scores, since it consists of the following:

(1) Autograph score of the first movement. On 16-staff *Hochformat* (upright) paper. The paper, as one might expect, was made in France; its watermark consists of a crowned shield enclosing a bunch

of grapes, and the words "FIN DE / M [fleur-de-lys] IOHANNOT / DAN-NONAY / 1777."[7] The score includes a substantial number of deleted and rewritten passages.[8]

(2) Autograph draft of the 6/8 slow movement, marked "Andantino." On 16-staff *Hochformat* paper with the same watermark as (1). There are a great many crossed-out measures, but the movement is in fact complete, so the draft can be called the first autograph score of the movement. Among the deleted passages is an episode in E minor following measure 48, with a long flute solo, and (after an 8-measure return of the opening theme) an episode in C major, with an oboe solo; this breaks off after seven measures.[9]

(3) Autograph score of the 6/8 movement in its final form, marked "Andante." On *Hochformat* paper; the staves have been drawn singly and vary between sixteen and twenty on each page. The paper is of Swiss origin; its watermark reads: "NIC : HEISLER." The text in general follows (2), but in writing out the movement again Mozart has incorporated a number of small improvements (for which see Beck's critical report and my note 19).

(4) Score of the finale, in the hand of a copyist. On 16-staff *Hochformat* paper with the same watermark as (1).

There is general agreement (which I share) that (1) represents the original score of the first movement; indeed its numerous deleted passages and alterations scarcely encourage any other interpretation. And paper with an identical watermark is found in several of the autograph scores that Mozart is known to have written in Paris, the paper being ruled either with sixteen staves, as here in (1), (2), and (4) (the copyist's score of the finale), in the Gavotte, K.300, and in the fragment known as "La Chasse," K.299d (Anh. 103), or with fourteen staves, as in the D-major violin sonata, K.306(300l), and the A-minor piano sonata, K.310(300d). The presumption is that this paper was bought by Mozart in Paris and that anything written on it will have been composed in Paris or in the weeks immediately following his departure from it.[10]

But we must view a score written on paper from Basel, as is the case with (3), the finished version of the 6/8 movement, rather differently. Mozart will not have bought this paper, which was made by the well-known Basel firm of Heisler (or Heusler, as it is better known), in Paris.[11] But Swiss paper traveled down the Rhine, in much the same way as Dutch paper traveled up the Rhine, and we find the young Beethoven using both Dutch and Swiss paper—some of it made by

Heusler[12]—in his earliest compositions written in Bonn in the 1780s and the beginning of the 1790s. Thus it is possible that Mozart acquired the paper for writing out the final version of the 6/8 movement in Strasbourg, which he reached on about 14 October 1778, eighteen days after he had left Paris, and where he stayed until 3 November.[13] Or he may even have waited until he reached Mannheim on 6 November; he was to remain there for over a month.

The other source that I bring forward as evidence was described in some detail by Ernst Hess in 1965.[14] It is a sketchleaf of Mozart's discovered in the music library of the monastery at Einsiedeln in Switzerland. One side of the leaf includes the melodic line of the 3/4 movement (here marked "Andante con moto"). Although the size and character of the writing identifies it as a "sketch," it differs but little from the finished form of the movement, as Hess showed. It is neatly written, is furnished with slurs, staccato marks, and dynamic signs, and has repeat marks after the first twenty-six measures.

Below this extended draft of the 3/4 slow movement there are a couple of short sketches for what are apparently dances, one in 2/4 meter, one in 6/8. It is, however, the other side of the sketchleaf that brings the greatest surprise. For it contains a sketch for measures 136–142 of the finale of the "Paris" Symphony. This passage too is not yet in its final form. The natural inference is that while Mozart's work on the finale of the symphony had still some way to go, the 3/4 slow movement was almost ready. That would put the date of the sketchleaf's contents to a time before 12 June, the day on which he informed his father of the symphony's completion. Noverre's ballet pantomime *Les petits riens,* to which Mozart contributed some music—K.299b (Anh. 10)—was performed for the first time in Paris on 11 June, and that commission may account for the presence of the two above-mentioned dance sketches on the leaf.

Today the sketchleaf measures 182 × 202 mm. and has eleven staves on each side. But it has been cut; for careful examination indicates that it was originally a 16-staff *Hochformat* leaf, identical with the paper of the symphony's first-movement autograph and other scores described above. The watermark can just be made out: it is "[DA]NNONAY / 1777."[15]

THERE IS, however, one document that might be thought to tell against the views that I am advancing here. That is a copyist's score of the symphony, now in the Mozarteum in Salzburg. Hitherto its prime claim to scholarly attention has been the fact that on the first six pages the wind parts (though not the string parts) were written in by Mozart; a facsimile of those pages has been published.[16] But what is equally relevant to the present discussion is that it is written on the same *Hochformat* paper made by Johannot of Annonay already referred to so often, though this time it is of the 14-staff and not the 16-staff variety. And although the Salzburg score is not complete, it includes the whole of the first movement and the first six measures of the 6/8 slow movement—not in its draft form but in its final form. Is this not strong evidence that the 6/8 movement was not only composed but was ready to be copied—indeed, *was* copied to the extent of six measures—before the time that Mozart left Paris?

A careful examination of the Salzburg score reveals a somewhat complex situation. It consists of two gatherings each of six bifolia, making twenty-four leaves in all, undoubtedly bought in Paris. But there is no need to suppose that they were all used at the same time, while Mozart was still in Paris—indeed, five pages at the end are still unused today. In fact there are not two hands in the score but three: Mozart's and those of two copyists whose work was quite separate both in time and in place. The hand of the first copyist is familiar to us; he copied the finale of the symphony in the Berlin "autograph," item (4) of the Berlin scores. In the Salzburg score he wrote the string parts (violins 1 and 2, viola, basso) from the beginning of the symphony down to the end of page 33—to measure 231 of the first movement. It is likely enough that this was copied before Mozart began to write in the score, and it is certain that it was copied in Paris during Mozart's residence there. For these string parts can be shown to have been copied from the autograph score of the first movement at a time before Mozart made a number of small changes in it—mainly ones of altering triplet eighth notes into sixteenth notes.[17] And we know that these changes, visible as alterations in the autograph, were made while Mozart was still in Paris because they are found in the first edition of the symphony, which was based on the material (whether a score or a set of parts) that he left with Legros on his departure from the French capital.

Thus we can speak of a "Paris" copyist. But it should not be assumed that the rest of the score, although on Paris paper, was written in Paris. From page 34 (measure 232 of the first movement) another copyist takes over. It is he who not only completes the string parts of the first movement but who also copies the wind parts that Mozart had stopped writing in at the end of page 6 (measure 40 of the first movement). This second copyist also wrote out the first six measures of the 6/8 movement on page 43, and then stopped; as has already been said, the last five pages of the score are left blank.

Unlike the first, this second copyist has a "Viennese" hand. His work is known from other Mozart scores, mainly from the Viennese years—for example, a score of the late string quintet K.593—but is not found among the "authentic" sources, the scores emanating from Mozart's immediate circle. There is no particular reason to suppose that he was close to Mozart himself, and some of his scores may have been copied after Mozart's death.[18] The matter need not be pursued here: what is relevant is that there is no reason for supposing the six measures of the 6/8 movement in the Salzburg score to have been copied before the 1780s (at the earliest), or to have been copied in Paris. They came from a later period, and have no bearing on the time and place at which the 6/8 movement was composed.

LET US THEREFORE return to the sketchleaf and the Berlin scores. As has already been pointed out, the natural inference from the former is that the 3/4 movement was more or less finished by the time at which the finale was still being worked out; thus the 3/4 movement was part of the symphony performed on 12 June 1778. And the natural inference from the Basel paper used for (3) of the latter, the revised version of the 6/8 movement, is that this revision was carried out in Strasbourg (where Mozart gave an orchestral concert on 24 October and seemingly another one on 31 October), or possibly in Mannheim—at all events, after Mozart had left Paris behind him for ever.

But there is nothing in this to prevent the further conclusion that the 6/8 movement was first written in Paris. It would seem to be the version represented by (2) of the Berlin scores that was played when the "Paris" Symphony was performed for the second time on 15 August. Later, apparently, while in Strasbourg (or Mannheim), Mozart felt that there were at least some small ways in which it could be improved, and accordingly produced the revised version of the movement, (3) of the Berlin scores.[19]

The difficulty, of course, is to reconcile this apparently straightforward state of affairs with the statements in Mozart's letters to his father. If Mozart left Paris with autograph scores of the first two movements of the "Paris" Symphony and a copyist's score of the finale, why should he have written to his father from Nancy implying that he had been unable to take any orchestral music with him—it had all been left with Legros—though he hoped when back home to write it all down from memory? The painful fact, which he attempted to conceal from his father in a variety of ways, seems to have been that he had written very little in Paris. If Zaslaw is right (as I believe), the "second" Paris symphony was not a new one; and although in his letter of 11 September to his father Mozart does not specifically state that it was, that is the clear implication. The aim here was therefore to deceive his father concerning what he had been able to produce in Paris.[20]

In the light of this, an element of suspicion may perhaps attach to Mozart's claim that he had completed a sinfonia concertante for four wind instruments, which Legros then retained. Certainly the work that formerly passed as this, Köchel[6], Anh. C 14.01 (for a different combination of instruments), can be only a pale reflection of anything that Mozart composed, although the possibility cannot be entirely excluded that it is derived somewhat remotely from a Mozart fragment.[21] But a completed "concertante," which Legros insisted on acquiring from Mozart and then denied to the world? A degree of skepticism is surely justified here.[22]

Other works, for long believed to have been composed by Mozart in Paris, such as the three piano sonatas K.330, 331, and 332, as well as the piano sonata K.333, have recently been claimed for a later period.[23] This makes the yield of the Paris months even more meager, and perhaps renders Mozart's attempt to deceive his father yet more understandable. But the reason for his lack of productiveness remains a mystery. One possibility is that he became deeply depressed and withdrawn as a result of his mother's death, so that for a while he was virtually unable to compose. Such a depression is almost completely concealed in his letters; but if one reads between the lines, it may not seem so surprising that Mozart should have left Paris with so few finished compositions to his credit.

10

Le nozze di Figaro:
Lessons from the Autograph Score

U NTIL recently it was probably the case that very few of those interested in Mozart had ever seen the complete autograph score of a mature opera. They could, it is true, have inspected *Don Giovanni* in Paris, and most of *La clemenza di Tito* in West Berlin. But that was about all. It was only portions of the other operas that were available: the last act of *Così fan tutte,* the last act of *Idomeneo,* and the middle act of *Die Entführung aus dem Serail* could be seen in West Berlin, and the first two of *Le nozze di Figaro*'s four acts in East Berlin.

The rest of these operas, as well as the whole of *Die Zauberflöte,* could be described as war casualties. At the outbreak of World War II their complete scores had been in the Berlin Staatsbibliothek, but the collection was then divided and parts of it were sent away from Berlin for greater security. One consignment, particularly rich in Mozart scores, was not recovered at the end of hostilities. For many years it was rumored to be in Poland; this was repeatedly denied but finally conceded in the spring of 1977. The score of *Die Zauberflöte* was promptly handed back to the Berlin Library from which it came, but the others are still in Poland, at the Biblioteka Jagiellońska in Kraków; fortunately they are now accessible to scholars.

But what difference, it is sometimes asked, does the recovery of a Mozart autograph score really make? Surely the operas were edited in the last century and in this by sound scholars who had access to the autographs? Is there anything really new that can be gained from those old scores? This chapter, by taking the newly accessible third and fourth acts of *Figaro* as its subject, may answer some of these questions.

EVER SINCE 1965 there has been lively discussion in certain circles about Act III of *Figaro:* about the inconsequentiality of some of the stage action, and about a bold means of overcoming its difficulties. For in that year Robert Moberly and Christopher Raeburn published a short but penetrating article in which they claimed that the present sequence of events cannot have been the one originally conceived, but resulted from a change of plan on the part of Da Ponte and Mozart.

The argument is complex as well as subtle, and the 1965 article deserves to be studied in full;[1] it cannot properly be summarized here. But its two main features can be stated simply. According to Moberly and Raeburn, the Countess's *recitativo accompagnato* ("E Susanna non vien!") and aria ("Dove sono"), as well as the short *secco* dialogue between Barbarina and Cherubino that precedes them ("Andiam, andiam, bel paggio"), originally came much earlier in the act, between the Count's aria and the sestetto. And an ingenious explanation of the change of plan was provided. In the first production the parts of Bartolo and Antonio were doubled by the same singer; and Da Ponte and Mozart must have found that, in the original sequence, there was no time at the end of the recitative following the sestetto for Bartolo to change into Antonio's clothes for the very next scene—Antonio's entry to the words "Io vi dico, signor, che Cherubino è ancora nel castello."

The implications of the article were quickly seen by opera producers. If the only reason for abandoning a first-conceived, more satisfactory order of the scenes was a difficulty caused by the doubling of two roles by one singer, why abandon it in any modern performance in which Bartolo and Antonio were sung by two different artists? So a number of productions reverted to what was claimed to be the original sequence of events. From time to time it was asserted that this also produced a more convincing sequence of keys within the act. That is an argument that merits further scrutiny, for it suggests that the music had already been composed before Da Ponte and Mozart were forced to rearrange the numbers.

This brings us to what some have held to be the greatest difficulty with the Moberly-Raeburn proposal: the total absence of any "source" evidence to support it. Is that what we should expect? It is true that after World War II the autograph score of the last two acts of *Figaro* was not available for inspection. Yet those who edited the opera for the old Gesamtausgabe in the nineteenth century, and who consulted the autograph at the time, evidently saw nothing to arouse their suspicion that the third act had been rearranged at a late stage. Nor does the libretto of the first production, although (as we shall see) it differs in places from the final version and preserves some discarded passages, show any sign that the sequence of the numbers has been switched. Accordingly, in editing *Le nozze di Figaro* for the *Neue Mozart-Ausgabe* in 1973 (when the autograph of Acts III and IV was not yet accessible), Ludwig Finscher felt obliged to retain the "traditional" sequence, while at the same time acknowledging the attractiveness of the 1965 "solution."

LIKE THE FIRST two acts of *Figaro* in the Deutsche Staatsbibliothek, Berlin, which are bound as one volume, the autograph score of Acts III and IV is contained in a single binding, with the pages numbered in a red crayon from 1 to 130 (Act III), 131 to 254 (Act IV), and 255 to 280 (leaves with extra wind parts that could not be accommodated within the score). But up to the time of the opera's first performance it probably consisted of a whole series of separate numbers, interspersed with recitatives, and written down on paper of various types. The individual numbers (arias and ensembles) were completed at different times and certainly not in the order in which they now stand in the score; except for Act I, which has a continuous foliation, they are almost always individually foliated in Mozart's hand, and at the beginning is usually to be found a note of the act and scene to which they belong. (Some of these indications were partly trimmed off when the score was bound, but they can usually be made out.) The recitatives have their correct position indicated by the numbers that precede and follow them; for instance, the recitative "È decisa la lite" has at the beginning "Dopo l'aria del Conte" and at the end "attacca subito il Sestetto," both indications being in Mozart's hand.

It is obvious, then, that to effect an alteration in the sequence of events no more might be needed than to shuffle the leaves of the score and to provide the necessary links with what comes before and after. Let us therefore look at the autograph of the third act up to the entry of Antonio. (The scene-numbering here and throughout the chapter is Mozart's own, not that of the NMA.)

The arrow indicates the relocation of the present scenes vi and vii at which Moberly and Raeburn claim to have been their original positions. But it at once becomes clear that the situation is more complex than might have been predicted.

First, they had said that scene vi "serves no obvious purpose except as a short *secco* fill-in between the Count's aria and the entry of the Countess." But this is to overlook the matter of Cherubino's arietta. No music has survived for it, and we do not know its key (or, if it was never in fact started, its intended key), but it was to follow directly on a cadence in C. And up to a late stage Mozart seems to have counted on its being in the opera. The words were even printed in the libretto for the first performance at the end of scene vi (see Figure 10.1).

In the autograph the arietta is duly cued in. At the end of the recitative on page 63 Mozart writes: "segue l'arietta di Cherubino." There follows a figure in red crayon that corresponds to its position within the opera—"20" (crossed out, however). And below this Mozart adds a further cue, this time for "Dove sono": "dopo l'arietta di Cherubino, viene Scena 7:ma—ch'è un Recitativo istromentato, con aria della Contessa"; this is followed by "21" in red crayon. Accordingly, "Dove sono" was in its present position at a time when the arietta was still to be part of the act.

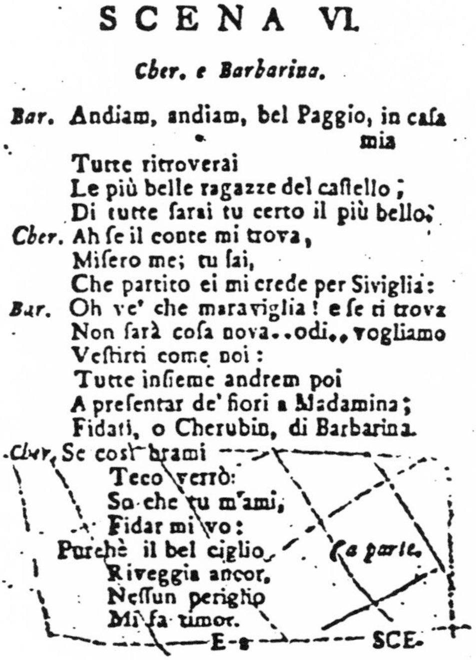

S C E N A VI.

Cher. e Barbarina.

Bar. Andiam, andiam, bel Paggio, in cafa
                          mia
Turte ritroverai
Le più belle ragazze del caftello ;
Di tutte farai tu certo il più bello.
Cher. Ah fe il conte mi trova,
Mifero me; tu fai,
Che partito ei mi crede per Siviglia:
Bar. Oh ve' che maraviglia ! e fe ti trova
Non farà cofa nova..odi,. vogliamo
Veftirti come noi :
Tutte infieme andrem poi
A prefentar de' fiori a Madamina ;
Fidati, o Cherubin, di Barbarina.
Cher. Se coft brami
Teco verrò:
So che tu m'ami,
Fidar mi vo:
Purchè il bel ciglio,   *(a parte.*
Riveggia ancor,
Neffun periglio
Mi fa timor.
                    E-s   SCE-

FIGURE 10.1. Part of page 67 in the libretto.
From the Library of Congress copy, Washington, D.C.

Second, it becomes clear that in its present form the autograph does not permit both scenes vi and vii to be relocated in the way proposed. For the start of scene vi is written on the same page—page 62—as the end of scene v, which must follow directly after the sestetto. How damaging is this to the Moberly-Raeburn hypothesis?

THERE SEEM to me to be two lines of escape, depending on the time in the collaboration between Da Ponte and Mozart at which a change of plan is thought to have taken place. If the problem arising from the doubling of roles was detected at a very early stage, *before* the numbers of the third act were written down, then there would be no reason why any "change of plan" should be reflected in the autograph score. But in that case one would expect Mozart to devise a sequence of keys suitable to the revised order of the numbers; if it happened to accord well with the original order as well, this would be no more than a coincidence. If, on the other hand, it is supposed that the score of the third act had been completed before the "change of plan," then it is necessary to assume that scene vi was rewritten in its new position.

Thus we shall be grateful for any help we can get in separating the various chronological layers of the autograph score. Our best guide here is the different types of paper on which the various numbers and connecting recitatives are written. A similar technique (though based on idiosyncrasies of the staff-rulings, not of the watermarks, and perhaps not so strictly directed) has already been used on the first two acts of *Figaro* by Karl-Heinz Köhler in 1967.[2] Köhler was handicapped by not having access to the autograph of the last two acts; nevertheless his conclusions as to the order in which Mozart tackled the numbers in Acts I and II appear to stand up well. What follows, then, is a highly condensed report of much detailed work on the autograph's various papers.

ABOUT THE TIME that he started to work on the third and fourth acts, Mozart acquired paper of a type that he had not used before. It can be distinguished from the other papers in the score most readily by its watermark: the letters GFA, with three moons over the word REAL as a countermark.[3] The total span (TS) of the staves, measured vertically, is either 186 mm. (sometimes 186.5) or, much less commonly, 182 mm. (sometimes 183). Moreover the pages of this paper-type with the 186 mm. staff-ruling have a recurrent irregular pattern in the "profile" created by the left ends of the staves. The fourth line of the third staff, for instance, projects further to the left than the other lines of that staff, as does also the second line of the ninth staff. The value of such banal observations is that the paper-type can be identified with a good degree of certainty from photographs.

Not that the whole of Acts III and IV is on paper of this New Type. In Act III the opening recitative, the duettino between the Count and Susanna (except its last page), the recitative that follows it, the sestetto, the second page of the dialogue between Barbarina and Cherubino (page 63), and the recitative after the chorus of village maidens are all on another paper-type found also in the first two acts, where it was used for some repair work and for a few recitatives—that is, *late* in the construction of those acts. But what of Act III? (It does not occur in Act IV, perhaps in itself a clue.) Can one say if it is earlier or later than the New Type? Some overlapping no doubt occurred, but the evidence points to its being in the main earlier. For Mozart, we

know, is likely to have tackled the less "soloistic" duettino and sestetto before undertaking the major solos in this act, the arias of the
Count and Countess; both these arias are on the New Type—as indeed is almost all the rest of the act, as well as the whole of the last act
(apart from Barbarina's Cavatina, seemingly a last-minute addition at
its very beginning), and also the supplementary wind parts at the end
of the score. In general terms, then, the New Type may be said to have
been the last paper that Mozart used for *Figaro*.

The instances of its use in the first half of the opera merely strengthen
that impression. It was used for the overture, and for three numbers at
the start of the second act—the Countess's aria "Porgi amor" at the
very beginning, Cherubino's arietta "Voi che sapete," and Susanna's
aria "Venite inginocchiatevi."[4] Köhler claimed all these as late additions to the score, and Finscher has pointed out that "Voi che sapete,"
which has the same meter as the text of Cherubino's lost arietta, may
have been a last-minute substitution for it.

It is not merely the major arias for the third act that are on paper
of the New Type; the same is true of their sketches. Figure 10.2 shows
a sketchleaf that is today in the Biblioteca Estense, Modena; the left-
hand "profile" of the staff-ends confirms the paper-type. The first
three staves contain sketches for the Countess's aria, while the rest
have sketches for the Count's. The opening of "Dove sono" on the top
staff (transcribed in NMA II/5/16, Part II, p. 634) differs a little from
the final text, but that this is not a sketch for an earlier but nevertheless completed version of the aria is indicated by measures 8–10 of
the third staff (omitted from the NMA transcription); these give the
voice part of measures 60–62 of the aria in a form that is to be found
in the autograph, where, however, it has been deleted and replaced by
the final text. (The bass line has had to be changed, but the other
strings and wind go only with the new notes, showing that for a time
the score consisted of vocal line and bass line alone.)

It is the destiny of paper-evidence to be suggestive rather than conclusive. All that has been established here is (*a*) that much of the autograph score of the third act (and some of its sketches) was written
rather late, after the first two acts had been more or less completed,
and (*b*) that in its present form the autograph score, as represented by
pages 62–63, is inconsistent with the Moberly-Raeburn hypothesis.
But it could always be argued that page 63 was a late insertion to enable scene vi to be recopied on pages 62–63. This is probably the best

FIGURE 10.2. Sketchleaf for the Countess's and Count's arias. Biblioteca Estense, Modena.

line of defense. That it is not on the New Type paper may not matter all that much, but it must have been recopied when Cherubino was still expected to sing "Se così brami," and any account of the "change of plan" is obliged to take the lost arietta into consideration.

THE KEY-SEQUENCE of the third act, since it has been adduced as evidence for the original order of the numbers, merits a few words. The present order, and the claimed original order, can be set out:

Duettino (Count, Susanna)	a–A
Count's aria	D
Sestetto	F
Arietta (Cherubino)	?
Countess's aria	C
Duettino (Susanna, Countess)	B-flat
Chorus	G
Finale	C

In what key was Cherubino's arietta intended to be? A cadence in C would normally be expected to be followed by a number either in the same key or a fourth higher. But C major is already usurped by "Dove sono," and F major is the key of the sestetto; possibly the key of G major, a relationship to the end of the recitative that has a few parallels, was what Mozart had in mind.[5]

The key-sequence ultimately adopted seems perfectly acceptable. The same is true of what is claimed to have been the original order; if we posit an arietta from Cherubino in G, we have an inexorable series of fourths, broken only once near the end in the transition from the "letter" duettino to the following chorus: A–D–G–C–F–B-flat–G–C. A fearful symmetry? Probably not, but at any rate Mozart settled for something else.

IT IS LIKELY that problems of key-sequence, and possibly some uncertainty as to the best arrangement of the numbers, arose also before Act IV was completed.

Figure 10.3 shows part of an incomplete score for an early version of Susanna's fourth-act aria. All that is known of this version will be found transcribed in NMA II/5/16, Part II, pp. 638–641: a sketch for part of the aria, and a score for the accompanied recitative (thirty-four measures) and the first thirty-six measures of the aria. It is described (at the end of this recitative score) as a "Rondò"—that is, as

FIGURE 10.3. Draft for Susanna's rondò in E-flat.

an aria with a slow section followed by a fast one, though we have no
sketches or score today that relates to the fast part.[6]

From Figure 10.3 we can see that it is on paper of the New Type,
and—more bewilderingly—that it is in E-flat. For the aria that replaced it ("Deh vieni non tardar") is in F major. Why the change of
key? In each case the preceding accompanied recitative has much the
same musical content, but that leading to the E-flat rondò makes
a cadence on B-flat; that leading to the F-major aria makes a cadence on F.

The clue would appear to lie in Figaro's aria, "Aprite un po' que-
gl'occhi." For in the completed opera this comes before Susanna's
aria, and is in E-flat. Clearly two arias in E-flat in succession would be
maladroit. But what if Figaro's aria was originally intended to be in a
different key, and to come *after* Susanna's E-flat aria? That would help
to mediate the otherwise brusque sequence of Susanna's aria in E-flat
being followed directly by the finale in D.

And there is evidence that Susanna's aria in its F-major form, and Figaro's E-flat aria, were among the last pieces in the opera to be completed. The recitative at page 161 of the autograph ends with the words: "Segue Recit: istrumentato con Rondò di Susana," so that when that was written her aria was still the rondò version in E-flat. But a sketch for the F-major version (NMA II/5/16, Part II, p. 641) is on the same page as a sketch for part of the overture (ibid., p. 628), surely a sign that it was written very late. And at the top of page 174, otherwise left blank by him, on the last side of the bifolium that he had used to complete the final version of the F-major aria, Mozart wrote: "Manca il Recitativo istromentato di Figaro avanti l'aria No. 30." Probably it had not yet been composed—seemingly another sign of last-minute rethinking.[7] In the autograph score, Figaro's aria has been placed *after* Susanna's F-major aria. It obviously does not belong there any longer, but perhaps this reflects in some way an earlier organization of the act, in which both the arias had different keys from their present ones. If Susanna's original aria in E-flat had been followed by an aria for Figaro in F, that would have given a key-sequence no different from the one that Mozart finally adopted.[8]

It may be that working with an autograph score solves some problems. But it also provides new ones in exchange. Perhaps that is why I find working with it so appealing.

11

The Mozart Fragments in the Mozarteum, Salzburg: A Preliminary Study of Their Chronology and Their Significance

THIS CHAPTER falls into three broad sections. In the first, I outline the history of Mozart's fragments, in particular those that came to rest at the Internationale Stiftung Mozarteum in Salzburg, and I review the various attempts that have been made to assign them their correct positions within the composer's oeuvre. In the second, I attempt to determine the dates of the Mozarteum fragments, relying particularly on the evidence afforded by paper-types. And I conclude by considering what such fragments can tell us of Mozart's working methods.

I

IN ADDITION to his very many completed compositions, Mozart left behind at his death a substantial number of unfinished scores or "fragments." Not surprisingly, perhaps, these fragments varied greatly in length; while some were the torsos of very substantial but unfinished works, others consisted of only a few measures of music. Yet taken together they were treated from the start as forming a significant part of the *Nachlass*. In 1799 Constanze Mozart arranged for a careful catalogue of them to be compiled by the Abbé Maximilian Stadler, and after she had disposed of all the available scores of her late husband's completed works to the publisher Johann Anton André in January 1800, the fate of the fragments, which had not been included in the sale, began to exercise her.

On 1 March 1800, therefore, she sent to Breitkopf & Härtel in Leipzig a list of the fragments, and invited them to include it in their journal, the *Allgemeine musikalische Zeitung*. The list was prefaced by the following paragraph:

> Report on Mozart's Surviving Fragments
> Submitted by His Widow
>
> Fragments of classical writers, of whatever category they may be, are objects of value. Among musical fragments those of Mozart certainly deserve every honor and respect. Had this great composer not left so many completed works in every genre (their total number is astonishing when one remembers that he was not thirty-six), these marvelous relics would by themselves be an enduring monument to his inexhaustible genius. What follows is an accurate list of those fragments that are of lasting value (for many others have been destroyed on account of their total unusability); with the exception of only twelve items expressly noted in the list, all the fragments are still in the possession of the composer's widow in Vienna.[1]

There followed a catalogue of thirty-two items "für das Clavier" (as well as a packet of thoroughbass exercises), twenty-seven items "für die Violine," nine items "für Blasinstrumente," fourteen items "von Singmusik," six items in the form of further fragments for "Clavier" that had been "completed by an amateur," and nine miscellaneous items no longer in Constanze's possession. A total, then, of ninety-eight items. It is clear that the list was based on Stadler's catalogue (he was also the "amateur" just referred to). But Breitkopf & Härtel chose not to print it in the *Allgemeine musikalische Zeitung*, and the list remained unpublished until 1828, when it appeared (with slight changes) in the Anhang to Georg Nikolaus Nissen's biography.[2]

Constanze's aim in having the list compiled and her desire to see it promulgated are sufficiently clear from her correspondence with Breitkopf & Härtel and with André, to both of whom at different times she offered the fragments for sale. She had set her heart on their publication—or at any rate publication of their incipits—both as further evidence of her husband's genius and as a protection against their appropriation by others. As early as 15 June 1799, indeed, she had suggested to Breitkopf & Härtel that they might care to publish them,[3] and her letter to André of 31 May 1800 makes her position even clearer:

I am concerned that everything that my husband wrote should be published. . . . Now when you bought those fifteen parcels from me, you also saw a quantity of fragments and draft material which I told you I was not giving you. And far from laying claim to them or expressing any wish to have them, you exclaimed: "Many people would be glad to have these things. What a fraud could be perpetrated with them! Why, one could have fine themes at a stroke!" I am carefully preserving them, and if my [elder] son [Karl] does not make use of them some day, then they will certainly never be used, and perhaps somebody may care to publish them in a collection, just as they are, as objects of curiosity. If that happened, no one could ever deck himself in borrowed plumes, and Mozart would retain the credit that is Mozart's due.[4]

The desire to have the fragments catalogued and thus made available to the public (as well as to have them protected against misappropriation) recurs in later letters to André, such as those of 10 September, 4 October, 16 and 26 November 1800, and 26 January 1801. But André's interest was confined to tracing missing portions of completed scores;[5] unfinished fragments evoked no response in him, nor—it would appear—in anyone else until collectors such as Aloys Fuchs appeared on the scene in the 1820s.

In the end, a few of the fragments found purchasers or grateful recipients. They were mostly the longer and more impressive pieces.[6] The rest remained with Constanze until her death in 1842. They then went to her younger son, Wolfgang; and on his death two years later, Frau von Baroni-Cavalcabò (Wolfgang's residuary legatee) and Aloys Fuchs arranged for them to pass into the custody of the Mozarteum in Salzburg. By that time the number of fragments in the collection had fallen to sixty.

T H E S E   S I X T Y   F R A G M E N T S are the central subject of the present study. At a very rough approximation they form a little less than half of the surviving autographs that qualify for the description of "fragment."[7] But in spite of having been kept together in the same collection for so long, they cannot be said to be well known. Constanze's modest wish that at any rate their incipits should be published was not fulfilled for more than a century, and even today scores of only about four-fifths of them are in print, most having become available within the last twenty-five years in the appendices to volumes of the *Neue Mozart-Ausgabe*.[8]

And it may be that their obscurity has been due in part to one of the themes of this chapter—their uncertain chronology. In publishing his famous catalogue in 1862 Ludwig von Köchel relegated the fragments—"unvollständige Compositionen"—to one of the five sections of the appendix (Anhang), and did not include their incipits. His reason was no doubt a practical one. For the catalogue was a *Chronologisch-thematisches Verzeichniss*, so he may have felt it an al-

most impossible task to find appropriate places within the chronological sequence of the main part of the book for all the undated and
seemingly undatable fragments.[9] And having relegated them to the appendix, he evidently felt that they had lost their claim to an incipit.
The editor of the second edition of Köchel's catalogue (1905), Paul
Graf von Waldersee, said at the end of his preface that he would gladly
have included incipits of the fragments but had been prevented by "in-
superable difficulties." Accordingly they remained in the Anhang for a
further generation.

It was Alfred Einstein, the editor of the third and greatly revised
version of Köchel (1937), who first intercalated the fragments at what
appeared to him to be appropriate places within the main part of the
catalogue. The fragments were provided with incipits, and for the first
time they received Köchel numbers—or rather "Köchel-Einstein numbers," newly devised combinations of a number and a letter that made
it easy for the editor, while retaining Köchel's basic chronological series running from 1 to 626, to insert new items and to rearrange old
ones in the light of the most recent conclusions of Mozart scholarship.
In fact the 1937 revision of Köchel resulted in a thoroughgoing rearrangement of the entire catalogue. For not a few users of that book,
indeed, the advantage of having the fragments numbered and provided with incipits must have been outweighed by the confusion that
resulted when compositions had to yield up their familiar, almost hal-
lowed, Köchel numbers, and to accept strange Köchel-Einstein numbers in exchange! In exchange—or in addition; for one consequence
was the cumbersome system of double numbers, Köchel *plus* Köchel-
Einstein, subsequently adopted in the Mozart literature, which the
further modifications of numbering introduced in Köchel[6] have rendered even more complicated today.

The question arises how Einstein tackled the problem which had
apparently defeated Köchel, that of finding convincing dates for the
fragments. This is an issue that has proved fateful for Mozart scholarship over the last forty years. For Einstein's 1937 datings were widely
accepted, and for the most part they have been retained in the latest
(sixth) edition of Köchel. It is only in recent years, in fact, that the
opinion has gained ground that many of them are seriously wrong.[10]
In this respect the Salzburg fragments are merely part of a wider context, though the discussion that follows will be restricted as far as
possible to them.

The preface to the third edition of Köchel goes some way to illuminating what was in Einstein's mind. It is clear that he was anxious to distinguish his own approach from those of his two great predecessors in Mozart bibliography, Otto Jahn and Köchel. Jahn, the "archaeologist and philologist," was criticized for being too much a man of learning and too little a musician; his picture of Mozart was characterized as one-sided and limited. And much the same judgment was passed on Köchel, for he was "not enough of a musician" and his approach was purely "archival." In contrast, the two volumes that had been published by Théodore de Wyzewa and Georges de Saint-Foix in 1912, covering Mozart's musical life and compositions up to the year 1777, were acclaimed by Einstein as evidence of a new "Aufschwung" in Mozart studies. They were "revolutionary" in that they focused on "Mozart's work, the influence of contemporary artists on that work, and his inner development." Their impact on Einstein cannot be overestimated; he regarded them as having rendered Köchel's approach out of date, and their "nouveau classement," based for the most part on considerations of style, is everywhere apparent as an influence upon the arrangement of Köchel[3].

This is not the place for an extensive critique of the approach of Wyzewa and Saint-Foix (whose work, after the premature death of Wyzewa in 1917, Saint-Foix eventually completed with the publication of the three final volumes in 1936, 1939, and 1946). There are observations of great value throughout the pages of that monumental enterprise. Yet it must be said that the confidence with which they applied stylistic criteria to chronology strikes many readers today as a little ridiculous. Of the piano sonatas K.330–332, for instance, they write that all three belong to the months spent by Mozart in Paris in the summer of 1778. K.331 is assigned on stylistic grounds to the period from May to July, and K.330 and 332 are allotted to the months of July–September. This very precise dating was accepted by Einstein without reservations; yet there is not the slightest evidence to support the idea that the sonatas date even from the year 1778.

Moreover, the techniques that Einstein himself applied, when he was not merely following the lead of Wyzewa and Saint-Foix, were fairly unsophisticated. Several Mozart fragments, he rightly perceived, are best understood as first attempts to write movements that were subsequently replaced by similar though different ones. The clues here are identity of scoring reinforced by identity (or appropriateness) of key as well. Two piano-concerto fragments, for instance, K.488b (Anh. 63) and K.488c (Anh. 64), are in the key of A major and are scored for an orchestra with two clarinets but no oboes. These, as Einstein saw, are likely to be first attempts at a finale for K.488, in the same key and with the same scoring.

Such an approach is perfectly sound so far as it goes, though scoring and key alone do not necessarily guarantee that the right context has been found. But in any case it can account for only a small number of the fragments.[11] In other cases, where the key was *not* suitable, Einstein was prone to suggest that the fragment was part of a *Gegenstück* (companion piece) or *Zwillingswerk* (twin work) to a completed composition; but in effect that meant all too often that the guide-line of identity in both scoring and key was abandoned for the less cogent link provided by scoring alone.

From here it was only a little way to a still vaguer conceptual frame where Einstein assigned fragments to a particular *Gedankenkreis* (loosely translatable as a "constellation of ideas") of Mozart's. Once again there is a core of common sense to this: it is readily observable that he worked on particular types of compositions at particular times—string quintets, for instance, in the spring of 1787 and symphonies in the summer of 1788. But where the dating of fragments is concerned such ascriptions require great caution and an awareness of the range of possible alternatives.

IN ATTEMPTING to date the fragments purely on the basis of their musical contents, Einstein was consciously rejecting other available techniques, and his grounds for doing so deserve to be understood. A few years earlier the fragments in the Mozarteum had been the subject of a dissertation by Mena Blaschitz, "Die salzburger Mozartfragmente." In Köchel[3] Einstein almost always cited Blaschitz's chronological conclusions when giving his own reasons for his placing of a fragment. But he did not often agree with her, and the consensus (referred to above) that has in very recent years moved against many details of Einstein's chronology is at least in agreement with him in rejecting most of Blaschitz's chronology as well.

Blaschitz chose to focus on physical aspects of the fragments: the paper-types, the rastrology (characteristics of staff-ruling), and the handwriting. Her investigation of the first two was both superficial and inconclusive; she therefore abandoned them as aids. Instead, she based her chronology largely on her impressions of Mozart's handwriting. In this she was guided by the book of her teacher Ludwig Schiedermair in Bonn, *W. A. Mozarts Handschrift in zeitlich geord-*

neten Nachbildungen, published in Leipzig in 1919. But Schiedermair (to judge from that work) was concerned with illustrating the changes that Mozart's handwriting underwent in the course of the years and briefly characterizing them rather than setting out in any great detail the precise criteria for dating them. Moreover, Blaschitz's knowledge of Mozart's handwriting—apart from the fragments she was studying—seems to have been confined largely to the examples provided by Schiedermair's plates.

Thus she was scarcely in a position to analyze the handwriting systematically. Her limitations here can be suggested by one not untypical example. Of the four Kyrie fragments in the Mozarteum, No. 3 (K.166g), No. 29 (K.196a), No. 56 (K.258a), and No. 57 (K.422a), she wrote that they "show in the notation of music and words so much resemblance that they must be chronologically very close to one another."[12] Her point of comparison was Schiedermair's Plate 20, a page of an aria from *La finta gardiniera,* K.196, dating from 1774; accordingly she assigned all four fragments to that year. But the recent work on both handwriting and paper-types which is discussed below is in agreement that whereas K.166g was probably written down a little before 1774 (the year 1772 has been suggested), the other three Kyrie fragments date from the late Vienna years and are certainly no earlier than 1787.

Einstein seems to have been grateful for Blaschitz's lead in rejecting the study of paper-types—and of the watermarks that are their main distinguishing feature—as a guide to chronology; in any case, his own account of their inadequacies as he saw them suggests that he had not himself persevered far with them.[13] And although he paid lip service to the usefulness of Mozart's handwriting in providing dating criteria, he did not in practice have much faith in it: "It is only rarely that the handwriting pattern by *itself* is decisive in regard to determining the exact chronology of one of Mozart's works."[14] In effect, then, Einstein fell back on his "internal" criteria, the limitations of which have already been discussed. It is time to consider whether the "external" criteria that he rejected may not in fact have a great deal more to offer.

A landmark in this respect is the 1978 article by Wolfgang Plath on the use of handwriting as a dating technique.[15] In it Plath aims at establishing by means of dated scores exact criteria for the identification of the changes in Mozart's handwriting through the course of the 1770s—criteria that are then systematically applied to the undated scores and fragments of scores. Although it will take a number of years fully to digest the results of Plath's investigations, it is already clear that no account of Mozart's productivity in the 1770s can afford to dispense with his conclusions. Numerous compositions, complete and incomplete, that were assigned a place in that decade in the various editions of Köchel (including the latest) have now been convincingly claimed by Plath either to belong to another time altogether or to be quite wrongly placed within that period. And a few other pieces traditionally assigned to dates after 1780 can be shown in fact to belong to the 1770s.

It may be asked why a method apparently discredited by Blaschitz should have proved so fruitful in the hands of Plath. The answer can only lie in the systematic and refined nature of Plath's investigations. With an unrivaled knowledge of Mozart autographs, he chose to focus on a single decade, one that saw Mozart pass from an adolescent of fourteen to a young man of twenty-four. Within that period, not surprisingly, Mozart's handwriting underwent a series of well-marked changes; the identification of these, and the chronological limits to be assigned to each of the variations, form the substance of Plath's article.[16]

It remains to be seen how far this technique can be extended to the years that followed, the period from 1781 to 1791, when Mozart resided in Vienna. That will depend on the identification of features in the handwriting that can be dated with some certainty. Naturally it is somewhat harder to find them in a mature style of writing, though the grosser differences between the hand of the earliest and latest Viennese years are not too difficult to characterize. Meanwhile, the results of Plath's *Schriftchronologie* for the 1770s will give Mozart scholars much to ponder. To cite but one of the more surprising conclusions: among the autograph material that has come down to us for the music to *Thamos, König in Aegypten,* K.345 (336a), the entr'actes are in a handwriting that dates from about 1777, that is, *before* the journey to Paris, whereas the choruses are in the writing of 1779 or early 1780, that is, *after* Paris.[17] What this means in terms of the stage-history of the work is not at all clear; yet there can be no doubt about the differences in the handwriting.

IT IS, HOWEVER, the other potential dating technique rejected by Einstein with which much of the present chapter is concerned. This technique consists in the establishment of a chronology that is based on the paper-types used by Mozart, these being identified by their watermarks and in some cases further refined by data derived from the rastrology. Once again it is necessary to ask why such a method, when applied today, is likely to prove more successful than in the days of Blaschitz and Einstein.

And once again the answer must lie in the systematic application of the technique—in this case, the identifying and distinguishing of the watermarks. The basic principles for achieving this are, in spite of an expanding literature,[18] still imperfectly understood. It needs to be grasped that each *leaf* of the paper used by Mozart is a quarter of a large *sheet* of paper; thus a single leaf can carry only a quarter, or "quadrant," of the sheet-watermark. As each watermark quadrant is likely to be unintelligible by itself, the aim must be to reconstruct the complete sheet-watermark, rather than to offer an inadequate description of part of it. A further complication is that the sheet-watermark is always to be found in two "twin" forms (since sheets of paper were made from a pair of similar molds used in alternation), one form usually being the mirror image of the other. These "twins" have to be distinguished from each other and identified separately. Only when the four quadrants of each of the "twin" forms have been completely worked out (and when, for preference, tracings or photographs have been made of them) can one claim to have total control of the watermark. But from that point on one can say with complete certainty, on encountering a new watermark, either that it is identical with the one that has been mastered or that it is quite distinct from it; intermediate categories, such as "similar to it" or "closely resembling it," have no place in the kind of research described here, any more than they have in the discipline of fingerprinting.

Once paper-types have been identified in this way, it is merely a matter of enquiry to ascertain what paper-types were used by Mozart, and at what times and in what places. A good start in dating the paper-types is provided by those autograph scores that Mozart himself dated either by an inscription or (indirectly) by an entry in his Verzeichnüss, the little catalogue of his works that he started in 1784 and continued up to the time of his death in 1791.[19] It is not necessary to have any preconceived notions about the way in which Mozart bought and used paper, though the variety of paper-types found in works completed at roughly the same time, and even within a single work, must suggest that he purchased it frequently, but in small quantities. There would be nothing surprising in that, for at the time paper was a costly item.

In fact a systematic cataloguing of the range of paper-types used by Mozart over the years yields some striking and stimulating results.

There are, for instance, a few paper-types that were in use for a very limited period: one of them, to judge from the autographs of K.497, K.498, and K.499 (the sole works in which it has been found), was in Mozart's hands only in the month of August 1786, while the evidence indicates that others were available to him only in the very last years of his life. On the other hand, there are some papers that appear to have been used by him for most of the Vienna years, or at any rate at a whole series of different times within them. In such cases the paper-type can offer no clue to the date, where that is in doubt. But instances like that must not be used to discredit the help to be derived from other paper-types that Mozart used within a circumscribed period.

A longer example may serve to illustrate the advantages of this technique, and perhaps a few of its limitations as well. There is one paper-type that has not so far been identified in any dated score of Mozart's before December 1787. From that moment it is to be found in almost all (perhaps, even, in all) of the autographs that he is known to have completed within the following fourteen months—but, with only two exceptions, in no dated score after that. It appears, therefore, to be a legitimate inference that Mozart's use of this paper was more or less confined to the fourteen months from December 1787 to February 1789. Here, first, is a list of these dated autograph scores in which it is found:

11 December 1787	K.531	Song: "Die kleine Spinnerin"
23 January 1788	K.535	Contredanse: "La Bataille"
24 February 1788	K.537	Piano Concerto in D (end of first movement, middle of last movement)
4 March 1788	K.538	Aria: "Ah se in ciel, benigne stelle"
5 March 1788	K.539	Song: "Ich möchte wohl der Kaiser sein"
19 March 1788	K.540	Adagio for piano in B minor
24 April 1788	K.540a	Aria for Ottavio: "Dalla sua pace"
30 April 1788	K.540c	Recitative and aria for Donna Elvira: "In quali eccessi"—"Mi tradì"
22 June 1788	K.542	Piano Trio in E
26 June 1788	K.543	Symphony in E-flat
25 July 1788	K.550	Symphony in G Minor
10 August 1788	K.551	Symphony in C ("Jupiter")
2 September 1788	K.553–K.561	Canons. Also drafts for K.553, K.557.[20]
27 October 1788	K.564	Piano Trio in G (piano part, 2 leaves)
February 1789	K.570	Piano Sonata in B-flat[21]

*   *   *

December 1789   K.585, Nos. 1–4: Minuets for 2 violins, bass
5 January 1791   K.595   Piano Concerto in B-flat (first, second, and
                           start of third movement)

It is only the last two items that fall outside the suggested time-span. The first of them, K.585, proves on examination to be no real exception. For the autograph in question consists of only the first four minuets, scored for two violins and bass; since the last page is blank, one must conclude that no more had been written at the time. The entry in the Verzeichnüss, on the other hand, which provides the "December 1789" date, relates to the *whole* of K.585, twelve minuets scored for a full orchestra. And there is independent evidence that the string-trio version of the first four minuets preceded the orchestral version.[22] The case of K.595 is more complex. It is clear that Mozart completed the score of this, his last piano concerto, in January 1791—but may he not have started it much earlier, for instance in 1788? This is a point which, together with some parallel examples, is discussed in my final section.

It looks, in fact, as if Mozart made use of this paper only in a period that began directly after his return to Vienna at the end of 1787 (following the first performance of *Don Giovanni* in Prague), and that ended before he set out on his trip to Prague, Leipzig, and Berlin in the spring of 1789. (Parts of the score of K.595 would be a possible exception.) What happens, then, if we apply the same time-limits to the other autograph sources on the same paper for which Mozart has provided no date?

The short answer is that we find a quite unexpectedly large group of finished scores, fragments, and transcriptions assigned to these months. Among the scores are the bass aria "Io ti lascio, o cara, addio," K.621a (Anh. 245), which Einstein placed in September 1791, and the string quintet in C minor, K.406 (516b)—an arrangement of the wind serenade K.388 (384a)—which he placed in the spring of 1787. It would seem that his dates for both of these must be wrong. The fragments on this paper, most of which are in the Mozarteum, include several drafts for piano sonatas and—more surprisingly—for a Mass or Masses; these, together with transcriptions of church works by Carl Georg Reutter, are discussed in the following section. But the point that needs to be made here is that in practically no instances do the dates assigned to these fragments and transcriptions by Blaschitz and Einstein fall within the period that we have allotted to this paper-type. And if the principle of dating by paper-type is a sound one, we can lay claim to a technique that promises to offer a more reliable guide to the dating of the Salzburg fragments.

I I

THE ''SIXTY FRAGMENTS'' of the Mozarteum, to which we can at last return, are today no more than fifty-eight; for No. 30, K.475a (Anh. 26), the song-fragment "Einsam bin ich," was given away in 1850, and No. 21, K.620a (Anh. 102), the fragment of an overture in E-flat which must have been intended for *Die Zauberflöte*,[23] disappeared more recently in circumstances that have not been explained. And we shall simplify our task by a somewhat summary treatment of the pre-1781 fragments. It is a striking fact about the fifty-eight surviving fragments that all but four, Nos. 3, 22, 31, and 60, belong to Mozart's Vienna years, the period from March 1781 to December 1791. This seems generally to have been recognized in the past (although Blaschitz dated five fragments to the pre-Vienna years, and Einstein seven).[24] No doubt it merely reflects the "usable" music that was mixed up with the autographs of finished works in Mozart's lodgings at the time of his death; indeed, when we reflect on the unpremeditated way in which Mozart settled in Vienna in 1781, it is perhaps a little surprising that any fragments from the Salzburg years should have found their way into the company.

In the classification that follows, the fifty-four fragments from the Vienna years are referred to in the first place by their Mozarteum numbers. These, it is true, seem to have been allocated some time before 1850 in a somewhat unsystematic way, but at least they have remained constant through the years; in any case Tables 11.1 and 11.2 at the end of this chapter provide concordances with the numberings of Köchel[3] and Köchel[6], as well as with the Anhang of Köchel[1]. The fragments are arranged under twenty-one different paper-types, to which the letters from (A) to (U) have been assigned for the purposes of this account.[25] Under each letter there are some comments on the dating of that particular type, and of the individual fragments grouped under it. In the case of some papers that Mozart used at several different times an additional chronological refinement within a type is provided by the rastrology: here the TS (total span)—the vertical distance (in millimeters) from the top line of the top staff to the bottom line of the bottom staff—may be described if it helps to determine a more exact chronology.

The four fragments from the pre-Vienna years are briefly discussed after the other fragments. They are on four different paper-types, which have been assigned the letters from (V) to (Y). Since each of the four fragments has been dated by Plath on the basis of its handwriting, his conclusions are recorded here alongside the datings suggested by their papers.

Fragments from the Vienna years (March 1781–December 1791)

(A) No. 1.   K.535b (Anh. 107)   Contredanse in B-flat. 24 mm.
     No. 40. K.593a (Anh. 35)   Adagio for mechanical organ. 9 mm.

A late paper-type. Apart from two scores (a full score and a piano score) of the soprano aria "Un moto di gioia," K.579, which probably date from August 1789 but which could possibly have been written out later, all the examples of this paper-type so far identified are from the last twelve months of Mozart's life. K.535b can perhaps be connected with other late contredanses, such as K.603, No. 2 (in the same key), and K.593a with K.608 (or with K.594, as Einstein suggested in Köchel³).

(B) No. 2.   K.522a (Anh. 108)   Rondo (strings, 2 horns). 24 mm.
     No. 5.   K.525a (Anh. 69)   Larghetto (2 vln, vla, vlc, cb). 16 mm.
     No. 7.   K.626b/32–33   Sketches, including ones for K.434
                                     (480b).
     No. 19. K.516a (Anh. 86)   String quintet in G minor. 8 mm.
     No. 48. K.495a (Anh. 52)   Piano trio in G. 19 mm.

This paper-type is found with two very similar but seemingly distinguishable TS patterns, one of 187–188 mm. and the other of 189. The latter, represented here only by fragment No. 7, is the earlier, and seems to be found from 1784 to 1786; the slightly shorter TS is apparently found in 1787, and possibly early in 1788.

In this case, therefore, the paper-type, even when reinforced by rastrology, does not supply a very exact dating. It seems that Einstein's procedures are for once more helpful. For two of these fragments can be related by scoring and tonality to movements that Mozart completed, though in an entirely different way: K.522a is obviously an attempt at the Rondo of K.522, "Ein musikalischer Spass," and K.525a is an attempt at a slow movement for K.525, "Eine kleine Nachtmusik." Nor can it seriously be doubted that K.516a was intended as a minor-mode finale for the G-Minor Quintet, K.516. All these identifications were suggested by Einstein (although in Köchel³ he had sup-

posed K.522a to be from before the Vienna years); but I do not think
that he was right in connecting K.495a with the piano trio in the
same G-major key, K.496.

K.626b/32–33 is not a "fragment" but a "sketchleaf." The unfinished terzetto "Del gran regno delle amazzoni," K.434 (480b),
which is sketched on it, may be dated a little too early in Köchel⁶; for
it was possibly written after *Figaro*, in the summer, fall, or winter
of 1786.

	No. 3. See (V).	
(C)	No. 4. K.458b (Anh. 71)	String quartet in B-flat. 10 mm.
	No. 6. K.589b (Anh. 73)	String quartet in F. 16 mm.
	No. 39. K.458a (Anh. 75)	String quartet minuet in B-flat. 9 mm.
	No. 47. K.546a (Anh. 47)	Violin sonata in G. 31 mm.
	No. 51. K.581a (Anh. 88)	Clarinet and strings in A. 89 mm.

Another late paper-type, not found in any dated autographs before
Così fan tutte, K.588 (completed January 1790). The three string-
quartet fragments must be regarded as drafts of movements for the
"Prussian" quartets: K.458a and K.458b for K.589 in B-flat, and
K.589b for K.590 in F.²⁶ (The autographs of both K.589 and K.590
also contain paper of this type.)

K.546a seems to be a fragment from 1790 or 1791 that is uncon-
nected with any surviving work. In Köchel³ Einstein suggested that
K.581a was an early idea for the finale of the Clarinet Quintet, K.581
("29 September 1789"), and that it was after that date that Mozart
decided to use its main theme for Ferrando's B-flat aria "Ah! lo veggio,
quell'anima bella" in the second act of *Così fan tutte*. But K.581a is
surely not an entirely serious piece of music; the thirteen changes of
clef in the clarinet part in mm. 51–69 suggest that it was intended for
domestic amusement,²⁷ perhaps even for the discomfiture of his friend
Anton Stadler, and is thus more likely to have been written after the
opera than before it. A date of 1790 is therefore probable.²⁸

	No. 5. See (B).	
	No. 6. See (C).	
	No. 7. See (B).	
(D)	No. 8. K.386d (Anh. 25)	Sketch for "Bardengesang auf Gibral-tar" by "Sined" (Denis). 58 mm.
	No. 54. K.384c (Anh. 96)	Allegro for winds. 16 mm.
	No. 59. K.370b (Anh. 97)	Horn concerto in E-flat. 35 mm.

A paper-type used mainly in the first Vienna years (up to the end of 1783), but unsatisfactory for dating purposes since Mozart occasionally had recourse to it in later years. A few scores have a TS of 186 (as K.370b here), and all of these date from the spring and summer of 1781. The rest have a TS of 188.5–189. K.386d, a "sketch" rather than a "fragment," can be dated by the reference to it in Mozart's letter to his father of 28 December 1782. K.384c, which in Köchel³ Einstein strangely assigned (as "K.196g") to the beginning of 1775, cannot be dated more precisely at present than to the "early Vienna years." K.370b, together with other fragments of the same first movement, now scattered, can be linked with the (not quite completed) rondo for horn, K.371, dated in the autograph "21 March 1781."

(E) No. 9.   K.587a (Anh. 74)   String quartet in G minor. 24 mm.
     No. 58. K.417c (Anh. 76)   String quartet in D minor. 11 mm.

A type which Mozart first bought about December 1785 or January 1786 in order to write down the last two acts of *Le nozze di Figaro* (where it is the predominant paper), and which he then used intermittently for the rest of his life, though most of the examples are from 1786 and 1787. Einstein's suggestion in Köchel³ that the fugal K.417c is a draft for the finale of the 1783 D-minor quartet, K.421 (417b), should be resisted. The fragment (which may be no more than an exercise)²⁹ could be from around the time of the "Hoffmeister" quartet, K.499, or later. The same is true of K.587a. The presence on the verso of sketches for the A-flat canon from the second act of *Così fan tutte* suggests that shortly before January 1790 this G-minor fragment, though doubtless written two or three years earlier, was under review as a possible start to a minor-mode quartet for the "Prussian" set. But the use of the leaf for sketching will have marked the abandonment of that plan, to which a quartet-fragment in E minor on paper-type (C), K.417d (acquired by the Mozarteum only in 1934), also bears witness.

(F) No. 10. K.589a (Anh. 68)   String quartet in B-flat. 65 mm.

This paper-type was available to Mozart at various times, but with the TS of the present fragment (182.5–183) it was used by him apparently only in 1782 and 1783. It is found inter alia in the first four of the "Haydn" quartets. This polonaise fragment is no doubt a draft finale for the "Hunt" Quartet, K.458, which was begun in 1783 and finished in 1784, and not for the late B-flat quartet, K.589, as Einstein supposed.[30]

| (G) | No. 11. K.502a (Anh. 60) | Piano concerto movement in C. 19 mm. |
| | No. 50. K.501a (Anh. 51) | Piano trio in B-flat. 25 mm. |

With the exception of the first eight leaves (= mm. 1–145) of the first movement of the A-major piano concerto, K.488, discussed later in this chapter, all the dated scores on this paper-type fall into the period from March 1784 to February 1785. Thus it is sensible to connect K.502a not with K.503 ("4 December 1786") but with the earlier C-major concerto, K.467 (autograph dated "February 1785"), or at least with the *time* of that concerto. And, in spite of the temptation to link K.501a with the B-flat piano trio, K.502 ("18 November 1786"), it should no doubt be placed earlier, in 1784 or early in 1785.

| (H) | No. 12. K.537b (Anh. 61) | Piano concerto movement in D minor. 21 mm. |
| | No. 20. K.504a (Anh. 105) | Orchestral movement in G. 10 mm. |

A rare paper-type, known so far only from the C-major piano concerto, K.503 ("4 December 1786"), the "Prague" Symphony, K.504 ("6 December 1786"), a first-trumpet part written out for a performance of the "Paris" Symphony, K.297 (300a), and these two fragments. But K.504a is readily identifiable as a rejected slow movement for the "Prague" Symphony. K.537b is more of a puzzle, since the scoring includes two oboes and two basset-horns. It is possible that Mozart was planning a piano concerto around the end of 1786 of which this was to be the slow movement.

| (I) | No. 13. K.491a (Anh. 62) | Piano concerto movement in E-flat. 3 mm. |

A unique paper-type, with sixteen staves, found elsewhere only in the autographs of the C-minor piano concerto, K.491, and of "Das Bandel," K.441. This fragment was an earlier idea for the slow movement of K.491, as is shown also by the scoring (two oboes plus two clarinets).

| (J) | No. 14. K.488c (Anh. 64) | Piano concerto movement in A. 20 mm. |
| | No. 15. K.537a (Anh. 57) | Piano concerto movement in D. 21 mm. |

No. 16. K.488a (Anh. 58)   Piano concerto movement in D. 10 mm.
No. 17. K.488b (Anh. 63)   Piano concerto movement in A. 23 mm.
No. 41. K.375d (Anh. 45)   Fugue for two pianos in G. 23 mm.
No. 43. K.426a (Anh. 44)   Allegro for two pianos in C minor.
                            22 mm.

Mozart's use of this paper-type seems to have been confined to the twelve months from December 1785 to December 1786. From the scoring (two clarinets but no oboes), K.488a is identifiable as a draft for the slow movement of the A-major concerto, K.488 ("March 1786"), and in the same way K.488b and K.488c as drafts for the finale.[31] The pair of two-piano fragments cannot be dated more closely than by the paper-type. But K.537a may come from the summer of 1786, since it is written in a reddish ink found also in the autographs of K.495 ("26 June 1786"), K.496 ("8 July 1786"), and K.507, with a draft for the finale of K.493 (June? 1786).

(K) No. 18. K.459a (Anh. 59)   Piano concerto movement in C. 37 mm.
     No. 46. K.385E (Anh. 48)   Violin sonata in A. 34 mm.

Mozart's use of this paper-type seems to have been confined almost entirely to the months of February, March, and April 1784 (there is one later instance, from February 1785). Thus it is likely that K.459a is a draft for the slow movement not of the F-major concerto, K.459, but of the G-major, K.453. (The last two movements in the score of K.453 are in fact on this paper.) K.385E probably dates from the same time as K.454, as Blaschitz suggested.[32]

    No. 19. See (B).
    No. 20. See (H).
    No. 21 = K.620a (Anh. 102), two leaves formerly in the Mozarteum,
        now lost.
    No. 22. See (W).
(L) No. 23. K.613b (Anh. 82)   String quintet in E-flat. 19 mm.
     No. 32. K.385h + K.576a   Piano music. 3 mm., 8 mm.
        (Anh. 34)

Hard to date with any precision. This paper-type is found with a variety of TS patterns. The earliest examples with this TS (186–187) come from November 1786, but the paper seems from then on to have been available to Mozart for most of the rest of his life. K.613b should be compared with No. 27, K.613a.

(M) No. 24. K.515a (Anh. 87)   String quintet in F. 10 mm.
    No. 25. K.515c (Anh. 79)   String quintet in A minor. 15 mm.[33]

A very late paper-type, confined to the year 1791, and found (for instance) in the E-flat string quintet, K.614. Could these be drafts for an opening Allegro and a slow movement of a planned A-minor quintet of 1791?

    No. 26. See (O).

(N) No. 27. K.613a (Anh. 81)   String quintet in E-flat. 71 mm.

Again, a paper-type found with two or more TS patterns, one of which is confined almost entirely to the year 1782. But the TS of the present fragment (188) is found in dated scores from 1785 to 1788. See also No. 23, K.613b (above) for the same instrumentation and the same key.

(O) No. 26. Köchel[6] Anhang A 23   Psalm by Carl Georg Reutter. 32 mm.
    No. 28. K.592b (Anh. 83)   String quintet in D. 19 mm.
    No. 29. K.196a (Anh. 16)   Kyrie in G. 13 mm. (21 further mm. not by Mozart).
    No. 33. K.569a (Anh. 31)   Piano sonata in B-flat. 19 mm.
    No. 34. K.590b (Anh. 30)   Piano sonata in F. 15 mm.
    No. 35. K.590a (Anh. 29)   Piano sonata in F. 8 mm.
    No. 36. K.383b (Anh. 33, 40) Fugue for piano in F. 17 mm.
    No. 38. K.590c (Anh. 37)   Rondo for piano in F. 33 mm.
    No. 52. K.484c (Anh. 93)   Adagio for clarinet and three basset-horns. 6 mm.
    No. 57. K.422a (Anh. 14)   Kyrie in D. 11 mm.

The reasons for dating Mozart's use of this paper-type to the period from December 1787 to February 1789 have been given on p. 134. Perhaps the most surprising of these late fragments are the two Kyries, to which can be added K.323 (Anh. 15), a Kyrie in C (in the Mozarteum but not among the "sixty fragments"), K.323a (Anh. 20), a Gloria in C (Berlin, Deutsche Staatsbibliothek)—both on this same paper-type—and No. 56, K.258a (Anh. 13), on paper-type (U). The evidence that Mozart was planning to write a Mass in the time between *Don Giovanni* and the 1789 journey to Prague, Dresden, Leipzig, and Berlin needs further investigation by biographers: was he hoping to obtain an ecclesiastical position?[34] Einstein sensibly linked the B-flat piano fragment, K.569a, to the finished sonata, K.570, in the same key. The three sonata fragments in F, K.590a, 590b, and 590c (see Figure 11.1) suggest that Mozart tried to write another sonata at the same time (the fugue, K.383b, may also possibly be related)—that is, *before* his 1789 journey. They cannot therefore be linked with the commission that he received later in Potsdam to write six "easy sonatas" for Princess Friederike of Prussia.[35] K.484c, dated by Einstein in Köchel[3] to 1783 and by Köchel[6] to the end of 1785, must have been written more than two years later; K.592b, on the other hand, is unlikely to be connected with the D-major quintet, K.593, as Einstein suggested, and is probably earlier. The transcription of Reutter's psalm, on a leaf that also includes some sketches for the finale of the "Jupiter" Symphony, K.551, may be compared with another Reutter transcription on the same paper-type, Köchel[6], Anh. A 22, which is in the British Library.

> No. 28. See (O).
> No. 29. See (O).
> No. 30 = K.475a (Anh. 26), given away by the Mozarteum in 1850.
> No. 31. See (X).
> No. 32. See (L).
> No. 33. See (O).
> No. 34. See (O).
> No. 35. See (O).
> No. 36. See (O).

(P)	No. 37. K.383c (Anh. 38) + K.383d (Anh. 39)	Organ and piano. 16 mm., 8 mm.
	No. 44. K.452b (Anh. 55)	Piano, horns, and strings. 29 mm.

The first of these is easier to date than the second. For this paper-type is found from 1783 to 1789, but various patterns of TS seem to have only limited time-spans. The TS of K.383c + K.383d (= 186.5) can be matched in three scores only, all from the summer of 1783; that of K.452b (= 183–183.5), on the other hand, occurs in scores of 1784, 1785, and 1786 (though not, it appears, outside those years).

> No. 38. See (O).
> No. 39. See (C).
> No. 40. See (A).
> No. 41. See (J).

(Q)	No. 42. K.375c (Anh. 43)	Sonata for two pianos in B-flat. 16 mm.
	No. 45. K.374g (Anh. 46)	Andantino for cello and piano. 33 mm.

FIGURE 11.1. Rondo for Pianoforte in F, K.590c (Anh. 37).
Internationale Stiftung Mozarteum, Salzburg, No. 38.

A paper-type used by Mozart almost exclusively in the early Vienna years, especially (but perhaps not before) 1782 and 1783. K.375b (Anh. 42), another two-piano fragment (Paris, Bibliothèque nationale) in the same key as K.375c, is on the same paper, as is also the fragmentary Larghetto and Allegro for two pianos in E-flat that came to light some twenty years ago.[36]

No. 43. See (J).
No. 44. See (P).
No. 45. See (Q).
No. 46. See (K).
No. 47. See (C).
No. 48. See (B).

(R) No. 49. K.580a (Anh. 94)   Adagio for four unnamed instruments, probably clarinet and three basset-horns.[37] 73 mm.

This is a leaf of 16-staff paper with a TS of about 205. No other specimen of such paper seems to be recorded, and the watermark cannot be matched. The scoring is uncertain, but may be identical with that of No. 52, K.484c. So a date of about 1788 is tentatively suggested.

No. 50. See (G).
No. 51. See (C).
No. 52. See (O).

(S) No. 53. K.484b (Anh. 95)   Allegro assai for two clarinets and three basset-horns. 22 mm.

This leaf again represents a unique paper-type, being 16-staff paper with a TS of 188.5, and a watermark that cannot be matched. The fragment is linked to the Adagio K.411 (484a), not only by identity of scoring but by a deleted musical incipit on the autograph of that work (see Köchel[6], p. 526: the third leaf had been used for the start of the clarinetto primo part to K.484b). K.411 is undated, though its paper-type (O) suggests that it could come from 1782 to 1783. But that does not perhaps form a sufficient basis for dating K.484b.

No. 54. See (D).

(T) No. 55. K.616a (Anh. 92)   "Fantasia" for harmonica, flute, oboe, viola, cello. 12 mm.

A paper-type used by Mozart in 1786–87 and again in 1791. Einstein correctly saw that K.616a is a first draft for the Adagio and Rondo, K.617, for the same unusual instrumental combination and in the same key.

(U) No. 56. K.258a (Anh. 13)   Kyrie in C. 9 mm.

A late paper-type: apart from one apparent instance from 1787, it is found only in scores from 1790 and 1791. For other evidence that Mozart was trying to write a Mass in the late Vienna years, see the commentary to (O).

> No. 57. See (O).
> No. 58. See (E).
> No. 59. See (D).
> No. 60. See (Y).

Fragments from the pre-Vienna years (before March 1781)

(V) No. 3. K.166g (Anh. 19)   Kyrie in D. 12 mm.

This paper, which was manufactured in Salzburg, is found in three dated sources from March through June 1772, K.126, K.127, K.164 (130a), and in the undated K.186 (159b), which could be about a year later. According to Plath (p. 151), the handwriting suggests the first half of 1772.

(W) No. 22. K.299d (Anh. 103)   La chasse. 32 mm.

The paper is a French one used by Mozart in Paris in 1778. Plath (pp. 169–170) accepts the date in Köchel[6] of "summer or fall 1778"; the place of composition given in Köchel[6] ("in Salzburg") is no doubt a slip. Einstein strangely identified this fragment as a probable finale to K.320e, No. 31 (see next item).

(X) No. 31. K.320e (Anh. 104)   Sinfonia concertante for violin, viola, and violoncello. 134 mm.

Mozart began to use this paper about July 1779, and continued to write on it until the time that he moved to Vienna. Plath (p. 172) offers no objection to the date suggested in Köchel[6], "summer or fall 1779."

(Y) No. 60. K.135a (Anh. 109)   Ballet "Le gelosie del serraglio"

The paper of these four leaves is one that Mozart used mainly in Milan during his third Italian journey (1772–73). The contents resemble sketches or rapidly written jottings, and according to Walter Senn may be Mozart's record of a ballet by Joseph Starzer.[38] Plath (p. 142) accepts the date proposed by Senn of "January–February 1773."

I I I

IN THESE DAYS the view is gaining ground that, in the words of his widow Constanze, "among musical fragments those of Mozart certainly deserve every honor and respect." But for a very long time they were neglected, and even today the literature about them is meager.[39] Perhaps it was felt that Mozart's surviving fragments had too little in common with each other to invite consideration as a "genre." But the same might be urged in the case of Beethoven's sketches—yet within the last twenty years the combination of a renewed interest in techniques for examining such difficult sources and an intense preoccupation with his "compositional process" has resulted in a very active scholarly concern with the Beethoven sketchbooks. It will at least be clear that any attempt to generalize about Mozart's fragments is bound to take us beyond the examples preserved in the Mozarteum. How, then, are they to be categorized?

The general consensus has undoubtedly been that the fragments represent compositions that Mozart had abandoned. And the reasons that caused him to break off work on a piece appear to fall into two main classes, which may, however, overlap in some cases. The first reason is the result of outside pressures—or perhaps the lack of them. For some pieces were undoubtedly abandoned when the external stimulus—a request, for instance, for an aria to be included in a current stage performance—was withdrawn. It seems likely that the majority of Mozart's operatic fragments fall into this category; the aria K.435 (416b), and the terzetto K.434 (480b), referred to elsewhere in this chapter, are no doubt typical examples. It would be unwise, at any rate, to conclude that Mozart was dissatisfied with his progress on those fragments. And it may be that not a few instrumental compositions were broken off when the concert for which they were intended was canceled (that would apply particularly in the case of a concerto), although our very limited knowledge of Mozart's concert plans, particularly in his later Vienna years, makes it almost impossible for us at present to attempt to identify any resulting fragments.[40]

The second reason for Mozart's abandoning a fragment does more to provoke one's curiosity. For here the cessation of work seems to have been due to internal scruples: Mozart became dissatisfied with the way his ideas were progressing and, unable to see his way forward, he discontinued the piece. Or he started it again in a different form (and on another piece of paper); this, as we have seen, was an assumption that Einstein was over-ready to make:

Every one of [the fragments], or almost every one, can be related to some complete movement written immediately afterwards. Mozart begins a work, and as soon as he has written the theme down this theme no longer appeals to him. He abandons it, and replaces it with a new one. And the new one is invariably more original, fresher, drawn from a deeper and purer spring of the imagination. Or the first theme does not give him space enough to gather the momentum he needs for the leap he has planned. So he goes back to take a longer run.[41]

There are a not inconsiderable number of cases in which Einstein is undoubtedly right. The clearest ones are those in which the rejected version is preserved alongside the improved version that has replaced it. We find this in a few scores in which Mozart has begun a slow movement or finale on the back of a leaf (or on a leaf conjugate with one) on which the preceding movement had ended. He did not approve of what he had just written down; but not wishing to recopy the end of the previous movement or to tear a leaf out, he simply deleted his false start and continued with its replacement, so that the deleted passage remained within the score. Good examples are to be seen in the autographs of K.415 (387b), 17 mm. of a slow movement in C minor—see Figure 11.2; K.542, 65 mm. of a finale in 6/8 meter; and K.589, 18 mm. of a finale, perhaps intended to be in variation form.

What is preserved in the score in these instances is essentially a "fragment," although one might not think of applying that term to it; and the connection between it and its replacement is incontestable. In a number of other cases, too, as we have already seen, Einstein established a convincing link between a fragment and a completed movement. The Mozarteum Nos. 2, 5, 6, 13, 14, 16, 17, 19, 20, and 55 seem to have been correctly identified by him as forerunners of movements that found their completion in a rather different form. And we can add an additional piece of confirmatory evidence that Einstein failed to draw on: in nine of these ten instances, the paper-type of the

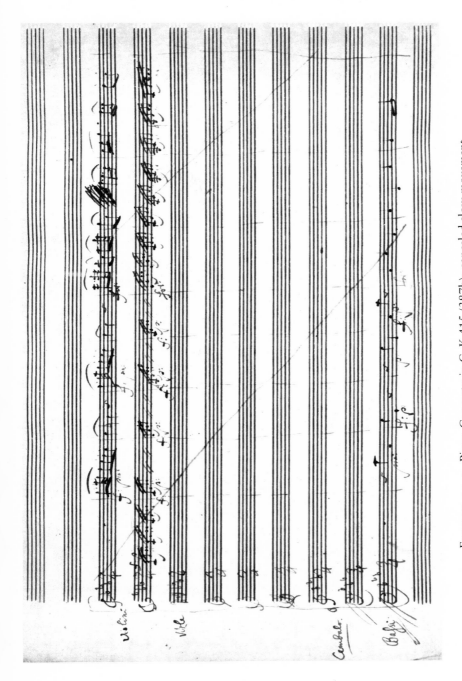

FIGURE 11.2. Piano Concerto in C, K.415 (387b): canceled slow movement, mm. 1–8 (fol. 19v). Biblioteka Jagiellońska, Kraków.

fragment is found within the completed score—and the tenth is scarcely an exception, since the paper-type of No. 19 (K.516a), the start of a G-minor finale for K.516, while unrepresented in the score of the G-minor quintet, is found in that of the C-major quintet, K.515, completed less than four weeks earlier.

THE NOTION that there is something "wrong" with the fragments, and that Mozart checked himself from compounding error just in time, is an exciting one; it is entertaining, too, to speculate in each case as to where exactly the fault may lie. But perhaps there are at least a number of fragments that represent something more positive. Instead of being abandoned work, could they be "work in progress"?

We should not be discouraged from such a view by the appearance of the Mozarteum fragments. Certainly these are nearly all very short: of the fifty-four from the Vienna years, all but seven (Nos. 15, 17, 18, 27, 29, 51, and 59) are on a single leaf of paper. But Mozart scarcely ever wrote down the start of a score on a single leaf; his unit of paper was a bifolium, or even a pair of gathered bifolia. Thus we should visualize each single-leaf fragment as being in Mozart's day on the beginning of a bifolium (or possibly two gathered bifolia), and thus with a large expanse of unused paper stretching invitingly ahead of it, and awaiting the next burst of inspiration. (The detachment and discarding of any unused leaves from the fragments was no doubt an episode that belongs to the story of the *Nachlass*.)[42] Other fragments may have lost not merely blank leaves but leaves with music on them: in the case of No. 14 (K.488c—see note 31), No. 25 (K.515c), and No. 51 (K.581a), we know that more of the fragment has survived elsewhere. And in the case of Nos. 14, 15, 17, and 18 (all piano-concerto fragments) we can tell from the sequence of the watermark quadrants that these pairs of leaves formed the beginnings of two gathered bifolia—that is, they were once units of four leaves.

In their original state, therefore, the Mozarteum fragments would have resembled "work in progress" more than they do today. And it is no coincidence that it is the shorter fragments that have ended up in the Mozarteum; for, as we have already seen, these were the ones that no one would take off Constanze's hands. Certainly some of the longer fragments in other institutions, such as K.516c (Anh. 91) in the Bibliothèque nationale, Paris, or K.514a (Anh. 80) and K.580b (Anh. 90) in the Deutsche Staatsbibliothek, Berlin, give a stronger impression of being works that Mozart had not abandoned but had merely laid aside for a while.

But perhaps the best evidence in favor of the view that fragments were not necessarily rejected forever would be some examples in which work was resumed on a fragment after a year or more of inactivity. Here are three cases in which it seems to me that the opening section of a completed piano concerto must have remained for some time in the form of a fragment:

1. K.503. Mozart entered this C-major piano concerto in his Verzeichnüss under the date of 4 December 1786. The three bifolia with which the autograph of the first movement originally began, fols. 1–2, 3–4, and 5 + 7 (fol. 6 being a later insertion), are of a rare paper-type, and when one looks around for other examples one comes up with only the following:

(a) K.459, piano concerto in F (Verzeichnüss: 11 December 1784). Last 14 leaves of finale.
(b) K.464a (Anh. 72), string quartet movement (fragment) in A major: 170 mm. Two leaves.
(c) K.464, string quartet in A major (Verzeichnüss: 10 January 1785). Two leaves added to Andante.
(d) K.466, piano concerto in D minor (Verzeichnüss: 10 February 1785). First 8 leaves of first movement.
(e) K.467, piano concerto in C (autograph: February 1785; Verzeichnüss: 9 March 1785). Last 8 leaves of finale.
(f) K.469, No. 6, aria for *Davidde penitente* (Verzeichnüss: 6 March 1785). Last 4 leaves.

The long undated fragment K.464a was no doubt an attempt to produce a finale for the A-major quartet. The dates show that all the other scores were completed within a period of less than three months between December 1784 and March 1785. And since that winter season saw the completion of three piano concertos, is it not likely that K.503 was started at this time too, but that it did not progress further than the first six leaves of the first movement? Perhaps the completion of another C-major concerto, K.467, in February 1785 provided a motive for setting the work aside. And Mozart appears not to have taken it up again next season, in the winter of 1785–86, but two seasons later, in the winter of 1786–87.

Thus for nearly two years the opening of K.503 will have remained a "fragment." That there is indeed something a little strange about these six leaves was recognized as long ago as 1954 by Walter Gerstenberg.[43] He drew attention to differences in the handwriting, ascribing some parts of the score to an earlier compositional stage, and reproducing a "particella" of mm. 1–127, which he described as "ein älteres Fragment eines Partitur-Entwurfes." The contribution of paper-studies in this case is to demonstrate the length of the period that seems to have elapsed between the writing-down of the "particella" at the start of the first movement and the subsequent resumption of work and completion of the concerto.

2. K.488. The Verzeichnüss date for this A-major piano concerto is 2 March 1786. Thus it is one of the three concertos completed in the winter season of 1785–86, the other two being K.482 (16 December 1785) and K.491 (24 March 1786). The orchestration of all three concertos, unlike those of any other season, calls for clarinets: K.482 and K.488 have clarinets instead of oboes, and K.491 is unique in having both oboes and clarinets. This affords us a useful clue—one, indeed, that we have already alluded to in dating the Mozarteum fragments Nos. 13, 14, 16, and 17.

The first eight leaves in the first movement of K.488 are on the paper already discussed as Paper-type (G). This type is found in a number of works dated between March 1784 and February 1785: K.450, 451, 452, 453, and 467. Thus it looks as though K.488 was begun at least as far back as the 1784–85 season—or even earlier, for the end of the 1783–84 season, an exceptionally productive one, cannot be entirely ruled out. The concertos from those two seasons have no clarinets. And if one examines the first page of K.488 one sees not only that the word "clarinetti" is written over an erasure, but that three sharps have been deleted at the beginning of their staves. Moreover, the passages assigned to them (mm. 9–18 and 62–66) are written at pitch, for nontransposing instruments, but are marked for deletion, and the same measures, now suitably transposed for clarinets in A, are added on a blank page at the end of the movement (fol. 26r).[44] It is clear enough what has happened: the scoring of the opening of K.488 was originally for oboes, but they were later replaced by clarinets. The fact that only fifteen measures required to be changed was no doubt due to the fragmentary nature of what Mozart had written down at the time; this, too, was evidently a "particella."

In this case, therefore, it is not only the paper-type but also the scoring which suggest that the opening of K.488 was started in 1783–

84 or 1784–85 but was then left as a "fragment" for a year or even longer.

3. K.449. This is the work with which Mozart began his Verzeichnüss, entering it under the date of 9 February 1784. Yet its scoring for a small orchestra, with the two oboes and two horns described in the Verzeichnüss as "ad libitum," reminds one of the concertos of 1782, K.413 (387a), K.414 (385p), and K.415 (387b), which Mozart advertised at the time as being playable "a quattro" (by four strings without winds).

And once again the paper for the first ten leaves of the first movement suggests a date considerably earlier than that given by the Verzeichnüss—the second half of 1782 rather than the beginning of 1784. This is a paper found, for instance, in the A-major piano concerto, K.414 (385p), and in the rondo for piano and orchestra K.386, the first page of which is dated 19 October 1782. But the autograph of K.449 offers further evidence of suspended work. For on fol. 9r Mozart started to "doodle" in the upper and right-hand margins, writing down a quantity of figures and symbols, and on the first four staves of fol. 10v (which must have been blank at that time) he sketched the vocal line of a tenor aria, "Müsst' ich auch durch tausend Drachen," K.435 (416b)—see Figures 11.3 and 11.4. This aria, of which an autograph survives with the voice-part and bass-line complete but with the rest of the scoring only intermittently written down, is not easy to date but perhaps comes from the early months of 1783.

Fols. 9 and 10, which form a bifolium, are the last leaves of the "1782" paper in the score of K.449. It looks as though Mozart started the first movement in 1782 and wrote it down, no doubt once again in a "particella," as far as measure 170 at the end of fol. 9r. He then apparently abandoned the piece, using the margins of this page for scribbling, and later turned the bifolium over to sketch the tenor aria K.435, on fol. 10v. But shortly after returning to Vienna from his visit to Salzburg at the end of 1783, he seems to have decided to resume work on the concerto. Fols. 9v and 10r were blank and offered no problem, but on reaching fol. 10v Mozart was obliged to delete the sketch for the tenor aria and to crowd his score on to the lower eight staves of the page. After that he took new paper and apparently completed the concerto by 9 February 1784.

Here, then, we have a third example of the start of a piano concerto being left as a "fragment" for a year or more. And one begins to wonder whether something of the kind happened with Mozart's last piano

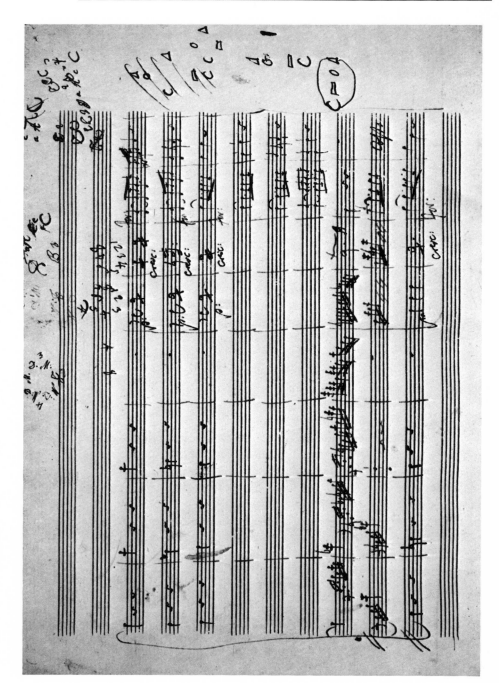

FIGURE 11.3. Piano Concerto in E-flat, K.449: first movement, mm. 162, 170 (61 9v) Biblioteka Jagiellońska Kraków

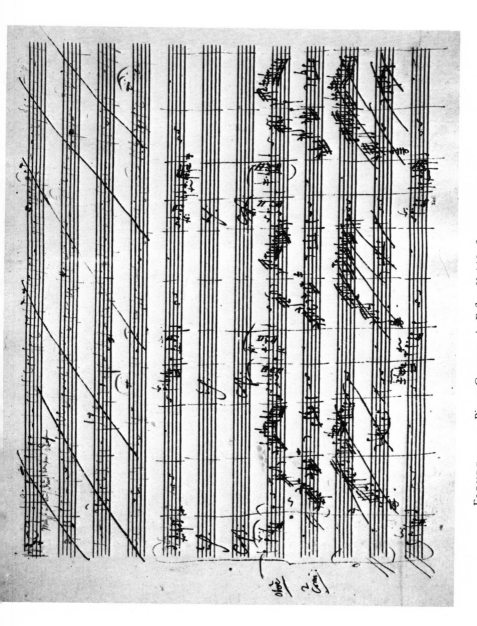

FIGURE 11.4. Piano Concerto in E-flat, K.449: first movement, mm. 193–203 (fol. 10v). Biblioteka Jagiellońska, Kraków.

concerto, K.595, which he entered in the Verzeichnüss under the date of 5 January 1791. But in this case more is involved than the opening of the work: the whole of the first and second movements and the first seven leaves of the finale are on a paper-type which is found in dated scores only between December 1787 and February 1789. Do we have here merely an exceptional use of Paper-type (O), two years after any of the other scores in which it is found were composed? Or was much of K.595 drafted long before the 1791 Verzeichnüss date—for example, in the summer of 1788 about the time of the last three symphonies, compositions that imply an expectation of concert performances?

Perhaps it is best to keep an open mind until the autograph (today in Kraków, Biblioteka Jagiellońska, and, until recently, inaccessible) has been more widely studied. My own view is that there are traces of a "particella" in much of the first movement, extending nearly to measure 300 on fol. 19, and also in the first two leaves (mm. 1–39) of the finale. But I cannot find it in the slow movement or in some later parts of the finale which are still on the same paper (the last twelve leaves of the finale are on a "1791" paper). And I cannot claim the support of *Schriftchronologie* in differentiating between a "ca. 1788" part of the score and a "1791" part.[45] Nevertheless the notion that some parts of a piano concerto were written months or even years before the rest no longer seems so strange as it once did.

But it is not only piano concertos that were at times written over a long period. We now know the same to have been true of some chamber works of the Vienna years. Such pieces cannot have been written easily. Mozart's own descriptions of his string quartets have often been quoted; the six "Haydn" quartets were "il frutto di una lunga, e laboriosa fatica," and his work on the three "Prussian" quartets was "diese mühsame Arbeit." Nor was it merely the composition of the complete sets that extended over a long time (the "Haydns" from the end of 1782 to the beginning of 1785, the "Prussians" from June 1789 to June 1790); a convincing case can be made that some individual quartets, too, took a long time to finish. The "Hunt," K.458, though not entered in the Verzeichnüss till November 1784, seems to have been started in the summer of 1783, and the other B-flat quartet, K.589, finished in May 1790, was probably started about a year earlier. These, then, must be added to the list of works which, though eventually completed, remained "fragments" for some time.[46]

It is in this light, surely, that we should view some scores which have remained fragments forever—for instance, the 100 measures of K.562e

(Anh. 66), the start of a string trio in G. It is clear enough from the paper-types that this impressive fragment was not started *before* the divertimento K.563 (Verzeichnüss: 27 September 1788) but *after* it, in 1790 or 1791.[47] Moreover, it represents two stages of work, as one can see from the ink. In the first, Mozart wrote down mm. 1−33 in at least one part, and in the second he added mm. 34−100 (and filled in parts omitted earlier); this took him nine measures into the development. We cannot tell how much time separated these two stages; it need not have been more than a few hours, or it could have been a year. And if the date was 1791, it needs little imagination to see how such "work in progress" could fall victim to the other pressures on the composer in that fateful year: the demands of operatic commissions, financial worries, illness, and an early death.

For Constanze, indeed, there was the possibility of life after death for the fragments; they were still "usable" in her eyes, and might one day be used by her elder son, Karl. She has often been mocked for the naivety of her attitude here. But if many of Mozart's fragments were in fact "work in progress," may she not have been drawing on a recollection of her former domestic life? It is possible that she had often seen her husband sifting through his collection of fragments, resuming work on an old piece, or deploring the fact that he could not find some scrap he was looking for. Clearly, then, they were "usable" and so deserved to be cherished.

I T S H O U L D be clear by now that a study of the chronology of Mozart's fragments brings us very close to the central question of how Mozart composed, especially in his Vienna years. Although it is beyond doubt that he often continued to compose with enormous rapidity and fluency, some kinds of works seem to have been written very slowly, and perhaps laboriously.

In the case of works that he ultimately finished, a long period of time may separate their first-written from their last-written pages. The date on the score or in the Verzeichnüss is likely to correspond to the time at which the work was completed, and we should bear in mind that some parts may be earlier. This is a point that must not be missed by those concerned with paper-studies; the Verzeichnüss date is a helpful guide to the dating of the latest paper within a score, but not to the dating of earlier papers in it. Perhaps, too, it is a point of some interest to those who can see its implications for stylistic analysis: must we learn to regard the beginning of K.449 as a part of the

TABLE 11.1. Catalogue numbers and dates assigned to the Mozarteum fragments.[a]

Mozarteum no.	No. in Köchel[6]	Dates				NMA
		Blaschitz (1924)	Köchel[3] (1937)	Köchel[6] (1964)	Suggested	
1	535b (Anh. 107)	1785	1788 (beginning)	1788 (beginning)	1790–91	—
2	522a (Anh. 108)	1788	pre-Vienna years	1787 (June)	1787	VII/18, p. 266
3	166g (Anh. 19)	1774	1773 (June)	1773 (June)	1772	—
4	458b (Anh. 71)	1782	1784 (November)	1784 (November)	1790	VIII/20/1/3, p. 138
5	525a (Anh. 69)	1782	1787 (August)	1787 (August)	1787	IV/12/6, p. 66
6	589b (Anh. 73)	1788	1790 (June)	1790 (June)	1790	VIII/20/1/3, p. 149
7	626b/32–33	1783	1783 (summer)	1785 (end)	1785–86	II/7/4, pp. 160–161 (in part)
8	386d (Anh. 25)	1782	1782 (December)	1782 (December)	1782 (end)	III/8, pp. 72–76
9	587a (Anh. 74)	1791	1789 (end)	1789 (end)	1786–1789	VIII/20/1/3, pp. 47–48
10	589a (Anh. 68)	1788	1790 (May)	1790 (May or June)	1783	VIII/20/1/3, pp. 148–149
11	502a (Anh. 60)	1790	1786 (November)	1786 (November)	1784–85	V/15/8, p. 196
12	537b (Anh. 61)	1789–90	1786 (February)	1788 (February)	1786 (end)	V/15/8, p. 198
13	491a (Anh. 62)	1788	"537c": 1788	1786 (March)	1786	V/15/8, p. 195
14	488c (Anh. 64)	1791	1786 (Feb.–March)	1786 (Feb.–March)	1785–86	V/15/8, p. 193
15	537a (Anh. 57)	1790	1788 (February)	1788 (February)	1785–86	V/15/8, p. 197
16	488a (Anh. 58)	1782	1786 (Feb.–March)	1786 (Feb.–March)	1785–86	V/15/8, p. 191
17	488b (Anh. 63)	1782	1786 (Feb.–March)	1786 (Feb.–March)	1785–86	V/15/8, p. 192
18	459a (Anh. 59)	1788	"466a": 1785 (beginning)	1784 (December)	1784 (April)	V/15/8, pp. 189–190
19	516a (Anh. 86)	1791	1787 (May)	1787 (May)	1787	VIII/19/1, p. 194
20	504a (Anh. 105)	1789–90	1786 (December)	1786 (December)	1786 (end)	—
21	620a (Anh. 102)	—	1791 (September)	1791 (September)	1791 (September)	II/5/19, pp. 372–373
22	299d (Anh. 103)	1788	"320f": 1779 (summer or fall)	1778 (summer or fall)	1778	II/6/2, pp. 112–113

No.	K.					Reference
23	613b (Anh. 82)	1791	1791 (April)	1791 (April)	1786–1791	VIII/19/1, p. 198
24	515a (Anh. 87)	1789–90	1787 (April)	1787 (April)	1791	VIII/19/1, p. 190
25	515c (Anh. 79)	1782	1787 (May)	1787 (May)	1791	VIII/19/1, pp. 190–194 (including Bergamo fragment)
26	A 23 (Reutter)	1777	"93a": 1771 (summer)	—	1787–1789	—
27	613a (Anh. 81)	1782	1791 (beginning)	1791 (April)	1785–1788?	VIII/19/1, pp. 196–97
28	592b (Anh. 83)	1782	1790 (end)	1790 (end)	1787–1789	VIII/19/1, p. 195
29	196a (Anh. 16)	1774	1775 (January)	1775 (January)	1787–1789	—
30	475a (Anh. 26)	—	1785	1785	?	III/8, p. 72
31	320e (Anh. 104)	—	1779 (summer or fall)	1779 (summer or fall)	1779–80	V/14/2, pp. 153–61
32	385h + 576a (Anh. 34)	1789–90	1782	1782 + 1789	1786–1791	IX/27/2, p. 170
33	569a (Anh. 31)	1790	1789 (beginning)	1789 (beginning)	1787–1789	IX/25/2, p. 181
34	590b (Anh. 30)	1791	1790 (June)	1790 (June)	1787–1789	IX/25/2, p. 182
35	590a (Anh. 29)	1790	1790 (June)	1790 (June)	1787–1789	IX/25/2, p. 181
36	383b (Anh. 33, 40)	1782	1782 (early)	1782 (early)	1787–1789	IX/27/2, p. 175
37	383c (Anh. 38), 383d (Anh. 39)	1782	1782 (early)	1782 (early)	1783	IX/26, p. 149 (transcription and facsimile of K.383c, facsimile only of K.383d)
38	590c (Anh. 37)	1790	1790 (June)	1790 (June)	1787–1789	IX/25/2, p. 182
39	458a (Anh. 75)	1786	1784	1784 (November)	1790	VIII/20/1/3, p. 138
40	593a (Anh. 35)	1788	1790 (end)	1790 (end)	1790–91	IX/27/2, p. 170
41	375d (Anh. 45)	1782	1782 (early)	1782 (early)	1785–86	IX/24/1, p. 50
42	375c (Anh. 43)	1782	1782 (early)	1782 (early)	1782–83	IX/24/1, p. 49
43	426a (Anh. 44)	1785	1783 (December)	1783 (December)	1785–86	IX/24/1, p. 51
44	452b (Anh. 55)	1785	"387c": 1782–83 (winter)	1784	1784–1786	—
45	374g (Anh. 46)	1791	1781 (summer)	1781 (summer)	1782–83	—

TABLE 11.1. *(continued)*

Mozarteum no.	No. in Köchel⁶	Dates				NMA
		Blaschitz (1924)	Köchel³ (1937)	Köchel⁶ (1964)	Suggested	
46	385E (Anh. 48)	1785	"480a": 1785 (end)	1782	1784	VIII/23/2, pp. 180–181
47	546a (Anh. 47)	1784	1788 (June)	1788 (June)	1790–91	VIII/23/2, pp. 184–185
48	495a (Anh. 52)	1781	1786 (summer)	1786 (June–July)	1786–87	VIII/22/2, p. 271
49	580a (Anh. 94)	1788	1789 (September)	1789 (September)	1788?	VII/17/2, pp. 238–241
50	501a (Anh. 51)	1786	1786 (November)	1786 (November)	1784–85	VIII/22/2, p. 272
51	581a (Anh. 88)	1781	1789 (September)	1789 (September) or later	1790–91	VIII/19/2, pp. 50–52
52	484c (Anh. 93)	1782	"440c": 1783	1785 (end)	1787–1789	VII/17/2, p. 237
53	484b (Anh. 95)	1786	"440b": 1783	1785 (end)	?	VII/17/2, pp. 236–237
54	384c (Anh. 96)	1786–beginning of 1788	"196g": beginning of 1775	1782 (July)	1781–1783	VII/17/2, p. 235
55	616a (Anh. 92)	1782	1791 (May)	1791 (May)	1791	VIII/22/1, p. 168
56	258a (Anh. 13)	1774	1776 (December)	1776 (December)	1787–1791	—
57	422a (Anh. 14)	1774	1783 (summer)	1783 (summer)	1786–1789	—
58	417c (Anh. 76)	1791	1783 (June)	1783 (June)	1786–1789	VIII/20/1/3, p. 133
59	370b (Anh. 97)	1782	1781?	1781 (March)	1781	—
60	135a (Anh. 109)	1782	1772 (December)	1772 (December)	1773 (Jan.–Feb.)	—

a. In this summary, terms of qualification, such as "probably," "perhaps," "circa," and question marks have been omitted; the original texts should be consulted for fuller information.

TABLE 11.2. Concordance of Köchel-Anhang numbers
and the Mozarteum numbers.

Köchel-Anhang	Mozarteum	Köchel-Anhang	Mozarteum
13	56	62	13
14	57	63	17
16	29	64	14
19	·3	68	10
22	26	69	5
25	8	71	4
26	30	73	6
29	35	74	9
30	34	75	39
31	33	76	58
33 (+ 40)	36	79	25
34	32	81	27
35	40	82	23
37	38	83	28
38 (+ 39)	37	86	19
39 (+ 38)	37	87	24
40 (+ 33)	36	88	51
43	42	92	55
44	43	93	52
45	41	94	49
46	45	95	53
47	47	96	54
48	46	97	59
51	50	102	21
52	48	103	22
55	44	104	31
57	15	105	20
58	16	107	1
59	18	108	2
60	11	109	60
61	12	109a	7

1782 concertos, and the rest of K.449 as belonging to the 1784 concertos? At all events, a more exact chronology of the fragments and of
the separate parts of each completed work carries with it both biographical and stylistic implications, which will need to be worked out
with some care in the coming years.

12

The Dates of Mozart's *Missa brevis* K.258 and *Missa longa* K.262 (246a): An Investigation into His *Klein-Querformat* Papers

IMMEDIATELY after his return to Salzburg from his third and last Italian journey in March 1773, Mozart began to make regular use of music paper of a size that he had scarcely ever employed before. Such paper was described by Köchel in the first edition (1862) of his catalogue as *Klein-Querformat*—that is, small oblong format. Its leaves measure approximately 170 mm. × 225 mm. (vertical dimensions first); all of them are ruled with ten staves, and the total span (or TS)[1] of the staves varies in different types of the paper from just under 137 mm. to just under 139 mm.

Although this paper was considerably smaller than almost anything that Mozart had used up to then,[2] he evidently took a liking to it. In the next four and a half years, in fact—the period from March 1773 up to his departure from Salzburg for Munich, Mannheim, and Paris in September 1777—the majority of his scores excluding operas are on *Klein-Querformat* paper. It is clear that he also had a quantity of it with him on his long sixteen-month journey (although from time to time he availed himself of other papers obtained locally in Mannheim, Paris, and elsewhere), and he continued to use it for one or two scores written after his return to Salzburg in January 1779. Soon after that, however, Mozart reverted to oblong paper that can no longer be described as "small," the leaves measuring very approximately 225 mm. × 305 mm. And with almost no exception he employed such larger papers till the end of his life. Until he moved to Vienna in March 1781 the papers were normally ruled with ten staves; but after he had settled there he almost always used 12-staff papers—a useful distinction which (in spite of a number of exceptions)[3] is of some practical use in problems of dating.

In the years from 1773 to 1779, the *Klein-Querformat* years, Mozart used at various times five different types of these small papers. A careful examination of the periods within which each of them was available to him may help in fixing the times at which he wrote some insecurely dated scores, such as the two masses named in the title of this chapter.

CERTAINLY there is no date today on the score of K.262, now in the Biblioteka Jagiellońska, Kraków (the first leaf has not survived in autograph, a point to be discussed later). But why should there be any problem over the date of K.258? For all the editions of Köchel from the first (1862) to the sixth (1964) indicate that the autograph score of that mass (Staatsbibliothek Preussischer Kulturbesitz, Berlin) is dated: "nel Mese Decembre 1776." (The writing is tentatively identified in Köchel[6] as Leopold Mozart's.) And we are given no hint that there is anything about this date to arouse suspicion.

Unfortunately this is an area in which Köchel's catalogue is not always a sound guide. There is, for instance, no hint in any edition of Köchel that there is something problematical about the dates on the autographs of the five violin concertos K.207, 211, 216, 218, and 219, all of which are assumed there to have been composed between April and December 1775. Yet in 1957 Ernst Hess drew attention to an obvious feature of the autograph of K.219 (Library of Congress, Washington): in the date on the first page, "li 20 di decembre/1775," the last two figures of the year had been tampered with.[4] Could we therefore be sure that K.219 was written in 1775? The whole matter was reviewed briefly by Wolfgang Plath not long ago,[5] and will certainly be discussed further now that the scores of K.207, 211, 216, and 218, for long inaccessible, are once again available (in Kraków) for study. For the dates on these four concertos have been changed in a similar way to that of K.219; according to Plath, the likeliest explanation is that the original dates on all the concertos—except for K.207[6]—were indeed "1775," but that at some stage they were changed to "1780" and then back again.

An examination shows that, in spite of Köchel's silence on this point, the year on the autograph of the *Missa brevis* K.258 has also been tampered with. And the same proves to be the case with the two other Masses that are still bound up with it: K.257 and K.259. The dates on their autographs are recorded in Köchel[6] as "nel Novb: 1776" and "Decembre 1776" respectively—yet in both cases the last figure of the year is suspect (with K.257, the last two figures). Did these three masses originally carry other dates—"1775," for instance? It looks at all events as if we should be grateful for any other clues to the times of their composition. And the same will apply to the *Missa longa* K.262, which carries no date, as well as several other *Klein-Querformat* scores of symphonies and other works from these years on which the dates have been made illegible by heavy crossings-out.

THE FIVE different kinds of *Klein-Querformat* paper used by Mozart in the years 1773–1779 can be divided into three common types and two rare types.

Type I. This is the paper that Mozart began to use immediately after his return from Italy to Salzburg on 13 March 1773. We can in fact take that date as the *terminus post quem* for our *Klein-Querformat* papers; for none of the scores that he had completed in Salzburg in the summer and autumn of 1772, nor any that date from his months in Italy in the winter of 1772–73, are on paper of this small size. The first of these *Klein-Querformat* scores that has come down to us is that of the divertimento K.166 (159d), dated "il 24 di Marzo 1773," that is, only eleven days after his return to Salzburg; and the second is probably that of the E-flat symphony K.184 (161a), for its date, though vigorously crossed out, has been read as "30 di marzo 1773."[7] Both scores are on paper of Type I, as are a large number of others that Mozart completed in the course of the next two years. They are listed in Table 12.1 at the end of this chapter. It is perhaps worth recording that whereas earlier visits of the Mozart family to Vienna had sometimes been characterized by the appearance of new paper-types in the scores written there, Mozart seems to have continued to use paper of Type I during the time from July to September 1773 which was spent in Vienna. Whether he had brought it all from Salzburg or whether he purchased more of it in Vienna cannot be determined, but the former seems more likely.

Here are the features by which paper of Type I can be identified:

Rastrology. 10-staff paper, with TS of 136.5–137 mm. A characteristic feature, recognizable in photographs, is that at its start the fifth line of the bottom staff projects a little further to the left than the fourth line.

Watermark (see Figure 12.1 at the end of this chapter). Mold A: on left, a crown over a shield that contains a lion rampant[8] facing to the left (that is, toward the outside of the paper); on right, a crown over the letters GF. Mold B: the same overall pattern in reverse, except that here the lion rampant is also facing to the left (that is, toward the middle of the paper).

A careful review of all the *Klein-Querformat* scores from these years with dates by Mozart (or by his father) that have not been tampered with makes it clear that he continued to use paper of Type I, and of that type only, at least until May 1775. From that month come the two dated tenor arias K.209 and K.210. Soon after that, however, the sources show that he had moved on to paper of Type II.

Type II. This paper was used by Mozart for at least a year and a half. The first scores that consist *wholly* of Type II paper are from August 1775: K.204 (213a), K.215 (213b), and K.214.[9] The list at the end of this essay shows that Mozart continued to employ it for the rest of 1775 and for the first nine months of 1776, as well as in two scores dated January 1777: the divertimento K.270, and the piano concerto K.271. And Type II is also found in the scores of the three masses K.257, 258, and 259—but whether the dates given to them in Köchel, November and December 1776, are correct is part of the subject of this chapter.

Type II paper can be identified as follows:

Rastrology. 10-staff paper, with TS of 138.5 mm. The fifth line of the bottom staff is normally a little shorter at the left-hand side than the other four lines of the same staff. Once again, this feature can be seen in photographs.

Watermark (see Figure 12.2). Mold A: on left, the letters FC; on right, three hats[10] over the letter R. Mold B: the same overall pattern in reverse.

Type III. Apart from the two scores of January 1777 mentioned above (K.270 and 271), all the *Klein-Querformat* scores that have come down to us bearing dates from the years 1777, 1778, and 1779 are on paper of this third type. It has the advantage of being readily identifiable in photographs; so it has been possible to add one or two scores which are no longer accessible to the list of Type III autographs at the end of this chapter (Table 12.1).

The earliest surviving score on this paper appears to be the divertimento K.287 (271H). Its date was cut off at a very early period; although André claimed to have evidence that it had been "February

1777," the consensus today is that the score was written out in June.[11] Mozart not only continued to use this paper up to the time when he set off on his long journey on 23 September 1777 (see the aria K.272 from August and the Graduale K.273 from 9 September), but he took a supply with him on his travels. For we find it in the four preludes K.284a = 395 (300g), seemingly written in Munich at the beginning of October, in the flute quartet K.285 (Mannheim, 25 December), and in the concerto for flute and harp K.299 (297c), apparently written in Paris in the spring of 1778. From time to time further supplies of such conveniently light paper may have been sent from Salzburg by Leopold; one such dispatch (to Augsburg) is mentioned by Leopold in his letter of 9 October 1777, and on the travelers' arrival in Paris Maria Anna Mozart reported to her husband (letter of 24 March 1778): "We managed to get through the customs examination all right except for Wolfgang's small music paper, for which he had to pay 38 sous."[12]

It is likely enough that Mozart kept such paper mainly for scores that might have to travel by mail—such as the bravura aria for Aloysia Weber, K.316 (300b), dated "Monaco [Munich] li 8 di gennaio 1779" but perhaps begun in Paris the previous June. Other works that he kept by him, such as the six violin sonatas K.301–306 (293a, 293b, 293c, 300c, 293d, 300l) or the A-minor piano sonata K.310 (300d), were written down on Mannheim or Paris papers. And when he finally returned to Salzburg in January 1779, he adopted *Querformat* paper of ordinary size for the majority of his scores, as he was to do for the rest of his life. There are a very few works, most of them apparently written soon after his return, that are still on Type III paper: the well-known "Coronation" Mass, K.317 (23 March 1779), the symphony K.318 (26 April 1779), and the church sonata K.328 (317c) (undated). From this time on, Mozart abandons not only Type III paper but almost without exception all *Klein-Querformat* paper.[13]

The features by which Type III paper can be recognized are as follows:

Rastrology. 10-staff paper, with TS of 138–139 mm. The individual lines in the staves are thicker than in Types I and II. Type III is very easily recognized in photographs by the presence of vertical lines ruled at the beginnings and ends of the staves—the only *Klein-Querformat* paper used by Mozart (apart from the score of K.61b) to have them.

Watermark (see Figure 12.3). Mold A: on left, three crescent moons; on right, the letters FS.[14] Mold B: the same overall pattern in reverse. The paper is thicker than that of the other *Klein-Querformat* types.

Summing up, then, we can set the following approximate limits to Mozart's use of Types I–III: Type I, from March 1773 to May 1775; Type II from August 1775 to January 1777; Type III, from June (or even February?) 1777 to about April 1779. The question next arises: what type or types did Mozart use in June and July 1775?

Three scores have survived that appear to be from those months. One, the church sonata K.212 (July 1777), is not on *Klein-Querformat* paper so it need not be considered here. A second, the violin concerto K.211, is on *Klein-Querformat* paper, but has to be treated with caution since—as we have already seen—its date, cited in Köchel[6] as "li 14 di giugno 1775," has been tampered with. But the third, the divertimento K.213, which is dated "nel Luglio 1775," gives rise to no such qualms.

The divertimento's six leaves prove on examination to be four leaves of Type II followed by two leaves of Type I. This seems entirely appropriate for a work written at the time when Mozart was passing from one paper-type to another. The violin concerto K.211 also contains the same mixture: sixteen leaves of Type I followed by twelve leaves of Type II. Surely this is strong evidence that in spite of the alteration of the date on its autograph, the concerto was written in June 1775.

And there is one other score in which a mixture of Types I and II is to be found. This is the *Missa longa*, K.262. For fols. 2–44 and 57–58 are of Type I, and fols. 45–56 are of Type II. (The present first leaf is in the hand of a copyist, evidently replacing an autograph leaf lost at some time before 1800.)[15] Thus we are, I believe, justified in assigning the composition time of K.262 to that period of two months in which we find Mozart changing from Type I to Type II paper, and using both within a single score. The *Missa longa* K.262, it seems, was written in June or July 1775, though at present it is not possible to identify the occasion that gave rise to a work of such size and splendor.[16]

IT IS TIME to turn to the autograph score of the *Missa brevis* K.258, which will at the same time introduce our remaining types of *Klein-Querformat* paper—the two rare ones.

This autograph consists of thirty leaves.[17] The first twenty-eight leaves form seven "single-sheet gatherings" (that is, gatherings consisting of two bifolia that come from the same original sheet of paper); the last two leaves are a bifolium. What is surprising is that no fewer than three different paper-types are involved.

Fols. 1–24 are of Type II paper. But fols. 25–28 are from a sheet of a different kind, which we can call *Type IV*. This rare type can be recognized by the following features:

Rastrology. 10-staff paper, with TS of 136.5–137 mm. No line in the
  bottom staff is conspicuously longer or shorter than the others.
Watermark (see Figure 12.4). Mold A: on left, a "Venetian" lion
  facing to the left (that is, toward the outside of the paper), over
  the reversed letter F; on right (but starting on left), the name F.
  CALCINARDI over TOSCOLANO. Mold B: the same overall pattern in
  reverse.

It is an obvious deduction that "F. Calcinardi" is the full name of the papermaker at Toscolano (on the west bank of the Lago di Garda) represented in Type II merely by the letters FC.

Type IV paper has been found in only one other score, the autograph of the violin concerto K.219 in Washington, already referred to earlier. Of its forty-six leaves, forty-two are of Type II paper; but fols. 37–40 are a single-sheet gathering of Type IV paper. The date on this autograph, "li 20 di decembre / 1775," we have already seen, must be treated with circumspection because of the changes (or attempted changes) to the last two figures of the year. Yet should "1775" turn out to be its correct date, that would suggest that the true date of the *Missa brevis* K.258 is December 1775 rather than December 1776.

The last two leaves of the K.258 autograph, a bifolium with fols. 29–30, introduce us to our final paper-type—or rather to half a sheet of it. For more complete examples of *Type V* we must turn to the soprano aria K.217, "Voi avete un cor fedele." The autograph of this aria (Staatsbibliothek Preussischer Kulturbesitz, Berlin) consists of fourteen leaves: fols. 5–8 are a gathered sheet of Type II, and fols. 1–4 and 9–14 are two gathered sheets and a bifolium of Type V. Type V can be identified as follows:

Rastrology. 10-staff paper, with TS of 136.5–137 mm. No line in the
  bottom staff is conspicuously longer or shorter than the others.
Watermark (see Figure 12.5). Mold A: on left, the letters FC: on right,

a posthorn shield, over the name L V GERREVINK, over the letter F. Mold B: the same overall pattern in reverse.

The letters FC indicate that this is yet another paper produced by F. Calcinardi of Toscolano. That the watermark also includes the name of a well-known Dutch firm, Lubertus van Gerrevink, should not mislead us, since the names of respected manufacturers were often appropriated without authority and included merely as a claim to quality.

The two leaves at the end of K.258, and ten of the leaves in the aria K.217, are the only known examples of Type V paper. And there is nothing problematical about the date of the aria, for Leopold wrote on the autograph "26 octob. 1775," and no one has tried to delete or to change the figures. That in itself must greatly strengthen the notion that the original date on the autograph of K.258 was not December 1776 but December 1775.

But the connection between the last two leaves of K.258 and the aria can be shown to be even more intimate than the sharing of a rare paper-type. For fols. 13–14 (a bifolium) of K.217 are the bottom half of a sheet (the watermark is that of Mold B), while fols. 29–30 of K.258 are the top half of a sheet (also Mold B); and from the fortunate fact that both scores are today in the same Berlin library, it is possible with a little care to establish that these are the *two halves of the very same sheet*.[18] The conclusion can hardly be avoided that both scores were written out in the last months of 1775. Accordingly, the date that Leopold originally wrote on the *Missa brevis* K.258 was "nel Mese Decembre 1775." And an extra bonus is that the violin concerto K.219 can be confirmed as having been completed in the same month and year.

To RECAPITULATE: an examination of the *Klein-Querformat* paper-types enables us to suggest (or to confirm) the following datings for two masses and two violin concertos:

Missa longa K.262 (246a)	June–July 1775
Missa brevis K.258	December 1775
Violin Concerto K.211	14 June 1775
Violin Concerto K.219	20 December 1775

And the date of a third mass can also be determined indirectly. For as long ago as 1964, Wolfgang Plath's elucidation of a Mozartian sketch-leaf in the Bibliothèque nationale, Paris, revealed the juxtaposition of

TABLE 12.1. Types of *Klein-Querformat* paper used by Mozart.

Köchel number	Composition	Date on autograph[a]	Location of autograph
	Type I		
K.166 (159d)	Divertimento	24 March 1773	Kraków, Biblioteka Jagiellońska (= BJ)
K.184 (161a)	Symphony	"30 March 1773"	Private collection
K.199 (161b)	Symphony	"10 (16?) April 1773"	Private collection
K.162	Symphony	"19 (29?) . . ."	Private collection
K.181 (162b)	Symphony	"19 May 1773"	Private collection
K.185 (167a)	Serenade	"August? 1773"	Disrupted: in various locations today.
K.189 (167b)	March	Undated	Berlin, Staatsbibliothek Preussischer Kulturbesitz (= SPK)
K.168	String Quartet	August 1773	Berlin, SPK
K.169	String Quartet	August 1773	Kraków, BJ
K.170	String Quartet	August 1773	Private collection
K.171	String Quartet	August 1773	Kraków, BJ
K.172	String Quartet	Undated	London, BL
K.173	String Quartet	1773	Kraków, BJ
K.173, finale movement	String Quartet	Undated	London, BL (Stefan Zweig Collection)
K.182 (173dA)	Symphony	"3 October 1773"	Private collection
K.183 (173dB)	Symphony	"5 October 1773"	Private collection
K.174	String Quintet	December 1773	Kraków, BJ
K.188 (240b)	Divertimento	Undated	Paris, Institut de France
K.201 (186a)	Symphony	"6 April 1774"	Private collection
K.202 (186b)	Symphony	"5 May 1774"	Private collection
K.190 (186E)	Concertone	"31 May 1774"	Private collection
K.193 (186g)	Dixit, Magnificat	July 1774	Vienna, Nationalbibliothek
K.194 (186h)	Missa brevis	8 August 1774	Vienna, Nationalbibliothek
K.203 (189b)	Serenade	"August 1774"	Private collection
K.237 (189c)	March	Undated	Paris, Institut de France
K.200 (189k)	Symphony	"17 (12?) November 1774"	Private collection
K.207	Violin Concerto	"14 April 1775"	Kraków, BJ
K.209	Tenor Aria	19 May 1775	Berlin, SPK
K.210	Tenor Aria	May 1775	Berlin, SPK

Other scores on *Type I* paper:
(a) Further undated autographs

K.293e	Cadenzas to arias by J. C. Bach: in Leopold's hand	Undated	Augsburg, Stadtarchiv

a. The dates are those on the autographs (as cited in Köchel[6]); altered or deleted dates are shown in quotation marks.

TABLE 12.1. *(continued)*

Köchel number	Composition	Date on autograph[a]	Location of autograph
K.320B	Divertimento (fragment)	Undated	Private collection
K.80 (73f), finale	String Quartet movement	Undated (first three movements dated 15 March 1770)	Kraków, BJ
K.113, added wind parts	Divertimento	Undated (original score dated November 1771)	Berlin, SPK
K.626b/36 and 44	Sketchleaf	Undated	Ithaca (USA), Cornell University
K.73w	Fugue (fragment)	Undated	Berlin, Deutsche Staatsbibliothek

(b) Arrangements or copies of music by other composers

Köchel[6], Anh. C 17.12 (Köchel[1]:187)	Music by Starzer and Gluck: in hand of Leopold	Undated	Kraków, BJ
Köchel[6], 626b/28	"Ballo gavotte" by Gluck: in hand of Leopold	Undated	Private collection
Köchel[6], Anh. A 14	Copy of "Ave Maria" by Michael Haydn	Undated	London, BL
Köchel[6], Anh. A 50	"Instrumental piece" by?	Undated	Vienna, Gesellschaft der Musikfreunde
Köchel[6], Anh. A 72–A 81	Copies of church music by Ernst Eberlin (A 80 = by Michael Haydn): in hand of Leopold	Undated	London, BL

Type II

K.204 (213a)	Serenade	"5 August 1775"	Private collection
K.215 (213b)	March	August 1775	Paris, Institut de France
K.214	March	20 August 1775	Paris, Institut de France
K.216	Violin Concerto	"12 September 1775"	Kraków, BJ
K.218	Violin Concerto	"October 1775"	Kraków, BJ
K.238	Piano Concerto	January 1776	Washington, Library of Congress
K.239	Serenade	January 1776	Paris, Institut de France
K.240	Divertimento	January 1776	Kraków, BJ
K.252 (240a)	Divertimento	Undated	Kraków, BJ
K.241 + 263	Church Sonatas	January 1776 (for K.241)	Leningrad, Public Library
K.246	Piano Concerto	April 1776	Kraków, BJ

TABLE 12.1. *(continued)*

Köchel number	Composition	Date on autograph[a]	Location of autograph
K.288 (246c)	Divertimento (fragment)	Undated	Private collection
K.247	Divertimento	June 1776	Kraków, BJ
K.248	March	June 1776	Paris, Institut de France
K.260 (248a)	Offertorium	1776	Vienna, Nationalbibliothek
K.250 (248b)	Serenade ("Haffner")	"July 1776"	Private collection
K.249	March	20 July 1776	Paris, Institut de France
K.101 (250a)	Contredanses	Undated	Paris, Institut de France
K.253	Divertimento	August 1776	Kraków, BJ
K.254	Divertimento	August 1776	Kraków, BJ
K.255	Alto Aria	September 1776	Veste Coburg, Kunstsammlungen
K.256	Tenor Aria	September 1776	Berlin, SPK
K.257	Missa	"November 1776"	Berlin, SPK
K.259	Missa brevis	"December 1776"	Berlin, SPK
K.270	Divertimento	January 1777	Kraków, BJ
K.271	Piano Concerto	January 1777	Kraków, BJ
K.365 (316a)	Cadenzas to Concerto for Two Pianos, in Leopold's hand, with additions by Wolfgang	Undated	Salzburg, St. Peter

Copies on *Type II* paper of music by other composers

Köchel[6], Anh. A 71, A 86–88	Copies of church music by Ernst Eberlin: in hand of Leopold	Undated	London, BL

Type III

K.287 (271H)	Divertimento	André: "February 1777" (June?)	Kraków, BJ
K.272	Soprano Aria	August 1777	Berlin, SPK
K.273	Graduale	9 September 1777	Berlin, SPK
K.395 (300g, = 284a)	Four Preludes	Undated	New York, Pierpont Morgan Library
K.311 (284c)	Piano Sonata	Undated	Kraków, BJ
K.285	Flute Quartet	25 December 1777	Kraków, BJ
K.315 (285e)	Andante for Flute	Undated	Paris, Bibliothèque nationale
K.299 (297c)	Concerto for Flute and Harp	1778	Kraków, BJ
K.316 (300b)	Soprano Aria	8 January 1779	Lisbon, Ajuda Library
K.317	"Coronation" Mass	23 March 1779	Kraków, BJ
K.328 (317c)	Church Sonata	Undated	Veste Coburg, Kunstsammlungen

TABLE 12.1. *(continued)*

Köchel number	Composition	Date on autograph[a]	Location of autograph
K.318	Symphony	26 April 1779	New York Public Library
Köchel deest (Sotheby, 12 December 1979)	Draft of a song	Undated	Private collection
K.413 (387a)	Cadenzas to Piano Concerto (in Leopold's hand)	Undated (not before end of 1782)	Salzburg, St. Peter

Autographs (untraced today) identified as *Type III* from photographs

K.296c	Sketch for Sanctus?	Undated	
K.626a, Part 2, F, G, H	Cadenzas to J. S. Schroeter, Op. III	Undated	

Types I and II in combination

K.211	Violin Concerto	"14 June 1775"	Kraków, BJ
K.213	Divertimento	July 1775	Kraków, BJ
K.262 (246a)	Missa Longa	Undated	Kraków, BJ

Types II and IV in combination

K.219	Violin Concerto	"20 December 1775"	Washington, Library of Congress

Types II and V in combination

K.217	Soprano Aria	26 October 1775	Berlin, SPK

Types II, IV, and V in combination

K.258	Missa brevis	"December 1776"	Berlin, SPK

Lost *Klein-Querformat* Scores

K.175	Piano Concerto	December 1773	
K.220 (196b)	Missa brevis	?	
K.279 (189d), first movement	Piano Sonata	Undated	
K.329 (317a)	Church Sonata	Undated	
K.314 (285d = 271k)	Oboe Concerto	?	cf. Bauer-Deutsch III, p. 256 (No. 728, 15 February 1783)—reference to "Das Büchel." For sketch (on Type II paper?), see NMA V/14/3, p. 174.

a group of sketches for the so-called "Credo"-Mass, K.257, and a sketch for the buffa aria "Clarice cara mia sposa," K.256.[19] This aria, which Alfred Einstein identified as one for insertion in Piccinni's "L'astratto ovvero Il giocatore fortunato" (text by Giuseppe Petrosellini), bears on the autograph the date of "nel Settemb: 1776," and makes it hard to avoid the conclusion that the month of November on the score of K.257 must be November 1776. Thus at present there is only one mass from these years surviving in autograph which cannot be dated with precision: for there seems no way to decide whether K.259 is from 1775 or 1776.[20]

It is to be hoped that future work on Mozart's paper-types, by establishing the period within which each type was used by him, will make an increasing contribution—along with other techniques, such as *Schriftchronologie*[21]—to the dating of those numerous scores (and score-fragments) which were left undated by him or by his father, or on which the date was falsified or made illegible.

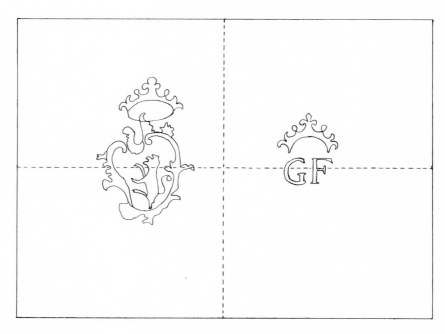

FIGURE 12.1. Type I.

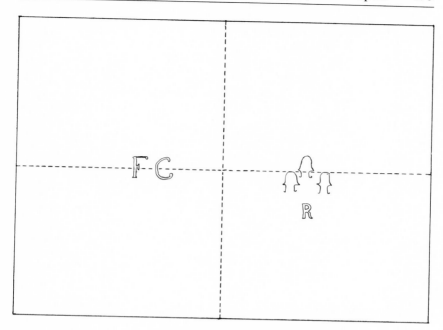

FIGURE 12.2. Type II.

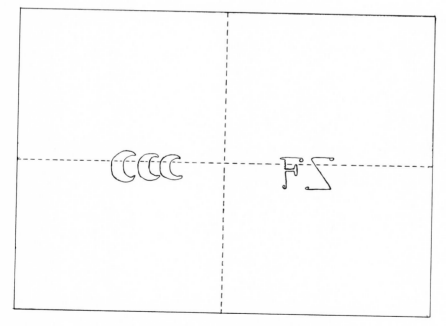

FIGURE 12.3. Type III.

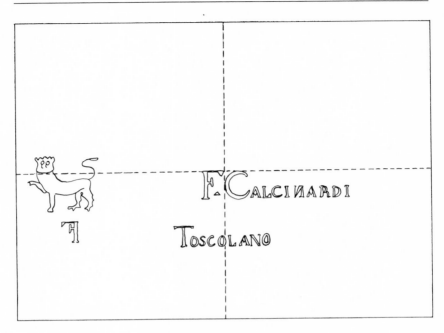

FIGURE 12.4. Type IV.

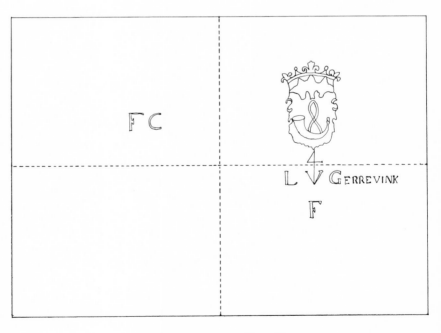

FIGURE 12.5. Type V.

13

On the Composition of Mozart's
Così fan tutte

Answers to the question as to how Mozart set about writing an opera do not lie wholly within the realm of speculation. For two of his mature operas, *Idomeneo* (1780–81) and *Die Entführung aus dem Serail* (1782–83), we have a detailed and exceedingly interesting correspondence between Mozart and his father; the subjects discussed range over the strengths and weaknesses of the singers engaged by the theater, the possibilities and potential limitations of the libretto, and—perhaps most enlightening of all—the composer's own intentions in particular ensembles and solo numbers, and his way of realizing them. Such a valuable source has naturally attracted a good deal of scholarly attention.[1] And some of the same topics are raised in other letters that concern themselves with operatic projects never completed, for instance, the 1783 plan to tackle an opera buffa on the subject of *L'oca del Cairo* (K.422).

For his other operas of the Vienna years, our evidence is much less copious. But for *Le nozze di Figaro* (1785–86) we have at least the reminiscences of Michael Kelly; and with *Don Giovanni* (1787) and *Die Zauberflöte* (1791) something, albeit of very uncertain value, has been contributed by anecdote or legend, to which Mozart's rather sparse letters have provided a framework. It seems that of all his mature operas it is *Così fan tutte* (first produced on 26 January 1790) that is—so far as its composition is concerned—the most obscure. There is very little in Mozart's correspondence, and no reminiscences from any of the singers; even the librettist Da Ponte's memoirs, always disappointing where his collaboration with Mozart is concerned, are particularly unforthcoming about *Così fan tutte,* "dramma che tiene il terzo loco tra le tre Sorelle nate da quel celeberrimo Padre dell'armonia."[2]

Thus we are left, in the main, to draw such inferences as are possible from the autograph score itself, from a few sketches and drafts that have also survived, and perhaps from the printed libretto of 1790. But here there have been difficulties throughout much of the last half-century. Although the autograph of the opera's second act is easily accessible in Berlin (Staatsbibliothek Preussischer Kulturbesitz), the first act was for long unavailable to scholarship, having disappeared at the end of World War II; it has only lately come to light in Poland (Kraków, Biblioteka Jagiellońska). The report that follows takes advantage of the recent accessibility of the first act's autograph score.

TODAY, when one asks to see the autograph of a Mozart opera, one will perhaps be presented with one, two, or three bound volumes. But their bindings are likely to date from the nineteenth century. What would one have seen immediately after the opera had been completed? By then the score might already have been contained in a simple paper binding or wrapper. Or it might have consisted merely of a large number of fascicles, no doubt provided with a simple numbering sequence to enable them to be kept in the correct order. (Some shorter scores were strung together by ribbon or twine.) In considering the collection of papers that make up the autograph score of Così fan tutte, it is helpful to visualize its condition just as Mozart was completing the opera, for that will serve to explain certain features in the score that are to be discussed.

The normal unit of paper used by Mozart in writing out almost any score is the bifolium, or pair of conjugate leaves. This is half a sheet (the sheet being the unit in which the paper was manufactured): either its upper or its lower half. In most of his scores of the Salzburg years, and in many of the earlier Viennese ones as well, the two bifolia from the same sheet were left to form a gathering of four leaves; but in the years after Figaro, Mozart usually separated the two bifolia before beginning to write, and filled all four sides of the one before moving on to the other.

Thus in a late score such as Così fan tutte, one will frequently find a bifolium directly followed by its "pair" from the same sheet—the pair being identified by the matching profile of its upper edge and by the complementary portions of the watermark. Frequently, but no more than that; for if leaves have been discarded for any reason, the tidy pattern is broken, and a bifolium will be followed by a bifolium from another sheet. When such a sequence is detected, it will suggest that Mozart may have thrown a bifolium away at that point, although usually nothing remains to show the nature of the change in plan or the correction involved. In spite of the binding, it is almost always possible to identify the individual bifolia and to see whether they are paired with their neighbors. From time to time, too, single leaves will be found; their presence needs to be accounted for. (Most of them will be seen to contain recitatives.)

So much for the basic make-up of a late operatic score by Mozart. How were its individual units placed and kept in their proper sequence?

When Mozart started to work on an opera, the libretto would have been no more than a handwritten text, possibly incomplete at some points. Passages with short lines and rhymes would show where an aria or an ensemble was intended. And these would be what Mozart first began to set to music, not without considering whether they were too frequent or too few, too undramatic or too muddled, in which case alterations in the text might be requested and made. Almost always he would begin each of these numbers with a new bifolium, every number being written separately and by no means in the order in which they were to stand in the completed score. When he had finished several numbers, he might try to place them in their proper sequence, fixing their positions by writing "No. 1," "No. 2," and so on, at the beginning of each number. He could also start to write *1, 2, 3,* and so on, on the individual bifolia and the occasional single leaves throughout the portions of the opera that he regarded as already finished. (In some opera scores every leaf was individually foliated from the beginning to the end.)

When most of the numbers (arias and ensembles) had been written, it was time for Mozart to turn his attention to the linking recitatives. A long one would have its own bifolium, but shorter ones might be entered on the blank pages at the end of the number that they followed. If, however, there were no blank pages there, or not enough of them to accommodate the whole recitative, Mozart would be obliged to insert a single leaf at that point. The location of such leaves (or bifolia) containing recitatives was almost always confirmed by a few words linking them with the numbers that preceded and followed them: at the beginning, a phrase like "Dopo il Sestetto," and at the end some words such as "segue l'aria di Ferrando No. . . ." (The figure was often added somewhat later.)

All of this will be familiar enough to anyone who has worked with the scores of Mozart's late operas. But it will serve as an introduction to the information displayed in Tables 13.1 and 13.2 (at the end of this chapter), which depict the autograph of *Così fan tutte,* Act I. The evidence that a finished score provides for the genesis of a work is hardly ever straightforward and is unlikely to take us as far as we desire. We may have to rely on minimal clues and to follow them farther than is comfortable. Still, in the case of this opera, we are likely to be grateful for any hints that we can gain as to the way in which Mozart set about writing it.

I T   I S   C E R T A I N L Y from the newly accessible score of Act I that the most promising clues can be gained. This consists of 174 leaves of 12-staff paper. The paper is not uniform; apart from two leaves,[3] all of it is of one or the other of two types distinguishable both by watermark and by the span of the twelve staves. The paper called here Type I has a sheet-watermark depicting a crown over the letter w in an ornamental frame (with a countermark of three moons over the word REAL) and a staff span of 187.5–188 mm.; Type II has a sheet-watermark showing the letters CS over C (a countermark again of three moons over the word REAL, but different in size from the elements in Type I) and a staff span of 182–183 mm. (see Figures 13.1a and 13.1b).

The distinction between the two paper-types is an important one, for it can be shown that Type I is the earlier; thus the distribution of the two papers within Act I might well suggest to us something about the order in which it was composed. Mozart was already using Type I in October 1789, when he wrote the two soprano arias K.582 and K.583 for Louise Villeneuve, the future Dorabella. It is also found in the bass aria "Rivolgete a lui lo sguardo," K.584, originally written for the role of Guilelmo in *Così fan tutte* and intended as No. 15 of the first act. Mozart entered this long D-major aria in his Verzeichnüss ("Eine arie welche in die Oper Così fan tutte bestimt war. für Benucci") under the date of December 1789. Its autograph is today bound up in Act I, of which it forms fols. 105–116, directly before the short G-major aria written to replace it, the new No. 15 ("Non siate ritrosi").[4] Almost half of Act I (78 out of the 174 leaves) is on Type I paper, but not a single leaf of Act II, which suggests that

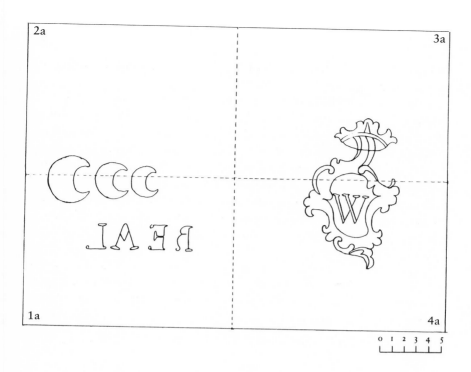

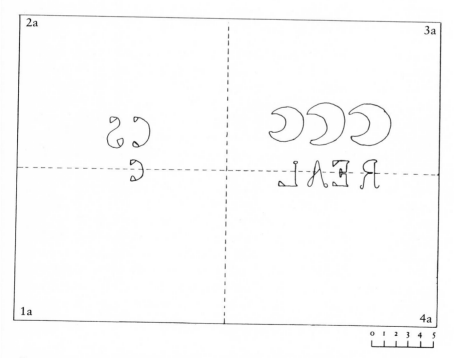

FIGURE 13.1b. Watermark on Type II paper, Mold A (Mold B is similar). The watermark drawings are schematic, and for clarity the chain lines have been omitted. Scale in centimeters.

Mozart's stock of that type had already been exhausted during his work on the first act.

This is likely to have been the point at which he turned to Type II, using it for 94 of the 174 leaves in Act I. He continued to use it almost exclusively in Act II (228 of the 238 leaves) as well as in parts of the next two works that he completed after the opera, the string quartets K.589 and K.590. But just as Type I is not found in any Mozart autograph after the first act of Così fan tutte, so Type II is not found anywhere before it. All of this is persuasive evidence that he started to use paper of Type II only after Type I was exhausted, that is, halfway through his work on Act I.

THE DISTRIBUTION of the two paper-types within Act I is shown in Table 13.2. Although at first sight the picture may seem somewhat confused, the separate numbers of the first act can be classified as follows:

A. Wholly on Type I paper: Nos. 1, 2, 3, 4, 6, 7, 10, 11, 13, 15a, and 16.
B. On a mixture of Type I and Type II: quintetto after No. 8, and No. 17.
C. Wholly on Type II paper: overture, and Nos. 5, 8, 12, 14, 15b, and 18 (except for two leaves).

One can argue that this classification represents more than one chronological layer. In Layer A, Mozart starts at the beginning of the libretto and works his way through much of the first act, stopping short only of the finale (No. 18). It is, however, noticeable that none of the numbers in this first layer, apart from No. 11 (Dorabella's aria) and No. 15a (Guilelmo's rejected aria), is a solo aria; instead they are all duetti, terzetti, quintetti, and sestetti. The solos come only in Layers B and C: No. 5 for Don Alfonso, No. 12 for Despina, No. 14 for Fiordiligi, No. 15b for Guilelmo (replacing No. 15a), and No. 17 for Ferrando. Even No. 11 for Dorabella belongs to Layer B rather than Layer A, if one includes the recitativo accompagnato that introduces it.

It appears, then, that as a matter of deliberate policy Mozart first tackled the ensembles in the first act and left the solo numbers until later. It has been possible to detect him doing the same thing elsewhere as well, for example, in La clemenza di Tito.[5] The explanation usually offered, that Mozart wished to familiarize himself with the special features of the singers' voices before writing their solo numbers, does not seem wholly applicable to the situation in *Così fan tutte*, where all the singers were known to him, and for all of whom (except the tenor Vincenzo Calvesi) he had already written several arias in the past. Adriana Gabrieli del Benè (known as "la Ferrarese"), who sang Fiordiligi, had been Susanna in the Viennese revival of *Figaro* in August 1789, and Mozart had written the rondò "Al desio, di chi t'adora," K.577, and the aria "Un moto di gioia," K.579, for her. For Louise Villeneuve, who is sometimes said to have been her sister,[6] and who sang the role of Dorabella, Fiordiligi's sister, in the opera, he had recently composed the concert arias K.578, 582, and 583 in August and October 1789. Dorotea Sardi Bussani, who sang Despina, had been Mozart's original Cherubino; her husband, Francesco Bussani, had been the original Don Bartolo and Antonio, as well as the Commendatore and Masetto in the Viennese *Don Giovanni;* Francesco Benucci, the Guilelmo, had sung the role of Figaro himself, and Leporello in the Viennese *Don Giovanni.* Only the tenor Calvesi, who sang Ferrando, was comparatively untested by Mozart, although he had been included in a terzetto and a quartetto (K.480 and K.479) written at the end of 1785 for insertion in Bianchi's *La villanella rapita.*

Although Mozart therefore knew the capabilities of these voices, he may nevertheless have wished to complete the principal arias in consultation with the individual singers, at a time when most of the ensembles were behind him.

Perhaps we should be asking why certain numbers such as No. 8, the very straightforward soldiers' chorus, or "Di scrivermi ogni giorno," a quintetto that comes shortly after No. 8 and was not given a separate number by Mozart,[7] are not in Layer A. That the overture and the finale of the first act are in Layer C is only to be expected.

ARE THERE any other ways in which we can detect chronological layers within Act I? An examination of the autograph suggests three possible leads:

1. There are two bass voices in the opera—those of Guilelmo and of Don Alfonso. (I write "bass," although in some modern scores Don Alfonso is described as a "baritone.") In eight of the eighteen first-act numbers they appear together, always with the tenor, Ferrando, and in four of them with female singers as well. But there is some inconsis-

tency on Mozart's part as to which of the two bass voices he writes lowest in the score.

In the first three numbers—all terzetti for male voices—Guilelmo's part is at the bottom. This is also the case with the sestetto No. 13 and with the first finale, No. 18. But in the unnumbered quintetto after No. 8 and in the terzetto No. 15, Don Alfonso's part is written lowest. And in No. 6, the first quintetto, we have a still more confusing situation: Don Alfonso's part is written at the bottom until m. 46, at which point Guilelmo's part takes the lowest staff.

Further reflection suggests that no chronological significance should be attached to any of this: Guilelmo has the lowest staff both in what are probably the earliest and in some of the latest first-act numbers. And that corresponds to his range relative to Don Alfonso's when they sing together. (In the quintetto No. 6, m. 63 and the first half of m. 64, for instance, Don Alfonso originally had the same notes as Guilelmo, until Mozart crossed them out and put them up an octave.) The numbers in which Guilelmo's part is written on a staff above Don Alfonso's are ones in which the voices on the whole sing not together but in alternation, so that the question of registral inversion does not arise.

This line of inquiry, then, has not led anywhere.

2. A possible clue to the internal chronology of the first act also lies in a certain confusion on Mozart's part over the names of the two sisters. Or is it rather a confusion over their voices? As the 1883 *Revisionsbericht* to the old *Gesamtausgabe*[8] explains (pp. 101–102):

Up to the finale of the first act, the first voice originally has Dorabella's name and the second voice Fiordiligi's. Later on the names are exchanged, probably merely for the sake of the names, since the well-known individuality of the singers mentioned above leaves no doubt which one was chosen as the first singer and which as the second. In Guglielmo's aria, too (Appendix I [= K.584]), their names were at first written down the other way around and altered only later.

An examination of the autograph more or less bears out that account. In the duetto No. 4, the quintetto No. 6, the terzettino No. 10, and the sestetto No. 13, the soprano staff that stands higher in the score originally bore the name "Dorabella," and the lower one "Fiordiligi," but a correction reversed the names in each case. These four numbers, we may care to note, as well as the rejected bass aria No. 15a—in which the sisters do not sing but are addressed in turn by Guilelmo, their names in the stage directions needing subsequently to be changed—are all written on paper of Type I. The finale, No. 18, on the other hand, where the names are right from the first, is (apart from a couple of leaves) entirely on paper of Type II. Nor did the names need to be changed in the unnumbered quintetto—this, too, ends on Type II paper (although it starts on Type I).

It is worth observing that in the recitative between Nos. 5 and 6, which begins "Stelle! per carità" and is on a single leaf of Type I paper, there is a very short passage in which the sisters sing together: "Ohimè! Che sento!" (fol. 38r). Here Fiordiligi has the higher part. And the same is true on fol. 54r-v at the end of the *secco* recitative and the beginning of the *recitativo accompagnato* that forms the unnumbered quintetto; this is on the first leaf of a bifolium of Type I paper. A possible implication here is that these passages of recitative, although on the earlier paper type, were nevertheless written rather late.

3. Scrutiny of the text of the Act I autograph exposes a third clue to its internal chronology, one of a rather unexpected kind. Who was Ferrando's fellow student at the *scuola degli amanti*? Today he is always referred to as "Guglielmo"—the form of the name found in the first published full score (Breitkopf & Härtel, Leipzig, 1810.) But the 1790 libretto writes "Guilelmo"—a more literal rendering of "Wilhelm"?—throughout, and so do the vocal scores published in the 1790s, such as those of Breitkopf (Leipzig, 1794) and Simrock (Bonn, 1799). (The vocal score of Schott [Mainz, 1795] has "Wilhelm" and German words.) Furthermore, this is the spelling that Mozart uses throughout Act II and in those parts of Act I that, for reasons already discussed, I believe to have been written later: in general, the parts on Type II paper.

But what of the parts on Type I paper? Here Mozart seems almost always to have written "Guillelmo" with three *l*s in all. The picture would be a clearer one if Mozart had always written the name in full. He nearly always does so at the beginning of a number, and sometimes at the head of a recitative. But the full name is not usually to be found *within* a number or a recitative (unless it is actually sung by one of the characters); there it is normally abbreviated to "Guil.," which may stand for either form of the full name that Mozart used.

It is "Guillelmo" with three *l*s at the start of Nos. 2, 3, 6, 7, 13, 15a, and 16, as well as three times in the middle of No. 6; and at the head of the recitative on fol. 18r and within the recitative on fol. 22v. All these passages are on Type I paper. The first place in the score where we find "Guilelmo" with only two *l*s is at the start of No. 1. For those who have followed my line of argument, this is, of course, a puzzle. Were the names of the characters added here somewhat later? Or was Mozart checking his spelling of the name against the manuscript of the libretto at the very start of the work—something that from then on he felt he had no need to do, until a stage was reached at which he realized he was repeatedly in error? One can do no more than speculate.

The other places in Act I where the supposedly later spelling is to be found are as follows: on fol. 35v within the recitative (which was probably added late, although it comes at the end of a number on Type I paper); on fol. 54v at the start of the unnumbered quintetto (this we have already guessed to be a later piece, even though it starts on Type I paper, because Fiordiligi's name stands above Dorabella's from the start, and in any case it ends on Type II paper);[9] in the recitative on fol. 70r-v (Type II paper); in a cue at the end of the recitative on fol. 104r (Type II paper); near the end of No. 15a on fol. 116r, where there is a stage direction "ferrando e guilelmo cominciano à ridere" (probably a late addition to this early Type I number— suggesting, incidentally, that it was a late decision to replace this long aria with the short No. 15b);[10] at the start of No. 15b and within No. 18 (both Type II): on fols. 136r, 150r, and 163r in that number, which is the first finale.

Three of these methods of inquiry—a chronological division of the first act according to which of two paper-types was being used by Mozart, whether Dorabella or Fiordiligi was originally assigned the higher part, and whether "Guilelmo" was spelled with three or two *l*s—all yield much the same results. Mozart tackled the ensembles first and then the solo arias; the recitatives were written at a fairly late stage; and No. 15a was eventually replaced by No. 15b (although No. 15a remained in the opera at least until he had settled on the spelling "Guilelmo," if I interpret the stage direction rightly). The ensemble on fols. 54–56 (the unnumbered quintetto) seems to have been late, as also the finale, No. 18; Dorabella's aria No. 11, the only one on Type I paper (apart from Guilelmo's rejected aria), may have been early. There is nothing to contradict one's guess that the overture was written last of all.

SOME FURTHER chronological clues can probably be extracted from Mozart's continuous numbering of the bifolia (and the occasional single leaf) that make up the first act; this is shown in the right-hand column of Table 13.2 and will be referred to here as the "bifoliation." Since this numbering will not have been begun before the general sequence of the incidents in the act was believed to have been settled, any arias or ensembles not included in it would appear to be late arrivals. And by this test we find, once again, that the solo arias and the overture are late; and the same is true of the soldiers' chorus, No. 8.

Almost all of these are on Type II paper; but not even Dorabella's aria No. 11, wholly on Type I paper, or Ferrando's aria No. 17, partly on Type I, are included in the bifoliation.[11] Thus the suspicion arises that perhaps the presence of Type I paper in these two arias may not commit them after all to a comparatively early date. Two or three sheets of Type I may still have been left when Mozart made his large purchase of Type II, and may have been mixed in with the new sheets. (The Type I bifolium that forms the pair with fols. 125–126 at the beginning of No. 17 turns up in the middle of a sequence of Type II paper in the finale of the act, No. 18, where it is fols. 140–141.) But it remains true that there is no Type I paper in Act II, or in any later Mozart autographs.

One small irregularity in the bifoliation calls for a different explanation. Fol. 27 and fol. 28, it can be seen, both carry the number *8*. When Mozart wrote out the terzetto No. 3 in short score, he probably required only four leaves, fols. 23–26; these received the bifoliation numbers *6* and *7*, and the duetto No. 4 that followed on fols. 28–35 was bifoliated *8, 9, 10,* and *11.* Subsequently, however, Mozart decided to enrich No. 3 with a postlude of fourteen measures, in which the men march off, bringing scene i to an end (and perhaps creating a break for the scene change?).[12] But this necessitated the insertion of a new leaf for its completion (the ink of this postlude is different from that of the preceding part).[13] It seems that this leaf, the fifth of No. 3, was at first given a *5*, but this was then changed to a bifoliation number *8*—resulting in two *8*s in succession.

Inscriptions at the top of one or two leaves may also contain hints as to the chronology of individual arias. No. 14 and No. 15b both have "Atto I.^{mo}" on their first pages; this suggests that when they were written out, Act II was already well under way. No. 5 and the march No. 8 have cues (the last words of the preceding recitatives) written by a copyist at the top of their first pages. (No. 5 has the same cue in Mozart's hand as well.) This, too, is a sign that they were written late; the Hoftheater's copyist, who will have had the responsibility of producing a correct version of the finished opera from the bits of Mozart's autograph, needed to record the places at which these two numbers were to be inserted.[14] More mysterious are the words "ist ganz instrumentirt" at the top of the first page of No. 11. It seems unlikely that when those words were written the aria was still in short score. Was it perhaps ready to be copied, but was the almost total absence of melodic phrases in the woodwinds creating the impression that the scoring had not yet been completed? There would seem to be something of a chronological clue here, if one knew how to interpret it.

MORE INTERESTING, perhaps, than evidence that bears merely on the sequence in which the various Act I numbers were written—for Mozart had to write something first and something later—are any hints of changes of plan within the act. Although there were undoubtedly some changes, little of the evidence has remained within the score, except for Guilelmo's rejected aria No. 15a. But there are traces at least of another abandoned solo number.

At the top left-hand corner of fol. 62r, the present beginning of scene viii, an amusing recitative in which Despina introduces herself and an aspect of her personality to us by tasting the chocolate she has prepared for her mistresses, there are (as Otto Jahn pointed out long ago)[15] some deleted words: "dopo la Cavatina di Despina / Scena 8ᵛᵃ" (see Figure 13.2). Furthermore, at the end of the preceding recitative of Don Alfonso's on fol. 61r, one can make out: "Segue scena / VIII. / Cavatina di / Despina," the last three words having been crossed out. So Despina was originally intended to make her entry with a solo number, of which no trace survives; it could, of course, be the case that it was never written. And since fol. 62 is of Type II paper, it must have been at quite a late stage in the construction of the act that the idea of Despina's cavatina was dropped. It must be assumed that the aria that she sings a little later, No. 12 ("In uomini, in soldati"), is a replacement for it; dramatically it is very effective, since it is a riposte to Dorabella's aria and the exaggerated grief of the two sisters, not merely a buffa autobiographical statement.

The sestetto that follows it, No. 13 ("Alla bella Despinetta"), is 219 mm. long. It was written early; was it ever planned as a finale?

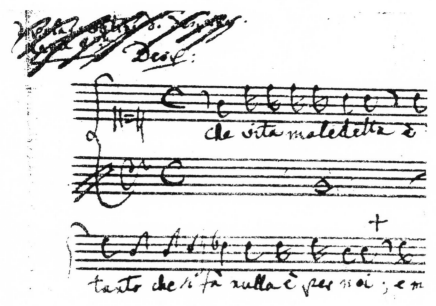

FIGURE 13.2. Fol. 62r of the Act I autograph.
Biblioteka Jagiellońska, Kraków.

Possibly it could once have been intended as the Act I finale in a three-act opera, with Guilelmo's long aria No. 15a easily accommodated within the middle act; but there is nothing in the autograph today to lend support to this. What can probably be excluded is the possibility that it was originally written as the first finale for a two-act opera. It is in C major, the tonic key of *Così fan tutte;* and in Mozart's mature two-act operas—*Don Giovanni, La clemenza di Tito,* and *Die Zauberflöte*—the first-act finale is always in another key.[16] But in *Die Entführung,* which is in three acts, the first act concludes in the tonic.

WHEN WE COME to consider the composition of Act II, the clues provided by its autograph score are very different from those that were of help in Act I. Here there is no Type I paper; except for a few leaves of miscellaneous papers containing only recitatives, it is all Type II. Fiordiligi's part is always placed above Dorabella's in the score. And the spelling "Guilelmo" is found throughout.

Some of the problems of Act II are probably insoluble, in the way that a jigsaw puzzle, several of the pieces of which are missing, cannot be completely solved. Yet it is interesting at least to examine the problems. Some consist of an apparent mismatch between the end of a recitative and the beginning of an aria that follows. The mismatch lies in the key relationship. And since there are good reasons for assuming that the recitatives were composed later than the numbers that they were intended to precede, any such mismatch suggests that a different aria was substituted for the original one—one in a different key—and that the join was not rewritten. But what happened to the original aria? Here, as I have said, some pieces of the jigsaw puzzle are missing.

More than that: not even the final version of Act II is fully represented by its autograph in Berlin. The duetto and chorus No. 21, Fiordiligi's *recitativo accompagnato* before her rondò No. 25, and Don Alfonso's No. 30, as well as the immediately preceding recitative, are all missing from it; and the recitative between Nos. 28 and 29 is not in Mozart's hand but in that of a copyist.

Luckily one of these missing sections has been recovered; in 1970 Wolfgang Plath announced that he had found a bifolium containing No. 30 and its preceding recitative among some uncatalogued papers from the *Opernsammlung* in the Stadt- und Universitätsbibliothek, Frankfurt am Main.[17] The bifolium is of Type II paper; according to Plath it is uncut and unfoliated, and has no trace of a previous stitching or binding. Only the *18* in *Rötel* (red crayon) on the first page links it in any way with the rest of the Act II autograph, since that figure is part of a bifoliation sequence running throughout the act.

Is there something to be learned from these gaps in the Berlin score? Are these numbers missing because they were written at the very last moment, possibly even after the long second finale, so that their scores had to be rushed to the theater copyist and never found their way back to the rest of the Act II autograph?

That can be no more than speculation, although No. 30 contains the words that may have led (as we shall see) to a last-minute change in the opera's title. It is noticeable, too, that Fiordiligi's *recitativo accompagnato*, ending with "e tradimento," omits six further lines that follow in the libretto, beginning "Guilelmo, anima mia!" and concluding "e il tuo tormento." Were those words perhaps set by Mozart in an earlier version of the scene, which was then rewritten? The matter is unlikely to be resolved unless an earlier draft of this kind turns up.

THERE ARE, in fact, only two surviving manuscripts that could be described as *drafts*—passages laid out in score and in ordinary writing—for any parts of the opera. These are both fragments that relate to Guilelmo's aria No. 26, and both, as one might have expected, are on Type II paper. One is a bifolium (Berlin, Deutsche Staatsbibliothek); it contains the first twenty measures in score, although only the bass line and voice, and from time to time a few other parts, are entered—as was usual before a number was "ganz instrumentirt." Although the meter is ₵ rather than 2/4, and the tempo not Allegretto but Allegro, most of the music (the first fifteen measures) corresponds almost exactly to the final version. The other fragment (Stanford, Memorial Library of Music) consists of eleven measures on one side of a single leaf; once again the meter is ₵, but the music is quite different from anything in the final version. The words found here, "à voi lo mostro, vi do marche d'amistà," represent a slightly different version from the ones finally set, "ve lo mostro, vi do segno d'amistà." But even in the autograph, Mozart retains *marche* instead of *segno* at one place (m. 46); and *segno* is not found at all in the libretto, which gives a somewhat confusing text and manages to leave out a line ("che credibile non è").

All that one can really conclude from this is that these were earlier attempts to produce a score of No. 26, and that they must have been along lines rather different from the final version.

Two leaves are also known that contain *sketches* for parts of the opera, both for sections of the Act II finale. As is often the case, the sketches—in a hard-to-read "private" style of writing—were entered on the backs of autograph score fragments (drafts), and there is good reason to suppose that this is why they were preserved: such leaves were saved from destruction because of the draft score in "public" writing, not for the sake of the sketches.

One group of sketches, for the A-flat canon quartet (mm. 173–204 of the second finale), is on the back of the string quartet fragment K.587a (Anh. 74). This fragment (Salzburg, Internationale Stiftung Mozarteum) is twenty-four measures of a quartet in G minor;[18] it is on a paper-type that Mozart could have used at any time after the beginning of 1786.[19] I have argued elsewhere that the presence of these sketches on its verso probably shows that when Mozart was working on the second finale, the fragment had been under consideration as a possible start to a minor-mode quartet for the "Prussian" set. (As was pointed out earlier, the second and third "Prussian" quartets, K.589 and K.590, were the first two works that he completed after *Così fan tutte*.) But the use of the leaf for sketching will have marked the abandonment of that plan.[20]

The sketches for the canon never give its melody to more than three voices; at an early stage Mozart seems to have decided that it would be best for Guilelmo to come in last with different material (indicated in one sketch).

The whereabouts of the other leaf with sketches for a passage in the second finale are not known today, but photographs of both sides are in the Hoboken Photogramm-Archiv, Österreichische Nationalbibliothek, Vienna. The leaf has on its recto the fragmentary Piano Fantasy in F Minor, K.383C (Anh. 32); the verso contains a sketch for mm. 545–558 on staves 1–3, and for mm. 559–574 on staves 4–6 (see Figure 13.3).[21] Although the leaf has been trimmed and consists only of the upper eight staves, it is possible to make an attempt at determining its paper-type by features of its rastrology; and this yields a somewhat unexpected result. It is not, as one might have anticipated, on Type II paper, but apparently on a paper-type found in the finales of the string quartets K.589 and K.590, completed shortly after the opera,[22] and also use by Mozart in writing out a simpler substitute for the canon quartet to be discussed later in this chapter. Since this last passage, and the finales of the quartets, were no doubt written after the opera had been completed, the fact that they are not on Type II paper is no surprise; but one might have expected a sketch for the finale, like the autograph score of the finale, to be on Type II. Could this by any chance be a sketch for a *rewriting* of the passage? That seems a forced explanation—until one finds that at a later stage Mozart apparently proposed to cut mm. 545–558, the very same measures that are sketched on staves 1–3 of this leaf. (This cut will be discussed below.) I am tempted, therefore, to conclude that this sketch is in fact later than the autograph score of the same passage; but it is a matter on which everyone will have to make up his own mind.

C H A N G E S of plan in the composition of Act II are from time to time exposed, as has already been pointed out, by curious mismatches between a recitative and the aria that follows it in the autograph.

The recitative of Act II, scene viii (which follows Fiordiligi's "Per pietà," No. 25), is a dialogue between Ferrando and Guilelmo; this

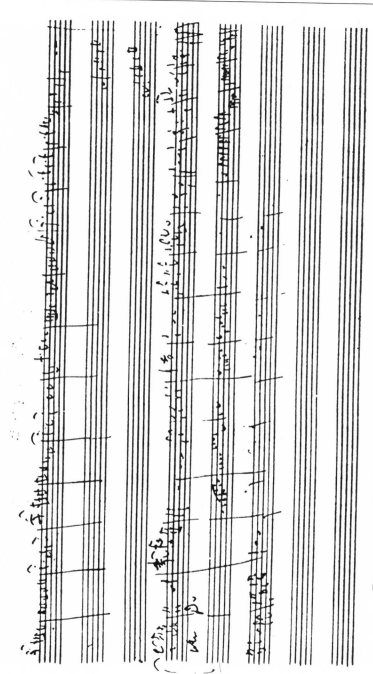

FIGURE 13.3. Sketches of Act II, No. 31, mm. 545–575. Hoboken Photogramm-Archiv, Österreichische Nationalbibliothek, Vienna.

takes on the greater intensity of a *recitativo accompagnato* at the moment when Ferrando learns that his Dorabella has been persuaded to yield the locket containing his portrait to the disguised Guilelmo. Originally it came to an end on fol. 231v with Ferrando's words: "Abbi di me pietà, dammi consiglio," and a cadence in C minor. This was followed by the link: "segue L'aria di Guilelmo" (with the number 26 added later in red crayon or *Rötel*). That this had originally been the ending of the recitative would in any case have been clear from its layout: only one system on the 12-staff page, on staves 4–8, whereas the preceding pages had two systems, on staves 1–5 and 7–11.

But Mozart chose later to extend the scene a little. So he deleted the last two measures and the linking words, inserted a new leaf (fol. 232), and on the recto wrote eight new measures with the following extra dialogue:

Guil: Amico, non saprei
        Qual consiglio a te dar
Ferr: Barbara, ingrata,
        In un giorno! in poch' ore!
Guil: Certo un caso quest' è da far stupore!

The last chord this time is the dominant of D, and the link is "attacca l'aria di Guilelmo, No. 26." This aria, "Donne mie, la fate a tanti," is in G, but begins with four measures on the dominant, D.

The puzzle here is what, in its *original* form, the recitative was intended to precede, after Ferrando's plea "Dammi consiglio" and a firm cadence in C minor. Could it have been Ferrando's despairing cavatina "Tradito, schernito," No. 27, which starts in C minor? It is certainly the case that the singer who concludes a recitative—especially a *recitativo accompagnato*—and remains on stage would expect to sing a solo aria that follows. But when Ferrando has asked for advice, it may have struck Mozart that it would be undramatic for him to prevent such advice being given by singing a cavatina; it would be more effective for Guilelmo to tender his counsel at this point in an aria on the subject of woman's nature. In this case he will have written "segue L'aria di Guilelmo" after the C-minor cadence, so that the aria he was about to write would be inserted at the right place; Ferrando's cavatina was simply postponed to a later position (and given a new *recitativo ac-*

compagnato to precede it). He will then have gone back later to build a better bridge to Guilelmo's aria, inserting fol. 232 with eight measures giving Guilelmo the last words of the recitative, and a correct cadence.

This, then, was a mismatch that Mozart corrected. But another one was not corrected in the autograph. The recitative that starts scene x of Act II ends on fol. 249v with Dorabella's words, "Credi, sorella, è meglio che tu ceda," and a cadence in E (major); the linking words are "Segue l'aria di Dorabella" and the number *28* in *Rötel*. But Dorabella's No. 28, "È amore un ladroncello," which follows, is in B-flat. The suspicion must arise that Dorabella originally had a different aria here—and one in a different key. The awkward juncture of E and B-flat was soon eliminated; in the version given by the early copyists' scores (*Abschriften*) the last six measures of the recitative are rewritten so that the cadence is not on E but on F. It seems likely that this emendation was sanctioned by Mozart himself, although that cannot be proved.

One further example of this kind is scarcely a mismatch but invites an explanation. The recitative of scenes xi and xii of Act II, mainly for Fiordiligi by herself, on fols. 258r–260r of the autograph, is in a copyist's hand; it ends with a cadence in E major. But curiously enough the early copyists' scores of the opera have a different version of the whole recitative, with a final cadence in A. The number that follows, the duetto No. 29, is also in A. Either version of the preceding recitative is therefore "acceptable"; the one cadencing in A is found in all editions of the opera. At present the reason for the existence of two versions, like their authorship, is unexplained.

A FINAL PUZZLE of the Act II autograph, which is discussed from time to time, is perhaps best explained by a lacuna in the Act I autograph.

When, in the second finale, Ferrando and Guilelmo make their entry in military uniform and totally confound the two sisters, they gradually reveal that they are no strangers to what the Albanian suitors experienced: Ferrando sings four measures of an Allegretto in D minor, Guilelmo eight measures of an Andante in F, which we recognize as a quotation from the duetto No. 23; and both join in the C-major music that accompanied Despina's miraculous cure with the magnet in the Act I finale.

From the context it would appear that Ferrando's four measures, to the words "A voi s'inchina, bella damina, il cavaliere dell'Albania" (addressed to Fiordiligi and, as the libretto says, accompanied by extravagant compliments) are also a quotation from an earlier scene. But neither the music nor the words occur anywhere else in the opera.

Thus it looks as though this is a quotation from an aria that was ultimately cut—perhaps one in D minor (for the other two citations retain the keys of their originals). Where could that aria have been placed? It cannot have been in the first part of Act I, since Ferrando must be in disguise; and even the beginning of Act II is too late. The best place would seem to be near the recitative that follows the sestetto No. 13, that is, about fols. 92–95 of the autograph. If Ferrando sang an aria introducing himself there, Fiordiligi's "Come scoglio," No. 14, would be her reply. Another possible place might be just after "Come scoglio," where both sisters start to leave and (according to the stage direction in the libretto) Ferrando calls back one while Guilelmo calls back the other. Guilelmo gets his aria of introduction; in No. 15b he, in fact, speaks on behalf of both men, as he had also done in the rejected No. 15a. But was there perhaps a time after No. 15a had been abandoned (but before No. 15b was written) when an aria was drafted in which Ferrando introduced himself?

Unfortunately Mozart has left no clues in this part of the Act I autograph. Apart from Guilelmo's rejected aria, everything from fol. 92 to fol. 120 is on Type II paper; and if the cancellation of an aria for Ferrando here once left any scars, they must have been eliminated by rewriting (or recopying).

THE PRINTED libretto has already been referred to several times as a source, and it deserves a few further comments, which will serve to remind us of Mozart's collaborator. It has survived in two very similar issues—an earlier and a later one, copies of both of which are to be found in the Stadtbibliothek, Vienna.

Apart from a few oversights in the later issue (such as the retention of the first line of the canceled aria No. 15a), both issues appear to accord well with the final version of the music. No doubt they were printed directly from the final version of Da Ponte's much-revised manuscript. One might see a hint of this in the spelling of Mozart's name at the beginning: "La musica è del Signor WOLFGANGO MOZZART." For the form "Mozzart" is also found in the *Don Gio-*

vanni libretto (Prague, 1787)[23] and throughout Da Ponte's *Memorie*, so that it may have been the librettist's own spelling of it.

It is noticeable that in his *Memorie* and elsewhere Da Ponte always refers to the opera as *La scola* [sic] *degli amanti*. One gains the impression that this was the original name of the opera as he conceived it and that the title *Così fan tutte* was Mozart's inspiration, the new title perhaps being adopted only after No. 30, the second-act number preceding the finale, had been set to music. The possibility that No. 30 (which is not in the Berlin autograph of Act II) was written very late— like the overture, where the musical setting of the words is cited as a kind of motto—has already been raised. And we shall find that what is apparently the earliest *Abschrift* at one time had on its title page no more than the words *La Scuola degli Amanti*. It would probably be a mistake, however, to see any ideological difference between Da Ponte and Mozart in their choice of titles; for the principal lesson in the "school for lovers" was obviously that "così fan tutte."

Yet personal allusions have not unreasonably been sought from time to time within the libretto. When it was being written, Adriana Gabrieli del Bene, who took the role of Fiordiligi, was Da Ponte's mistress; she was known as "la Ferrarese," which probably explains why the two sisters were from Ferrara, "dame ferraresi," in the opera. But another geographical point still calls for an explanation. As Jahn pointed out long ago,[24] the recitative of Act I, scene ix, originally included the words, "da Trieste partiti sono gli amanti nostri"; but Mozart changed this to "da Napoli . . ." in the autograph, altering the note values to fit (see Figure 13.4). Was there any personal allusion behind the change from Trieste to Naples? Or had Trieste—a more likely place than Naples to encounter rich Albanians—become to the Viennese in 1789 a city not all that distant from an unpopular war zone? The libretto, as one might have expected, states: "La Scena si finge in Napoli"; a further surprise, however, is encountered in the earliest *Abschriften* and the first published full score, where there is a return to the Adriatic, with the reading "da Venezia," and a reversion to the original note values.

One minor discrepancy between the later issue of the libretto and the autograph version of a passage in a recitative has recently been attributed to Mozart's inventiveness.[25] It comes in the dialogue between Don Alfonso and Despina in scene x of Act I. In that libretto the passage runs:

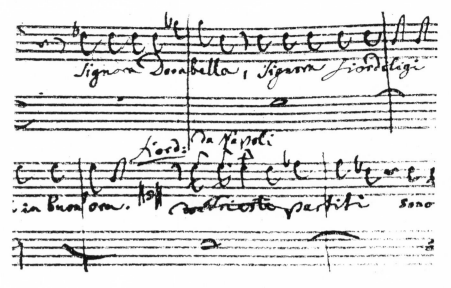

FIGURE 13.4. Fol. 70r of the Act I autograph.
Biblioteka Jagiellońska, Kraków.

D. Al. Despina mia,
        Di te bisogno avrei.
Desp.   Ed io niente di lei.
D. Al. Ti vo fare del ben:
Desp.   Non n'ho bisogno
        Un uomo come lei non può far nulla.

But in the autograph, and in the earlier issue of the libretto, Despina's
last lines are a bit more tart:

A una fanciulla
Un vecchio come lei non può far nulla.

It would seem more likely that the softening of this sharp reply in the
libretto's later issue was due rather to a wish not to get into trouble with
the censor. There are also cuts in this recitative in many *Abschriften*.

   Later in the same scene Mozart appears to have omitted a line of
the libretto, but to have tried subsequently to insert it. The passage
runs:

Desp. Hanno una buona borsa
           I vostri concorrenti?
           (Per me questa mi preme:)

It was the last line that was omitted. Mozart squeezed the necessary seven notes into the recitative on fol. 79r but did not add the words; the early *Abschriften,* on the other hand, inserted the words without the notes (see Figures 13.5 and 13.6). It should be possible to include both words and music in a modern performance.

THE CHANGES that a composer makes in his opera as it goes into production, or during its initial run, or perhaps even in the course of preparations for its revival at a later date, could, on a generous interpretation of the word, still be regarded as part of the work's "composition"—even if this activity were to be expressed largely in the form of cuts. I propose to conclude these notes on the composition of *Così fan tutte* by considering what later changes Mozart may have tried to make in his score.

My first example is of a short but significant revision that was certainly carried out by Mozart, although I cannot find it discussed in the literature. This newly composed music is never heard today. It will soon be clear, however, that there is little surprising in that.

For at some stage Mozart decided to eliminate the A-flat canon quartet in the Act II finale. The reason may have been that it was proving difficult in performance, as well as holding up the action with a Larghetto section. To replace it, he extended the preceding Andante by adding thirteen new measures after m. 172; these ended with a modulation to E major and a change of the tempo to Allegro, leading into m. 208. Thus mm. 173–207, thirty-one measures of Larghetto plus four of Allegro, were replaced by thirteen measures of Andante. The new music is based on the music beginning at m. 153 ("Tutto, tutto o vita mia"), but the words are those of the canon quartet ("E nel tuo, nel mio bicchiero"). It goes without saying that it is a clever revision. But even if the music were readily accessible—it is reproduced here in Figures 13.7–13.9—today's performers and audiences would probably be unwilling to forfeit the celebrated canon quartet.

The autograph of this revision, neatly written on the first three sides of a bifolium, is in the Deutsche Staatsbibliothek, Berlin. Since its last

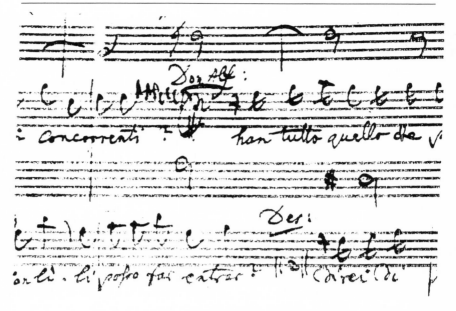

FIGURE 13.5. Fol. 79r of the Act I autograph.
Biblioteka Jagiellońska, Kraków.

FIGURE 13.6. A page of *Abschrift* S, copied by the firm
of Wenzel Sukowaty.

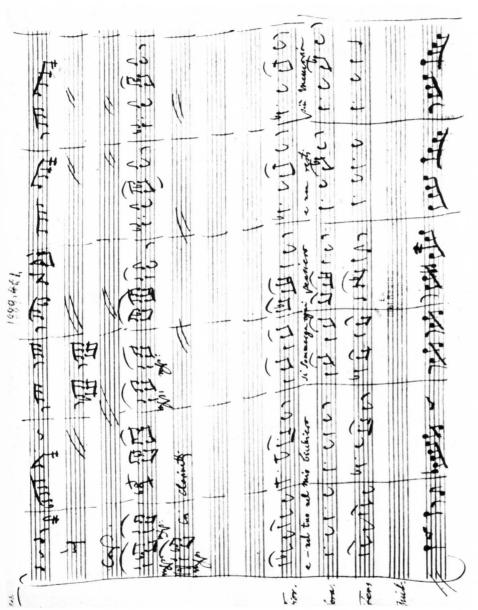

FIGURE 13.7. Mozart's autograph replacement for the canon quartet, mm. 1–6.
Deutsche Staatsbibliothek, Berlin.

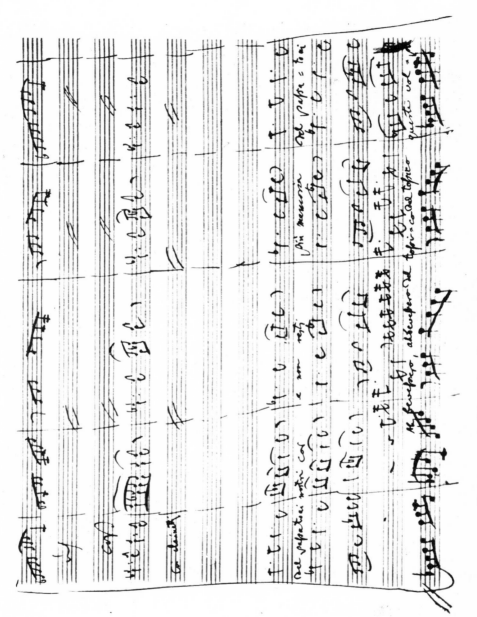

FIGURE 13.8. Mozart's replacement for the canon quartet, mm. 7–11.

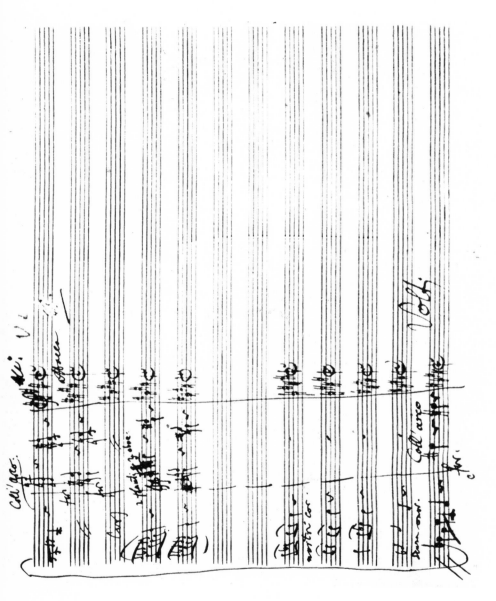

FIGURE 13.9. Mozart's replacement for the canon quartet, mm. 12–13.

measure ends with "attacca," "Vi-," and "Volti" (only the first of
these in Mozart's hand), it was no doubt at first inserted in a score of
the opera—although not in the Act II autograph, since that score has
no corresponding "-de" or similar marking at the appropriate passage. One must presume that it was inserted in a copyist's score (*Abschrift*), from which it later became detached.[26]

The precise stage at which this replacement for the canon quartet
was composed cannot now be determined. The bifolium on which it is
written is one of the paper-types discussed above—the type apparently used to sketch a revision of a passage in the second finale, and
found also in the finales of the string quartets K.589 and K.590, completed shortly after the opera. What may be a more helpful clue is the
fact that the early *Abschriften* (with one or two exceptions, shortly to
be described) and printed versions seem to know nothing of this
substitute passage; this would suggest that the traditional text had
already been widely dispersed before Mozart produced his revision.
(It is, of course, possible that the revised version was intended for
a particular performance or production, but not as a permanent
substitute.)

If we were in search of further evidence that Mozart was under
pressure to shorten his opera, we might feel that we had found it in
virtually all the *Vervielfältigungen,* or duplicated copies, in which the
text of the opera first circulated. For in these *Abschriften* a number of
passages (some admittedly very short) are missing; and the same is
true of the eighteenth-century vocal scores, such as those published by
Breitkopf in 1794 and by Simrock in 1799, as well as of the first full
score of the opera, issued by Breitkopf & Härtel in 1810. The passages usually omitted include the following:

(a) Overture: mm. 81–88, 140–156, 194–201.
(b) Soldiers' chorus, No. 8: the first twenty-four mm., for orchestra
    alone.
(c) Ferrando's aria No. 17: mm. 50–57, 63–66.
(d) Act I finale, No. 18: mm. 461–475.
(e) Ferrando's aria No. 24: mm. 57–91.

(Some of the omissions led to minor adjustments to the text at the
new joins.)

The problem posed by these widely distributed cuts was briefly discussed in the *Revisionsbericht* to the *Gesamtausgabe,* pp. 99–100.

There is nothing in the autograph score that corresponds to them, except in the case of (d), where there are a couple of markings at the appropriate place in *Rötel*—although these are probably not in Mozart's hand. It was thus a matter of speculation whether any of the cuts corresponded to Mozart's wishes, whether he accepted them only with reluctance, or whether they were arbitrarily introduced by others without his knowledge, perhaps even after his death. The triviality of the cuts in the overture, for instance, suggested that at least in those Mozart could have had no hand.

S o m e   p a r t s of this problem may remain insoluble today, for a deletion that Mozart made contentedly in a score is unlikely to be distinguishable from one to which he assented reluctantly. But in my view, a great deal of light can be thrown on the cuts by a source that appears to have escaped scrutiny up to now. This is an *Abschrift* in Vienna (Österreichische Nationalbibliothek, O.A. 146), described in the sixth edition of Köchel as the "Direktionsexemplar der k. k. Hoftheater." Since its singular features can best be described by comparing it with one of the more usual *Abschriften,* I shall discuss it together with a score made by the firm of the court copyist Wenzel Sukowaty,[27] referring to the Hoftheater score as "H" and to Sukowaty's as "S." Each of the scores is in two volumes, the title pages of which carry the same wording (except that Sukowaty added his name and address to the first volume).[28]

At first glance the two *Abschriften* appear almost identical. No doubt the explanation is that both were produced by Sukowaty's team of copyists. It is not merely that the handwriting in both scores is extremely similar (although the copyists are not in fact the same): both are made up from more or less the same "ternions" (gatherings),[29] and the layout of almost every number is the same, with identical line breaks and page turns. Is it possible to establish a connection between the two? At the end of the recitative before No. 12 ("In uomini, in soldati") H has "attacca subito / L'Aria di Des," the trimming of the margin having removed the rest of Despina's name. At the same place in S one finds the identical words, with Despina's name similarly truncated, but ending this time an inch from the margin. It is a reasonable deduction, then, that S was copied directly from H.

It is when one makes a page-by-page comparison between H and S that significant differences are detected. Four of the five passages listed above as cuts are indeed missing from S (which retains the orchestral introduction to the soldiers' chorus). But in H they were first copied out in the full form seen in the autograph and were then crossed out, although not so vigorously as to obscure the text; in the overture alone the measures were obliterated by being pasted over. It seems clear that the deletions made in H formed the basis of the cuts to be found in the *Vervielfältigungen,* including S. Where there are cuts marked in H, the layout of pages in S, which otherwise follows H faithfully, is modified, the reduced number of measures being distributed over a slightly reduced number of pages.

Thus the problem of the cuts can be restated: Who authorized the deletions that were made in H? One difficulty is that by no means all the markings in this score date from Mozart's time: as the official Hoftheater copy, it continued to be of service for several decades after his death, reflecting productions of the early nineteenth century, in which arias were often cut, transferred to different positions, or even assigned to other characters.[30] Moreover, the score is incomplete: although Köchel[6] says that H contains "numbers 1–31," ternion 21 from Act I (Ferrando's aria No. 17 and the recitative that follows it) and ternions 10 and 11 from Act II (Guilelmo's aria No. 26 and the preceding recitative) are missing.

But since the cuts that concern us here were made very early, we cannot escape the question: Did Mozart at one time hold H in his hands and give instructions as to where he was prepared for cuts to be made? I think that on the basis of the following evidence our answer must be yes.

1. The passage of thirteen measures replacing the canon quartet is also found in H, where it is in a copyist's hand. It is placed in the score just before the canon quartet (which is also written out in full). At one time, as one can see, the pages containing the canon were stitched together, so that they would be omitted; and mm. 206–207, which could not be concealed in this way because of the measures on the same page following them that needed to be seen, were eliminated by being pasted over: see Figure 13.10.

Scrutiny reveals, however, that the leaves with the replacement for the canon are not contemporary with the rest of H, but are a later insertion, probably from about 1804–1805 (to judge by the watermark). Why were they inserted in H at that time? Treitschke's handwritten note of 1804 (cited in footnote 26) springs to mind. It looks as

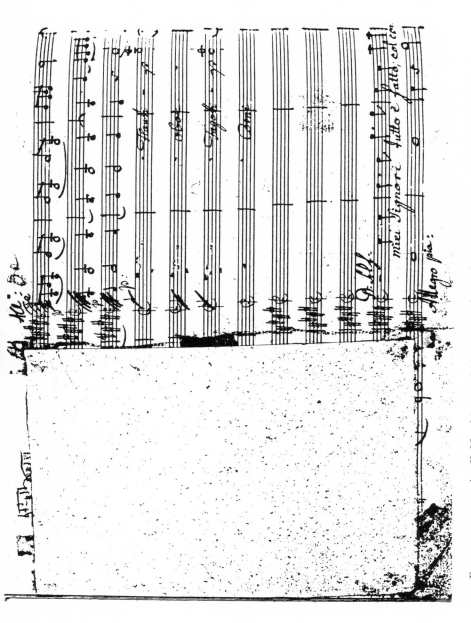

FIGURE 13.10. Act II, No. 31, mm. 208–210, in the Hoftheater *Direktionsexemplar, Abschrift* H. Österreichische Nationalbibliothek, Vienna, O.A. 146.

though the two autograph leaves with the thirteen measures were originally placed in H by Mozart himself and remained there until Treitschke discovered them in 1804, at which time they were removed and replaced by the two leaves in a copyist's hand (with the same music) that now stand there. In that case the "-de" at m. 208 in H would have matched the "Vi-" at the end of the autograph of the thirteen measures (compare Figures 13.10 and 13.9). Moreover, the tempo marking "All?" at m. 208 in H is surely in Mozart's hand.

If H contained the autograph of the thirteen measures until about 1804, and after that the same measures in a copyist's hand, this may explain how two *Abschriften* of the opera in the Conservatorio di Musica, Florence—both probably from the beginning of the nineteenth century—should happen to include them too.

2. More of Mozart's handwriting is found in H in connection with a cut of fourteen measures toward the end of the second finale. The cut starts with m. 545 and extends to m. 558; but some changes in the words and the deletion of a few notes in mm. 559, 560, and 561 were also called for, in order to patch up broken phrases: see Figure 13.11. Mozart himself entered these changes directly into H,[31] yet the cut and the alterations are not included in the *Vervielfältigungen,* except for one *Abschrift* in the Conservatorio di Musica, Florence. The reason cannot be that those copies were all made *before* Mozart altered H, for in m. 561 of S the copyist first wrote the three notes for the new word *bella* before erasing them and writing a single quarter note for the original word *vò*. Thus when S was copied from H, the changes at this place in H had already been made, but the copyist of S decided (or was instructed) to ignore them.

3. It is likely (although probably impossible to prove) that Mozart's handwriting appears at two other places in H, again in connection with cuts. The more interesting of these cuts is the deletion of fifteen measures from Act I, No. 18 (the first finale), listed above as (d), the only one for which there are any corresponding markings in the autograph. But the markings in the autograph here, probably not by Mozart, are very discreet—a couple of circled crosses made in *Rötel* above the score at the beginnings of mm. 461 and 476 (and "NB" before the former). No notes and no words within the score have been altered, leaving it unclear precisely how the new join is to be effected.

As with the cut in the second finale just discussed, the problem here is that the removal of mm. 461–475 leaves lacunae in the text, for at the beginning of m. 461 Despina and Don Alfonso lose two eighth

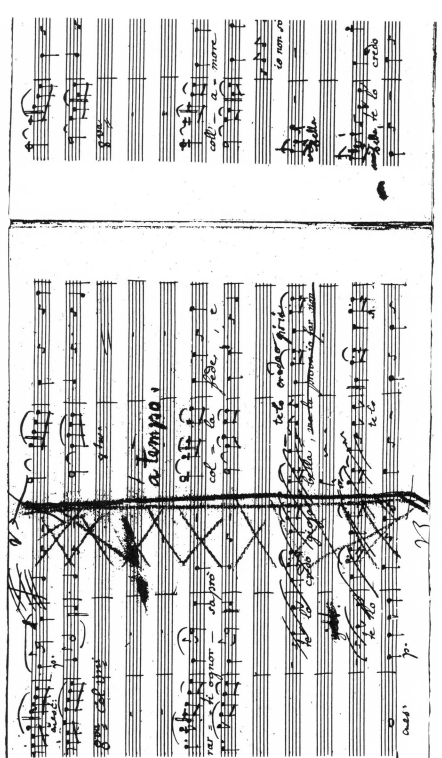

FIGURE 13.11. Act II, No. 31, mm. 556–561 in H: end of a cut, with Mozart's alterations.

notes with the necessary word *tosco* (the faulty form in which the word appears in this passage in the autograph), and at the beginning of m. 476 Fiordiligi and Dorabella would appear to enter with a meaningless *io*. The necessary changes were made in H: the sisters' superfluous *io* was replaced by a rest; and *tosco*, with its two eighth notes, was restored to Despina and Don Alfonso at the beginning of this same measure (see Figure 13.12). A little later, however, some-one—was this Mozart?—seems to have realized that the word for poison was *tossico*, the three-syllable form found in the libretto and used by Mozart elsewhere in the autograph. So in m. 476 *tosco* was changed to *tosico* (the right number of syllables even if not yet the correct spelling), and the first eighth note was changed to a dotted sixteenth followed by a thirty-second note.

The other place where Mozart's hand perhaps makes a brief ap-pearance is in connection with the cut listed above as (e), the deletion of mm. 57–91 in Ferrando's aria in Act II, No. 24. This cut deprived the word *pietà* of its final syllable in m. 57, so that "-tà" has been added, probably by Mozart, at the beginning of m. 92.

By now there can be little doubt that Mozart himself collaborated in cutting certain passages in the opera and helped to repair some of the jagged edges.[32] But the reasons that led to the cuts, and the frame of mind in which he made them, must remain matters for speculation.

AFTER THIS lengthy review of the cuts in the opera, it is pleasant to be able to *add* a few measures to *Così fan tutte*. Julius Rietz, the editor of the opera for the *Gesamtausgabe*, wisely chose to disregard the cuts preserved in the full score of 1810, and to print the full text of the work according to the autograph. Only in the case of those few numbers missing from the autograph—the duetto con coro No. 21, Fiordiligi's *recitativo accompagnato* before No. 25, and the short No. 30 just before the second finale—was it necessary to supplement it by turning to secondary sources. (He used an *Abschrift* from the Dresden Hoftheater.)

The texts of the *recitativo accompagnato* before No. 25 and of No. 30 are more or less identical in H and S (not unexpectedly, if S was copied from H). But a surprise awaits one when comparing No. 21 in the two scores. For S has the seventy-one measures of this number that are found not only in the *Gesamtausgabe* and in all mod-ern scores, but in all the early scores as well. But in H, No. 21 origi-

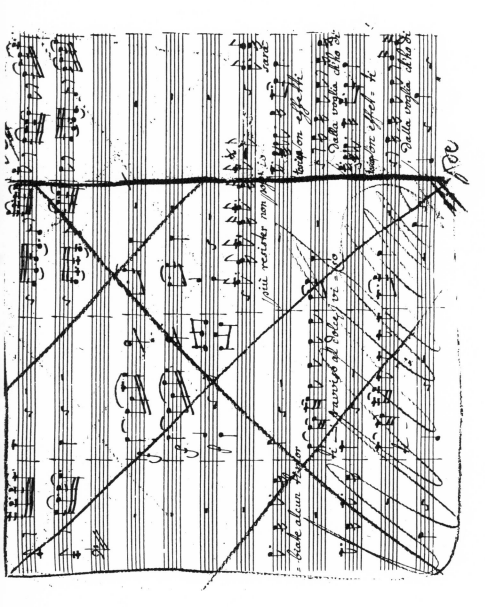

nally consisted of eighty-four measures; after m. 24, but before the voices enter, there are thirteen extra measures for winds alone: see Figures 13.13–13.15. These measures are, however, crossed out (and the measure count at the end of the number reads "71," not "84"), so that they were not copied by S and are not to be found in the *Vervielfältigungen*—or for that matter in any printed score, old or new. (They are reproduced here for the first time.)

Yet they were surely not invented by the copyists of H, who elsewhere carefully followed the autograph, even though some of the measures within the opera that they copied were later dropped from performance and so were struck out in the *Abschrift*. Rather it seems clear that the thirteen measures must have been in the long-lost autograph score of No. 21. And since all the other passages crossed out in H and omitted from the scores subsequently made from it were ultimately restored in the *Gesamtausgabe*, it would seem logical to restore these thirteen measures as well.[33] From a practical point of view they present no problem; they are the same as mm. 59–71, but without the two flutes (and without the chorus).

It seems quite clear that these measures should be included in all modern performances that aspire to be complete. The only way to guarantee that is to have them printed in modern editions of the opera, as the other excised material has been for more than a century. Any measures of Mozart must surely be worth rescuing, even if in at least some of these cases one may be rescuing them from Mozart himself.

EXAMPLE 13.1. Mozart, *Così fan tutte*, Act I, No. 14, mm. 76–77:
(a) autograph;
(b) *Abschrift* H, Vienna, Österreichische Nationalbibliothek, O.A. 146.

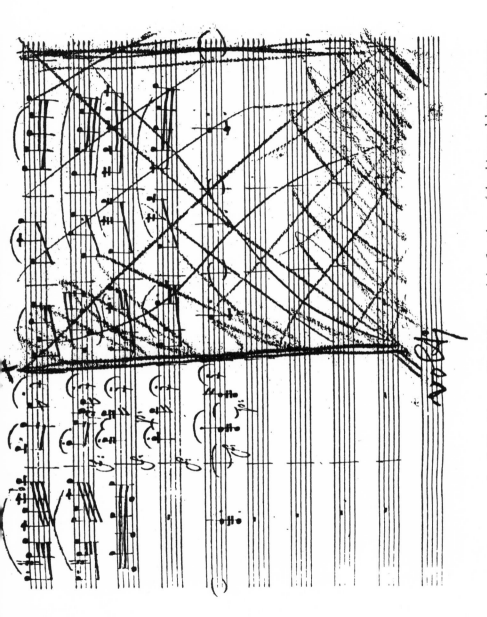

FIGURE 13.13. Act II, No. 21, mm. 23–24 in H, and the first three of the thirteen deleted measures.

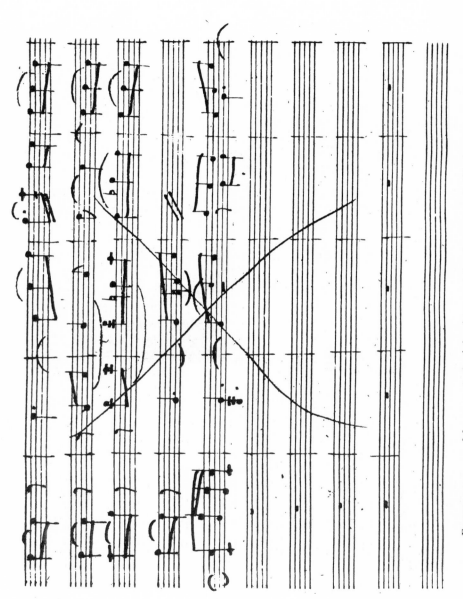

FIGURE 13.14. Measures 4–8 of the thirteen deleted measures in H, Act II, No. 21.

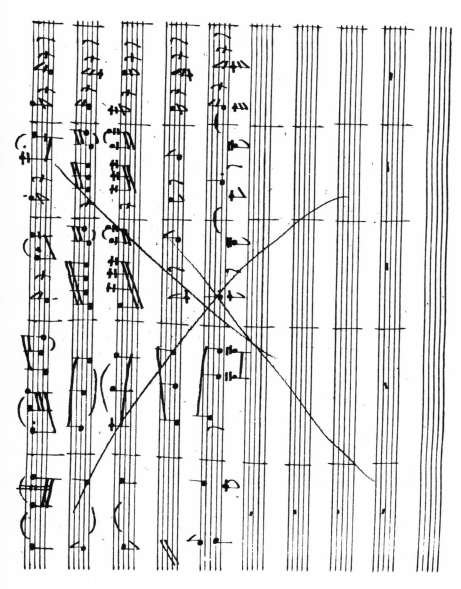

TABLE 13.1. *Così fan tutte:* sequence, numbering, and keys.

Overture		C
Act I		
No. 1	*Terzetto:* "La mia Dorabella" (Ferr., Guil., Don Alf.)	G
No. 2	*Terzetto:* "E la fede delle femine" (Don Alf., Ferr., Guil.)	E
No. 3	*Terzetto:* "Una bella serenata" (Ferr., Guil., Don Alf.)	C
No. 4	*Duetto:* "Ah, guarda, sorella" (Fior., Dor.)	A
No. 5	*Aria:* "Vorrei dir, e cor non ho" (Don Alf.)	F minor
No. 6	*Quintetto:* "Sento oddio" (all except Desp.)	E-flat
No. 7	*Duettino:* "Al fato dan legge" (Ferr., Guil.)	B-flat
No. 8	*Coro:* "Bella vita militar!"	D
(—)	*Quintetto:* "Di scrivermi" (all except Desp.)	F
No. 9	= Da capo of No. 8	D
No. 10	*Terzettino:* "Soave sia il vento" (Fior., Dor., Don Alf.)	E
No. 11	*Aria:* "Smanie implacabili" (Dor.)	E-flat
No. 12	*Aria:* "In uomini, in soldati" (Desp.)	F
No. 13	*Sestetto:* "Alla bella Despinetta" (all)	C
No. 14	*Aria:* "Come scoglio" (Fior.)	B-flat
No. 15a	*Aria:* "Rivolgete a lui lo sguardo" (Guil.) (cut)	D
No. 15b	*Aria:* "Non siate ritrosi" (Guil.) (its replacement)	G
No. 16	*Terzetto:* "E voi ridete?" (Don Alf., Ferr., Guil.)	G
No. 17	*Aria:* "Un' aura amorosa" (Ferr.)	A
No. 18	*First finale:* "Ah che tutta in un momento" (all)	D
Act II		
No. 19	*Aria:* "Una donna a quindici anni" (Desp.)	G
No. 20	*Duetto:* "Prenderò quel brunettino" (Dor., Fior.)	B-flat
No. 21	*Duetto con coro:* "Secondate aurette amiche" (Ferr., Guil.)	E-flat
No. 22	*Quartetto:* "La mano a me date" (Don Alf., Ferr., Guil., Desp.)	D
No. 23	*Duetto:* "Il core vi dono" (Guil., Dor.)	F
No. 24	*Aria:* "Ah! lo veggio quell' anima bella" (Ferr.)	B-flat
No. 25	*Rondò:* "Per pietà" (Fior.)	E
No. 26	*Aria:* "Donne mie, la fate a tanti" (Guil.)	G
No. 27	*Cavatina:* "Tradito, schernito" (Ferr.)	C minor
No. 28	*Aria:* "È amore un ladroncello" (Dor.)	B-flat
No. 29	*Duetto:* "Fra gli amplessi" (Fior., Ferr.)	A
No. 30	*Andante:* "Tutti accusan le donne" (Don Alf., Ferr., Guil.)	C
No. 31	*Second finale:* "Fate presto o cari amici" (all)	C

Ferr. = Ferrando; Guil. = Guilelmo; Don Alf. = Don Alfonso
Fior. = Fiordiligi; Dor. = Dorabella; Desp. = Despina

TABLE 13.2. The structure of Mozart's autograph for
Così fan tutte, Act I.

| | Present foliation | Watermark | | Mozart's "bifolia-tion" |
		Type	Quadrant	
Overture	1	II	3b	*1*
	2		2b	
	3		4b	*2*
	4		1b	
	5		2b	*3*
	6		3b	
	7		1b	*4*
	8		4b	
	9		2a	*5*
	10		3a	
	11		1a	*6*
	12		4a	12v blank
No. 1, *Terzetto:* "La mia Dorabella" (= scene 1)	13	I	4b	*1*
	14		1b	
	15		3b	*2*
	16		2b	
Recit. (18r–v): "Fuor la spada"	17		1b	*3*
	18		4b	
No. 2, *Terzetto:* "E la fede delle femine"	19	I	1a	*4*
	20		4a	
Recit. (bottom of 21v; 22r–v): "Scioccherie di poeti!"	21		2b	*5*
	22		3b	
No. 3, *Terzetto:* "Una bella serenata"	23	I	1b	*6*
	24		4b	
	25		2b	*7*
	26		3b	
	27		4a	27v blank	*8 (5?)*
No. 4, *Duetto:* "Ah, guarda, sorella" (= scene 2)	28	I	3a	*8*
	29		2a	
	30		4a	*9*
	31		1a	
	32		4b	*10*
	33		1b	
	34		3b	*11*
Recit. (35v, 36r): "Mi par che stammattina" (scene 3 = bottom of 35v)	35		2b	
	36		1a	36v blank	*12*

TABLE 13.2. *(continued)*

	Present foliation	Watermark			Mozart's "bifoliation"
		Type	Quadrant		
No. 5, *Aria:* "Vorrei dir, e cor non ho"	— 37	II	4a		
Recit.: "Stelle! per carità"	— 38	I	2a	38v blank	13
No. 6, *Quintetto:* "Sento oddio" (= scene 4)	⌐ 39	I	4b		14
	⌐ 40		1b		
	⌐ 41		3b		15
	⌐ 42		2b		
	⌐ 43	I	3a		16
	⌐ 44		2a		
	⌐ 45		4a		17
Recit. (46v): "Non pianger, idol mio"	⌐ 46		1a		
No. 7, *Duettino:* "Al fato dan legge"	⌐ 47	I	2a		18
	⌐ 48		3a		
Recit. (49r): "La comedia è graziosa"	— 49	I	3a	49v blank	19
No. 8, *Coro:* "Bella vita militar!" (= scene 5)	⌐ 50	II	2a		1
	⌐ 51		3a		2
	⌐ 52		1a		3
	⌐ 53		4a	53r–v blank	4
Recit.: "Non v'è più tempo"; then *Quintetto* (54v): "Di scrivermi ogni giorno"	⌐ 54	I	1b		20
	⌐ 55		4b		
	— 56	II	1a		21
(No. 9 = repetition of "Bella vita militar!" not scored) Recit.: "Dove son?" (= scene 6)	— 57	II	3a	57v blank	22
No. 10, *Terzettino:* "Soave sia il vento"	⌐ 58	I	1a		23
	⌐ 59		4a		
Recit. (60v): "Non son cattivo comico" (= scene 7)	⌐ 60		2a		24
	⌐ 61		3a	61v blank	

TABLE 13.2. *(continued)*

	Present foliation	Watermark		Mozart's "bifolia-tion"
		Type	Quadrant	
Recit.: "Che vita male-detta" (= scene 8 → scene 9) → recit. accomp.	⌐ 62 L 63	II |	4a 1a	25
No. 11, *Aria:* "Smanie implacabili"	⌐ 64 L 65	I	2a 3a	1
	⌐ 66 L 67	|	2b 3b	2
	⌐ 68 L 69	|	1b 4b	3
Recit.: "Signora Dorabella"	⌐ 70 L 71	II |	3b 2b	26
No. 12, *Aria:* "In uomini, in soldati" (71r, below end of the recit.)	⌐ 72 L 73	|	3a 2a	(Rötel) 2
	⌐ 74 L 75	|	3a 2a	(Rötel) 3
	⌐ 76 L 77	|	3a 2a	76v, (Rötel) 4 77r–v blank
Recit.: "Che silenzio!" (= scene 10)	⌐ 78 L 79	II |	4b 1b	27 79v blank
No. 13, *Sestetto:* "Alla bella Despinetta" (= scene 11)	⌐ 80 L 81	I	1a 4a	28
	⌐ 82 L 83	|	2a 3a	29
	⌐ 84 L 85	|	3a 2a	30
	⌐ 86 L 87	|	4a 1a	31
	⌐ 88 L 89	III III	3a 2a	32
	⌐ 90 L 91	I |	3a 2a	33
Recit.: "Che susurro!" → recit. accomp.	⌐ 92 L 93	II |	3b 2b	34
	⌐ 94 L 95	|	1a 4a	35 95v blank

TABLE 13.2. *(continued)*

	Present foliation	Watermark		Mozart's "bifoliation"
		Type	Quadrant	
No. 14, *Aria:* "Come scoglio"	⌐ 96	II	3b	*1*
	∟ 97		2b	
	⌐ 98		1b	*2*
	∟ 99		4b	
	⌐ 100		1b	*3*
	∟ 101		4b	
	⌐ 102		2b	*4*
	∟ 103		3b	103v blank
Recit.: "Ah, non partite!"	— 104	II	2a	104v blank *36*
No. 15a, *Aria di Guilelmo,* "Rivolgete a lui lo sguardo" (= K.584, December 1789)	⌐ 105	I	3a	*1*
	∟ 106		2a	
	⌐ 107		4a	*2*
	∟ 108		1a	
	⌐ 109		2b	*3*
	∟ 110		3b	
	⌐ 111		1a	*4*
	∟ 112		4a	
	⌐ 113		1a	*5*
	∟ 114		4a	
	⌐ 115		2a	*6*
	∟ 116		3a	
No. 15b, *Aria:* "Non siate ritrosi"	⌐ 117	II	3a	(Rötel) *1*
	∟ 118		2a	
	⌐ 119		1b	(Rötel) *2*
	∟ 120		4b	120v blank
No. 16, *Terzetto:* "E voi ridete?" (= scene 12)	⌐ 121	I	2a	*37*
	∟ 122		3a	
Recit. (124v): "Si può sapere"	⌐ 123		1a	*38*
	∟ 124		4a	
No. 17, *Aria:* "Un' aura amorosa"	⌐ 125	I	2b }	*1*
	∟ 126		3b }	
	⌐ 127	II	1b	*2*
	∟ 128		4b	
(bound in wrong way)	— 129		4a	129v blank –
Recit.: "Oh, la saria da ridere!" (= scene 13)	⌐ 130	II	4b	*39*
	∟ 131		1b	131v blank

TABLE 13.2. *(continued)*

	Present foliation	Watermark		Mozart's "bifoliation"
		Type	Quadrant	
No. 18, *Finale I* (= scene 14)	132	II	3b	40
	133		2b	
	134		4b	41
	135		1b	
Scene 15: "Si mora sì, si mora"	136		3b	42
	137		2b	
	138		4b	43
	139		1b	
	140	I	1b	44
	141		4b	
	142	II	4b	45
	143		1b	
	144		3a	46
	145		2a	
	146		3b	47
	147		2b	
	148		4a	48
	149		1a	
Scene 16: "Eccovi il medico"	150		4b	49
	151		1b	
	152		2b	50
	153		3b	
	154		1b	51
	155		(copyist)	155v blank	—
	156		4b	
	157		3a	52
	158		2a	
	159		3b	53
	160		2b	
	161		1a	54
	162		4a	
	163		2a	55
	164		3a	
	165		2a	56
	166		3a	
	167		1a	57
	168		4a	
	169		4b	58
	170		1b	
	171		3b	59
	172		2b	
	173		2a	60
	174		3a	

End of Act I

14

Mozart's Use of 10-Staff
and 12-Staff Paper

IF ONE SURVEYS the whole corpus of Mozart's surviving auto-graph scores, one may permit oneself certain generalizations about the characteristic features of their outward appearance. Here are four such generalizations:

1. The format that he preferred, along with most of his contemporaries, was an oblong (*Querformat*), not an upright (*Hochformat*) one. The main use of the upright format was not for scores, but for individual instrumental and vocal performance parts.
2. Wherever it was possible, Mozart preferred to have the staves mechanically ruled. In such cases all the staves were ruled simultaneously by the rastration machine. If no such machine was available, Mozart had to rule the staves with a hand rastrum, usually singly but occasionally with an instrument that ruled two staves at a time.
3. In his Salzburg years—a term to cover all the time up to his arrival in Vienna on 16 March 1781—Mozart generally used machine-ruled oblong paper with ten staves to the page.
4. But in his Vienna years he almost always used oblong 12-staff paper.

It is the third and the fourth of these generalizations that I propose to examine in detail here, by considering what appear to be the more striking exceptions to them. In the light of the first and second, moreover, I shall take no account of the few scores by Mozart that are in upright format, or of those scores in which the staves have been ruled not by machine but by hand.

THE STATEMENT that the great majority of Mozart's machine-ruled oblong-format scores from the Salzburg years have ten staves to the page can scarcely be challenged. It is true that some of his earliest scores have only eight staves, but it will be found that the staves were ruled singly (as is also the case with a few early 12-staff scores, such as the cassation K.63). That the machine-ruled scores generally have ten staves is as true of the paper in the "small" oblong format (*Klein-Querformat*) that he frequently adopted in the years from 1773 to 1779 as it is of the larger oblong paper that he used throughout his life.[1]

Certainly 10-staff paper seems to have been more than adequate for most of Mozart's purposes before his final move to Vienna. Many of the symphonies that he composed in the 1770s, for instance, required no more than seven or eight staves, the others remaining blank. But occasionally he found himself writing a score in which a greater number of staves would perhaps be useful: a church work with a large orchestral accompaniment to four voices, for instance, or a chorus or ensemble in the finale of a stage work. In such circumstances Mozart would sometimes select paper ruled with twelve staves. What is surprising here is that this paper seems in almost every case to have been purchased in the first instance somewhere other than at Salzburg, leading one to suspect that machine-ruled 12-staff paper could not be obtained in Salzburg itself. For that reason he may even have kept a small hoard of it.

The best way to investigate this is to review all the 12-staff (machine-ruled, oblong-format) paper that Mozart used before he went to Vienna in March 1781, with special attention to the place at which it appears to have been purchased.

FIRST there are three scores that were written out in London in 1764 and 1765: the Symphony in E-flat, K.16, the Motet "God is our Refuge," K.20, and the transcription of a symphony in E-flat by Carl Friedrich Abel, which was for long believed to be an original work by Mozart and assigned the number K.18, but is now in the Anhang to Köchel[6] as "A 51." In writing down K.16, we note, Mozart used the twelve staves for two systems of 6 staves,[2] and in K.20 he used them for three systems of four staves. Thus the 12-staff paper proved convenient for him, even though he used no system with as many staves; such paper seems to have been readily available in London.

The next time that he used 12-stave paper was in 1768, and once again he was away from Salzburg. One paper-type is found in all three finales of the opera *La finta semplice,* K.51 (46a), which was intended for performance in Vienna in the summer of 1768, but which never reached the stage. It was also used at a few other places in that opera; and over half the leaves of *Bastien et Bastienne,* K.50 (46b), the one-act Singspiel from the same summer, and the first sixteen leaves of the Mass in C Minor, K.139 (47a), are of the same type. The date of the Mass is uncertain, but it may well have been at least begun before the end of the year.[3] This, then, was a Viennese paper. Another 12-staff paper-type seems to have been used by Mozart very slightly later, since it is to be found in a new version of the aria No. 23 in *La finta semplice,* and in the rest of the Mass in C Minor. Clearly this was a second Viennese paper.

It is obvious, however, that he took some of the latter paper back with him to Salzburg, for over two years later, in May 1771, he used it for writing out the *Regina Coeli,* K.108 (74d), a work the scoring of which required all twelve staves. On further leaves of the same paper-type he entered three church sonatas, K.67 (41h), 68 (41i), and 69 (41k), and at a later time two more, K.144 (124a) and 145 (124b).[4] It was suggested by Hanns Dennerlein in 1953 that the first three date from 1772–73, and by Wolfgang Plath in 1978 that these are from 1771–72 and the latter two from the beginning of 1774, all no doubt composed in Salzburg long after the paper had been purchased in Vienna.[5]

When the Mozarts went to Milan on their second Italian journey in the summer of 1771, Wolfgang wrote the "serenata" *Ascanio in Alba,* K.111, and for the choruses he used 12-staff paper, obviously purchased in Milan. Once again he took some of the 12-staff paper back to Salzburg. Part of it he used soon afterwards in March 1772 for writing out his *Litaniae de venerabili altaris sacramento,* K.125. But some more of it was retained for much longer, and remained unused until about 1780, when Mozart drew on it for writing out the last chorus of the Singspiel *Zaide,* K.344 (336b). So the valuable 12-staff paper was kept this time for up to nine years before being used.

Yet another type of 12-staff paper is found in two choruses of a second "serenata," *Il sogno di Scipione,* K.126, and in the three divertimenti for string quartet, K.136 (125a), 137 (125b), and 138 (125c). The autograph of the divertimenti is dated "Salzburg, 1772," and a date of "1772" on the cover of the K.126 score appears to be in Leopold Mozart's hand. Until very recently, in fact, the accepted view was that *Il sogno di Scipione* was composed at Salzburg in about March 1772, and performed there early in May of that year as part of the celebrations to welcome the new prince-archbishop, Hieronymus

Colloredo. But it has now been shown that the name "Girolamo" (= Hieronymus) in the recitative preceding the first version of the "Licenza" aria is a replacement for "Sigismondo," the erased name of Colloredo's predecessor, the prince-archbishop Sigismund von Schrattenbach, who had died on 16 December 1771.[6] This provides a *terminus ante quem* for the composition of K.126, and accords well with *Schriftchronologie,* since the whole autograph (except for the second version of the "Licenza" aria) appears to Plath to date from 1771.[7] Today the composition of the serenata has been tentatively assigned to the period from April to August 1771, between the Mozarts' first and second Italian journeys.

That certainly allows for the possibility that the unusual 12-staff paper was bought and ruled outside Salzburg, perhaps toward the end of the Mozarts' first Italian journey, which finished on 28 March 1771. The paper itself does not resemble the others that had been bought in Milan or elsewhere south of the Alps; possibly only a small quantity of it was acquired on the homeward journey, which would explain its scarcity—its occurrence in only two scores around this time.

The next time that Mozart purchased 12-staff paper, he was again on his travels. It was early in 1778, and he was in Mannheim. The leaves of this paper-type were particularly large, measuring approximately 255×370 mm.[8] On it he wrote the soprano recitative and aria "Alcandro, lo confesso" and "Non sò d'onde viene," K.294,[9] the tenor aria "Se al labbro mio non credi" K.295, and several violin sonatas, K.296, 301 (293a), 302 (293b), 303 (293c), 304 (300c), 305 (293d), and a draft for the first movement of K.306 (300l). In the middle of March 1778 he left Mannheim for Paris, taking with him the scores of the violin sonatas; it is evident that not all of them had been completed, for the autograph of K.304 (300c) is inscribed "Sonata IV à Paris," and that of the final version of K.306 (300l) is on a different paper-type from the rest, not paper from Mannheim but French paper from the firm of Johannot of Annonay. The first two movements and a draft of the third movement are on 14-staff upright-format paper; but the final version of the third movement is on 12-staff oblong-format paper. Mozart had evidently reached France (and no doubt Paris) when he acquired this last paper.[10]

THAT CONCLUDES our survey of the oblong-format, machine-ruled 12-staff paper from Mozart's Salzburg years; he purchased no more of it until he had finally settled in Vienna. We have seen that it was acquired in London in 1764–65, in Vienna in 1768, in Milan in 1771, and in Mannheim and Paris in 1778; only in the case of the 12-staff paper used in *Il sogno di Scipione* and the divertimenti of 1772 is the exact provenance unknown. Not that it was necessarily the case that the machines for ruling 12-staff paper could be found in all the larger musical cities. It seems, for instance, that Mozart could not buy any 12-staff paper ruled by them in Munich or in Prague. There is none of it, for example, in the two acts surviving in autograph of *La finta giardiniera,* K.196, produced in Munich in January 1775. Perhaps none was needed, not even for the finales;[11] but the autograph score of *Idomeneo,* produced in Munich almost exactly six years later, included both 12-staff and 14-staff paper. Most of it, however, can be seen to have been hand-ruled with a 2-staff rastrum. And the same holds good of the 12-staff paper purchased by Mozart in Prague for completing the scores of *Don Giovanni* in 1787 and *La clemenza di Tito* in 1791.

Thus it is perhaps not so surprising that he could buy no such paper in Salzburg. There is a somewhat comic confirmation of this in a score from February 1766, the so-called "Lodron" Concerto for Three Pianofortes, K.242. If ever he needed 12-staff paper in Salzburg, it was surely in writing out this autograph, since he required six staves for the three pianofortes, and six more for the four strings and for the oboes and horns. But it was a long time since he had been to any of the cities listed at the beginning of the previous paragraph, and such paper as he had brought back was evidently exhausted. So he fell back on 10-staff paper, but with a single-staff rastrum drew in two extra staves on each page, one at the top and the other at the bottom.[12]

IF MOZART had for many years been nursing a secret wish to use 12-staff paper for writing every one of his scores, it certainly found expression the moment that he arrived in Vienna. From that time on, the vast majority of his scores were on 12-staff paper, in oblong format and machine-ruled. And just as in the Salzburg years, when 10-staff paper was the norm, it is the exceptions to the prevailing pattern that have invited our attention, so now it will be the (machine-ruled, oblong-format) 10-staff paper of the Vienna years that calls out for explanation.[13]

The immediacy of the change from ten to twelve staves is emphasized by the fact that for a short time the paper-type remained unchanged. For we find 10-staff paper with a particular watermark in some of the works written in Munich at the end of 1780 or early in

1781: not only in Acts I and III of *Idomeneo* and in the ballet music to that opera, but also in the recitative and aria for soprano "Misera, dove son!" and "Ah! non son' io che parlo," K.369, dated "Munich, 8 March 1781." Only two weeks later, we find paper with an identical watermark, but now ruled with twelve staves. Mozart used it in the rondo for horn, K.371, dated "Vienna, 21 March 1781," and also in the fragmentary movement of a violin sonata in B-flat, K.372, dated "Vienna, 24 March 1781." It is possible, indeed, that he possessed a stock of unruled sheets of this paper, which from time to time was ruled for him locally: with ten staves in Munich, and then, when he presented it a little later for ruling in a city that had more sophisticated rastration machines, with twelve staves in Vienna.

AS HAS BEEN SAID above, it is Mozart's scores from his Vienna years on 10-staff paper that invite explanation. And since a cursory scrutiny of them indicates that most of them are probably from the earlier Vienna years, a possible explanation is that a number of them derive from the second half of 1783, when Mozart and his wife left Vienna to visit Salzburg, and remained there from the end of July to 27 October. No doubt Mozart took some 12-staff paper along with him, but when that was exhausted he would have had to rely on 10-staff paper purchased locally.

There is one paper-type with ten staves that clearly dates from this return to Salzburg. It is found, for instance, in nine leaves at the end of the unfinished score of the C-Minor Mass, K.427 (417a), containing extra wind parts for the work. The Mass was performed in the Peterskirche on 26 October, the day before Mozart and his wife started their return journey from Salzburg. Thus it is hard to reject the notion that this was a Salzburg paper. More of it, moreover, is found in the surviving material for the uncompleted opera buffa *L'oca del Cairo*, K.422, on which he was obviously working that summer in Salzburg: in the scores of Nos. 1, 2, 3, the recitative to No. 4, and No. 5, as well as sketchleaves for Nos. 2 and 3.

Once it has been established that this was a Salzburg paper, we must assume that other 10-staff scores on the same paper were written either in Salzburg in the second half of 1783 or perhaps immediately after the visit there. These scores include:

K.393 (385b), No. 3, Solfeggio
K.610, Contredanse
Köchel[6], Anh. A 11, "Pignus futurae gloriae," by Michael Haydn

The first of these has traditionally been connected with Mozart's tuition of his wife for the solo soprano part of the C-Minor Mass, and the third can easily be related to Mozart's desire to acquire in Salzburg suitable fugal music with which to gratify the Baron van Swieten on his return to Vienna. (Another setting by Michael Haydn of this text was also copied out by Mozart in these months: Köchel[6] Anh. A 12.)[14] The Contredanse K.610 was entered by Mozart in his Verzeichnüss under the date "6 March 1791," but the autograph (in the Newberry Library, Chicago) was obviously written out several years earlier.[15]

Another 10-staff paper-type may also date from these months spent in Salzburg in 1783, though it is not possible to link it with any works that it is certain he composed there. The following scores and fragments are written on it:

K.463 (448c), Minuet 2 and Contredanse 2
K.153 (375f), Fugue in E-flat (fragment)
K.375h + K.417B, No. 6, Fugue in F (fragment), and start of a
    four-part Fugue
K.331 (300i), Piano Sonata, final leaf.

The first of these is found in combination with a Viennese paper (which contains Minuet 1 and Contredanse 1). The autograph includes a citation of the melody of K.462 (448b), No. 5, suggesting that K.462 and K.463 are closely linked in time. The date proposed for both in Köchel[6] is "January 1784"; there is not much evidence for this, except that such dances were popular at that time of year. It might be possible to imagine that Mozart started work on the present ones before returning to Vienna.

The fugue fragments, too, are hard to date, though it is clear that they belong to the early Viennese years.[16] For K.331 (300i), see below.

NOT THAT ALL the 10-staff paper used in the Vienna years needs to be explained by reference to the 1783 Salzburg visit. One obvious exception is the recitative and aria for soprano "A questo seno deh vieni" and "Or che il cielo a me ti rende," K.374, which Mozart seems to have written almost immediately after his arrival in Vienna; for the aria, described as "new" in his letter of 8 April 1781, had been sung by the Salzburg castrato Francesco Ceccarelli at the Deutsches Haus in Vienna that same day.[17] The paper's ten staves are easily explained: this was Salzburg paper, of two types that Mozart had used there from July 1779 until his departure for Munich in November

1780, and also for working on *Idomeneo* in Munich. (No doubt the paper, though used by him there, had been bought earlier in Salzburg.) Thus the thirteen leaves of K.374 were either brought to Vienna by Mozart, or perhaps more probably were readily available to him in the Deutsches Haus, where Prince Colloredo and his retinue—including, for a time, Mozart—were lodged.

Another score that surprisingly is on 10-staff paper but cannot in any way be linked with Salzburg is the scena with rondò "Ch'io mi scordi di te" and "Non temer, amato bene," K.505, written (as Mozart says in his Verzeichnüss) "für Mad.selle Storace und mich," and entered under the date of "27 December 1786." This score is on two different paper-types; the first four leaves are of a type that has not been identified anywhere else in Mozart's works, and the remaining leaves appear to be a variant of a type found with twelve staves in scores from December 1785 to December 1786. A possible explanation here is that a little time before his departure from Vienna for a short visit to Prague, Mozart found himself out of paper, and had to borrow these uncharacteristic types from a friend.

Two further leaves of 10-staff paper are found, together with two 12-staff leaves, among the autograph material in the Deutsche Staatsbibliothek, Berlin, for the music to a pantomime, K.446 (416d). But this material consists of no more than an incomplete first-violin part. Our information about the pantomime comes from Mozart's letters of 15 February and 12 March 1783;[18] it was apparently written for a "masquerade" on 3 March. Once again the 10-staff paper is unmatched elsewhere in Mozart's scores, and may be accounted for by the "improvised" nature of the occasion for which the music was produced. (The size of the paper is larger than that which he normally bought, each leaf measuring about 240 × 330 mm.)

THE LAST two examples show that in certain situations Mozart did in fact use 10-staff paper in Vienna, even if it must be counted a rare event. That should be borne in mind when we come to consider four 10-staff scores to which Köchel[6] assigns dates of "1778" and "1780." Three of these scores are on the same paper-type and share the same rastrology: they are those of the piano sonatas K.330 (300h) —see Figure 14.1—and K.332 (300k), and of the three orchestral minuets K.363. Of the fourth score, the piano sonata K.331 (300i), only one leaf—the final one—has survived; although this too has ten staves, and a similar rastrology, it has a different watermark, showing

FIGURE 14.1. Piano Sonata in C, K.330 (300h): second movement. Biblioteka Jagiellońska, Kraków.

that it is in fact of the same paper-type as K.463 (448c), K.153 (375f), and K.375h + 417B, no. 6, discussed and provisionally dated above. It seems likely that the three piano sonatas and the orchestral minuets were written about the same time, but when was that?

In the first edition (1862) of Köchel, K.363 was assigned the provisional date of "1780," which has been accepted in all subsequent editions. For the piano sonatas Köchel[1] offered the equally provisional date of "1779." Their location a year earlier, during the time that Mozart was in Paris, was proposed by Georges de Saint-Foix in 1936; he claimed that the A-major sonata (K.331) had been written between May and July, and that the C-major (K.330) and F-major (K.332) sonatas dated from the period from July to September 1778.[19] This chronology was immediately adopted by Einstein in Köchel[3], and has been retained in Köchel[6]. But there is little or nothing to be said for it; unlike the other works known to have been written by Mozart in Paris, these sonatas are not even on French paper. Recent studies of Mozart's handwriting, moreover, have suggested a later date than 1778. In 1978 Plath claimed that the summer of 1780 was the earliest possible time that they could have been written.[20] He also suggested very tentatively that the summer of 1780 seemed the earliest possible date for K.363, adding that the early Vienna years, "up to 1782/83," appeared to him a likely time for that work's composition.[21]

Since the handwriting evidence is not completely conclusive, we are left in doubt whether these four works are from the last Salzburg years or from the first Viennese ones. It is at this point that the fact that their autographs all have ten staves is likely to influence our dating. The view seems to be gaining ground that these are not works of his last Salzburg years; but I wish to suggest that they are "Salzburg works" in another sense—compositions of the summer of 1783. The sonatas would then take their place as teaching works prepared for the busy season that awaited Mozart on his return to Vienna (the use of the soprano clef may possibly suggest a didactic purpose), and the minuets of K.363, perhaps first performed at Salzburg that summer, may also have been composed with the Viennese balls of the coming winter in mind.

The dating of these four works to the second half of 1783 is not entirely free from difficulty. Since it seems to be accepted now that the piano sonata in B-flat, K.333 (315c), a work also formerly assigned to Mozart's 1778 stay in Paris, probably in fact dates from the end of 1783,[22] there is a problem in that its handwriting is somewhat different from that of K.330–332—though it should be noted that it is written on paper of a very different size and shape. Moreover, in a letter to his father of 9–12 June 1784, Mozart refers to K.330–332 as "the three piano sonatas that I once sent to my sister"; if he had composed them in Salzburg, would Nannerl not have been given a copy there? However, they may not have been finished, or he may not have had the time to have a copy made; and it is significant that in the same letter he refers to the fact that the firm of Artaria was going to publish them, and that Torricella was going to publish K.333 (together with the very old piano sonata K.284 and the brand-new violin sonata K.454). If K.330–332 had been composed some time before the Salzburg visit, would he not have offered them to Artaria much earlier?

It should be clear by now that the useful distinction for Mozart scholars, "ten staves = Salzburg years; twelve staves = Vienna years," to which there are evidently not many exceptions, is blurred a little by the complication of the Salzburg visit within the Vienna years. But its utility should not be underestimated; additions made in Vienna, for instance, to Salzburg works are often exposed by their 12-staff paper, and other evidence, such as the handwriting and watermarks, may then help us to date the additions more precisely. In this way we can see that the minuet to the Symphony in B-flat of July 1779, K.319, was written in 1784 or 1785; the clarini parts to the Symphony in G of April 1779, K.318, were added in 1782 or 1783; a similar dating applies to the cadenzas for No. 10, "L'amerò, sarò costante," in *Il Rè pastore*, K.208, first produced in 1775; and two of the cadenzas to the 1777 Piano Concerto in E-flat, K.271, were probably composed in 1784.[23]

My final example concerns the date of the concert aria "Ah se in ciel, benigne stelle," K.538. The claims of this aria to be a late work, and probably the very last piece that he wrote for his sister-in-law Aloysia Lange, née Weber—for whom he had had an intense but unrequited passion ten years earlier, in 1778—seem very strong, as has been explained in Chapter 2. For there exists an autograph score on 12-staff paper of a type that he used largely in 1788; he inscribed this "per la Sig.ᵗᵃ Lange. Aria. Vienna li 4 di Marzo. 1788," and entered the work in his Verzeichnüss under the same date.

But in addition to the score a "particella" has also survived, consisting of the voice-part and bass-line only.[24] One might expect this to be on the same paper-type (or on one of the same period) as the score. It is described in Köchel[6] as having twelve staves.[25] But this is not the case, as one can see from the illustration of its first page in NMA II/7/4 (= *Arien*, Band 4), page xix. More surprising still, the paper-type is not one that Mozart used in Vienna; the watermark shows a shield and the name CANDER.[26] The last time that he had used paper of this kind was in completing *Idomeneo* in Munich at the beginning of 1781.

It is in such a situation that the help of an expert on Mozart's hand-writing is particularly welcome. Any notion, for instance, that Mozart had perhaps produced (or had planned to produce) the aria at some concert in Munich (or perhaps in Mannheim) shortly before or after the coronation of the Emperor Leopold II at Frankfurt in October 1790 cannot stand up to a scrutiny of the particella's writing. Plath has confirmed that it must have been written *long* before the full score; and we have together reached the conclusion that K.538 was really composed by 1778, and the particella written in Munich at the end of that year, with Aloysia *Weber* in mind. So there was no real dishonesty in describing it almost ten years later as "per la Sig.^ra Lange"—it was still the same voice, even though the singer had changed her name.

Thus we must regard the 1788 score as a revised version of a 1778 composition. But the revisions cannot have been very extensive. The differences in the vocal line are small ones, being largely confined to changes in the underlay. The particella starts where the voice enters, at m. 24 of the 1788 version, so we cannot tell whether the preceding ritornello was different in 1778. But the end seems to have been shorter; the particella stops with the first quarter note of m. 193 (the word "ben"), and it would appear therefore that the voice in the rest of m. 193 and mm. 194–207 is an addition of 1788.

That K.538 is essentially a work of 1778 might not have been detected, had its 10-staff paper not aroused suspicion and led to further investigation. It is the possibility of making such discoveries that would seem to justify the attention devoted here to what might otherwise appear the arid topic of Mozart's use of 10-staff and 12-staff paper.

15

Notes on the Genesis of Mozart's "Ein musikalischer Spass," K.522

To anyone who takes more than a passing interest in Mozart's psychology, it would be a matter of surprise if the death of his father Leopold on 28 May 1787 did not arouse deep emotional feelings and conflicts within him. For the extremely important part that Leopold had always played in nearly every aspect of his son's life is a commonplace of biographers. When Wolfgang was twelve, Leopold wrote to a friend about the "miracle that God allowed to happen in Salzburg," and the young Wolfgang was wont to declare that "next after God comes Papa."[1] Although the bond began to prove somewhat irksome to both parties when Wolfgang reached manhood, it could not be said to have been totally severed even after he went his own way, first abandoning Salzburg and settling in Vienna in 1781, and then marrying a girl of whom his father disapproved in 1782.

The years that followed provoked a degree of bitterness on both sides, sometimes masked by a steely formality on Wolfgang's part. Yet the impressive letter that he wrote to Leopold on 4 April 1787 when the news first reached him that his father was seriously ill is not merely "correct" but in places apparently filled with true tenderness—even if it can be shown that many of the sentiments contained in it are freely lifted from the writings of Moses Mendelssohn.[2] (Why not? There is little reason to expect total originality from anyone in such a predicament. Perhaps one should be grateful that it was not merely filled with sentiments drawn from Metastasio.)

In the preface to the second edition (1909) of his greatest single book, *Die Traumdeutung* (first edition: 1900), Sigmund Freud identified the writing of it as a portion of his own self-analysis, his reaction to his father's death, "that is to say, to the most important event, the most poignant loss, of a man's life." In Mozart's case, in the light of the very significant role that his father had always played in his life, it would not be unreasonable to search his music for some reflection of Leopold's death.

Such responses can of course take a wide variety of forms, not excluding a total or partial cessation of productiveness. Or compositions of a "memorial" character could be created. It has, for instance, been noticed that the start of the second movement of the A-major piano concerto K.414(385p), apparently from the second half of 1782, very closely follows the opening bars of a D-major overture by J. C. Bach, who had died on 1 January 1782; and that the finale of the A-major violin sonata K.526, entered in Mozart's Verzeichnüss under the date of 24 August 1787, is modeled on the last movement of a sonata by C. F. Abel, who had died on 20 June 1787.[3]

I F   O N E   H A D to select a work to serve as a memorial of this kind to Leopold, one's choice might well fall on the peerless "Eine kleine Nachtmusik," K.525, completed two months later, the perfect serenade to recall all those serenades and divertimenti of the Salzburg years. But it is the more ambivalent aspects of the son-and-father relationship that have guided recent speculation in the attempt to identify Wolfgang's musical reaction to Leopold's death. A popular interpretation is that the greatest work of 1787, the "dramma giocoso" *Don Giovanni,* was composed under the shadow of Leopold's last illness and demise, and draws its overwhelming power partly from the intensity of feeling and sense of liberation that filled its composer in those months. For it has not escaped notice that in the opera a "vecchio" is killed off in the first ten minutes, so that a "cavaliere," described as "estremamente licenzioso," can proceed on his course of sexual indulgence, even though in the second finale he has to pay the penalty for it—a fate that elicits from him no sign of repentance. (The opera's first title is in fact *Il Dissoluto Punito.*)

It has further been argued that so ambivalent a reaction to his father's death later gave way to more positively charged feelings. For it has at least been noted that in Mozart's last three operas we encounter father figures altogether more benign than the understandably enraged Commendatore: the elderly philosopher Don Alfonso in *Così fan tutte,* the enlightened Sarastro in *Die Zauberflöte,* and the Em-

peror Titus, who manifests clemency even to his enemies. Nevertheless, the relation between characteristics of operatic figures and the
composer's inner world must remain a problematical area.

IN RECENT YEARS another candidate has been proposed as Mozart's musical response to his father's death. This is "Ein musikalischer
Spass," K.522, a parody both of poor compositional techniques and
of poor instrumental performance. It is undeniably the first work entered by Mozart in his Verzeichnüss after the news of Leopold's death
at Salzburg had reached him in Vienna, for it is assigned the date there
of "14 June 1787."

Certainly the form of K.522—a composition for two violins, viola,
bass, and two horns, as depicted in the vignette on the title page of
J. André's first edition (1802, see Figures 15.1 and 15.2)—is highly
reminiscent of many works written in Mozart's later Salzburg years,
such as K.205 (167A), 247, 251, 287 (271H), 334 (320b). So was he
dealing with his father's death by parodying the weaker works of his
former acquaintances in Salzburg and the more inadequate performers of those works? Such a notion has gained some force from the discovery by H. W. Hamaan that the first movement of K.522 shares a
figure with Leopold's "Sonate sei per chiesa e da camera a tre, due
violine e basso" (published in Salzburg, 1740).[4] It might seem that
part of Mozart's response to his father's death was to poke fun at his
father's compositions.

MY AIM in this chapter is to invoke evidence from the discipline of
paper-studies which at least suggests that much of "Ein musikalischer
Spass" was conceived and written down by Mozart some considerable
time before he received news of his father's terminal illness. Even if it
appears to be the case that the work was not *completed* before the
date of 14 June 1787 given in the Verzeichnüss, it also seems clear that
much was composed and possibly even performed long before then.
To demonstrate this, a very careful examination of the autograph material for the work is called for. All of it is today in the Musikabteilung
of the Staatsbibliothek Preussischer Kulturbesitz, Berlin.[5]

This material consists of a curious mixture of instrumental parts
and of scores. So far as the first movement is concerned, we only have
individual parts: first and second violins, viola, bass, and first and second horns.

There are two peculiarities here, however. One is that the first-

First edition

FIGURE 15.1. Title page of André's first edition of K.522.

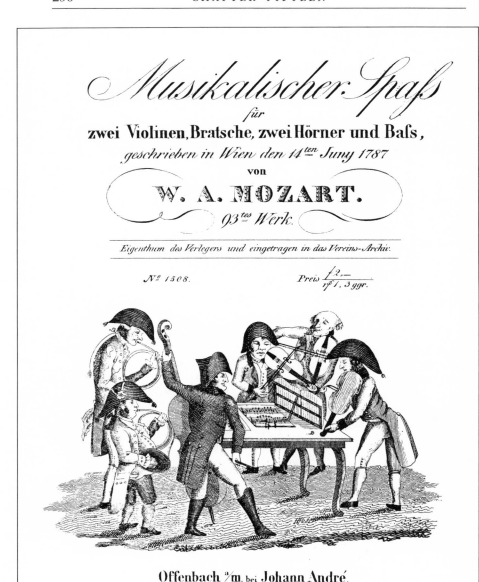

FIGURE 15.2. Title page of a later edition by André.

violin part is not merely for the first movement, but for the second
and third movements as well. Changes in the colors of the inks that
he used suggest that Mozart continued from time to time to extend
the part.[6] It is likely that this part was written before any of the
others, because the coda of the first movement shows a lengthening by
seven measures (five measures deleted, and twelve added); the other
parts have the longer form of the coda without any changes having
been made.

The other peculiarity is the existence of not one but two somewhat
different second-violin parts for the first movement. In editing K.522
in the *Neue Mozart Ausgabe,* Albert Dunning wrote:

Why Mozart wrote out two versions of the second violin's first-movement
part is not clear. Neither of the versions is crossed out or carries any declara-
tion of invalidity. It seems necessary therefore to give both of them equal
status in the NMA's main text. Since the two parts significantly supplement
each other in some passages, it can be suspected that there are meant to be
two second violins.[7]

The rest of the material consists not of parts but of scores: for the
second and third movements, scores *without* the first violin, and for
the fourth and last movement a score for all the instruments.

A little reflection will make it clear that there is no duplication here,
apart from the two second-violin parts to the first movement—and
even those contain differences in thirty of the eighty-eight measures.
For we have only instrumental parts for the first movement, and only
a full score for the last movement; the two middle movements have
scores that lack the first violin—but that is no loss, since the first-
violin part is not merely for the first movement, but for the second
and third as well.

IT IS WHEN one applies the techniques of paper-studies to this
source material that a more complex picture emerges. For in effect the
sources can be shown to fall into three categories or paper-types:

Type 1. Paper with a watermark of the letter w in an ornamental
    shield surmounted by a crown, and three moons over the word
    REAL in reverse, with a total span of 183–183.5 mm. for the twelve
    staves. (See Figure 15.3.)

On paper of this type one finds the first-violin part for the first
movement—eventually extended to include the second and third move-

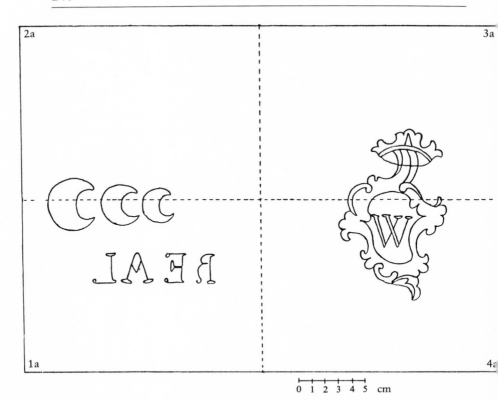

FIGURE 15.3. Paper-type 1, Mold A (Mold B is mirror image).

ments—and the "basso" part for the first movement. Each part is on a bifolium, and the two bifolia once formed a single sheet of paper.

The other instances of this paper-type among Mozart's autographs that can be dated are either from 1784 (the orchestral minuets K.461 (448a), and sections of *Lo sposo deluso*, K.430 (424a), which seem to be from the same year), or from the second half of 1785 ("Das Veilchen," K.476, the trumpet and timpani parts to the piano concerto K.482, the two opening duettini for Act I of *Le nozze di Figaro*, K.492, some of the earliest exercises set for Thomas Attwood).[8]

Thus it seems a reasonable inference that Mozart started to write out parts for at least the first movement of K.522 before the end of 1785.

Type 2. Paper with a watermark of GF under a crown, and three moons over the word REAL, with a total staff-span of 189 mm. (See Figure 15.4.)

On this paper-type we find one of the second-violin parts, the viola and bass parts, and the parts for the two horns—all for the first movement only. Every part is on a bifolium; the two bifolia for second violin and viola once formed a single sheet of paper, and the same is true of the two bifolia of the horn parts. This second-violin part is the one found in André's first edition and used in the old Mozart *Gesamtausgabe* (AMA); in the NMA VII/18 it is printed *above* the other second-violin part on pp. 223–228, and illustrated on p. xxiii.

All the other datable examples of this paper-type are from before the end of 1786. They include portions of autographs completed in 1784 (the piano concertos K.453 and 459), and in 1786 (the string quartet K.499, the piano trio K.502, and the "Prague" Symphony, K.504; also a couple of leaves with corrections to Attwood's compositions).[9]

The impression is therefore gained that the whole of the first move-

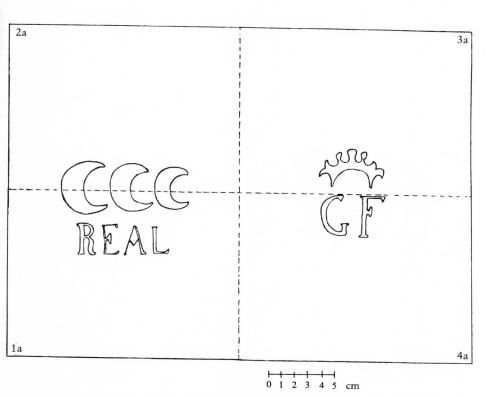

FIGURE 15.4. Paper-type 2, Mold A (Mold B is mirror image).

ment was written out in parts, presumably with a performance in mind, at any rate before the end of 1786.

Type 3. Paper with essentially the same watermark as Type 2, but with a total staff-span of about 187.5 mm.

Mozart used this paper-type for the scores of the second, third, and fourth movements. He also wrote on it a further second-violin part to the first movement; in the NMA VII/18 it is printed *below* the other second-violin part on pp. 223–228, and illustrated on p. xxii.

The datable examples of this paper-type straddle the date of "14 June 1787" in the Verzeichnüss for K.522, for they include portions of the string quintet K.515 (19 April 1787), and the whole of the violin sonata K.526 (24 August 1787). The first scenes in Act I of *Don Giovanni,* K.527, are also on this paper, and the same is almost certainly true of the serenade "Eine kleine Nachtmusik," K.525 (10 August 1787).[10]

Accordingly the portions of K.522 that are on this paper were probably written down around the time at which Mozart first heard of his father's illness, or a little later, when he was coming to terms with his death. So it would be possible—though far from necessary—to regard those parts of K.522 as being linked in some way with the sad event in Salzburg. But that is not a possible explanation for the genesis of those portions of K.522 written on the other two paper-types described here.

READERS who have followed my argument this far may be wondering whether there are risks in attempting to draw a chronological distinction between paper with a total staff-span of 189 mm. and paper with a span of about 187.5 mm. For can one be certain that this minimal difference in the staff-span will always remain detectable? Fortunately there are two other small clues to aid us in discriminating between the paper of Types 2 and 3—clues that it seems worthwhile to mention here:

(a) Although I believe that all the paper of Types 2 and 3 was produced (at rather different times) from the same pair of molds, the passage of time seems to have resulted in very slight changes in the watermark wires in at least one of the molds, so that some of the leaves of Type 3 have a slightly different watermark. This can be detected in leaves with the watermark-quadrant lb. In what is here claimed to be the later paper-type, with the total staff-span of about

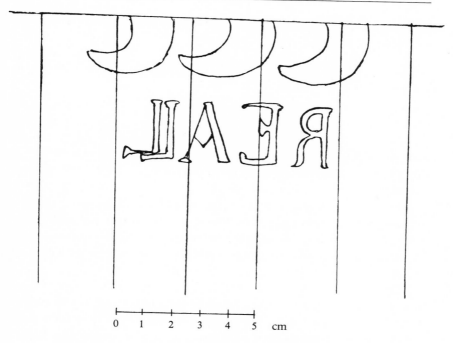

0 1 2 3 4 5 cm

FIGURE 15.5. Paper-types 2 and 3, Mold B, Quadrant 1b,
showing the two positions of the letter L.

187.5 mm., the letter L of the word REAL has come to lie slightly closer
to the letter A than it did in the apparently earlier paper-type, with a
span of 189 mm. (See Figure 15.5.)

(b) A comparison of the rastrology (staff-ruling) in the two paper-
types also reveals some small differences in addition to that of the
staff-span. For the lines of the staves are rather thicker in our Type 2
than they are in Type 3. And the "profiles" of the staff endings at their
left-hand edge are not the same in the two groups. In the third paper-
type, for instance, the left-hand ends of the lines of the twelfth (bottom) staff on each page can be categorized as

long
short
long
short
long

whereas in Type 2 the same lines of the same staff, though almost all the same length, could be described as

short
long
long
long
long

See, for example, the illustrations on p. xxiii, and on p. xxii, in NMA VII/18. Similar distinctions can be found for most of the other eleven staves.

All this serves to prove that we are in reality dealing with two distinguishable batches of paper, produced by the same paper mill but at different times, and ruled at different times. This merely corroborates the evidence already presented that Mozart used the two paper-types at different times.

WE ARE BECOMING more used to the notion that many of the works of Mozart's Viennese years were begun a considerable time before they were completed and entered in the Verzeichnüss. Quite apart from the three distinguishable and separately datable paper-types in K.522, the complexities of the autograph source material would surely suggest a protracted compositional phase.

Something of the same kind is also suggested by the many changes in the colors of the inks that Mozart used. Although there are no doubt perils in this, it is tempting to try to date at least loosely some of these inks. A cerise-colored ink, for instance, is a conspicuous feature of several autographs from the middle of 1786, such as the horn concerto K.495, the piano trio K.496, the canon K.507, and the piano concerto fragment K.537a (Anh. 57). And it is notable that the sequence of a yellowish-brown ink followed by a slate-colored ink, found in the first violin part to K.522, occurs elsewhere in one or two scores that Mozart completed before the end of 1786, such as the string quartet K.499, the piano trio K.502, and the C-major piano concerto K.503.

But it was a dark ink that Mozart used for the scores of the second, third, and fourth movements of K.522. This dark ink is found in the second violin part that is on Type 3 paper—all of which suggests to me that that part was intended as a late replacement for the other second violin part (I find it hard to view it merely as a supplement to it).

We also encounter the same dark ink in a rondo fragment in Salzburg (Mozarteum). This is K.522a (Anh. 108), a score laid out for two violins, viola, bass, and two horns, and consisting of no more than twenty-four measures, for the first violin only.[11] Once again the paper is Type 3, which more or less proves that Franz Giegling was correct in identifying it in 1959 as a rejected draft for the start of the last movement of K.522.[12]

It seems to indicate, too, that Mozart did not turn his attention to the composition of a finale for K.522 till at least the second quarter of 1787. That is some time after the composition of a fugue which, Daniel Heartz has suggested, is being mocked in this finale. This was a fugue in C major by Thomas Attwood, dated "August the 13."[13] "Its theme, key and order of entries reappear," writes Heartz, "with only a slight variant in the third bar, as the fugato of the last movement of Mozart's *Ein musikalischer Spass* . . . which could be taken as a commentary on the fledgling composer."[14]

By the time that the finale of K.522 was being written, Attwood had left Vienna and returned to London. All of which helps to remind us how ignorant we remain concerning the occasion (or occasions) for which Mozart conceived and started to write out instrumental parts or scores of the movements that were finally assembled as "Ein musikalischer Spass." But at least we can now set aside the notion that the work as a whole can be regarded in any way as a reaction, whether poignant or whimsical, to the death of his father Leopold.

Mozart's D-Major Horn Concerto: Questions of Date and of Authenticity

MOZART has long been credited in the literature with having completed four horn concertos: three in E-flat, and one—the prime subject of this investigation—in D. These are, to give them their traditional Köchel numbers, K.412 in D, and K.417, 447, and 495 in E-flat. There are also three fragmentary concerto movements for the horn. K.371 is a rondo in E-flat that reaches its conclusion after 219 measures but is only partially scored up. The other two are incomplete first movements: K.370b in E-flat is the greater part of a movement, and K.494a in E major is the first 91 measures of one.[1] The scoring of both, like that of K.371, has been only partially completed.[2]

I

CONSIDERABLE uncertainty prevails concerning the dating of two or three of these concertos and fragmentary movements. But others are precisely dated. The rondo K.371 is inscribed "Viene ce 21 mars 1781," only five days after Mozart had arrived in the city that was to be his home for the rest of his life. There is general agreement that the fragmentary first movement K.370b belongs with this rondo, and is therefore also from the spring or early summer of 1781, a view supported by the paper-type of the dismembered score.[3] The autograph of the concerto K.417 bears the date "Wien den 27 May 1783," and the concerto K.495 was entered by Mozart in his Verzeichnüss—the little thematic catalogue of his finished compositions from February 1784 onwards that he continued up to his death—under the date of 26 June

1786. But the autographs of the two other concertos, K.412 and K.447, were not dated by Mozart, and neither work was entered in his Verzeichnüss. The E-major fragment K.494a (like almost all of Mozart's fragments—K.371 is here an exception) is also undated.

Today it is possible to offer new datings for both K.447 and K.494a. Ludwig von Köchel's number of "447" for the concerto in Köchel[1] has not been changed in any of the later editions of his catalogue. It seems to have been chosen in order to keep the piece earlier than the start of the Verzeichnüss, which begins with the entry for the E-flat piano concerto K.449 on 9 February 1784. But the horn concerto K.447 must surely be a later work. In 1939 the French scholar Georges de Saint-Foix, who based his arguments mainly on what are now regarded as far-from-infallible stylistic considerations, proposed that K.447 was probably not composed before 1788.[4] Paper-studies certainly confirm that it is a latish work: the autograph includes paper of a type found elsewhere only in *Don Giovanni*, apart from two leaves in the string-trio score of the six German dances K.571.[5] Probably, then, the concerto dates from 1787 rather than from 1788. Why it was not entered by Mozart in his Verzeichnüss is a problem of a different kind.

It would seem to be a mistake to attempt to assign a date to the E-major fragment K.494a by connecting it either with K.412, as in Köchel[3], or with K.495, as in Köchel[6]. Paper-studies suggest that it could have been written out in the middle or latter half of 1785,[6] although a somewhat later date, such as the middle of 1786, cannot be entirely excluded.

I I

THERE IS GOOD evidence that all four concertos were written with the same soloist in mind. This was Joseph Leutgeb (or "Leitgeb," in Mozart's spelling).[7] He was born in a Vienna suburb on 8 October 1732. From about 1763 he played in the orchestra of the Prince-Archbishop of Salzburg. Thus he was well known to the Mozart family. On 2 November 1760 he had married Barbara, the daughter of a Viennese cheese and sausage merchant, Blasius Plazzeriani; and in 1777 he settled in Vienna, apparently in order to carry on his wife's family business. He also enjoyed some financial support around that time from Leopold Mozart.

It is not clear what aspects of Leutgeb's personality, or perhaps
of his educational deficiencies, resulted in his becoming the butt of
Mozart's teasing. But this was already manifest by the spring of 1783,
when Leutgeb was fifty and Mozart only twenty-seven. At the top left-
hand corner of the first page of the concerto K.417, Mozart wrote
"Leitgeb Esel" in *Rötel* (red crayon), and went on to date the work by
writing in ink: "Wolfgang Amadè Mozart hat sich über den Leitgeb
Esel, Ochs, und Narr, erbarmt zu Wien den 27. May 1783." The six
surviving leaves from the autograph of the concerto K.495 contain
passages written in red, blue, green, and black ink; the work is listed
in Mozart's Verzeichnüss as "Ein Waldhorn Konzert für den Leitgeb."[8]
Although there are no diverting marginal comments or color schemes
in the autograph of the concerto K.447, Leutgeb's name appears twice
in Mozart's hand in the last movement.[9] And it is notorious that
Mozart's autograph of the rondo of the D-major concerto K.412 has a
running commentary of insulting remarks above the horn part from
beginning to end. The first measure of the rondo is marked "Adagio"
in the horn part but "Allegro" in the other parts; and where the horn
enters at measure 8, we find: "à lei Signor Asino. Animo—presto—sù
via—da bravo—coraggio—e finisci gia? [above four measures' rest]—
à te [where the horn resumes]—bestia—oh che stomatura," and so
on, with a final "basta, basta!" over the last notes (see Figure 16.6).
Although Leutgeb is not actually named here, the analogy with the
marginalia or colored inks in the other three concerto autographs
surely suggests that it is he who is once again the recipient of Mozart's
teasing and sarcasm.

                                I I I

A L L   T H I S is a necessary preliminary to a discussion of the date of
the D-major concerto. That there must be some problem here is
indicated by its placement in the sixth edition (1964) of Köchel's catalogue, where it is listed as "K.386b = 412 (und 514)." The explanation of this complex listing takes us back over a hundred years to the
first edition of Otto Jahn's Mozart biography and the first edition of
Köchel's catalogue.[10] For at that time there seemed to be one undated
autograph of a first movement, no slow movement, and two autographs
of a rondo, one of which was really only a draft, since large sections
were only minimally scored. Nevertheless it apparently reached a con-

clusion. But the other autograph presented a fully scored and somewhat different and slightly longer rondo.

The first movement had been assigned a speculative date of 1782 by
Johann Anton André.[11] Both Jahn and Köchel accepted this and applied it also to the draft of the rondo. Hence the Köchel number 412.
Köchel himself listed the uncertainly dated works from each year *after*
the precisely dated ones. But in revising Köchel's catalogue for its third
edition, Köchel[3] (1937), Alfred Einstein inserted the uncertainly dated
works at what he deemed appropriate places among the precisely
dated ones. And since K.387, the G-major string quartet, was dated
by Mozart "li 31 December 1782," Einstein slipped the D-major concerto in before it with the new number "K.386b."

The completed version of the rondo, however, did carry a date—
though evidently one about which there was no exact agreement. In
1858 Jahn wrote in his Mozart biography: "Frau Baroni-Cavalcabo
has the original score of a rondo in D major for horn, composed for
Leitgeb on 6 April 1791—it is missing from Mozart's thematic *Verzeichnüss*."[12] But four years later, in 1862, Köchel stated in the first
edition of his catalogue: "Composed in 1787, on 6 April, in Vienna.
The autograph erroneously states: '1797.' . . . In the possession of
Frau Baroni von Cavalcabò at Gratz. . . At the end: 'Vienna Venerdi
Santo li 6 Aprile 1797.'"[13] Since Mozart could not have written anything in 1797, and since he was prone to be mischievous where Leutgeb
was concerned, and often transposed the figures of dates in jest,[14]
Köchel assumed that by "1797" Mozart meant "1787," and therefore
gave the rondo the separate Köchel number 514. He may have been
encouraged in this view by the fact that in 1787, though not in 1791
or in 1797, Good Friday ("Venerdì Santo") did indeed fall on 6 April.

To summarize this tangled tale so far: For many years the received
view has been that it was in 1782 that Mozart completed the first
movement of the D-major horn concerto and drafted the rondo. Five
years after that, he apparently wrote out another score of the rondo,
this time a complete one, playfully dating it "Good Friday, 6 April
1797"—by which he meant 1787. It is the second version of the rondo
that was published in 1881 in the old *Gesamtausgabe* (AMA) and is
the one that concert audiences have always heard played. Scarcely any
Mozart scholars appear to have been worried by the absence of a slow
movement, or by the fact that in the first movement the strings are
supported by oboes and bassoons, but in the rondo only by oboes.

THE RECEIVED VIEW has not been called into question till recently. The chief reason for this may have been the fact that the sources
themselves were not always available for examination. In the 1860s,
as already mentioned, the completed rondo score had been in the possession of Frau Baroni di Cavalcabò, who inherited the *Nachlass* of
Mozart's son Wolfgang; but afterwards its whereabouts were unknown. The autographs of the first movement and of the draft of the
rondo were in the Berlin Staatsbibliothek until World War II, but they
were among the scores that disappeared in 1945; only in 1977 was
it revealed that those scores were safely preserved at the Biblioteka
Jagiellońska in Kraków, Poland, where today they can be inspected.
And an article by Dmitri Kolbin in *Sovetskaia muzyka* (1966), reprinted in an expanded form in the *Mozart-Jahrbuch 1967* with
the title "Ein wiedergefundenes Mozart-Autograph," declared that the
score of the completed rondo is today in Leningrad (Institute for Theater, Music, and Cinematography).[15] The articles included a few not
very distinct illustrations of some of its pages. Attention was drawn to
some parallel fifths in the movement, which the author supposed had
been intentionally included by Mozart as a kind of jest—like some of
the oddities in "Ein musikalischer Spass," K.522. A short time later it
was recognized that the Leningrad score was no Mozart autograph. In
an interesting essay that appeared in 1973, Wolfgang Plath discussed
the process by which Mozart scholars had come to deceive themselves
in regard to the handwriting.[16] For although the score, authenticated
by Aloys Fuchs,[17] had passed for a Mozart autograph in the nineteenth century, it was clearly not in his hand. Plath went on to exclude
Anton Eberl, Franz Xaver Süssmayr, Franz Jakob Freystädtler, Thomas
Attwood (four pupils of Mozart), and the Abbé Maximilian Stadler as
the writer of the score; but he held firm to the view that the "1797"
date meant 1787 and that the score had therefore been written out in
Mozart's lifetime. Since it exhibited signs of compositional changes,
the following scenario was suggested by Plath: Mozart could not find
his rondo draft, or for some other reason was disinclined to complete
the movement for Leutgeb; and Leutgeb, who at least had the main
theme of the rondo draft in his head, went to some other Viennese
composer and was successful in having "his" rondo, with Mozart's
theme, composed anew by another hand, presumably in 1787.

V

THE DIFFICULTIES in Plath's 1973 conjectural view become clearer when the two autograph movements that are in Kraków—the completed first movement and the draft of the rondo—are carefully examined. One can find facsimiles of both movements, as well as of all the surviving autograph leaves from Mozart's other horn concertos and fragments, in a book published by Hans Pizka in 1980.[18] But Pizka does not reproduce blank pages, the positions of which are essential to an understanding of the make-up of the manuscript.

Several features of the two autograph movements, including aspects that the facsimiles do not show, can be displayed in a diagram (see Table 16.1). It will be seen that the manuscript consists of four paper-types. Type I has the main text of most of the first movement, with nearly all the text up to measure 128 (fifteen measures before the end), as well as a number of rejected passages. Type II has the concluding fifteen measures (129–143), and also twelve measures (85–96) replacing a deleted passage in the middle of the movement. Type III

TABLE 16.1. Make-up of the autograph of Mozart's D-major horn concerto. Kraków, Biblioteka Jagiellónska.

Movement	Folio	Mozart's foliation	Paper-type	Remarks
I	1	"1"	I	Fols. 1–4 have main text of first
	2	"2"	I } =	movement, up to m. 84 and
	3	"3"	I } one sheet	from 97 to 128, but with
	4	"4"	I	several deleted passages.
	5	"5"	II	Fol. 5 has mm. 85–96, and
	6	"6"	II	mm. 129–143 (the ending). Fols. 6r and 6v are blank.
	7	–	III	Fol. 7 has oboes and bassoons
	8	–	III } =	for the first movement. Fols.
			one sheet	8r and 8v are blank.
II (Rondo draft)	9	"1"	III	
	10	"2"	III	
	11	"3"	IV	
	12	"4"	III	Rondo ends on 12r; 12v is blank.

straddles the two movements, giving the lie to the idea sometimes raised that the two movements did not originally belong together;[19] it contains the wind parts to the first movement and the first two leaves and the last leaf of the rondo. The wind parts to the first movement and the start of the rondo are on two bifolia that once formed a single sheet of paper. Type IV is represented by only one leaf, with thirty-six measures (and four deleted ones) towards the end of the rondo.

The surprises come when one tries to date these papers. Type I is a paper that Mozart started to use for the first time when about half of *Le nozze di Figaro* had been written—so it can scarcely be earlier than the beginning of 1786.[20] Indeed, it is probably quite a bit later: Mozart continued to use it, though to a decreasing extent, in the years that followed. But Type II, with the ending and part of the middle of the first movement, was used by him only from March to December of 1791, being found inter alia in the autographs of K.612, 614, 616, 620 (*Die Zauberflöte*), 623, and 626 (the *Requiem*). Thus it is certain that the first movement, even if it was begun some two, three, four, or possibly as long as five years earlier but then remained a fragment for a time, was not finished till 1791.

Type III is also a late paper, used by Mozart for the first time in working on *Così fan tutte* after some of the first act had already been written, and available to him throughout 1790 and 1791.[21] But since the oboe and bassoon parts here must have been written out only after the first movement was completed in 1791, we can limit the Type III paper here to 1791.

Thus the rondo draft will have been begun in 1791. Type IV is another late paper, used by Mozart almost exclusively in 1790 and 1791.

We are obliged, then, to conclude that the first movement was finished, and the rondo drafted but not completed, at some time in 1791, probably in the last ten months. (Mozart's contacts with Leutgeb in the summer and fall of 1791 are mentioned in several of his letters of that year.) Since the latter part of the rondo needed further work on it, this is doubtless why Mozart never found himself in a position to write oboe and bassoon parts for it.

V I

TO RETURN to the Leningrad score: who was its composer? The illustrations of it reproduced in Kolbin's two articles appear to me to be entirely consistent with the handwriting of Mozart's pupil Franz

Xaver Süssmayr from these years.[22] Among the Süssmayr autographs in the British Library there are, for instance, two fragmentary drafts for the first movement of a clarinet concerto in D that provide a good basis for comparison.[23] The later of these drafts is dated "Vieña li   Jan 792" (the day of the month being omitted), and the earlier draft is on Bohemian paper identical in watermark (though ruled with a slightly different 2-staff rastrum) to that used by Mozart in completing *La clemenza di Tito* at Prague in September 1791—probably Süssmayr's concerto was started at that time. If one compares features such as the system-braces and other characteristics of these drafts (and of other Süssmayr scores from around this time) with the same items in the Leningrad score, the similarities will be apparent (compare Figures 16.1 and 16.2 with 16.3 and 16.4).

There remains the problem of the date at the end, usually taken to be "1797." The words appearing before the year need to be taken seriously: "Venerdì Santo li 6 Aprile" (see Figure 16.4). For Good Friday fell on 6 April in only three years between 1708 and 1849: these were 1787, 1792, and 1798. And since the rondo draft has now been shown to have been written by Mozart in 1791, we can accordingly rule out "1797" as a slip or a joke for "1787." In 1791 Good Friday fell on 22 April, and in 1797 on 14 April. But what about 1792? I feel sure that this is, in fact, the date on the Leningrad score. It so happens that the writer (in my view, Süssmayr) made a small horizontal line to the right on the bottom of the "7," making it look a little like a "2" (see Figure 16.4). But that does not mean that when he wrote a "2," he meant it to be a "7"!

Here, then, is my scenario: We find Süssmayr completing an incomplete Mozart score in Vienna only four months after his revered teacher's death. Not that there is anything so strange about that; for almost the only thing many people recall about Süssmayr is that he was charged at one time with completing Mozart's unfinished *Requiem*.[24]

What is striking, however, about the Leningrad score is that it is a rather free completion. For it deviates to quite an extent from Mozart's draft, even in places such as the opening measures, where the draft is fully scored.[25] And whereas Mozart's draft is only 135 measures long, Süssmayr's movement has 141 measures.

At measure 67 in the Leningrad score there begins a passage for the solo horn which has been identified as the Gregorian chant for the Lamentations of the prophet Jeremiah.[26] There is nothing that corresponds to this in Mozart's draft, so we must assume that it was an

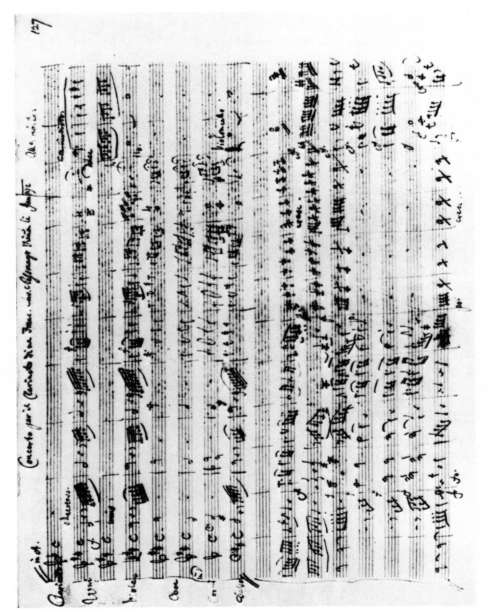

FIGURE 16.1. First page of the second draft of a clarinet concerto in D by Franz Xaver Süssmayr. British Library, London, Add. MS 32181, fol. 127r.

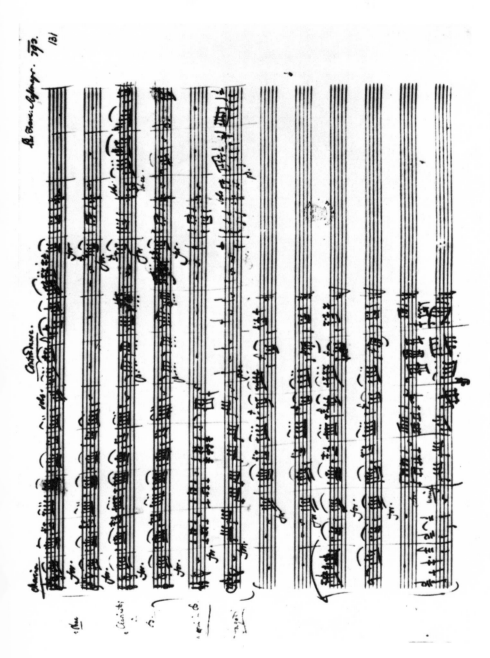

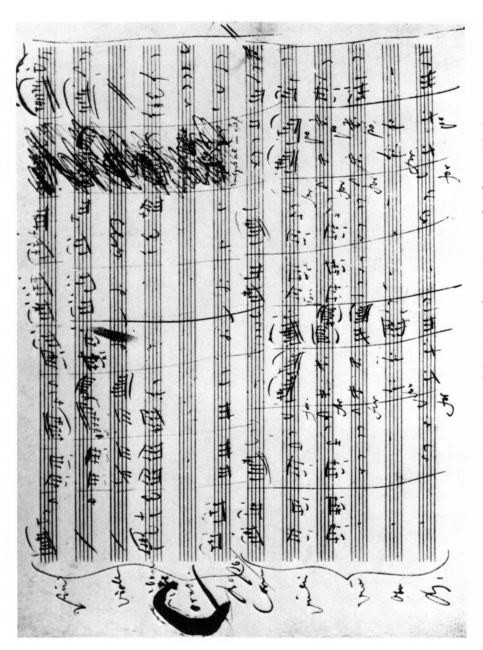

FIGURE 16.3. Second page of the Leningrad score (Institute for Theater, Music, and Cinematography), with mm. 18–32 of the rondo.

FIGURE 16.4. Penultimate page of the Leningrad score, with the final thirteen measures of the rondo and the date.

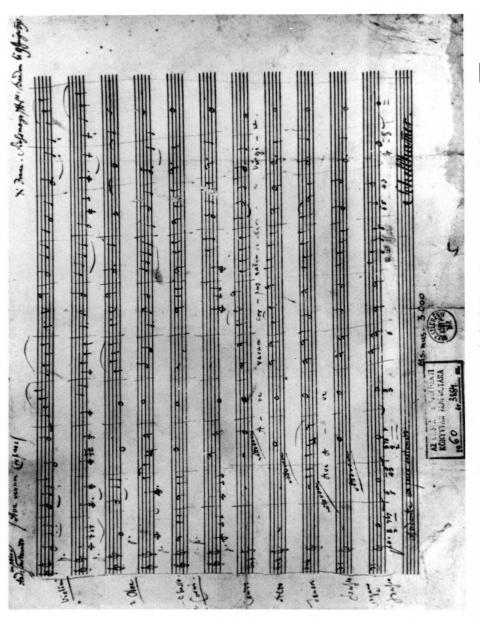

FIGURE 16.5. An *Ave verum corpus* inscribed "di Franc. Siessmayr mpr: Baaden li 9 Giugno 792." Országos Széchényi Könyvtár, Budapest, Ms. mus. 3000.

inspiration of Süssmayr's. Those versed in liturgical matters will have no difficulty in connecting the melody with the "Good Friday" date; in the Catholic Church the Lamentations were appointed for use on three days in Holy Week. But there is perhaps a further message here. Is this an allusion not merely to the date of the score's completion, but to the lamentable death of Mozart four months earlier?

V I I

FOR WHAT OCCASION was this score completed? Was Süssmayr merely tidying up parts of his teacher's *Nachlass?* Or did he have a particular performer in mind? One recalls the rude remarks addressed to Leutgeb all through Mozart's rondo draft. The Leningrad score also had a few facetious remarks in the margins, including "Leitgeb bitt um Hilf" under a measure crossed out in all the parts (see Figure 16.3). So probably this score too was intended for a performance by Leutgeb. One cannot even exclude the notion that it was for a performance on Good Friday, 1792, Holy Week being a time when the Viennese theaters were not used for opera or drama and so were available for memorial or charitable concerts.

But there is a small puzzle in the solo horn part here, as was pointed out to me by Robert Levin, who showed me the value of charting the ambitus of the horn's notes in this work. One can do this separately for the first movement, for the rondo draft, and for Süssmayr's rondo; and one should also record any other pitches that occur in deleted passages (see Example 16.1). For the first movement we have just over an octave from *g′* to *a″;* on folio 4v of the autograph, which has sev-

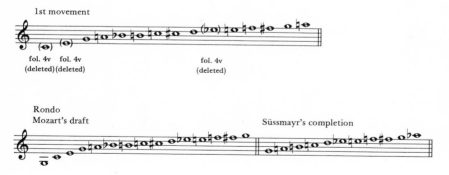

EXAMPLE 16.1. Notes for the horn in the D-major concerto.

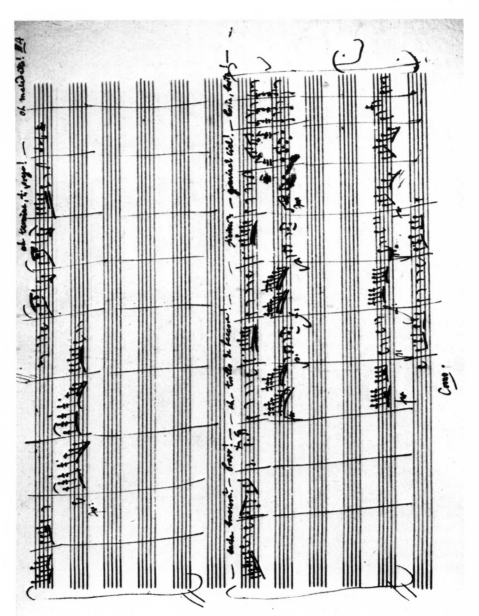

FIGURE 16.6. Last page (fol. 12r) of Mozart's draft of the rondo. Biblioteka Jagiellońska, Kraków.

eral deleted measures, we find two lower notes, c' and e', as well as an $e^b{}''$ not in the finished version. In Süssmayr's rondo the range is just over an octave, from g' to $a^b{}''$, the latter note occurring in the "Lamentations" passage. Mozart's rondo draft, which does not have this $a^b{}''$, has three low notes, g, c', and e' (see Figure 16.6). In mm. 35–36 Süssmayr pointedly avoids the g in a passage that he otherwise lifts from Mozart.

Was the elimination of the three low notes simply an accident of the revision by Mozart and recomposition by Süssmayr? (They were assigned to Leutgeb in the three other concertos that Mozart wrote for him, and in two of them there are high notes up to c'''.) Or was he, in his fifty-ninth or sixtieth year, experiencing technical difficulties at the extremes of his range? (In that case, Mozart's revision and completion of the first movement would have occurred after he had drafted the rondo.) According to the article on Leutgeb in the *New Grove*, "He apparently retired from playing in 1792."[27] Little is known about the rest of his life, except that he died at his house in a Viennese suburb on 27 February 1811, leaving debts of 1286 gulden.[28] But his connection with Mozart, even though he was often the victim of his teasing, is enough to guarantee Joseph Leutgeb's immortality. As for Süssmayr, his immortality is already secure as a result of what he did for Mozart's *Requiem*—to which we can now add what he chose to do for the rondo of the D-major horn concerto.

17

The Rondo for Piano and Orchestra, K.386

O NE DAY near the end of March 1980 I was at the British Library, London, looking through a volume in the Department of Manuscripts that consisted of miscellaneous pieces of music by Franz Xaver Süssmayr. The contents of the volume, Add. MS 32181, formed part of a large collection of manuscripts by various composers that had been purchased by the British Library (then the British Museum) on 9 February 1884 from the Leipzig antiquarian firm of List and Francke. These manuscripts, catalogued as Add. MS 32169–32239, were said to have come from the library of Johann Nepomuk Hummel (1778–1837), and the majority of them (Add. MS 32184–32237) are in fact compositions by Hummel, or arrangements made by him of music by other composers.

The volume Add. MS 32181, one of two consisting of music by Süssmayr, contains a large number of his autograph scores, though many are incomplete, and also a few other compositions by him in the hand of copyists. But after looking through 249 leaves of music by Süssmayr, I was astonished to come across three leaves in Mozart's handwriting. They had been catalogued (as I discovered later) as a "fragment of what appears to be the end of a piano concerto in A, by Süssmayr: *Autograph.*" But that identification did not seem plausible, and indeed I quickly recognized the main theme of Mozart's rondo for piano and orchestra in A major, K.386. Further examination indicated that the three leaves, Add. MS 32181, fols. 250–252 (and a final blank leaf, fol. 253), contained the final forty-five measures of the rondo, and must have formed the end of its autograph score.

But another cause for astonishment awaited me. For I found the music somewhat unfamiliar, and I soon discovered that it did not correspond to the ending of the rondo that was normally played. At that point it became clear to me that a radical revision was required in our understanding of K.386's history, and of the basis for its textual tradition.

BEFORE INVESTIGATING and discussing this textual tradition in detail, it will probably be helpful to provide a summary of the work's history from Mozart's death until the present day:

(a) An autograph score of K.386 was included in the great collection of her deceased husband's autographs that Constanze Mozart sold to the publisher Johann Anton André of Offenbach under the contract dated 8 November 1799.[1]

(b) But, as was the case with quite a lot of other autographs bought by André, the score of K.386 was incomplete; the ending was missing.

(c) Attempts to trace the autograph's missing ending, or to replace it from other sources, were unsuccessful. This may well be a reason why no edition of the rondo was ever published by André's firm.

(d) But a reduction of the rondo for piano solo was made by Cipriani Potter (1792–1871) and published in London in 1838.[2] Potter composed an ending of his own for the work, it now seems clear.

(e) At about the same time as the appearance of Potter's edition (or, as will be suggested below, a little earlier), the autograph of K.386 was among a number available to be bought from a "Mr. French" in London. It found a purchaser.

(f) The purchaser, or at any rate the subsequent owner, was William Sterndale Bennett (1816–1875). No doubt because the autograph was incomplete, Sterndale Bennett felt no inhibitions against breaking it up; he frequently removed leaves and even divided some, and gave these fragments away to friends. Thus the autograph became widely dispersed. None of it was known to Ludwig von Köchel when he published the first edition of his catalogue in 1862; his only source of information about the work was its entry in André's manuscript catalogue of 1833,[3] and he was unaware of the existence of Potter's 1838 edition.

(g) It is in the last half century that attempts have been made to reconstruct the original version of the rondo. Several portions of its text are preserved on those leaves of the autograph that have survived, and they can also be used as a basis for rescoring Potter's piano reduction in the passages for which no autograph leaf has been found. This task was first attempted by Alfred Einstein in 1936,[4] and it has become easier as more leaves, or parts of leaves, from the autograph have come to light. What was therefore a sounder reconstruction, by Paul Badura-Skoda and Charles Mackerras, was published in 1962.[5]

(h) The rondo was also published in 1960 in the Anhang to the eighth volume of piano concertos in the *Neue Mozart-Ausgabe*.[6] In accordance with the principles of that edition, its editor, Wolfgang Rehm, presented in full score only those passages for which leaves of Mozart's autograph were then available; the rest of the piece was presented only in Potter's piano reduction. Rehm also printed Potter's text under the passages that survived in autograph; that enables those who are interested to assess the accuracy of Potter's version, and to see what techniques he used to condense the orchestral score.

(i) In general the emergence of autograph leaves from various sections of the movement has confirmed the accuracy of Potter's piano reduction. But the conclusion of the rondo in Mozart's handwriting that came to light in the British Library in 1980 shows that the ending in Potter's edition must have been an invention of his composed in the 1830s.

AFTER THAT SUMMARY of the work's history, we are now in a position to examine each of the many stages in greater detail.

The autograph's first leaf, today in the possession of a descendant of Sterndale Bennett, proves to have some interesting inscriptions on it, two by Mozart and one or two others evidently from the last decade of the eighteenth century. Mozart's entries consist of the work's title, "// Rondeaux //,"[7] at the top of the page in the center, and in the upper right-hand corner the inscription "di Wolfgango Amadeo Mozart mp / Vieña gli 19 d'Oct.^bre 1782." Of the other entries, the most important for us is "das Ende fehlt," in the handwriting of someone who obviously had worked with the Abbé Stadler and Georg Nikolaus Nissen in sorting out Mozart's *Nachlass;*[8] for this shows that the autograph was recognized as lacking its conclusion before it was sold to André in 1799. Another phrase, "zu ergänzen," is in Nissen's hand; the same words by him are to be found in the same place on the autograph of the E-flat piano concerto, K.449. In the top left-hand corner there is a reference number, "N°26," similar numbers being found in the same position on the autographs of the other piano concertos.

An interesting clue suggesting that Nissen and his helpers had been searching for the rondo's missing ending before the collection of autographs was sold to André is to be found in an inscription on fol. 26r of the autograph of the A-major piano concerto, K.414(385p) (see Figure 17.1). It appears that fols. 26 and 27, a bifolium containing the last thirty measures of its slow movement, were at one time an unidentified "fragment," before they were restored to their correct position within the autograph of K.414. For the Abbé Stadler wrote on fol. 26r the words "zu ein Clavierconzert," and Nissen wrote there not only his usual formula, "Von Mozart und seine Handschrift," but also the interesting though somewhat misguided sentence:

Ein Ende, welches vielleicht irgendwo fehlt, vielleicht zu dem mangelhaften Rondò gehörig.

[An ending that is perhaps missing somewhere, perhaps belonging to the defective rondo.]

Nissen evidently failed to observe that this fragment of the K.414 slow movement was in 3/4 meter, not 2/4 meter, and ended in D major rather than in A major.

There appear, moreover, to be at least two references to the rondo, and to the attempt to find its missing ending, in the surviving correspondence between Constanze Mozart and Johann Anton André of the year 1800, though they seem mainly to have been unrecognized. In her letter of 21–27 February 1800 Constanze wrote:[9]

Das Rondo im Clavierconzert N.26. kann vielleicht der Abbé Stadler durch seine Correspondenz mit der Ployen ergänzen.

[Perhaps the Abbé Stadler can complete the rondo in the piano concerto No. 26 through his connections with Fräulein Ployen.]

By "Ployen" is meant Barbara Ployer, for whom Mozart wrote the two piano concertos K.449 and K.453; but the "N.26" seems to indicate that the autograph of K.386—which, as we have seen, carries this number—is what is referred to.

Barbara Ployer is also alluded to in Constanze's letter of 31 May 1800. In a section that discusses pieces requiring completion that had evidently been enumerated by André, she wrote:

4. Clavier Rondò mit begleitung des Orchesters. dieses wird seyn in den handen der vormaligen fräulein Ployen, izigen verheiratheten Bojanowich, welche lebt *unweit* Kreuz in Croatien. Der Vater ihres Mannes ist hiesiger Ungarischer Hofagent. Ich habe vorhin vergebens an sie schreiben lassen.[10]

[4. Rondo for piano with orchestral accompaniment; this will be in the hands of the former Fräulein Ployen, now Frau Bojanowich, who is living *not far*

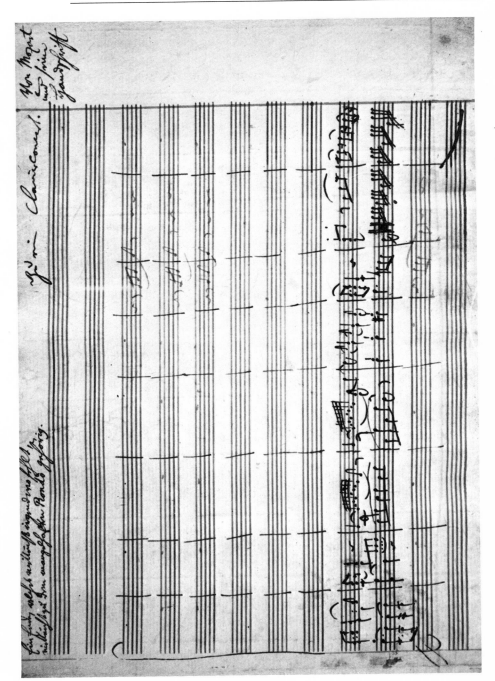

FIGURE 17.1. The A-Major Piano Concerto, K.414 (385p): fol. 26r, near the end of the slow movement. Biblioteka Jagiellońska, Kraków.

from Kreuz in Croatia. Her husband's father is the representative of the Hungarian court here. I have already had letters sent to her, but to no effect.]

If I am correct in identifying these passages as referring to K.386,[11] it is evident that there is some hitherto unsuspected connection between Barbara Ployer and the rondo. Was that too written for her? The problem remains unresolved at present.

S OME INTERESTING light on the history of K.386 near the end of the 1830s was contributed in 1963 by a couple of articles in the *Festschrift Otto Erich Deutsch*.[12] In his survey of "Cipriani Potter's Edition of Mozart's Pianoforte Works," Cecil B. Oldman discussed inter alia the publication date of the edition's fourteenth and most important number, Cipriani Potter's arrangement of K.386 for solo pianoforte—the first appearance in print of the rondo in any form. Nos. 10–13 of Potter's Edition had been entered at Stationers Hall in July and August 1837. Although somewhat surprisingly No. 14 was never entered at Stationers Hall, the evidence from contemporary advertisements is that it had already been published by February 1838.[13]

As part of his own contribution to the same *Festschrift,* Wolfgang Rehm discussed "A Catalogue of Musical Manuscripts" offered for sale in London around this time. The manuscripts, the majority of which were autographs by Mozart, were described as being "mostly unpublished" and "from the collection of Mr. A. André, Offenbach," and they included K.386. The catalogue stated that "Mozart composed this Rondo in 1782, and completed all but the last page."

Alfred Einstein wrongly described the offering of these autographs for sale as an "auction," and unconvincingly assigned to it the date of 1840. The catalogue carries no date, but its cover includes the words: "Apply for the Purchase of any of these MSS. at Mr. French's, 9, East Street, Red Lion Square." And since nothing is known of a Mr. French in London at this time, Wolfgang Rehm argued that he was no doubt J. A. André's son Gustav (1816–1874), who went to London early in 1838 and worked there as a music dealer, publisher, and importer until at least September 1839. Thus it would follow that it was 1838 or 1839 when "Mr. French" offered K.386 and the other autographs for sale.

But there is an obvious difficulty here, since Potter's piano reduction of K.386 had already been published before the apparent arrival of Gustav André in London; thus Potter must have had access to the autograph no later than 1837. And since K.386 is listed in "Mr. French's" catalogue among the "unpublished" works, it would appear that the catalogue too must have been prepared by 1837. Indeed, as Rehm pointed out, the typography of the page in the catalogue with the musical incipits of the autographs makes it likely that that page was prepared by the house of André at Offenbach, though the typography of the rest of the catalogue indicates that it was printed in England. Perhaps, then, the catalogue was put together in 1837 by a Mr. French who acted as agent for André's firm, at any rate until Gustav André arrived in London. Sterndale Bennett spent several months from October 1836 to July 1837 in Leipzig and elsewhere in Germany. It might be suggested that he stopped at Offenbach on his journey back to England that summer and acquired the autograph of K.386 from the house of André there, or else bought it from "Mr. French" after his return to London.[14] The assumption would be that he then lent it to his former teacher at the Royal Academy of Music, Cipriani Potter, so that it could be included in the latter's Mozart edition.

A new piece of evidence, however, appears to assign a somewhat earlier date to Potter's concern with the publication of K.386—a date in the spring of 1837. The evidence is contained in a document recently acquired by the British Library, and to be found in Add. MS 63814; this is a contract between Johann André of Offenbach and Messrs. Coventry & Hollier, the publishers of Potter's "Chefs D'Oeuvre de Mozart," assigning to them—for a payment of £30—the copyright for England of five Mozart works. The main text, probably written in Germany, is as follows:

Document

The underwritten transfers herewith of the following compositions of Mozart wich are his property, the copyright for England to Messrs Coventry & Hollier in London for the sum of thirty Pounds Sterling—

The titles and the incipits of five works follow, and then come the words:

Offenbach o/M the 26th of April 1837

Johañ André

The five works listed here all consist of fragmentary autographs. "No. 1, Trio for Piano, Violon, Violoncello" is K.442, three fragmentary movements for piano trio; "No. 2, Sonata for Piano & Violon" is

K.403(385c), a violin sonata with a fragmentary finale; "No. 3, Sonata for Piano & Violon" is K.372, a fragmentary violin-sonata movement; "No. 4, Allegro for Piano solo" is K.400(372a), a fragmentary
piano movement; and "No. 5, Rondo, for Piano, Concerto Rondo" is
K.386, a work then lacking its ending.

All five of the fragmentary works listed in the contract were published in completed versions by Potter in his Edition: No. 10 = K.442,
No. 11 = K.400, No. 12 = K.372, No. 13 = K.403, and No. 14 =
K.386. As stated above, Nos. 10−13 were entered at Stationers Hall
in July and August 1837. It is regrettable that No. 14 was never entered there; but the contract between Johann André and Coventry &
Hollier is valuable evidence that Potter's publishers acquired for him
the right to publish K.386 as early as April 1837.

As some of the inscriptions on the now widely scattered leaves of
the autograph suggest, it was not very long after acquiring it that
Sterndale Bennett began to dismantle it and give sections of it away.
On one leaf he wrote: "Mozart—Rondo in A. with orchestra / recently published by Coventry—71. / Dean St. Soho." Another leaf
was inscribed by him: "Original M.S. / of Mozart. / I have the title /
page / W S Bennett," a phrase that suggests that the autograph had by
then been largely disrupted. Some leaves were even cut into small
pieces; an envelope containing about a quarter of a leaf bears the
inscription in another hand: "Mozart's Autograph / given to me by
Mr Sterndale Bennett / Thursday Feb[ry] 26th 1846 in 4 Wigmore Street
/ London."

With the leaves so widely dispersed and most of them then apparently lost, it must have seemed that there was no possibility of reconstructing the work in the form that Mozart wrote it. Yet this was
proposed in the latter part of the last century by William Warde
Fowler (1847−1921), as explained by him in a privately printed pam-
phlet of 1910.[15] Fowler had encountered Potter's arrangement in
1860, when he was twelve. He goes on to explain:

When first at Oxford my old friend Professor Case (now President of Corpus)
[Thomas Case, 1844−1925] showed me the collection of musical autographs
which belonged to his father-in-law Sterndale Bennett, great was my astonishment and in one sense my delight at finding among them two fragments
of the original score of the Rondo, of which I had read in Köchel that the
autograph had disappeared.[16] It was scored for strings with two oboes and

two horns as well as piano, and there seemed to me to be enough of it to
enable a skilful musician, familiar with Mozart's methods, to reconstruct the
whole from these fragments together with Potter's arrangement for piano
solo. I tried to interest Sir John Stainer in it, but he was too much occupied
with other things. There is therefore some probability of its being lost to the
world, since the owner of the autograph, whoever he may have been, thought
fit, as it would seem, to cut it up in pieces to be given away as curiosities.

It was not until 1936, however, that a reconstruction of the original
version of the work was attempted. The courageous pioneer here was
Alfred Einstein. But at that time he knew of only two autograph
leaves, the ones containing measures 136–171. In 1962, when they
undertook their own reconstruction, Paul Badura-Skoda and Charles
Mackerras knew of six and a quarter leaves. Since then, four and a
quarter more leaves (one of them blank) have come to light. Thus today ten complete leaves, and parts of two more leaves, are known to
have survived. And it is not unlikely that one or two further lost
leaves, or parts of leaves, may at any moment reappear.

E N O U G H of the autograph is already available to justify an attempt
to reconstruct its original make-up. All the surviving leaves and parts
of leaves seem to be of the same paper-type, with the sheet-watermark
of a crown over the letters $^{C}_{C}$, and three crescent moons over the word
REAL (see Figure 17.2); they have (or had) twelve staves, with a total
span of 182.5–183 mm. It is a reasonable assumption, on the analogy
of other autographs from this period of Mozart's life, that the structure of K.386 will have been a series of gathered pairs of bifolia, each
pair being from the same sheet. And although the suggestion is made
in Köchel[6], p. 427, that the autograph originally had fourteen leaves,
it seems more likely that there were sixteen leaves, the last of which
was not used.[17] My proposed reconstruction is shown in Table 17.1.
Even though parts of leaves 6 and 7 are missing, the only ones that are
today totally lost are leaf 5 and leaves 10–12. Yet it cannot be doubted
that they were available to Cipriani Potter in 1837; there is no reason
to suppose that anything was missing in his day except the ending of
the work.

Some evidence for this comes from an investigation into the exact
place at which Mozart's true ending, preserved in the British Library,
fits onto Potter's piano reduction, revealing the extent of his own invented ending. This would appear to be after m. 224. For the first measure of Add. MS 37181, fol. 250r, is a two-octave descending A-major

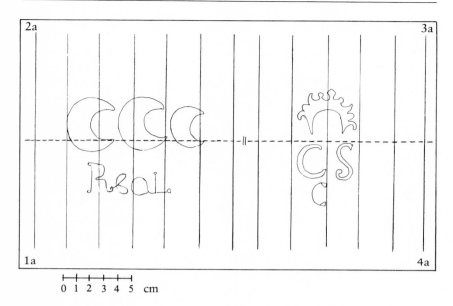

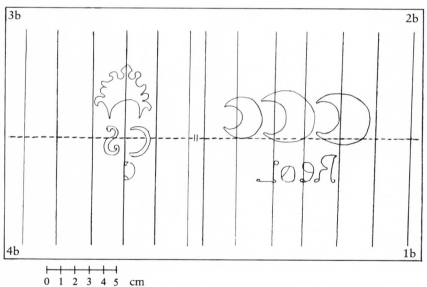

FIGURE 17.2. The watermark of the paper-type in K.386's autograph.
(K.386 apparently has only Mold A.)

TABLE 17.1. Proposed reconstruction of the
autograph of K.386.

Leaf	Measures	Recto	Verso	Watermark quadrant
1	1–22	1–11	12–22	2a
2	23–41	23–31	32–41	[1a]
3	42–62	42–53	54–62	[4a]
4	63–78	63–70	71–78	3a
5	79–100	?	?	[4a]
6	101–115	101–107?	108?–115	[3a]
7	116–135	116–124	125–135	[2a]
8	136–154	136–145	146–154	1a
9	155–171	155–161	162–171	4a
10		?	?	[3a]
11	172–224	?	?	[2a]
12		?	?	[1a]
13	225–239	225–231	232–239	1a
14	240–258	240–248	249–258	2a
15	259–269	259–266	267–269	3a
16	blank			4a

Leaf 1: in the possession of Mr. T. G. Odling, Gloucestershire, England.

Leaf 2 and Leaf 3: auctioned at Sotheby's, London, on 14 June 1976 (No. 142; side with mm. 54–62 illustrated in the catalogue), and now owned by a private collector.

Leaf 4: in the library of the Royal College of Surgeons, London.

Leaf 5: missing.

Leaf 6: a fragment of this leaf, with the bottom five staves (with pianoforte, cello, and bass) of mm. 101–104 and 110 (last few notes)–115, was auctioned at Sotheby's, London, on 17 November 1983 (No. 142); it is now in the Music Library of The University of Western Ontario, London (Canada).

Leaf 7: a fragment of this leaf, with the bottom six and a half staves of mm. 118 (last few notes)–124, and 125–132, is in the possession of Mr. T. G. Odling.

Leaf 8: in the Sibley Library, Eastman School of Music, Rochester, N.Y., U.S.A.

Leaf 9: auctioned at Sotheby's, London, on 27 February 1973 (No. 362; side with mm. 155–161 illustrated in the catalogue), and now owned by Mr. Bin Ebisawa, President of the Kunitachi Music College, Tokyo.

Leaf 10, Leaf 11, and Leaf 12: all missing.

Leaf 13, Leaf 14, Leaf 15, and Leaf 16: in the Department of Manuscripts, British Library, London, Add. MS 32181, fols. 250–253.

scale, followed by two measures with a rising series of appoggiaturas and a 7th chord on the leading note. And these three measures find a close parallel in mm. 219–221 of Potter's arrangement, for m. 219 is a two-octave *ascending* A-major scale, and mm. 220–221 contain a *descending* series of appoggiaturas and the same 7th chord on the leading note. There are also parallels between mm. 217–218 (with the melody in the right hand) and mm. 223–224 (with the same melody in the left hand): see Example 17.1. Thus the five measures 217–221 are closely matched by mm. 223–224 and the first three measures of Mozart's ending, leading one to deduce that the twenty-eight measures that follow m. 224 in Potter's arrangement and bring the piece to a conclusion must have been devised by him. The fact that most of the measures that Potter used in composing his ending were lifted from earlier passages in the work, where they came from Mozart's pen, accounts for that ending having hitherto been accepted as "Mozartian" and not merely dismissed as "Potteresque."[18] Yet if (as we assume) Potter knew nothing of Mozart's ending, he would never have invented mm. 219–221 that are so clearly echoed by the first three measures of Mozart's ending. Thus we can conclude that Potter had every part of Mozart's autograph up to m. 224.

TODAY, then, we can be sure enough that K.386 was conceived by Mozart as a rondo of 269 measures, rather than as one of 252 measures (as in Potter's version). And of these 269, we have Mozart's full scoring for 159 measures, and part of his scoring in 9¼ and 13¼ further measures. That is surely sufficient to justify attempts to orchestrate Potter's piano reduction for the 110 measures in which we lack Mozart's scoring, or at least part of it.

One difficulty, it is true, arises from an unusual feature of Mozart's scoring here: the highly independent part that he wrote for the violoncello. For this provides a problem in instrumenting the "tutti" version of the "second subject," the two passages that begin with m. 91 and m. 171; of these only m. 171, the first measure of the second passage, is preserved in Mozart's autograph.[19]

Yet we are in a position today to dismiss what might appear to be another source of difficulty by correcting an apparent misunderstanding by J. A. André of Nissen's inscription on the first page of the autograph, consisting of the words *zu ergänzen*. For that no doubt meant that the missing ending of the rondo needed to be found, or else to be replaced somehow. But André, as we learn from his 1833 catalogue, took it to mean that the instrumentation needed some degree of supplementation (or augmentation);[20] and this view was repeated by Köchel in 1862 and by Einstein in 1937. Rehm, however, doubted this; and the word *Entwurf* in his 1960 edition is therefore followed by a question mark. Now that we have Mozart's ending, we can see that it is scored no less fully than the rest of the rondo; the light scor-

(a) Mm. 217-224 of Potter's arrangement, plus the first three measures invented by him.

(b) Mm. 1-4 of Add. MS 32181, fol. 250r = mm. 225-228 of the work.

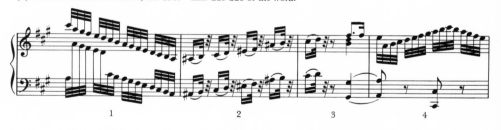

EXAMPLE 17.1. The link between Potter's arrangement and the autograph ending of K.386.

ing of the piece as a whole makes it analogous with the three piano concertos of the end of 1782, K.413, 414, and 415.

Today, therefore, *zu ergänzen* can be taken as an invitation to score those parts of the work that survive merely in Potter's reduction, although they were *not* missing at the time that Nissen wrote *zu ergänzen* on the score; he was referring to the work's then missing *ending*.

SINCE MOZART was not only working on, but probably completed, the A-major piano concerto K.414(385p) in the last months of 1782, the question inevitably arises whether K.386, also in A major and bearing the date of 19 October 1782, is somehow related to it—and if so, in what way.

Einstein was the first to express an opinion on the matter. In the preface to his 1936 edition of K.386 he stated: "The composer wrote this Rondo as a last movement for his pianoforte-concerto K.414, though whether it formed the original finale or was intended to replace the Allegretto that now concludes the work in all editions, is not certain." The same two possibilities were also raised in his 1937 edition of Köchel. Even in his 1945 book on Mozart he did not reach a decision between them; but he suggested why K.386—which he believed Mozart had left in the form of a nearly complete sketch—could have been at least ultimately rejected as a finale for K.414: "No doubt the reason for abandoning it was that it repeated certain melodic turns of phrase that had appeared in the first movement."[21] Yet he did not find it inferior to the movement with which the concerto now ends: "To us it seems at least as attractive as the Rondo Mozart used for this work, and perhaps even superior to it."

Another consideration was raised by Rehm in his edition of 1960. Although K.386 shares with the finale of K.414 the tempo of Allegretto and the 2/4 meter (and of course the key of A major), it has an unusual feature in its scoring already referred to: the highly independent violoncello part. In his announcement in the *Wiener Zeitung* of 15 January 1783 that manuscript copies of his three new piano concertos (K.413, 414, and 415) could be obtained at the beginning of April by those who subscribed in advance, Mozart declared that they could be performed "either with a large orchestra with wind instruments or merely *a quattro*, viz. with 2 violins, 1 viola and violoncello." But K.386 could not be performed *a quattro*; so if it had been the original finale of K.414, it would, as Rehm observed, have had to be replaced. And Einstein's suggestion that K.386 might have been intended as a substitute for the concerto's original finale seems, in the light of its peculiar scoring, to be fairly unlikely.

FOR A LONG TIME after World War II the autograph of K.414, and those of the other two piano concertos that Mozart composed around the same time, K.413 and K.415, were feared to have been permanently lost; but since 1980 they have been available for study in the Biblioteka Jagiellońska, Kraków. The question therefore arises whether their relative chronologies, and the true relation between K.414 and K.386, could now be established by a scrutiny of these autographs and a study of the various papers on which they were written.

The three concertos are made up from five types of paper. The distribution of these papers can be summarized as follows:

K.414, in A	*K.413, in F*	*K.415, in C*
Fols. 1–28 = Type A	Fols. 1–8 = Type A	Fols. 1–20 = Type B
Fols. 29–34 and 39 = Type D	Fols. 9–26 = Type B	Fols. 21–24 and 29–40 = Type C
Fols. 35–38 = Type E	Fols. 27–38 = Type C	Fols. 25–28 = Type D
(And two separate horn parts = Type C)		

Each type has a characteristic total span (TS) of its twelve staves in these concertos.[22] Type E is the paper that Mozart apparently also used for the whole of the autograph of K.386; its watermark is illustrated above in Figure 17.2

It seems a plausible inference from the distribution of the paper-types that Mozart was working on all three concertos at the same time; he did not complete one before starting work on another. Some further clues to the same effect can be gained from Mozart's letter to his father of 28 December 1782:

nun fehlen noch 2 Concerten zu den Suscriptions Concerten.—die Concerten sind eben das Mittelding zwischen zu schwer, und zu leicht—sind sehr Brillant—angenehm in die ohren—Natürlich, ohne in das leere zu fallen—hie und da—können auch *kenner allein* satisfaction erhalten—doch so—daß die nicht-kenner damit zufrieden seyn müssen, ohne zu wissen warum.[23]

[Two concertos for the series of subscription concertos are still lacking. These concertos are in fact a happy medium between what is too difficult and what is too easy; they are very brilliant, and agreeable to the ear, natural, without being vacuous. There are passages here and there that can bring satisfaction *only to connoisseurs*, but they are written in a way that must bring pleasure to non-connoisseurs, without their knowing why.]

The letter implies that much work must have been done on all three concertos by 28 December 1782, even though only one of them had been completed by then. It is generally agreed (though we cannot be certain) that this will have been K.414; it is notable, too, that when the firm of Artaria published all three concertos in Vienna in 1785 as Mozart's "Oeuvre IV, Livres 1–3," K.414 was "Livre 1."

But even if K.414 was finished first, it is impossible to date the completion of the various parts of the three concertos with greater precision. For all these five paper-types were used quite a lot by Mozart around this time, as well as earlier and later. Types A, B, and C, for instance, as well as Type D with a different TS, are all found in *Die Entführung aus dem Serail*, K.384, completed in May 1782; and Type B, and also Type D with the *same* TS, are to be found in the "Haffner" Symphony, K.385, written in July 1782.

Nor, unfortunately, does it appear that much can be inferred from the presence of Type E, the paper of K.386, in the autograph of K.414. For paper with this watermark and TS is found in a number of other scores, though all of them are, regrettably, hard to date with precision. (In fact it is only K.386 that bears a date!) These scores, or parts of scores, are as follows:

K.375	Serenade for wind in E-flat: second version, for octet. The whole work except for the two minuets, which are in a copyist's hand.
K.388(384a)	Serenade for wind in C minor: fols. 9–12 = finale (except for the last 23 mm., a replacement in another hand).
K.410(484d)	Adagio for 2 basset-horns and 1 bassoon.
K.414(385p)	Piano Concerto in A: fols. 35–39, in finale.
K.427(417a)	Mass in C minor: fols. 11–14 (= start of "Laudamus Te").
K.449	Piano Concerto in E-flat: fols. 1–10 (= start of first movement).[24]

The structure of the K.414 autograph and the distribution of the paper-types within it are shown in Table 17.2, and their watermarks are illustrated in Figures 17.2 (above), 17.3, and 17.4. The leaves were not foliated by Mozart, but he numbered the four-leaf gatherings.

Movement	Gathering	Folio	Type	Watermark quadrant			
I (1r) Allegro	1	1	A	3a			
		2		4a			
		3		1a			
		4		2a			
	2	5		2a			
		6		1a			
		7		4a			
		8		3a			
	3	9		2b			
		10		1b			
		11		4b			
		12		3b			
	4	13		3a			
		14		4a			
		15		1a			
		16		2a			
	5	17		3b			
		18		4b			
		19		1b			
		20		2b			
II (21r) Andante	6	21		1a			
		22		2a			
		23		3a			
		24		4a			
	7	25		2b			
		26		1b			
		27		4b			
III (28r) Allegretto		28		3b			
	8	29	D	4a			
		30		1a			
		31		4a			
		32		1a			
	9	33		4b		Kroměříž:	
					→	A	Type D	3b
						B	Type D	2b
		34		1b			
	10	35	E	1a			
		36		2a			
		37		3a			
		38		4a			
		39	D	3b			

Mold A

Mold B

FIGURE 17.3. Type A.

Mold A

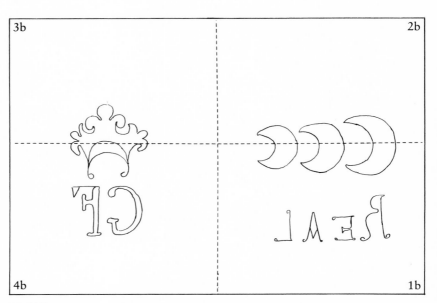

Mold B

FIGURE 17.4. Type D.

(The ninth gathering consists of only a single bifolium, because after concluding fol. 33r with m. 107, Mozart drafted ten measures on fol. 33v and a further eight on the first side of the inner bifolium that followed it; but he then revised his plans for this section, deleted these eighteen measures, and after withdrawing and discarding the inner bifolium he continued the movement in a different way, starting with m. 108 on fol. 34r.)[25]

It will be seen that Type E, the paper-type of K.386, is found in only one gathering in the finale of K.414, beginning at m. 131 on fol. 35r, and continuing up to the conclusion of the movement on fol. 38r. A later expansion of the coda resulted in additions being made on fol. 38v (mm. 182–192), and on the verso of a newly added leaf of another paper-type (Type D), fol. 39 (mm. 193–197).[26] It might be suggested by someone that after concluding the finale of K.414 on Type E, Mozart then proceeded to write K.386 on paper of the same type. But the evidence for this sequence is far from convincing, especially when it appears that he was possibly using that paper some months earlier than October—for example, for the wind octets, on which it is likely that he was working in about July.

It is worth noting, too, that the finale of K.414 does not begin on a new gathering, but starts on fol. 28r, the last leaf of the second gathering on which Mozart wrote the slow movement. If K.386 had been the original finale of K.414, would he not have begun to write it down on fol. 28r, immediately following the end of the slow movement? That was certainly his usual practice, although there are one or two exceptions; these appear to be instances when a finale was started before the preceding movement had been completed. (The finale of K.413, for instance, is on a different paper-type from the rest of that concerto, and its ink is of a different color; its leaves moreover are foliated from "1" to "12" rather than from "27" to "38.")

But the start of the finale of K.414 (see Figure 17.5) seems to be in the same ink as the preceding slow movement, and thus it seems likely that it was written directly after it.

To conclude: it looks as though paper-studies cannot provide a definite solution to the problem of K.386's relation to K.414. But such evidence as there is suggests that it was neither the concerto's original finale nor a proposed replacement for the movement that now ends the concerto. And unless they were added only at a late stage, Mozart's inscriptions on the first page of the K.386 autograph would tend to suggest that he did not conceive it simply as a finale.

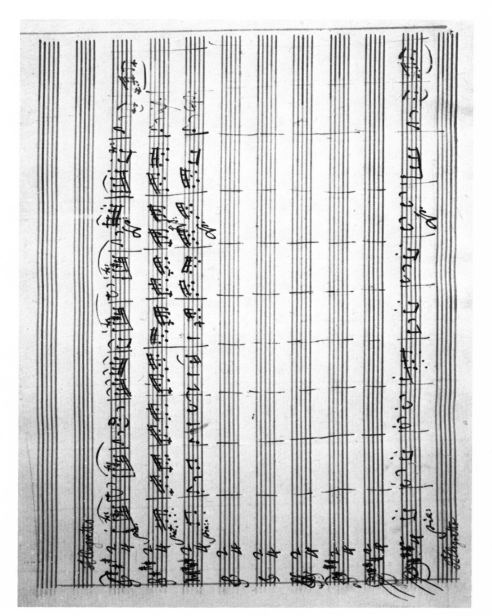

FIGURE 17.5. The A-Major Piano Concerto, K.414 (385p): fol. 28r, beginning of the finale. Biblioteka Jagiellońska, Kraków.

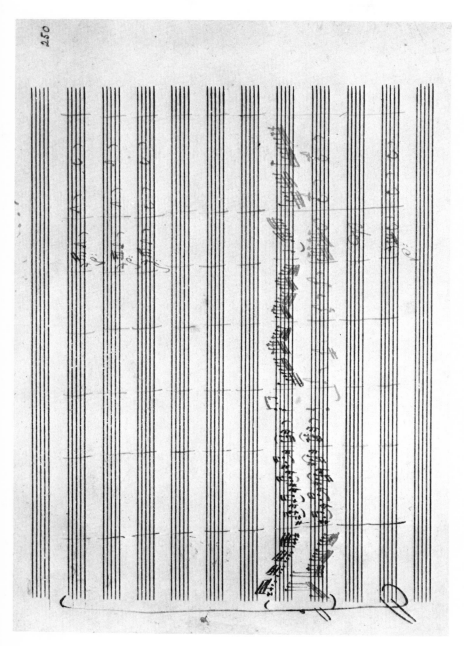

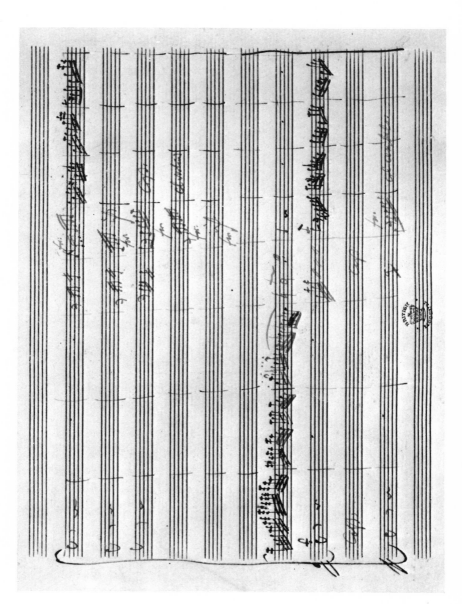

Figure 17.7. British Library, Add. MS 32181, fol. 250v.

251

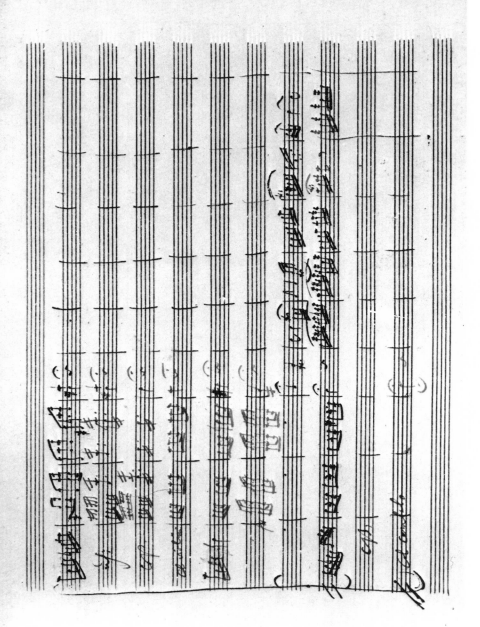

FIGURE 17.8. British Library, Add. MS 32181, fol. 251r.

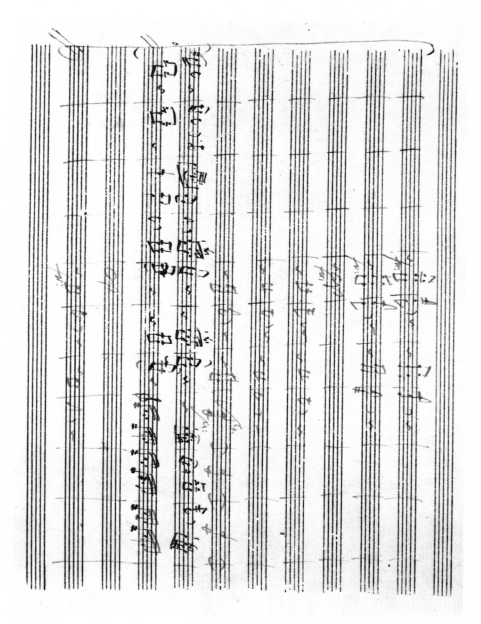

FIGURE 17.9. British Library, Add. MS 32181, fol. 251v.

252

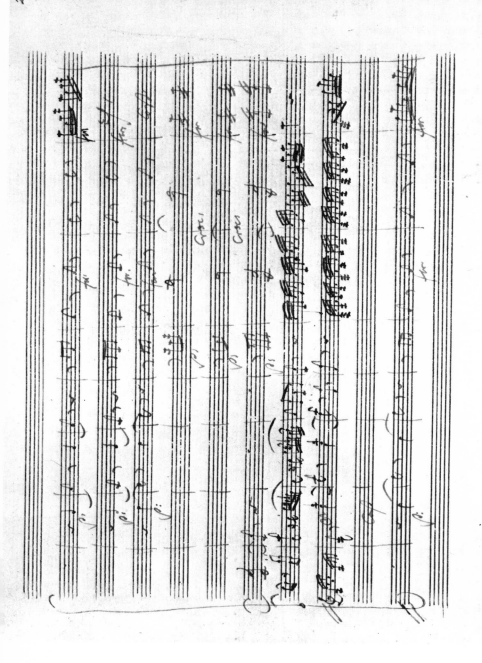

FIGURE 17.10. British Library, Add. MS 32181, fol. 252r.

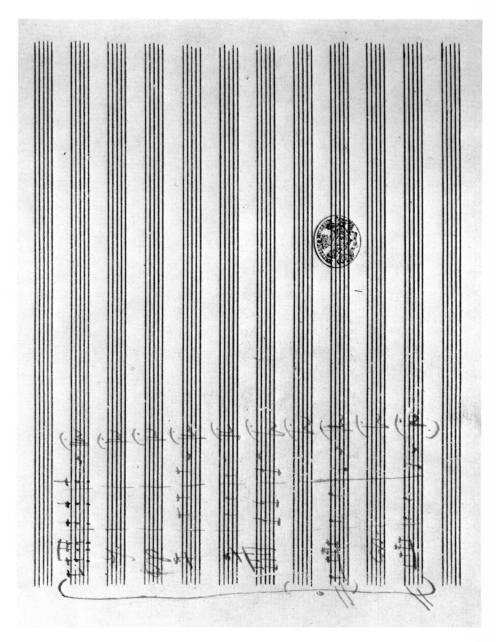

FIGURE 17.11. British Library, Add. MS 32181, fol. 252v.

THUS one gains the impression that K.386 is an independent work—independent not merely in regard to its unique scoring, but perhaps also conveying a musical atmosphere of self-sufficiency. C. M. Girdlestone has pointed out that (for a finale) "it opens with a tutti of unusual length"[27]—a possible clue that it was written for performance as a rondo movement on its own. From near the beginning of 1782 the piano concerto rondo K.382, a new finale that Mozart had written in Vienna for the D-major piano concerto of 1773, K.175, had been enjoying a great popular success whenever he played it in public; so he may have been encouraged to compose another concerto rondo, for performance as a single piece, before he had had time to complete any new concertos. Today, at any rate—perhaps for the first time since the 1780s—we are in a position to study every one of the 269 measures of K.386, and to make an assessment of the rondo as a whole. The autograph leaves with its long-lost ending are illustrated in Figures 17.6–17.11.

18

Some Problems in the Text of *Le nozze di Figaro:* Did Mozart Have a Hand in Them?

A FEW PUZZLING features in the text of *Figaro* have been discussed for a very long time within the vast literature on this opera.[1] Nevertheless, there is little in the libretto that Lorenzo Da Ponte based on Beaumarchais's revolutionary play *La Folle Journée, ou Le Mariage de Figaro,* and in the music that Mozart then provided for it, which is really problematical. After all, almost the entirety of Mozart's long autograph score has come down to us, even though today Acts I and II are divided geographically from Acts III and IV—the first two acts being in the Deutsche Staatsbibliothek, Berlin (DDR), and the last two (which left the Berlin library in World War II) being at present in the Biblioteka Jagiellońska at Kraków in Poland. (The whole autograph is fortunately accessible today.) It would seem that the only portions that have not come down to us in Mozart's handwriting are a couple of passages for recitative and some of the supplementary wind parts for the last act's finale; we have these merely in the handwriting of copyists, included inter alia in scores made for early performances or for sale in Vienna and other cities. Several of these copyists' scores will shortly be discussed here.

Thus the text of the opera is basically in very good shape. But if one approaches it in an enquiring, or suspicious, frame of mind, it is possible to discover some loose ends or slightly ambiguous elements. Nor is that altogether surprising when one reflects on the complexity of putting together a work like *Le nozze di Figaro.* Indeed, some of the problems of changing Beaumarchais's extended play into a shorter opera, with fewer characters and four acts instead of five, are discussed by Da Ponte in his preface to the libretto. In his turn, Mozart will have written different numbers at different times, *not* in their final sequence—occasionally revising them to improve their dramatic effectiveness or to adapt them more closely to a particular singer's vocal skills or limitations. He may have pressed Da Ponte to make small changes in the libretto; and late in his work on the opera he will have completed the scoring and composed the *secco* recitatives linking the numbers—but only after the sequence of the numbers was thought to have been finally settled, since the recitatives provide the links between their keys.

All these loose leaves of the autograph (or rather, in most cases, bifolia—that is, double leaves) will then have needed to be assembled in the right sequence, perhaps paginated or foliated, and sent to the court copyist (*Hofkopist*) for an official working copy of the score to be made, along with copies of the vocal and orchestral parts, for use in the court opera house. In the case of most operas it seems to have been this copy of the score made by the court copyist or his team of assistants, and not the opera composer's original autograph, that served as the basis for the making of other manuscript scores for circulation to other cities, or for sale in Vienna and elsewhere.

THUS IT IS NOT unlikely that the complicated process of assembling all the parts of an extended work may result in a few loose ends or ambiguous features. One or two discarded passages may not have been destroyed, and may survive to perplex us. A number of alterations may have been made within the autograph score, so that it displays a first and a second version of certain passages, probably superimposed. On the other hand, a few short sections, written or revised at the last minute, may not have found their way into the autograph score—at least, not in Mozart's handwriting, though a copyist may have inserted them later.

Furthermore, in the course of an opera's first run, its composer may be persuaded to make certain changes in his already completed score, perhaps altering notes that a singer unexpectedly found difficult, or making cuts in order to tighten the dramatic effect of certain scenes or merely to shorten the length of the evening's entertainment. (And of course a revival of the opera in a later year, with a different cast, could also result in some small alterations, or even in the insertion of new numbers.)

Where would a composer record such changes? In Mozart's case we naturally turn to his autograph scores and scrutinize them very carefully. But I have come to the conclusion that after Mozart had completed a first version of an opera, and had had it copied in score by professional copyists, with performing parts also copied out for the singers and orchestral players, there would have been little point in entering most of the changes in his autograph score. Instead, he would have marked the changes in the singers' own parts, and perhaps also in the *Hoftheater*'s official score made by the court copyist. In that way the changes would be circulated from then onwards, as interested parties consulted the official copy.

My views have been shaped by my experience with *Così fan tutte*, described in Chapter 13. For in 1871, when the first critical edition of that opera was prepared, using Mozart's autograph score as the basic source, it was discovered that every manuscript copy and every printed edition of *Così* made between 1790 and 1870 was characterized by a series of smallish cuts within some numbers. These cuts were unexplained (and of course since 1871 always disregarded) until about four years ago, when I examined a copyist's score in the Österreichische Nationalbibliothek, Vienna—no doubt the *Hoftheater* copy—which reproduced the autograph score's full version, but had the cuts marked in and the cut measures crossed out in pencil; in some cases the cuts were clearly marked in Mozart's writing. So Mozart evidently entered one or two changes in the official opera-house score, but not in his autograph score.

W E M U S T therefore be alert to the possibility of late changes that Mozart made in an opera—changes that are not reflected in his autograph but are to be found instead in certain copyists' full scores (which I shall refer to here as *Abschriften*). Yet the aesthetic aspects of such changes are sometimes a bit perplexing to us. For in several cases the alterations, even if it is clear that Mozart himself made them, may not gain our complete approval. We do not, for instance, like the cuts in *Così*, and perhaps we would hope to claim that he was forced to make them, against his better judgment or against his wishes. Sometimes, too, new numbers for a new singer in an opera's revival, however effective purely as vocal pieces, may seem a little inappropriate to the stage character as we have hitherto viewed him or her.

We ought therefore to be looking at the early *Abschriften* of the operas for clues as to possible changes that Mozart made in the works after the autograph score had been copied and even the first version of the music distributed. The principal problem here, of course, is that people apart from Mozart may have introduced changes: how are we to tell Mozart's from those of producers, or singers, or even of inaccurate copyists? There is no absolutely certain way, it would appear; we need to judge each case separately and with much care; and we should do our best in the first place to determine the approximate dates and the provenance of every one of all such scores.

It is hardly surprising that a lot of old *Abschriften* have survived in the case of an opera as popular as *Figaro*. Nine of them are listed in Köchel[6]. Yet with the partial exception of four of them—the ones at Donaueschingen, Florence, Berlin (DDR), and Budapest—practically nothing seems to have been published that attempts to identify their places of origin, or to date them, or even to describe any unusual features within them. So for the purpose of the present investigation I shall now provide some brief notes on thirteen early *Abschriften*, including the nine listed in Köchel[6].

Unless stated otherwise, the text originally entered by the copyist was Italian (though a German text was often added later in another hand). But a few *Abschriften* have the original text in German, usually without any *secco* recitatives; the opera was evidently performed as a Singspiel. The appraisal of each score's place of origin, and the estimate of its approximate date, derive from an examination of the types of paper (and their watermarks) from which it is made up. For although the times at which copyists used certain paper-types are not necessarily identical with the times at which these were used by the great composers Mozart, Haydn, and Beethoven for their easily dated scores, they are usually pretty similar.

H ERE THEN are brief notes on thirteen *Abschriften:*

(1) Modena, Biblioteca Estense, Mus.F.791. All four acts, in two volumes. The Act I title page runs: "Le Nozze di Figaro / Comedia per Musica / in Quattro Atti / Rappresentata nel Teatro di Corte / a Vienna L'Anno 1786 / La Musica è del Sig^{re} Wolfg. Ama: Mozart."

Apparently of Viennese origin, and very early; a date of 1786, or 1787, or perhaps 1788 is probable.

(2) London, British Library, Add. MS 16055 and 16056. All four acts, in two volumes. The Act I title page, a faulty replacement (on English "Whatman" paper) of the original one, which was no doubt damaged, runs: "Le Nozze di Figaro / o sia / La folle giernata / Comedia per Musica / Tiratta dal Francese / in quattro Atti / La Musica à del Signor Wolffgango Mozart."

This *Abschrift* was bequeathed to the British Museum in 1846, along with a great many other opera scores, by the famous double-bass player Domenico Dragonetti. Apparently of Viennese origin, and very early: probably 1786 or 1787.

(3) Berlin, Deutsche Staatsbibliothek, K-H/M 3056. Acts I and II only. The Act I title page runs: "Le / Nozze di Figaro / Comedia per Musica / Tratta dal Francese / in quattro Atti / Rappresentata nel Teatro di Praga l'Anno 1787. / La Musica è del Signor Volfgango Mozart."[2]

The paper on which this is written is a Bohemian one. The score may well have been copied in 1787 or 1788. It was used for a performance at Potsdam in 1790.

(4) Budapest, Országos Széchényi Könyvtár, Ms. mus. OK-11/a-3. Acts III and IV only.

This *Abschrift* (together with some accompanying vocal parts) is certainly no later than 1789—for which there is some useful external evidence. As is described in detail in Dénes Bartha's and László Somfai's book on Haydn as the director of operas, Haydn planned to produce *Figaro* at Eszterháza in 1790. There is a bill presented to Eszterháza on 13 July 1789, with Haydn's signature on it, in which the theater director, Nunziato Porta, reports on his expenditure of 120 florins in buying in Vienna three opera scores, one of them being *Le nozze di Figaro*, and also the singers' parts for the same opera. But for reasons that are not clear, *Figaro* was not produced at Eszterháza in 1790.[3]

(5) Donaueschingen, Fürstlich Fürstenbergische Hofbibliothek, Mus. Ms. 1393 and 1393/II. Acts I and II only, in two volumes. The Act I title page runs: "Le Nozze di Figaro / Comedia per Musica / in quattro Atti / La Musica del Sig.re Volfg: Amad: Mozart."[4]

The paper on which the two acts are written is a Bohemian one—the same type that Mozart used in Prague in the late summer of 1787 to finish *Don Giovanni*. The text is in Italian. But the opera was performed in German at Donaueschingen on 23 September 1787, as is indicated both by the local libretto and by locally produced parts for the singers. It would appear that this *Abschrift* was produced in Prague in 1786 or 1787.

(6) Florence, Conservatorio di Musica "Luigi Cherubini," F.P.T. 262 (formerly A.262). All four acts, in four volumes. The Act I title page merely states: "Partitura. / Le Nozze di Figaro. / Atto Primo / Del Sig.r Mozart."[5]

The paper-types suggest a Viennese origin; and on the Act I title page are the penciled words (later inked over): "Lausch copista del tempo Di Mozart." The watermarks are those found in Viennese manuscripts around the years 1803–1806, so a date close to the middle of the first decade of the nineteenth century seems likely.

(7) London, British Library, Royal Music Library, R.M. 22. i. 3–5. All four acts, in three volumes (Acts III and IV bound together). The Act I title page runs: "Le Nozze di Figaro / Opera / in / Quattro Atti / Del Sig: Wolfg: Ama: Mozart. / Atto Primo."

The paper-types suggest a Viennese origin, and a date close to the middle of the first decade of the nineteenth century.

(8) Bergamo, Conservatorio di Musica "Gaetano Donizetti," 627/10551. All four acts, in four volumes. The Act I title page runs: "Le Nozze di Figaro / Opera / in Quattro Atti / Del Sig. Wolfg. Amadeo Mozart." The text is in German (except for Basilio's Act IV aria, which was first given an Italian text); there are no *secco* recitatives.

According to Köchel[6], the copyist was Johann Elssler, junior. The paper-types suggest that this *Abschrift* originated in Vienna in the early years of the nineteenth century.

(9) Vienna, Österreichische Nationalbibliothek, O.A. 295. This copy is described in Köchel[6] as the "Direktionsexemplar der k.k. Hoftheater." All four acts, in four volumes (with modern binding). Most of the text is in German.

No doubt this *Abschrift* is from Vienna. Much of it is on a type of Bohemian paper from the firm of Kiesling, but that became widely used in Vienna, though not before the second decade of the nineteenth century. The whole of Act II, however, except for the finale, is on a much older paper, used in Vienna in the second half of the 1780s, and therefore worthy of our attention.

(10) Vienna, Österreichische Nationalbibliothek, KT 315 (that is, from the Kärnthnerthortheater). This is a collection of thirteen volumes, the contents being different parts of the opera, copied at very different dates, sometimes including music not by Mozart, as well as scoring that includes harps and trombones. Some volumes have a German text and no *secco* recitatives (only the words, on tipped-in blue letter paper). But others have the Italian text and the *secco* recitatives.

Most of the volumes are from Vienna, on paper of the first, or more often the second, decade of the nineteenth century. But portions of two volumes, one containing Act III, and one Act IV, probably date from the 1780s, and merit investigation.

(11) Brno, Moravské Museum, A 17037 a-d. All four acts, in four volumes. German text throughout, and no *secco* recitatives.

This *Abschrift* probably originated in Vienna in about 1803, to judge from the principal paper-type.

(12) Brno, Moravské Museum, A 17970 a-c (also known as A 339). Acts I–III only, in three volumes. The basic text is Italian, but there are no *secco* recitatives; a German text has been added.

This *Abschrift* seems also to have come from Vienna, and to have been made in about 1802–03.

(13) Berlin, Staatsbibliothek Preussischer Kulturbesitz, Mus. ms. 15150. All four acts in two volumes.[6]

Most of this *Abschrift* appears to have been assembled in Vienna in about 1802 or 1803. But one or two sections are older, from about 1790. Some numbers appear originally to have been copied for individual sale, with separate title pages (not carrying any music); but the wording on each of these title pages was later erased, and the page rendered blank in this way was then used for entering part of the number's preceding recitative. Thus certain numbers that had been copied individually earlier were taken into this *Abschrift*.

IT WOULD APPEAR, therefore, that five of these thirteen *Abschriften* were totally copied in the first four years of the opera's existence: three of them (the ones in Modena, Budapest, and London—Dragonetti's copy) were produced in Vienna; and the other two (the ones in Donaueschingen and in the Deutsche Staatsbibliothek, Berlin) were copied in or near Prague. It is appropriate accordingly to recall the early performances of the opera in these two cities. After the first performance in Vienna on 1 May 1786, it was given there three more times in May, and once in each of the months of July, August, September, November, and December. But these nine Viennese performances of 1786 were not followed by any others in that city in 1787 or 1788. In Prague, however, *Figaro* enjoyed great popularity from the time of its first performance there, probably in late November or at the beginning of December 1786; and four days after his arrival at Prague on a visit, Mozart wrote the famous letter of 15 January 1787 to his friend in Vienna, Baron Gottfried von Jacquin, in which he reported: "For here nothing is talked about except *Figaro;* nothing is played, blown, sung, and whistled except Figaro; no opera draws the crowds like *Figaro*—it's always *Figaro*. Certainly it's a great honor for me."[7] It was not until 29 August 1789 that *Figaro* was revived in Vienna; and since the cast was different from that of 1786, Mozart revised the opera in a number of small ways. For Susanna he wrote two new numbers: the aria "Un moto di gioia," K.579, to replace "Venite, inginocchiatevi" in Act II, and the rondò "Al desio, di chi t'adora," K.577, to replace "Deh vieni non tardar" in Act IV. But we need to consider carefully whether there were other changes as well.

If one can get two *Abschriften* together on a desk, or perhaps view them together on microfilms or in print-outs, one is often in for a surprise. Naturally any differences between them will stimulate one's curiosity. But one *may* see, on page after page, exactly the same text, exactly the same page-turnovers, perhaps even the same mistakes. Thus it will be obvious that one is copied from the other—or more likely, both from a common source. (Could that be the *Hoftheater* copy?) One will often find, too, that the gatherings from which the score is made up are identical in size and in contents: there will be in the upper left-hand corner of the first side of each gathering, say in the third act, the figures 1/3, 2/3, 3/3, and so on. The word that was apparently used to describe these gatherings (as mentioned above in Chapter 13) was "ternions," a word that can elsewhere mean a gathering of three double leaves, but that seems to have been used by Viennese copyists to describe a gathering of approximately twelve leaves—for three large sheets of paper produced six bifolia, or twelve leaves.[8]

In addition to the early *Abschriften*, some interesting information is provided by a few of the early libretti shown in Figure 18.1. The libretto produced for the opera's first performance (in Vienna) survives in only two or three copies: the most familiar is the one in the Library of Congress, Washington, D.C. There are copies of the libretto for the first Prague production, near the end of 1786, in the Museum české hudby, Prague, and in the Vienna Stadtbibliothek. The libretto for the 1787 Donaueschingen performance is to be found in the Hofbibliothek at Donaueschingen, and there is also a slightly defective copy in the Gesellschaft der Musikfreunde, Vienna.

Some early manuscript vocal scores can also provide helpful information. An arrangement of most of the numbers for voice and pianoforte was advertised in the *Wiener Zeitung* by the copying firm of Laurent Lausch as early as 1 July 1786. Two Prague musicians also produced vocal scores of the opera: Johann Baptist Kucharz and Vincenz Maschek (Mašek). Kucharz's manuscript copies were advertised in the *Wiener Zeitung* on 6 June 1787. Yet a few may have been made earlier; for although in some copies—the one in the New York Public Library, for instance—the title page describes the opera as "Rappresentata nel Teatro di Praga l'Anno 1787," in others, such as the one in the Vienna Nationalbibliothek, that year is given as "1786" (Figure 18.2).[9] The Kucharz manuscripts, and some of the Maschek ones too, include the recitatives as well as the individual numbers.

FIGURE 18.1.
Title pages of three early libretti.
(a) Vienna, 1786. Library of Congress, Washington, D.C., Schatz 6826.
(b) Prague, 1786. Museum české hudby, Prague, B 4715.
(c) Donaueschingen, 1787. Hofbibliothe Donaueschingen, I UB 3g.

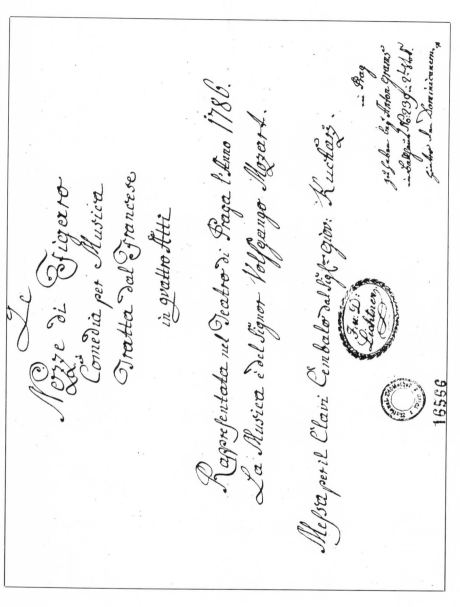

FIGURE 18.2. Title page of vocal score by Kucharz. Österreichische Nationalbibliothek, Vienna, Mus. Hs. 16566.

FIRST I propose to investigate a problem that surrounds No. 15 of
Act II, the short G-major duettino for Susanna and Cherubino, who
are nervous at finding themselves locked together in a room, while the
Count has left to fetch some tools to break down the door.[10] It begins
with Susanna's words "Aprite presto aprite" and ends with Cherubino
jumping out of the window and landing (as we later learn) on some
carnations, before fleeing into the distance.

What is the problem? In 1970 Karl-Heinz Köhler drew attention to
a curious feature of the *Abschrift* in the Deutsche Staatsbibliothek,
Berlin, listed above as an early score of Acts I and II only, written on
Bohemian paper.[11] After the recitative that concludes with the Count's
(and Countess's) exit, the Berlin score has the words of the following
duettino, "Aprite presto aprite," in the form of a *secco* recitative, although that is later followed by the familiar G-major duettino version.
Köhler claimed that Mozart's original setting of the words was as a

FIGURE 18.3. First page of recitative version of duettino, Act II,
No. 15. British Library, London, Add. MS 16055, fol. 209r.

FIGURE 18.4. First page of duettino, Act II, No. 15, tipped in on Prague paper. British Library, London, Add. MS 16055, fol. 202r.

recitative, and that the dramatic nature of the stage situation encouraged him later to compose the familiar duettino version.

I first came across "Aprite presto aprite" set as a recitative elsewhere: in the British Library's *Abschrift* presented by Dragonetti, a score described above as apparently copied very early in Vienna, probably in 1786 or 1787. Curiously enough, some leaves with the duettino version had also been tipped into that score after it had been completed; but unlike the rest of the *Abschrift,* they are on Prague paper (and in a different handwriting—see Figures 18.3 and 18.4).

Köhler described what he had found in the Berlin *Abschrift* as "ein sonst nirgends überliefertes Rezitativ," a recitative that had not been transmitted anywhere else; and he also repeated the claim made much earlier by Strasser that the Berlin score contained a number of features showing that it had been copied *directly* from the autograph.[12] But I cannot accept either of these viewpoints. For the features that are thought to link the Berlin score closely with the autograph are found in most other early *Abschriften* of Viennese origin, suggesting that they are all derived from a master copy (the *Hoftheater* copy?). And the recitative version of "Aprite presto aprite" is to be found in most of the early Viennese manuscripts: not only in the Dragonetti copy, as already mentioned, but also in the early *Abschrift* in Modena.[13] And although only Acts III and IV of the Budapest *Abschrift* have survived, we have a separate performance part for Cherubino which contains the recitatives for all four acts; here too we have the recitative version, not the duettino.

Thus I have reached the conclusion that the early *Abschriften* of Viennese origin all included the recitative version, and that the Berlin score, although on Prague paper, must have been copied directly from a Viennese *Abschrift*.

WHAT, then, is the relation between the two versions, whether or not we choose to think they are both by Mozart? I cannot accept Köhler's view that the recitative version was the first to be written. For not only was the duettino, to judge from its paper-type,[14] obviously composed quite early among the individual numbers of the opera, but (as Köhler himself points out) there are several melodic similarities between the recitative and the duettino versions; and these must surely represent an adaptation of the duettino as a recitative, not a conversion of the recitative into the duettino. It seems a plausible notion, therefore, that the recitative version was prepared as a "stand-by," after difficulties had been experienced with the performance of the duettino. Conductors and producers still sometimes describe it as a difficult number.

Here is some evidence that it was found to be difficult in Mozart's day. Before the opera was completed, Mozart started to draft an alternative version of the duettino (Figure 18.5). These four and a half measures are labeled: "invece del Duetto di Susaña e Cherubino"; perhaps he thought that an opening in contrary motion was a good way to depict the contrary movements of Susanna and Cherubino. That it was written fairly late in his work on *Figaro* is indicated by its paper-type;[15] but that the opera had not yet been totally finished when he started and later abandoned this new duettino is shown by the late sketches that he subsequently wrote on its other side: these are sketches for Susanna's "garden" aria in its final form, and a brief sketch for the second subject of the overture.[16]

But can we connect the recitative version with Mozart himself?

FIGURE 18.5. Draft by Mozart to replace the duettino, Act II, No. 15.
In private ownership, New York.

There are clues within the autograph score, which I myself came across before I discovered that Köhler had noticed them earlier. The opera's preceding number, No. 14, the terzetto, ends on the page of the autograph bearing the page number 215; page 216 carries the recitative that precedes the duettino, although strangely enough that short recitative is not in Mozart's hand but in the hand of a copyist. The first page of the duettino has the page number 219, so today there is no leaf with the page numbers 217–218 within the score.

So I suspect that at one time the autograph included this missing leaf, on which was probably written the short recitative that follows the terzetto, in Mozart's hand, and then the recitative version of the duettino, also in Mozart's hand. In other words, it would seem that at one time there were settings by Mozart of "Aprite presto aprite" both as a recitative and as a duettino next to each other in the autograph, and that they were duly paginated. Some copies reproduce this. But later someone decided to remove the recitative version, making a gap in the page numbers. (Was that "someone" Mozart?) The short recitative before it, on the same leaf, was also removed, and had therefore to be replaced by a copyist on the blank page at the end of the preceding terzetto (No. 14). Does that not explain all the facts?

Moreover, as Köhler pointed out, the leaves of the Act II autograph with recitatives on them have their own separate foliation in pencil, which runs from 1 to 12—but there is no fol. 8, which should have come at about this point in the autograph. This is further evidence that a leaf of the autograph has been removed; it is even possible to predict the paper-type and the watermark quadrant of the missing leaf.[17]

These clues that the autograph once contained a leaf with the recitative version of "Aprite presto aprite" are the strongest evidence that that version was in fact written by Mozart.

THE NEXT PROBLEM that I want to consider concerns the number preceding the duettino that we have just examined: this is No. 14 in Act II, the terzetto for the Count, the Countess, and Susanna, beginning with the words "Susanna or via sortite." The problem posed by one feature of this terzetto is well known, having been discussed in the literature from the time of Jahn onwards.[18] It concerns the relative roles of the Countess and Susanna: when they sing together, who has the higher part?

The facts about the autograph's version (or rather, versions) have not always been accurately described. There are not many scenes in the opera in which the Countess and Susanna are both on the stage, and sing together. But where they do, it is important to examine the autograph to see what Mozart first wrote, and what changes, if any, he later introduced. If one does that, one sees that in the terzetto, No. 14, and in the Act II finale, the Countess was always in the first place given the upper staff, and (except in a very few short phrases) the higher part. But later in the opera, in the Act III "letter" duettino, for instance, and throughout the Act IV finale, one can observe that Susanna was from the first always given the upper staff and almost all the higher notes.

So by the time he was writing out Acts III and IV, Mozart seems to have known that the singer who was to take the role of Susanna should be given the higher part. This, however, had evidently not been the case a little earlier, when he was first writing down the Act II finale. A scrutiny of that finale is instructive; for it can be seen that again and again Mozart made further entries in order to exchange the notes originally assigned to each of the two characters. He would often write "Sus:" before some passage on the higher staff (the Countess's), and "La Con:" on Susanna's staff below it. Such an exchange of notes was easy to introduce, for instance, at places where the sopranos were singing the same words in thirds; but in a few passages where the Countess's words were different from Susanna's it was not enough for Mozart merely to reallocate the staves—he had to delete each character's words and replace them by the other's (as in mm. 246–253).

It seems to be the case that these changes made by Mozart in the autograph of the Act II finale have never been questioned or challenged, and (with one exception)[19] have been adopted by all scores of the opera from Mozart's time to the present day. But the problem of the terzetto, No. 14, is less straightforward.

When he first wrote down the terzetto, as already stated, Mozart gave the Countess the upper staff and the higher part. But he later began to reverse the roles of the two characters at several places: in mm. 12–14, for instance, he crossed out some of the Countess's high notes and entered them on Susanna's staff, Susanna's lower notes being then entered on the Countess's staff; and in m. 30 he wrote "La Con:" against Susanna's notes, and in m. 32 "Sus:" against the Countess's notes (see Figure 18.6). Here new words had also to be given to the two sopranos. But although there were one or two further

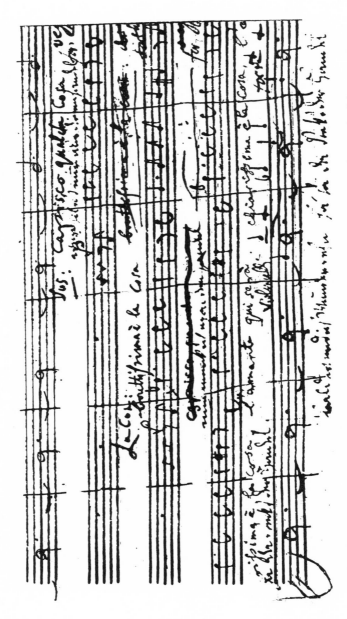

FIGURE 18.6. Part of page 204 of the Act II autograph, showing some changes by Mozart in mm. 30–34 of the terzetto, No. 14. Deutsche Staatsbibliothek, Berlin, DDR.

changes made by Mozart to his autograph (for example, in mm. 40–45), the Countess still retained most of her part, running up in coloratura passages to c''' at mm. 117 and 132. Thus the autograph version, even though amended in places, did not rob the Countess of most of her high notes.

Yet the text of the terzetto provided by the autograph's final version seems to have been virtually unknown until this century. All the old *Abschriften* (with one exception already mentioned) and all the printed scores of the opera, including the one in the AMA, provide a different text in which Susanna has the higher part throughout this number, just as she has in Mozart's amended version of the Act II finale and in Acts III and IV. It is, for instance, Susanna who sings the runs ending with c''' in mm. 117 and 132. Thus we should search for the reason why this version of the terzetto (which I shall call "the conventional version") has had an almost exclusive circulation for practically two centuries, while for much of that time the autograph's text has remained almost unknown.[20]

My conclusion is that the version of the terzetto found in virtually all manuscript copies and printed scores is indeed by Mozart, and that it represents a continuation by him of the changes that he started to make in the autograph but then ceased to carry out there. One can imagine a scene at a rehearsal of *Figaro*, at which Luisa Laschi, the soprano who sang the Countess, was having some difficulty with her part in places; Mozart would have said to her, and to Nancy Storace, the soprano who was Susanna: "Lend me your solo parts for a minute or two; I've thought of some changes that will make this number easier for you both." He would then have entered several changes in the *Hoftheater Abschrift* and in the performance parts; the result of this would have been that all the other copies subsequently made from the *Hoftheater* copy would incorporate these changes. But there is no likelihood that at the rehearsal Mozart would have said: "Before I make any changes I must go back to my apartment and get my autograph and make the changes first in that." In other words, I believe that the conventional version of the terzetto incorporates quite a large quantity of Mozart's revisions to that number—far more than he found it convenient, or practical, to make in his autograph.

In referring above to some of the cuts to be found in *Così fan tutte*, I suggested that even if they can be shown to derive from Mozart, they may not have our approval; perhaps indeed Mozart was forced to make them against his better judgment. In the same way we may accept the fact that Mozart found himself obliged to give Susanna a higher vocal line than he had given to the Countess at various places in the opera; but although he did it for practical purposes—it might seem that Nancy Storace was better to be trusted with the high notes than Luisa Laschi[21]—he may not have done it very willingly, and we too may regret the seemingly permanent nature of his amendments. In the terzetto, as some have pointed out, Susanna is supposed to be in hiding; should she be singing those shrill chromatic passages near the end that lead to a high c′′′? And as others have claimed, some of the melodic figures given at first to the Countess are more dignified, more legato, or more soaring than the lower broken-up phrases given at first to Susanna. If Mozart then exchanged the parts, was he perhaps blurring his own sophisticated musical characterization of the two characters?

Perhaps Mozart himself felt that if he continued to alter his autograph throughout the terzetto, it would never be possible to restore his original musical characterization, even when at a later date he had a Countess who found the original high notes easy. And perhaps this is the reason why he gave up making changes in the autograph; it may have seemed wiser to continue them in the opera-house's working copies. Nevertheless, there are difficulties for us today in recreating a Countess with the higher role; for although in the terzetto and in the Act II finale it is always possible to perceive what was Mozart's original version before his changes were made, in Acts III and IV he had apparently abandoned the notion of giving the Countess the higher role before anything was written down. The NMA text simply adopts the present version of the autograph, accepting the small number of changes in the terzetto and the ones that run through the Act II finale. To restore the concept of the Countess in the higher role would mean to reject all these changes within Act II, and to amend Acts III and IV in a way for which Mozart provides no earlier model.

If the heavily amended conventional version of the terzetto was the one that found a place in virtually all *Abschriften* and printed scores, was the original version totally unavailable, except to those who continued to have access to the autograph? I have found some evidence to the contrary. The Budapest *Abschrift,* described above, consists of Acts III and IV only, but there are some performance parts made, like the score, in 1789, for all four acts; the Countess's part has the three voices and the bass for the terzetto, written on the same paper-type as the *Abschrift*. This performance part has mm. 1–96 of the conventional version, and then mm. 97–146 (the end) in what is mostly the autograph's version, followed by mm. 97–146 in the conventional version. The gathering structure and the handwriting show that both versions were written out at the same time; the version of mm. 97–146 that corresponds closely to the autograph has no words, only the notes, and the leaves were at some stage stitched together so that it was hidden. Thus the Viennese copying house evidently knew both versions of the last third of the terzetto, but presented them in a way that would encourage the singers to perform the amended version. Is it likely that the copying house—probably the team of the *Hofkopist* Sukowaty—had made a very early master copy of the original version of the terzetto, before Mozart started to alter it? (Yet it was only the measures from 97 to the end that were circulated in two versions.)[22] Although it seems clear that the main changes in the terzetto were made as early as 1786—probably even before the first performance of the opera—since they are found in the earliest *Abschriften*, the evidence offered by the Budapest vocal part for the terzetto is that something of the earliest version was still known in a Viennese copying house in 1789.

Yet it was virtually always the amended version that was circulated. Curiously enough, the conventional version also includes a long series of small rhythmic deviations from the autograph which are suggestive of changes made at rehearsals. Instead of a half note followed by a quarter note, for instance, there is a half note tied to an eighth note, and then followed by an eighth note, in the following measures: 43 (Susanna and Countess); 52 (Count); 84, 85, 87, 88 (Count). These and many other small deviations from the autograph help to confirm the impression that the conventional version is the one that Mozart authorized in 1786.[23]

Thus there seems to me to be a strong case for continuing to perform the conventional version of the terzetto, even if we would have preferred the Countess to have retained the higher soprano part.

THE *Abschrift* of the first two acts of *Figaro* in the Fürstlich Fürstenbergische Hofbibliothek at Donaueschingen is an interesting though in some ways a puzzling score. Its peculiarities have received some attention in the literature: Anheisser, for instance, thought that its singular features identified it as a version of the opera even earlier than the autograph, as the *"Urfassung"* of *Figaro*. The unusual aspects that have attracted most attention are (a) the omission of sixty-nine measures (mm. 398–466) in the Act II finale, the whole of the Andante in 2/4 meter beginning "Conoscete Signor Figaro"; (b) the omission of Cherubino's first aria, "Non so più cosa son, cosa faccio," No. 6 of Act I; and (c) the inclusion of a strange cavatina in C major for Marcellina, "Signora mia garbata," as a replacement for the preceding number, No. 5, the A-major duet between Marcellina and Susanna in which they curtsey to each other and then fall out. Alfred Einstein published this cavatina in 1931, believing it to be an unknown piece by Mozart, though he later changed his mind about that.[24]

It seems likely that Einstein's second thoughts were better here than his first ones. But at least we are in a good position today to identify the place where this cavatina and the other peculiarities of the Donaueschingen *Abschrift* originated. It was clearly Prague. As mentioned above, the copy was made on Bohemian paper, and its peculiar features are found in other Prague sources: the Prague libretto of 1786, and the vocal score of Act I by Vincenz Maschek,[25] both of which omit Cherubino's first aria and include "Signora mia garbata" instead of the duettino No. 5 for Susanna and Marcellina.

Another peculiarity of the Donaueschingen *Abschrift* is the general granting of a higher part to the Countess than to Susanna in the terzetto, No. 14, and the Act II finale. But a careful examination of this score should convince one that it is not the *Urfassung* of the first half of the opera; its version of the terzetto, for instance, includes several of the later changes that Mozart made in his autograph, cuts out quite a number of measures, and assigns the higher part to the Countess even in places where the autograph gave the higher part to Susanna from the very first (for example, mm. 9–12). This would suggest that the Prague opera house was prepared to make a number of unauthorized changes in the score: the Prague libretto and the Donaueschingen *Abschrift* show that words of the recitatives were also changed or cut in a number of places.

Although only Acts I and II of the Donaueschingen *Abschrift* have come down to us, it is possible to gain some idea as to the contents of Acts III and IV, from the libretti of Prague, and of the 1787 Donaueschingen performance (though this was in German and was given as a Singspiel, with the recitatives not sung), and from a number of the 1787 performance parts. The latter are not on Prague paper, but on paper made by the firm of Georg Schild of Stein am Rhein, who took over the princely paper mill near Donaueschingen in 1785; nevertheless, their contents are a good indication as to the characteristic features of the Prague version of the opera in all four acts.[26]

The only question is whether Mozart had any hand in the peculiarities of the Prague version. I am inclined to suppose that he did not—not least because the vocal scores by Kucharz, produced in Prague at the end of 1786 or in 1787, seem to reproduce the conventional version of the opera.

WHATEVER problems are raised by versions of the opera that originated in Prague, we are naturally more concerned about peculiar features deriving from Vienna. One of these is a puzzle associated with the Fandango, the forty-three Andante measures in 3/4 meter near the end of Act III. During this short passage there is some dancing on stage; the Count, who has pricked his finger on the pin sealing the letter of "assignation" that he has just received from Susanna, shows that he understands what role the pin has still to play; and Figaro, who has joined in the dancing, makes some comments on the situation to Susanna.

The words of the Count and Figaro amount to only eight lines of text; these are included both in the Viennese and in the Prague libretti of 1786. The puzzle here is that a great many *Abschriften* do not contain the Fandango: it is not to be found, for instance, in those listed above as being in Modena, Budapest, Florence, West Berlin, Brno (two scores), or in the Royal Music Library (British Library). Even though it is in the Dragonetti *Abschrift* in the British Library, it is not part of the score's original leaves, but is tipped in on Prague paper.

The implication of this last fact would seem to be that the Fandango was suppressed in Vienna but survived in Prague. One finds it, for instance, in the vocal scores by Kucharz produced in the latter city. It is clear, moreover, that it was heard at the 1787 performance in Donaueschingen; for although Acts III and IV have not come down to us in score from there, the locally produced vocal parts for the Count and for Figaro include the Fandango, and the eight lines that they sang during it are in the 1787 Donaueschingen libretto.

From the point of view of the autograph, the Fandango was never a separate piece or number: it begins in the middle of page 117 in the Act III autograph and ends after the first measure on page 123, where it is followed by a Maestoso *recitativo accompagnato*. Although the Fandango is basically in the key of A minor, and ends in that key, its very first measure is in C major, the key of the passage that preceded it. So when it was decided to leave it out, an embarrassing confrontation was produced between C major and A minor. In the autograph the Maestoso's first measure passes from A minor to the dominant of G major; but in the *Abschriften* that omit the Fandango it is changed, passing instead from C major to the dominant of G major (see Figure 18.7). It would appear, therefore, that some master copy (the *Hoftheater* copy?) was prepared in a way to facilitate the omission of the Fandango.

If one searches for a reason for the omission of the Fandango from so many *Abschriften*, one finds a possible explanation in the contents of an anecdote told by Da Ponte in his memoirs.[27] Count Rosenberg sent for Da Ponte just a couple of days before the opera's dress rehearsal and asked whether it included a ballet. Da Ponte replied that it did, and Rosenberg asked him whether he knew that the Emperor did not wish to have ballets in the theater. When Da Ponte denied this, Rosenberg told him that the ballet in *Figaro* must be removed. He also asked to be shown the ballet scene in the libretto, and tore out two leaves and threw them on the fire.

Two days later, however, the Emperor accepted Da Ponte's invitation to attend the dress rehearsal, and he was puzzled when near the end of Act III the Count and Susanna were gesticulating on the stage; for since the orchestra was silent, it looked like a puppet show. Da Ponte, asked to explain the situation, merely presented the Emperor with his libretto, in which he had restored the torn-out scene. The Emperor then asked Rosenberg why there was no dancing and was told that the opera had no dancers; he proposed that ballerinas should be obtained from other theatres, "and in less than half an hour twenty-four dancers and extras had arrived, and the end of the third act,[28] which had been omitted, was repeated, and the Emperor cried: 'Now it's fine like that!'"

Assuming that this and other anecdotes in Da Ponte's memoirs are to be trusted, it would appear that an effort by Count Rosenberg and his friends to suppress the Fandango—part of a general campaign to damage the opera—was unsuccessful, since the Emperor welcomed Mozart's music; and it seems that nothing was cut near the end of Act III in the opera's first production. But did Rosenberg perhaps use his powers to control the version of the opera circulated by the *Hofkopist?* Or had a number of copies already been made by the time of the dress rehearsal, with the Fandango neatly cut out, and was the need to restore the omitted passage overlooked? The fact that the version of the opera known in Prague apparently included the Fandango would seem to indicate that its elimination from copyist scores was by no means universal: Prague was evidently provided with an uncut version of the Act III finale.

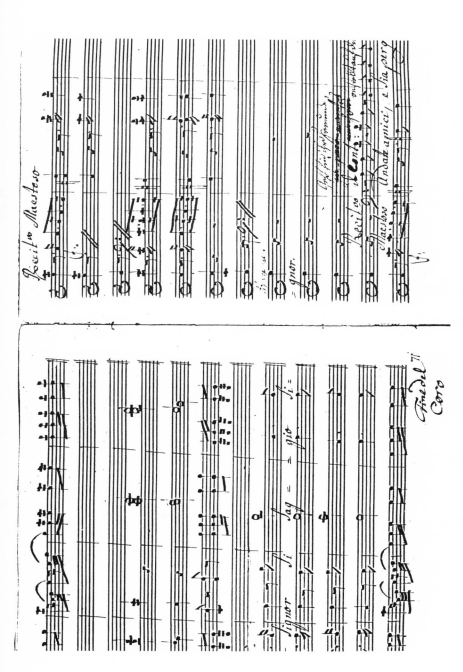

FIGURE 18.7. A score that omits the Fandango near the end of Act III. Országos Széchényi Könyvtár, Budapest, Ms. mus. OK-11/a-3, fols. 89v and 90r.

ONE OF THE SCENES in the opera that has not survived in the autograph—not having been inserted there even in the hand of a copyist—is the short one preceding the Act IV finale. But it is found, set as a recitative of a dozen measures, in a great many copyists' scores, including several of those listed earlier in this chapter (see Figure 18.8). So the omission of this recitative from the autograph has not caused any distress; the copyists' text is assumed to be what Mozart himself wrote.

Yet an inspection of this passage in the 1786 Vienna libretto raises a query regarding Cherubino's words on his entry here—his first appearance in Act IV. For whereas most *Abschriften* give him merely the words, "La la la la la la la la lera," without any notes to which to sing them, the Vienna libretto (Figure 18.9) prints those ten syllables and then the verse: "Voi che intendete / Che cosa è amor, / Donne vedete / S'io l'ho nel cor." No doubt the purpose of these lines was to enable

FIGURE 18.8. The recitative before the Act IV finale. Országos Széchényi Könyvtár, Budapest, Ms. mus. OK-11/a-3, fol. 150v.

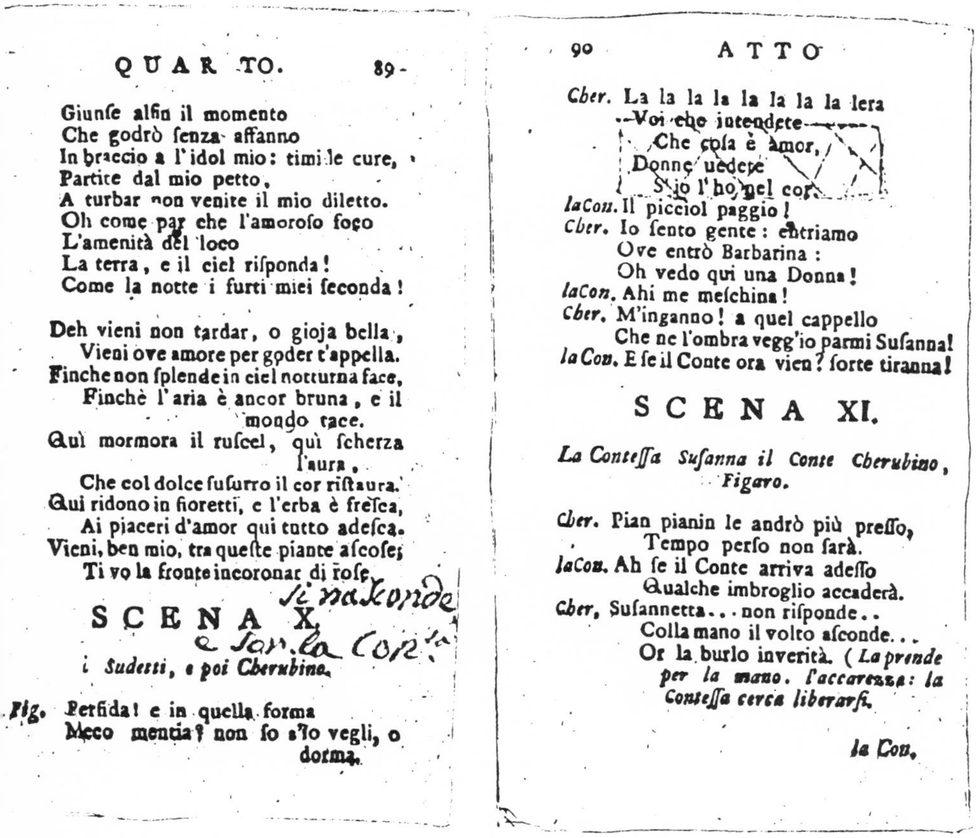

QUARTO.　　89-

Giunfe alfin il momento
Che godrò fenza affanno
In braccio a l'idol mio: timile cure,
Partite dal mio petto,
A turbar non venite il mio diletto.
Oh come par che l'amorofo foço
L'amenità del loco
La terra, e il ciel rifponda!
Come la notte i furti miei feconda!

Deh vieni non tardar, o gioja bella,
　Vieni ove amore per goder t'appella.
Finche non fplende in ciel notturna face,
　Finchè l'aria è ancor bruna, e il
　　　　mondo tace.
Quì mormora il rufcel, quì fcherza
　　　　l'aura,
Che col dolce fufurro il cor riftaura.
Qui ridono in fioretti, e l'erba è frefca,
Ai piaceri d'amor qui tutto adefca.
Vieni, ben mio, tra quefte piante afcofe;
　Ti vo la fronte incoronar di rofe,
　　　　　　　　　　　si naßconde

SCENA X.　　　*e Son la Con*

i Sudetti, e poi Cherubino.

Fig.　Perfida! e in quella forma
Meco mentia? non fo s'io vegli, o
　　　　　dorma.

90　　ATTO

Cher. La la la la la la la la lera
　--Voi che intendete------
　[--,Che cofa è Amor,
　|Donne uedete--
　|　S'io l'ho nel cor--

laCon. Il picciol paggio!
Cher. Io fento gente: entriamo
　Ove entrò Barbarina:
　Oh vedo qui una Donna!
laCon. Ahi me mefchina!
Cher. M'inganno! a quel cappello
　Che ne l'ombra vegg'io parmi Sufanna!
la Con. E fe il Conte ora vien? forte tiranna!

SCENA XI.

La Conteffa Sufanna il Conte Cherubino,
　　　Figaro.

Cher. Pian pianin le andrò più preffo,
　Tempo perfo non farà.
laCon. Ah fe il Conte arriva adeffo
　Qualche imbroglio accaderà.
Cher. Sufannetta... non rifponde..
　Colla mano il volto afconde...
　Or la burlo inventà. (La prende
　per la mano. l'accarezza: la
　Conteffa cerca liberarfi.

la Con.

FIGURE 18.9. Pages 89 and 90 of the Vienna 1786 libretto.
Library of Congress, Washington, D.C.

the character who was making his entry to be identified as Cherubino, the natural setting for them being his "signature tune." Since, however, these four lines are not to be found in any of the copyists' full scores, it has up to now been taken for granted that Mozart neglected to set them while writing this recitative passage. (Nor are the words even to be found in the 1786 Prague libretto.)

Nevertheless, there is one early source in which they are to be found, set to the melody that we would expect. In 1789, as has already been mentioned, Haydn obtained from Vienna a score of *Figaro* and a set of performance parts for a planned production at Eszterháza in 1790; these manuscripts are now in Budapest. Although the score of Act IV has the usual copyists' version of this scene, Cherubino's

FIGURE 18.10. The recitative before the Act IV finale in Cherubino's
solo part. Országos Széchényi Könyvtár, Budapest, Ms. mus.
OK-11/b-5, fol. 9r.

own part includes the verse "Voi che intendete," set to the melody of
"Voi che sapete" (see Figure 18.10).[29] Thus a setting of these lines,
otherwise known only from the Vienna 1786 libretto, was included in
performance parts copied in Vienna in the 1780s.

It remains puzzling that the Budapest copy of Cherubino's part, and
the Budapest copy of the Act IV score, have different versions of this
scene; for they were produced at the same time by the same copyist
firm—almost certainly that of Wenzel Sukowaty, the *Hofkopist*.[30] We
should ask ourselves which source is more likely to have preserved the
original version of this scene. It is possible, for instance, that Mozart
first set the whole of the libretto's text here, in the form shown in
Cherubino's part, but was later for some reason induced to cancel
Cherubino's "signature tune," a decision that resulted in the version
found in the score. And if we conclude that this cut, like some others,
was made by Mozart somewhat reluctantly, it is possible for us to restore the missing measures.

FOR MANY years now, at any rate since Michael and Christopher Raeburn published their 1959 account of "Mozart Manuscripts in Florence," interest has been expressed in one of the *Abschriften* of *Figaro* in the Conservatorio di Musica "Luigi Cherubini" in that city. This is the score mentioned above which was apparently made by the Viennese copying firm of Lausch; its date, I have suggested, is the early 1800s. It contains the new aria and the new rondò (K.579 and K.577) that Mozart wrote for the new Susanna, Adriana Gabrieli del Bene ("la Ferrarese"), when the opera was revived at Vienna in August 1789. There are, however, other deviations from the autograph's original version that need to be investigated, especially since they are found in many other *Abschriften*. The three most significant variants are the altered versions of the Act III arias both for the Count and for the Countess, and the shortened version of the Act I duettino for Marcellina and Susanna.

The best known of these variants is a high version of the latter part of the Count's aria. Although the first part, the forty-seven measures of the Allegro maestoso "Vedrò, mentre io sospiro, felice un servo mio?" is unchanged, the following Allegro assai section, "Ah no, lasciarti in pace," has been rewritten for a much higher vocal range from m. 55 onwards (see Figures 18.11 and 18.12). This high version, reproduced in the 1959 article of Michael and Christopher Raeburn, is to be found in a number of *Abschriften* dating at least from the early 1800s.

Was it written for the singer, or for one of the singers, who took the role of the Count in the 1789 Viennese revival? It is apparently not yet known who sang the Count in 1789. Although it has been suggested that it was Francesco Albertarelli, that baritone does not appear to have had a high range—to judge at any rate from the arietta that Mozart wrote especially for that voice in May 1788, "Un bacio di mano," K.541. Perhaps the part was sung (sometimes, at least) by Francesco Morella, the Don Ottavio in the Vienna performance of *Don Giovanni,* for he had made his debut in March 1788 as the Count Almaviva in Paisiello's *Il Barbiere di Siviglia.*

This high version of the end of the Count's aria is not to be found in the early *Abschriften*—those, for instance, in Modena, Budapest, and the British Library (Dragonetti)—although a quite different high version occurs in the 1787 performance part for the Count at Donaueschingen (it was sung by a tenor). But several of the *Abschriften* of Viennese origin dating from the early nineteenth century include the version found in the Florentine score. An interesting example, for in-

FIGURE 18.11–18.12. The high version of the Count's Act III aria, measures 54–61
Conservatorio di Musica "Luigi Cherubini," Florence, F.P.T. 262,
fols. 24r and 24v of Act III.

stance, is in one of the volumes in the Vienna Nationalbibliothek's collection KT 315. It has a ternion beginning at m. 54 that is numbered "3/3," with the high version; it is then followed by another ternion also beginning at m. 54, and numbered "3½/3," with the lower, regular version. Thus one forms the impression that in the early nineteenth century the Viennese copyists were in a position to provide scores that included both versions of the end of the Count's aria: the original version (as found in the autograph), and another one which may well be Mozart's revised version for the opera's 1789 revival.

THE FLORENTINE *Abschrift* is also one of many that includes an altered version of the Countess's famous Act III aria, "Dove sono." This version seems not to have been discussed in the literature, and it has remained unpublished; the changed passages of the vocal line are presented in Example 18.1, and the full score of a couple of passages in the Florentine *Abschrift* is shown in Figures 18.13 and 18.14.

* *recte*: l'in-gra-to

EXAMPLE 18.1. Variant versions of two passages in "Dove sono."

FIGURE 18.13–18.14. The new version of the Countess's aria "Dove sono":
nine measures that come after m. 83 of the regular version. Conservatorio di Musica
"Luigi Cherubini," Florence, F.P.T. 262, fols. 67r and 67v of Act III.

Apart from small changes in the cadenza near the end, the high version of the end of the Count's aria follows the basic structure of the autograph's version, even though the orchestral accompaniment has had to be modified throughout. But in the new version of "Dove sono" the melody is entirely recast in several places, with impressive new orchestral accompaniments, at first from the first violins and in a later passage from the first oboe and the first bassoon.

As with the high version of the Count's aria, it is important to note that this new version of "Dove sono" is not to be found in those *Abschriften* of the opera that have been identified as the early ones—the scores in Modena, in Budapest, and in the British Library (Dragonetti). But it is in many *Abschriften* of Viennese origin from the early nineteenth century: in two in Brno, in two in the Vienna Nationalbibliothek's collection KT 315 (in one of which four leaves with the new version's measures are inserted in the middle of a score containing the earlier version), and in the Royal Music Library score in the British Library (Figures 18.15 and 18.16). Once again, one is tempted to reach the conclusion that this revised version of "Dove sono," which evidently came from Vienna, was probably made by Mozart for the 1789 revival of the opera there.

ANOTHER VARIANT to be found in the Florentine *Abschrift* also seems to have received wide distribution. This is a cut version of the duettino, No. 5 in Act I, for Marcellina and Susanna. In Mozart's autograph it consists of seventy-four measures; but in several *Abschriften* these are reduced to forty-five, the only measures remaining being 1–16, 21, 43–58, 59 (or 63), and 64–74.

Once again the *Abschriften* that include these cuts are not among the earliest ones; in addition to the score in Florence they include the Royal Music Library's copy in the British Library, and the copy in the Staatsbibliothek Preussischer Kulturbesitz, Berlin (Mus. ms. 15150). Thus one is once again left with the impression that, since the scores containing these cuts are all of Viennese origin, the shortened version of this Act I duettino was probably prepared by Mozart for the 1789 revival of *Figaro*.

In a letter to his wife in the first half of August 1789 Mozart wrote: "*Figaro* is going to be performed very soon, and as I have some alterations to make, my presence will be required at the rehearsals."[31] What were these alterations? We know about the two new arias for Susanna, both of which are entered in his *Verzeichnüss*. But other departures

FIGURE 18.15–18.16. The new version of the Countess's aria "Dove sono":
mm. 33–36 of the regular version and six new measures. British Library, London,
R.M. 22. i. 5, fols. 66v and 67r of Act III.

from the original versions in this revival of the opera have not hitherto been detected; no record of them would necessarily be found anywhere other than in the later *Abschriften*. I am convinced that we should consider very seriously the suggestion that in August 1789 Mozart not merely supplied Susanna with a new aria and a rondò, but also provided the Count with an alternative higher version of the end of his aria, gave the Countess a new version of "Dove sono," and organized a shortened version of the duettino that is No. 5 of Act I.

To RETURN to the opera's autograph score: there are at least three places where the early pagination, found on all its leaves, shows gaps—a feature that invites some speculation as to the reason for this.

The lack of a leaf bearing the page numbers 217–218 in Act II has already been discussed. An explanation for the loss of a leaf at this place was offered: it may have contained the recitative version, found in several *Abschriften,* of the duettino No. 15, "Aprite presto aprite" (and perhaps also the preceding recitative, "Dunque voi non aprite?"), and it may well have been removed when it was found that the proper orchestral version of No. 15 could after all be successfully performed.

There is also a gap of two pages—pages 165–166—near the beginning of Act II, just after the Countess's "Porgi amor." The loss of a leaf with those page numbers is less worrying, because it was probably blank. It seems clear that in writing Act II Mozart started with the recitative "Vieni, cara Susanna," and that he decided only later to compose an opening aria for the Countess, "Porgi amor." The aria appears to have been written down on two gathered bifolia, but since it ended on the verso of the third leaf (page 164), the fourth leaf (pages 165–166), doubtless being blank, was evidently removed, although its stub still remains in the score. Mozart often used the blank pages at the end of the separate numbers for writing down the following recitatives; but I believe that this did not happen in the present case because the recitative "Vieni, cara Susanna" had already been written, beginning on page 167.

A more puzzling gap in the pagination is the lack of a leaf with the page numbers 83–84 just before the "letter" duettino for the Countess and Susanna, "Su l'aria." Page 82 of the autograph here has some odd features: the last two measures of the recitative, containing a text not to be found in the libretto or in any other score, are crossed out, and their replacement in the version that has always been adopted is entered below in the hand of a copyist. Mozart has also added the words: "Dopo il Duettino manca ancora il piccolo Recitativo." The next four leaves in the autograph, pages 85–92, have the final version of the "letter" duettino, and the short recitative that follows it.

Page 67 of Angermüller's 1986 book, *Figaro*, reproduces in color the first side of the leaf in the Internationale Stiftung Mozarteum, Salzburg, which contains a draft of the duettino, preceded by three measures of recitative. (A transcription of both sides of this leaf will be found in the NMA edition.) [32] A puzzling feature of this leaf is Mozart's words (not quoted in the NMA) in the top left-hand corner of the first side: "Dopo il Duettino." How are they to be explained? I do not believe in the theory, sometimes advanced, that Mozart originally planned to have *two* duettini here, the first now being lost (if ever written), and the second, "Su l'aria," being "dopo il [primo] duettino." That explanation seems very unlikely.

I have come to the conclusion, however, that the Mozarteum leaf probably once formed a bifolium with pages 81–82 of the autograph; thus it may well be the lost pages 83–84. [33] Possibly Mozart at first wrote only "Dopo il Duettino" in its top left-hand corner, intending to insert several leaves with "Su l'aria" before it (and after pages 81–82), and later to write on it the short recitative following that duettino. But he then started to write on it a new ending for the earlier recitative, to replace the one he had cancelled on page 82, and to follow that with a score of the duettino; later, when the score ran into difficulties, he removed the leaf and inserted the four leaves, pages 85–92, with the duettino's final version, and its following recitative as well. There is today what is apparently the stub of a lost leaf in the autograph after page 92; if I am right, it is the stub of a leaf that was originally pages 83–84, and is today in the Mozarteum in Salzburg.

THERE IS ONE more problem in the Act III autograph that appears to have escaped discussion so far. It relates to some small changes temporarily made by Mozart in the words that were to be sung by the six characters near the end of the sestetto, one of Mozart's favorite pieces. In the text that he set, Susanna, Figaro, Bartolo, and Marcellina have the following lines:

Al dolce contento
Di questo momento
Quest' anima appena
Resister or sà.

The Count and Don Curzio have their own variant:

Al fiero tormento
Di questo momento
Quest' [Don Curzio: Quell'] anima appena
Resister or sà.

But in the libretto, the first two lines given to all six characters are different. Susanna, Figaro, Bartolo, and Marcellina have:

Al dolce diletto
Che m'agita il petto

whereas the Count and Don Curzio have:

A l'ira, al dispetto
Che m'agita il petto

(The other two lines agree in both variants with the words in Mozart's autograph.)

Page 54 of the Act III autograph is shown in Figure 18.17. In three of the parts on this page, those of Susanna, Marcellina, and Don Curzio, Mozart has crossed out his original words and replaced them by the libretto's; but subsequently he has deleted these new words and restored his original ones. How are we to understand this situation? Is the version printed in the libretto a revision by Da Ponte of what he had originally written, a revision that Mozart attempted to accept but then quickly decided to reject? Or did Mozart start by setting an improved version made by Da Ponte, an improvement that was too late to get into the libretto, and then for some reason (perhaps through a misunderstanding) begin to restore the libretto's original words, a decision that he soon abandoned? Certainly the autograph's version here has always been accepted, whereas the libretto's wording has never found favor.

IT SHOULD be clear from the whole of the above that while a careful scrutiny of the well-preserved *Figaro* autograph can yield much information as to how it was put together, nevertheless a great many useful clues to the opera's history, and perhaps to the changes that Mozart himself was induced to make in it, can come from a careful

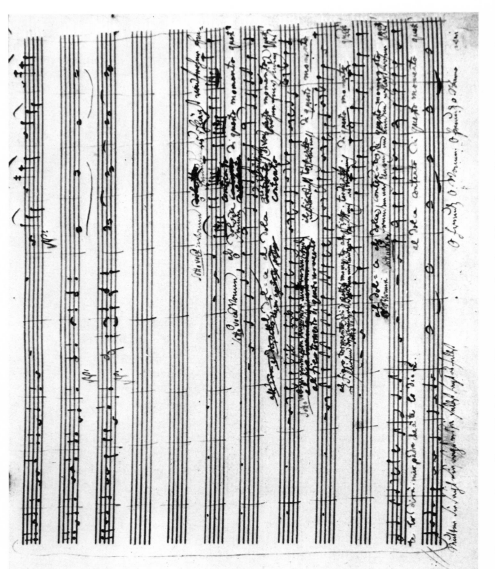

FIGURE 18.17. Page 54 of the Act III autograph, showing Mozart's small changes to some words in the *recitativo Biblioteca Jagiellońska, Kraków*

study and comparison of the many *Abschriften* that have come down to us from his lifetime, or from a few years after his death. Further investigations are needed into the various copyists who produced these *Abschriften*.[34] It should be clear that the more information we have about the datings and the places of origin of this opera's secondary sources, the better we shall be able to grasp its somewhat complicated textual tradition and, by investigating some problems in the text, to assess whether Mozart himself had a hand in them.

Notes

1. New Dating Methods

1. See, in particular, the work of Wolfgang Plath on Mozart's changing handwriting, especially his essay "Beiträge zur Mozart-Autographie II: Schrifchronologie 1770–1780," *Mozart-Jahrbuch 1976/77* (Kassel, 1978), pp. 131–173.

2. A. H. Stevenson, "Watermarks Are Twins," *Studies in Bibliography* (Charlottesville), 4 (1951), 57–91, 235.

3. *Journal of the American Musicological Society,* 28 (1975), 332–334.

4. See NMA IX/27/1, pp. xxx–xxxiii, Nannerl Mozart's Music Book (Notenbuch).

5. See, for instance, NMA II/5/17, p. xxi (the overture to *Don Giovanni*).

6. See Chapter 3 for a description of the paper found in the first two of Mozart's "Prussian" quartets.

7. For a fuller discussion of the number of staves in Mozart autographs, see Chapter 14.

8. NMA I/3, p. xx.

9. NMA I/2/1, p. xxi.

10. NMA V/15/1, p. xiv.

11. NMA I/1/2/1, p. xviii.

12. NMA V/15/7, p. xiv.

13. Cf. Dmitri Kolbin, "Ein wiedergefundenes Mozart-Autograph," *Mozart-Jahrbuch 1967* (Salzburg, 1968), pp. 193–204; Karl Marguerre, "Das Finale von Mozarts 'Erstem Hornkonzert,'" *Acta Mozartiana*, 26 (1979), 34–36. For a detailed examination of the puzzles posed by the D-major horn concerto, see Chapter 16.

14. For a fuller discussion of examples 1, 2, and 3, see Chapter 11.

15. Margaret Crum, comp., *Catalogue of the Mendelssohn Papers in the Bodleian Library Oxford*, II (Tutzing, 1983), 78.

16. Bauer-Deutsch, IV, No. 1173; Anderson, No. 605.

17. F. X. Niemetschek, *Lebensbeschreibung des K. K. Kapellmeisters Wolfgang Amadeus Mozart, aus Originalquellen*, zweite vermehrte Auflage (Prague, 1808), p. 41. Niemetschek's 1st ed. (Prague, 1798) speaks only of a D-major symphony.

2. Redating Mozart

1. Plath, p. 173.

2. The church sonatas K.274(271d) and 278(271e), a cadenza for the piano concerto of January 1777, K.271, the contredanses K.267(271c), and the trio for two violins and a bass, K.266(271f).

3. Plath, p. 173.

4. Plath, p. 172, describes *Thamos* as "unter allen Werken Mozarts vielleicht das mit der kompliziertesten und dunkelsten Entstehungsgeschichte."

5. Cf. NMA V/14/1, *Violinkonzerte und Einzelsätze*, p. xi.

6. Monika Holl, "Nochmals: 'Mozart hat kopiert!'" *Acta Mozartiana*, 30 (1983), 33–36.

7. It is also significant that Giuseppe Bonno, Hofkapellmeister, had died on 15 April 1788.

8. Bauer-Deutsch, IV, No. 1082; Anderson, No. 557.

9. The Danish visitor was Joachim Daniel Preisler; see O. E. Deutsch, *Mozart: Die Dokumente seines Lebens* (Kassel, 1961), pp. 284–285; Eng. trans., *Mozart: A Documentary Biography* (London and Stanford, 1965), pp. 323–325. The term "operetta" may have referred to the Singspiel season.

10. In his letter to his father of 12 April 1783 (Bauer-Deutsch, II, No. 739), Mozart refers to the fact that musical taste is constantly changing, and adds that "this extends even to church music, which ought not to be the case."

11. Wolfgang Plath, "Zur Datierung der Klaviersonaten KV 279–284," *Acta Mozartiana*, 21 (1974), 26–30.

12. Bauer-Deutsch, II, No. 386; Anderson, No. 256.

13. For a full discussion of the D-major horn concerto, and of the completion of its rondo by Süssmayr, see Chapter 16.

3. New Light on Mozart's "Prussian" Quartets

1. Facsimiles of all ten autographs were distributed by the Robert Owen Lehman Foundation, New York, in 1969. A new facsimile edition of them is now published by the British Library, London (1985 and 1987).

2. Bauer-Deutsch, IV, Nos. 1105, 1113, 1123, 1125, and 1130; Anderson, Nos. 567, 572, 578, 580, 582.

3. Köchel[3], p. 725.

4. Alec Hyatt King, "Mozart's 'Prussian' Quartets in Relation to his Late Style," *Music & Letters*, 21 (1940), 328–346 (quotation on 330–331).

5. Alfred Einstein, ed., *W. A. Mozart: The Ten Celebrated String Quartets, First Authentic Edition in Score* (London [1945]), p. xi. The presence of an alto clef on the cello staff at the ninth measure is indeed a puzzle; it does not seem to be accounted for merely by the reversal of parts. But a number of explanations are possible; and even if one assumes with Einstein that Mozart was here writing for a cello in the alto clef, there are no parallels within Mozart's chamber music, so that logically the practice cannot be used as an argument for *any* dating. It looks as if by 1945 Einstein had forgotten some of the arguments for an early date that he had used in 1937, and was searching around for new ones!

6. NMA VIII/20/1/3 (1961), ed. Ludwig Finscher, p. vii, n. 8; see also ibid., Kritischer Bericht (1964), p. 33.

7. See NMA VIII/20/1/3, Kritischer Bericht, p. 33: "Fragmente eines ornamentalen Wasserzeichens (nicht das übliche mit drei Halbmonden und 'REAL'!) sichtbar, aber nicht zu entziffern."

8. See František Zuman, "České filigrány XVIII. století," *Rozpravy České Akademie Věd a Umění*, třída I, číslo 78 (Prague, 1932), p. 22, and plate XXXV/2; also Zuman, "Papírna v Dolní Poustevně," *Papír a celulóza* (1950), 130–132. I am extremely grateful to Dr. Miroslav Vykydal of Plzeň for these references and for other information. Recently I have found another example of this same watermark in the Museum české hudby, Prague, in a manuscript vocal score of Mozart's *Le nozze di Figaro* made by Johann Baptist Kucharz (call-mark XL-F:288).

9. See the so-called "Kafka Sketchbook," British Library, Add. MS 29801, fols. 73, 84, 85 (Prague papers), and 48, 49, 81, 82, 83 119(?), 142 (Berlin papers); I am indebted to Douglas Johnson for much of this information.

10. Possibly it was in 1787, for what appears to be the same watermark is found in the autograph of the aria K.513.

11. NMA VIII/20/1/3, p. 131.

12. The fragment is printed in NMA VIII/20/1/3, p. 149.

13. See NMA VIII/20/1/3, pp. 139–146.

4. *La clemenza di Tito* and Its Chronology

1. Tomislav Volek, "Über den Ursprung von Mozarts Oper 'La Clemenza di Tito,'" *Mozart-Jahrbuch 1959* (Salzburg, 1960), pp. 274–286.

2. Illustrated in Alexander Buchner et al., *Mozart und Prag* (Prague, 1957).

3. See in particular: Franz Giegling, "Zu den Rezitativen von Mozarts Oper 'Titus,'" *Mozart-Jahrbuch 1967* (Salzburg, 1968), pp. 121–126; Stanley Sadie, "Mozart's Last Opera," *Opera*, 20 (1969), 837–843; Robert Moberly and Christopher Raeburn, "The Mozart Version of *La Clemenza di Tito*," *Music Review*, 31 (1970), 285–294; Robert Moberly, "Mozart and His Librettists," *Music & Letters*, 54 (1973), 161–169; Robert Moberly, "The Influence of French Classical Drama on Mozart's 'La Clemenza di

Tito,'" *Music & Letters*, 55 (1974), 286–298; and, for an excellent summary of the problems, Helga Lühning, "Zur Entstehungsgeschichte von Mozarts 'Titus,'" *Die Musikforschung*, 27 (1974), 300–318. The complete music, together with sketches and drafts for several numbers, was published in 1970 in NMA II/5/20, ed. F. Giegling (the Kritischer Bericht has not yet been published).

4. See Giegling (1968).

5. In Paris, for example: the "Paris" Symphony, K.297 (first and last movements and draft of the 6/8 slow movement); the A-Minor Piano Sonata, K.310; the march K.408, No. 1; the song K.468 (an instance of old paper being used?). In Mannheim: the aria K.295 (paper probably from Kandern in Baden). In Munich: the 12-staff and 14-staff "Cander" (Kandern) paper in *Idomeneo*, K.366; possibly the aria K.368 ("H Blum" paper). For these (or similar) Mannheim and Munich papers, mostly produced by Swiss-owned firms, see Eugene K. Wolf and Jean K. Wolf, "A Newly Identified Complex of Manuscripts from Mannhein," *Journal of the American Musicological Society*, 27 (1974), 424, 425, 427. (From 1735 to 1819 the paper mill at Kandern was owned by the Basel firm of Heusler.)

6. This paper-type is found in the cantata K.619 (July 1791). It is also the principal one in the Act II autograph of *Così fan tutte*, K.588; the identical watermark, but sometimes with a slightly different TS, occurs in numerous other scores, for example, in the autographs of the string quartets K.589 and K.590, and in the *Abschrift* of the adaptation of Handel's *Alexander's Feast*, K.591 (all 1790).

7. The identical watermark and TS are found among Beethoven's sketchleaves in the "Kafka Sketchbook," British Library, Add. MS 29801, fols. 131–134; in his edition of this sketch-miscellany (London, 1970) Joseph Kerman assigns a date of 1795 to the sketches on these four leaves.

8. The identical watermark, but with a different TS, is found in the aria K.513 (1787), in the autographs of K.589 and 590, and in the *Abschrift* of K.591.

9. The composition that immediately preceded *Tito* was *Die Zauberflöte*, K.620 (July 1791). But there is almost no overlap in the paper-types found in the two operas, although some sketches for *Tito* at Uppsala are on leaves first used for drafts of the Act II finale of *Die Zauberflöte*. They include a sketch for the definitive version of No. 1 (in F major, with Sesto as a soprano); NMA, p. 324. Paper-type II is not found in any Mozart autographs apart from *La clemenza di Tito*.

10. The third (No. 8) is on Prague paper; this suggests a last-minute decision by Mozart to expand Tito's part.

11. Moberly and Raeburn (1970), p. 288.

12. See Dénes Bartha and László Somfai, *Haydn als Kapellmeister* (Budapest and Mainz, 1960), p. 441, watermark No. 81; H. C. R. Landon, *The Symphonies of Joseph Haydn* (London, 1955), p. 613, watermark No. I:87.

13. Giegling (1968), p. 126.

14. It was also written for a different singer. Volek (1960), p. 278, points out that Josepha Duschek had a deeper voice than Maria Marchetti-Fantozzi, who sang Vitellia; and that "Non più di fiori" has a lower compass than most of the rest of Vitellia's music.

15. Lühning (1974), p. 313, gives reasons why the fact that the last six measures of Vitellia's preceding recitative are on Prague paper may be of little significance. Another aria sometimes associated with Mozart's last visit to Prague is K.621a, "Io ti lascio, o cara, addio." But the only surviving leaf of the autograph, containing the last seventeen measures, is not on Prague paper but on "Viennese" (North Italian) paper, of a type that he used almost entirely in 1788. It seems unlikely, therefore, that this aria was written just before Mozart left Prague in the middle of September 1791, as is stated on an early copy.

16. Volek (1960), p. 280.

17. Giegling (1968), p. 126.

18. For one of the first, see Karl-Heinz Köhler, "Mozarts Kompositions-weise—Beobachtungen am Figaro-Autograph," *Mozart-Jahrbuch 1967* (Salzburg, 1968), pp. 31–45.

5. A Reconstruction of Nannerl Mozart's Music Book (Notenbuch)

1. See *Leopold Mozart, Nannerl-Notenbuch 1759*, ed. Erich Valentin (Munich, 1956). This edition omits all of Wolfgang's contributions. A complete edition of the Notenbuch, edited by Wolfgang Plath, was published in 1982 in the NMA IX/27/1 (Die Notenbücher). I am greatly indebted to Dr. Plath for his help in a number of matters connected with the following discussion.

2. A copy of the Notenbuch made for Otto Jahn in February 1856 shows that then it had exactly the same leaves as it has at present. (This copy is today in a private collection in Bonn.)

3. For a diagram showing the make-up of the Kessler Sketchbook, see Douglas Johnson, Alan Tyson, and Robert Winter, *The Beethoven Sketchbooks* (Berkeley and Oxford, 1985), p. 127.

4. These drawings are to some extent schematic: the watermarks are over-large in relation to the size of the sheet as indicated by the frame, and chain lines have been omitted. The four quadrants (each corresponding to a leaf) in the two molds are numbered and lettered in accordance with my "Ground Rules for the Description of Watermarks": see "The Problem of Beethoven's 'First' *Leonore* Overture," *Journal of the American Musicological Society*, 28 (1975), 332–334.

5. The same watermark is found in a number of Mozart autographs dating up to about 1772. In all of these the staves are drawn singly with a rastrum. The following have ten staves: K.36(33i), the recitative; K.37; K.38; K.39–41;

K.43; K.65(61a), the last leaf; K.66; K.70(61c); K.73; K.89(73k), draft; K.99(63a), the Marcia; K.100(62a); K.107; K.110(75b); K.114; K.117(66a); K.118(74c); and K.124. The following have twelve staves: K.63; and Köchel[6], Al, A2, and A3 (Eberlin)—the last three copied by Leopold Mozart.

6. All four sides of the two leaves are reproduced in facsimile—in the somewhat bizarre order 1v, 2r, 2v, 1r—in Edward J. Dent and Erich Valentin, *Der früheste Mozart* (Munich, 1956); and also in an English edition with the title *The Earliest Compositions of Wolfgang Amadeus Mozart* (Munich, 1956). I am most grateful to Rigbie Turner and Paul Needham for identifying these watermarks.

7. *Salzburger Mozart-Album* (Salzburg, 1871), No. XIII.

8. See J. A. Stargardt (Marburg), Catalogue 602 (28 November 1973), item 771. A facsimile of one side of the leaf appears on p. 193. The suggestion is made there that the autograph may be identical with K.626b/10 in Köchel[6].

9. Georg Nikolaus Nissen, *Biographie W. A. Mozarts* (Leipzig, 1828).

10. See Bauer-Deutsch, IV, Nos. 1268, 1293, and 1313, pp. 298, 342, and 373; and Eibl's commentary on these passages, VI, 507, 535, and 554.

11. This information was kindly supplied by Prof. Burgemeister and Dr. Landmann.

12. Plath, pp. 160–161.

13. Ibid., p. 153.

14. Ibid., p. 161.

15. For the original sizes of some Beethoven sketchbooks, see Alan Tyson, "A Reconstruction of the Pastoral Symphony Sketchbook," *Beethoven Studies [1]*, ed. Alan Tyson (New York, 1973), pp. 86–87; the literature cited there; and Johnson, Tyson, and Winter (1985). On 5 October 1782 Mozart dispatched from Vienna to his father in Salzburg five *Bücher* of 12-staff paper ("5 bücher 12 linirtes Papier"), unobtainable in Salzburg, so that *Die Entführung* could be copied there. Since the autograph score of the opera has almost exactly 240 leaves (less than 240 if paper for the extra wind parts is excluded), this suggests that at that date a Viennese *Buch* of music paper consisted of forty-eight leaves (twenty-four bifolia).

16. The argument has even been reversed: some resemblances of the March in F (an anonymous piece written by Leopold on fol. 10v and on the recto of the first Paris leaf) to K.1b—and even to No. 6 of the 1768 Singspiel *Bastien et Bastienne*, K.50(46b)—have been claimed as evidence that the march is in fact by Wolfgang.

6. The Date of Mozart's Piano Sonata in B-flat, K.333(315c)

1. Georges de Saint-Foix, *Wolfgang Amédée Mozart*, III (Paris, 1936), 140.

2. Plath, pp. 131–173, esp. p. 171.

3. For illustrations see, for example, Georg Eineder, *The Ancient Paper-Mills of the Former Austro-Hungarian Empire and Their Watermarks*, Monumenta Chartae Papyraceae Historiam Illustrantia, VIII(Hilversum, 1960), Nos. 1454–1616; and Joseph Schmidt-Görg, "Wasserzeichen in Beethoven-Briefen," *Beethoven-Jahrbuch*, V (1966), Nos. 43–82.

4. See Eineder, pp. 64–65, and Friedrich Berndt, "Steyrer Paper-Wasserzeichen," *Veröffentlichungen des Kulturamtes der Stadt Steyr* (November 1950), pp. 19–23.

5. It is probable that a leaf in the National Library, Jerusalem, which contains a sketch for the terzetto "Che accidenti!" from the unfinished opera buffa *Lo sposo deluso*, K.430(424a), is the same paper. Unfortunately the top of the leaf, which would have displayed the watermark, has been cut off.

6. Eineder, No. 1693 (in a document from the town of Steyr). Cf. Edward Heawood, *Watermarks Mainly of the Seventeenth and Eighteenth Centuries*, Monumenta Chartae Papyraceae Historiam Illustrantia, I (Hilversum, 1950), No. 3232, where the source of the paper is not identified.

7. See *L'oca del Cairo*, NMA II/5/13 (1960), p. x.

8. For some examples see Plath, pp. 169–173, and the literature cited there.

9. K.449 is also the first work to be entered in Mozart's Verzeichnüss (under the same date). I accept the arguments of Daniel N. Leeson and David Whitwell in "Mozart's Thematic Catalogue," *The Musical Times*, 114 (1973), 781–783, that the Verzeichnüss was not in fact begun by Mozart until some months later.

10. I am omitting K.426 (see note 11).

11. I am assuming here that the date on the autograph of K.426 (now in the Pierpont Morgan Library, New York)—"di Wolfgango Amadeo Mozart mpa Vienna li 29 di decembre 1783"—is correct. Yet the last figure was originally a "2." If K.426 was in fact written near the end of December 1782 (see also the very similar inscription on the autograph of the G-major string quartet, K.387, "di Wolfgango Amadeo Mozart mpa li 31 di decembre 1782 in viena"), Mozart may have composed it not with Baron van Swieten but with his pupil Josepha Auernhammer in mind.

7. Mozart's "Haydn" Quartets

1. This system of numbering and lettering is explained in my "Ground Rules for the Description of Watermarks," *Journal of the American Musicological Society*, 28 (1975), 332–334.

2. NMA VIII/20/1/3 (1961), ed. Ludwig Finscher.

3. The same may also be true of K.587a (Anh. 74), in G minor. But its paper suggests that it was written down somewhat earlier, perhaps in 1786 or

1787; and the fact that its verso was used by Mozart for sketching the A-flat canon in the second finale of *Così fan tutte*, K.588, shows that by the very end of 1789 he had abandoned the quartet fragment.

8. The Origins of Mozart's "Hunt" Quartet, K.458

1. *Allgemeine musikalische Zeitung*, 1 (September 1799), cols. 854–855. The story was confirmed by Constanze when Vincent and Mary Novello visited her in Salzburg in 1829: see their travel diaries, *A Mozart Pilgrimage*, ed. Nerina Medici di Marignano and Rosemary Hughes (London, 1955), p. 112.

2. Intrigues prevented a Vienna performance of *La finta semplice* in 1768, but it was performed in Salzburg in 1769. See O. E. Deutsch, *Mozart: Die Dokumente seines Lebens* (Kassel, 1961), pp. 82–83; R. Angermüller, "Ein neuentdecktes Salzburger Libretto (1769) zu Mozarts 'La Finta semplice,'" *Die Musikforschung*, 31 (1978), 318–322. In his edition of the masses, Walter Senn fixes the composition of the C-Minor Mass K.139(47a) between the autumn of 1768 and the middle of 1769; see NMA I/1/1 (1968), p. xi.

3. The Robert Owen Lehman Foundation (New York, 1969); British Library Music Facsimiles, IV (London, 1985); and Documenta Musicologica, Series II, No. IX (Kassel, 1983).

4. For a fuller discussion of the internal chronology of *L'oca del Cairo*, see Chapter 6.

5. The number of staves and their total vertical span are important qualifications here. For in Salzburg in 1783 Mozart used paper with the same watermark but with ten staves, not twelve, their total span being 183 mm. Later in Vienna he used 12-staff paper with a total span of 188.5–189 mm. in 1785, and again in 1791. The 1791 paper can be recognized by the vertical lines at the beginnings and ends of the staves.

6. I am assuming here that K.426 is correctly dated by Mozart. In fact the autograph (Pierpont Morgan Library, New York) shows that the year was originally written down as "1782."

7. NMA VIII/20/1/3 (1961), ed. Ludwig Finscher, p. 138.

8. The watermark is found a little earlier in copyists' scores—e.g., in the March 1789 score (with additions by Mozart) of Handel's *Messiah*, K.572.

9. NMA VIII/20/1/3, pp. 148–149.

9. The Two Slow Movements of Mozart's "Paris" Symphony, K.297

1. See Hermann Beck, "Zur Entstehungsgeschichte von Mozarts D-Dur-Sinfonie, KV. 297," *Mozart-Jahrbuch 1955* (Salzburg, 1956), pp. 95–112 (esp. pp. 97, 108–109), and his 1957 edition of the symphony (NMA IV/11/5, pp. ix and 128; cf. also the critical report, p. 40); O. E. Deutsch, *Mozart: Die Dokumente seines Lebens* (Kassel, 1961), p. 160 (Eng. trans., p. 178); and Eibl, V, 537.

2. Georges de Saint-Foix, *Wolfgang Amédée Mozart: sa vie musicale et son œuvre*, III (Paris, 1936), 79–83.

3. See, e.g., *The Musical Times*, 116 (1975), 128.

4. Neal Zaslaw, "Mozart's Paris Symphonies," *The Musical Times*, 119 (1978), 753–757.

5. It is hard to evaluate Legros's reported complaint that the movement played on 18 June contained "too much modulation." Some might suppose that to apply more readily to the 6/8 movement than to the 3/4 one; but in fact there is very little modulation in either.

6. See the cover of *The Musical Times*, 119 (1978), September (where the publisher's name and address are not shown).

7. For the firm of Johannot at Annonay, see H. Gachet, "Vieilles papeteries françaises: les papeteries d'Annonay. 1. Les Papeteries Johannot," *Courrier graphique*, No. 41 (1949), pp. 27–34. Annonay was (and is) a papermaking town in the hilly region of Vivrais, some forty miles south of Lyons. It was there, in 1782, that the brothers Montgolfier, both papermakers, first experimented with hot-air balloons made partly of paper.

8. For the deleted passages, see NMA IV/11/5, pp. 133–136.

9. Ibid., pp. 137–138.

10. There are perhaps two known exceptions. The march for orchestra, K.408, No. 1 (K.383e), probably dates from Mozart's early Vienna years, and the Masonic song "Gesellenreise," K.468, was entered by Mozart in his Verzeichnüss under the date of 26 March 1785. The autographs of both (three leaves and one leaf respectively) are on 14-staff paper of this same type.

11. See W. F. Tschudin, *The Ancient Paper-Mills of Basle and Their Marks*, Monumenta Chartae Papyraceae Historiam Illustrantia, VII (Hilversum, 1958).

12. These include the autographs of the 1785 piano quartets, WoO 36, the 1783 organ fugue, WoO 31, the four-handed Variations on a Theme of Count Waldstein, WoO 36, and the piano part, in the hand of a copyist, of the very early E-flat piano concerto, WoO 4.

13. At the time Strasbourg was, from the tariff point of view, a special enclave even within Alsace. French paper would have been very expensive there, since it was subjected to French export duties and probably internal tariffs en route. There was a large trade between Strasbourg and Basel, not only by river but also by road. See F. L. Ford, *Strasbourg in Transition, 1648–1789* (Cambridge, Mass., 1958), p. 132 for the tariffs, and p. 147 for the overland trade with Basel.

14. Ernst Hess, "Ein neu entdecktes Skizzenblatt Mozarts," *Mozart-Jahrbuch 1964* (Salzburg, 1965), pp. 185–192.

15. I am very grateful to Pater Lukas Helg of Kloster Einsiedeln for his help in establishing this.

16. *W. A. Mozart, Symphonie parisienne: Fragment* (Lucerne, [1949]).

17. For instance, in violins 1 and 2 in measures 82, 93–98, 101–102,

178–185, and elsewhere. The fourth and the eighth of the violins' notes in measure 53 (and measure 207) were originally quarter notes, not eighth notes.

18. For information about this second copyist and for details of the scores that he copied I am greatly indebted to Dr. Wolfgang Plath.

19. This is the version that is normally heard today—although orchestras occasionally use a text based on the old *Gesamtausgabe* of 1880, which followed (2), the first version. (The most easily recognizable feature of the first version is that measures 73–74 are in the major and measures 75–76 in the minor; Mozart reversed this in the later version.)

20. Cf. my letter on "Mozart's Truthfulness," *The Musical Times*, 119 (1978), 938.

21. See Martin Staehelin, "Zur Echtheitsproblematik der Mozartschen Bläserkonzertante," *Mozart-Jahrbuch 1971/72* (Salzburg, 1973), pp. 56–62; Daniel N. Leeson and Robert D. Levin, "On the Authenticity of K. Anh. C 14.01(297b), a Symphonia Concertante for Four Winds and Orchestra," *Mozart-Jahrbuch 1976/77* (Kassel, 1978), pp. 70–96; and for a more recent review of the evidence, Wolfgang Plath's introduction to his edition of the work in NMA X/29/1.

22. But Mozart's letter of 1 May 1778 specifically states that the work had been completed and was ready to be copied, and that the soloists had already learned their parts. Perhaps we should believe him here.

23. See Plath, "Schriftchronologie," p. 171; and Chapter 6 of this book on the date of the B-flat piano sonata K.333(315c).

10. *Le nozze di Figaro:* Lessons from the Autograph Score

1. Robert Moberly and Christopher Raeburn, "Mozart's 'Figaro': the Plan of Act III," *Music & Letters*, 66 (1965), 134–136; see also R. B. Moberly, *Three Mozart Operas: Figaro—Don Giovanni—The Magic Flute* (London, 1967), pp. 103–104.

2. Karl-Heinz Köhler, "Mozarts Kompositionsweise—Beobachtungen am Figaro-Autograph," *Mozart-Jahrbuch 1967* (Salzburg, 1968), pp. 31–45.

3. All seven paper-types in *Figaro* have versions of this countermark; they can be differentiated by its size and spacing.

4. The paper of Susanna's second-act aria—like that of the third-act "letter" duettino, and of the start and one later passage in the fourth-act finale—has the TS of 182 mm. There is evidence to suggest that this paper was available to Mozart slightly earlier than the New Type, with a TS of 186 mm.

5. Cf. the recitatives before "Aprite presto aprite" in *Figaro*, Act II, and before the chorus "Giovinette" in *Don Giovanni*, Act I. But precedents must be handled with care. Masetto's aria "Ho capito," in F, is preceded by a recitative with a cadence in D—a strange relationship. It is possible, however,

that this aria was originally written in G, and was later transposed down a tone for the singer's benefit. This finds support in the fact that it is the only part of the first-act score of *Don Giovanni* that is on Prague paper.

6. The Countess's "Dove sono," too, seems originally to have been designated a Rondò in the autograph. It is certainly in the requisite two tempos, but at both places in the score where the word was apparently used (pp. 67 and 68), it was neatly scratched out and the word "Aria" substituted.

7. The autograph of this recitative is today in the Memorial Library of Music, Stanford University.

8. But Figaro would then have had two solo numbers in F, since his first-act Cavatina is also in that key. Mozart seems usually to have avoided this.

11. The Mozart Fragments in the Mozarteum, Salzburg

1. Bauer-Deutsch, IV, 324–331 (= No. 1288).—Finished compositions of Mozart listed in Köchel[1] are identified here by their original Köchel number followed (in parentheses) by their number in Köchel[6]. Fragments, on the other hand, are referred to first by their number in Köchel[6], with the Köchel-Anhang number usually added. The fragments in the Internationale Stiftung Mozarteum, Salzburg, are also identified by their Mozarteum numbers. For further details and concordances, see Tables 11.1 and 11.2 at the end of this chapter.

2. Georg Nikolaus Nissen, *Biographie W. A. Mozarts* (Leipzig, 1828), Anhang, pp. 10–20.

3. Bauer-Deutsch, IV, 250–251 (= No. 1245).

4. Ibid., pp. 352–353 (= No. 1299).

5. Though André's letters to Constanze have not survived, a part of their contents can be inferred from her replies. For his anxiety that some of her fragments could be missing portions of the scores that he had bought, see her letters of 31 May 1800 and 4 March 1801: Bauer-Deutsch, IV, 354 (= No. 1299) and 401 (= No. 1333).

6. At the end of the section "für die Violine" in the list sent to Breitkopf & Härtel on 1 March 1800, Constanze singled out eleven fragments for special mention. Only one of these has fewer than fifty measures. It is significant, therefore, that three of them are now in the Deutsche Staatsbibliothek, Berlin: K.464a (Anh. 72), K.514a (Anh. 80), and K.580b (Anh. 90); and one is in the Fitzwilliam Museum, Cambridge: K.562e (Anh. 66); while one cannot now be traced: K.383g (Anh. 100), no doubt because it was sold early in the nineteenth century. The fragment Anh. 101 has been identified by Wolfgang Plath as being part of the present autograph of *König Thamos,* K.345(336a); perhaps it was claimed by André as soon as it was recognized as belonging to that score (which André had purchased). A further fragment on the list, K.417d, is in the Mozarteum today but was not acquired until 1934. Thus of

the eleven fragments specially selected by Constanze, only four remained unsold and accordingly reached the Mozarteum in the last century (Nos. 21, 25, 27, 31; No. 21 has subsequently been lost).

7. I shall not attempt an exact description of the term "fragment" here. But, however tentative and incomplete they may be, fragments are set out in the same manner as a finished score, and are in the same "public" handwriting. Sketches, on the other hand, are almost always in a "private" handwriting, which may be very hard to decipher, and they are normally not set out in formal score.

8. See Table 11.1 at the end of this chapter.

9. Köchel, it must be recorded, was somewhat arbitrary in deciding what was to be relegated to the Anhang as an "unfinished composition." In his main series from K.1 to K.626 he found room not only for large unfinished (though easily datable) scores such as the Mass in C Minor, the two operas of 1783 (*L'oca del Cairo* and *Lo sposo deluso*), and the *Requiem,* but also for numerous small fragments such as K.153, K.396, K.402, K.403, K.443. (Most of these, it is true, had been "completed" by Stadler.)

10. A warning concerning some of Einstein's dates was sounded by Wolfgang Plath in 1964: see "Der gegenwärtige Stand der Mozart-Forschung," *Bericht über den Neunten Internationalen Kongress Salzburg, 1964,* I (Kassel, 1964), 47–55.

11. Einstein was much more sanguine: "In most cases the correct context can be recognized with certainty by the identity of key and scoring" (Köchel[3], Preface, p. xl).

12. Mena Blaschitz, "Die salzburger Mozartfragmente" (diss., University of Bonn, 1924), p. 175; part of the dissertation was published in *Jahrbuch der philosophischen Fakultät Bonn* (1924–25).

13. Köchel[3], Preface, p. xl. Einstein claimed there that "the paper most frequently used by Mozart has a watermark with three moons of unequal size," and he cited instances of such paper in scores dating from as far apart in time as 1727 and 1785. Such a dismissal shows a total unfamiliarity with the material. There were literally thousands of eighteenth-century Italian papers with different forms of the "tre lune" watermark (an indication neither of provenance nor of date, but of quality) used in combination with other marks. The comparatively few (about fifty?) that were used by Mozart need to be distinguished carefully from one another and dated separately.

14. Köchel[3], Preface, p. xli.

15. Plath, "Schriftchronologie."

16. Plath's work on the *Schriftchronologie* of Mozart has parallels in recent investigations into Beethoven's early handwriting: see in particular Douglas Johnson, *Beethoven's Early Sketches in the "Fischhof Miscellany,"* *Berlin Autograph 28* (Ann Arbor, 1980), I, 25–64. Some of the changes in

Beethoven's musical handwriting in the years 1785–1800 are distinct—and datable; after 1800 the writing changes much less.

17. Plath, "Schriftchronologie," p. 173.

18. See, for instance, Alan Tyson, "The Problems of Beethoven's 'First' *Leonore* Overture," *Journal of the American Musicological Society*, 28 (1975), 292–334, esp. 307–309 and 332–334, and the literature cited there; and Johnson (1980), I, 65–70.

19. A slight qualification to this procedure is suggested at the end of the chapter.

20. The date in the Verzeichnüss is no doubt that of the completed canons, not of these drafts.

21. Only one leaf survives of this autograph (London, British Library); it contains mm. 65–132 and 161–209 of the first movement.

22. See Köchel[6], p. 661, for an *Abschrift* (with autograph wind parts) of minuets 1, 2, and 4 (Vienna, Gesellschaft der Musikfreunde); no doubt it once contained all of the first four minuets. On it is the following inscription: "Mozart composed these minuets for two violins and bass in the year 1789; but since they met with such a warm reception, Mozart was asked to orchestrate them. He had the trio version put in score, and the present orchestration is in his own handwriting. He made me a present of it 14 days before his death. Franz Roser mp."

23. An early copy of this fragment, still in the Mozarteum, preserves its musical content. An autograph leaf in Berlin (Deutsche Staatsbibliothek) continues the music for a further eight measures; it is of a paper-type that Mozart did not use before his return to Vienna from Prague in September 1791.

24. Blaschitz, "Die salzburger Mozartfragmente," Nos. 3, 26, 29, 56, 57 (No. 31 not discussed). Einstein, Köchel[3], Nos. 3, 22, 26, 29, 31, 56, 60.

25. Descriptions and illustrations of the individual watermarks have been dispensed with here. A full catalogue of paper-types used by Mozart, with illustrations of their watermarks, under preparation by me, will eventually be published in the NMA.

26. For a recent interpretation of Mozart's quartet fragments, see Christoph Wolff, "Creative Exuberance vs. Critical Choice: Thoughts on Mozart's Quartet Fragments," in *The String Quartets of Haydn, Mozart, and Beethoven: Studies of the Autograph Manuscripts*, Isham Library Papers, III, ed. Christoph Wolff (Cambridge, Mass., 1980), 191–210.

27. Not all of these changes are shown in NMA VIII/19/2, pp. 50–52, where the fragment is published. Mr. Mischa Donat drew my attention to twenty-one further measures of this fragment (like the rest, only partially scored) on an autograph leaf at Stift Göttweig; it is of the same paper-type.

28. The 93-measure fragment, K.516c (Anh. 91), for clarinet—or bassetclarinet?—and strings in B-flat (Paris, Bibliothèque nationale) is also on the

same paper-type, and dates therefore from 1790 or 1791. It is possible that the movement was in fact completed, for the ninety-three measures are fully scored, and the music continues to the very end of the bifolium, with ties leading over to a presumed continuation, now lost. See NMA VIII/19/2, pp. 41–43.

29. Compare K.405a (Anh. 77), another fugal fragment for quartet (Berlin, Deutsche Staatsbibliothek). This is on Paper-type (C) and dates therefore from 1790 or 1791.

30. For the probable connection of the polonaise with K.458, and for the dating of the individual movements, see Chapter 8.

31. A second leaf of the fragment, K.488c, containing a further seven measures, is today in the library of the Karl Marx University in Leipzig. At that point the music breaks off.

32. Another fragment for violin and piano, K.403(385c), in the Bibliothèque nationale, Paris, is on the same paper. Because of an inscription on it that runs, "Sonate Premiere. Par moi W: A: Mozart pour ma très chère Epouse," it has been assumed that several of these fragments represent an attempt by Mozart to write a set of "easy" violin sonatas for his wife soon after their marriage in August 1782. The assumption does not seem to be justified. Mozart's use of "épouse" was certainly not confined to 1782. He used the word, for instance, in inscribing a drawing that he had made in Linz on 13 November 1783—an *Ecce homo:* see Constanze's letter to Breitkopf & Härtel of 21 July 1800, Bauer-Deutsch, IV, 360(= No. 1301)—and in several of his letters to his wife in 1791.

33. The first 57 mm. of this fragment are on a bifolium of the same paper-type in Bergamo, Conservatorio di Musica "G. Donizetti."

34. It is possible that the powerful D-minor Kyrie, K.341(368a), also belongs to this period, but the autograph is lost. All the editions of Köchel have followed Otto Jahn in assigning it to Mozart's stay in Munich from November 1780 to March 1781, but there is little to be said in favor of this.

35. On the other hand, the G-minor piano-sonata fragment, K.312(590d), in the Bodleian Library, Oxford, is on Paper-type (C) datable 1790–91, and is thus a possible result of this commission. It was Einstein in his 1947 supplement to Köchel[3] who first suggested that K.312 was in fact a late work.

36. Köchel[6] *deest:* see NMA IX/24/1, Supplement (1964), ed. Gerhard Croll; and Croll's reports in the *Mozart-Jahrbuch 1962/63* (Salzburg, 1964) and the *Mozart-Jahrbuch 1964* (Salzburg, 1965).

37. For a discussion of the scoring of this piece, the melodic line of which is complete, see Marius Flothuis, "Mozarts 'Adagio für Englischhorn,'" *Mitteilungen der Internationalen Stiftung Mozarteum,* 15 (1967), Heft 1/2, pp. 1–3.

38. Walter Senn, "Mozarts Skizze der Ballettmusik zu 'Le gelosie del ser-

raglio' (KV Anh. 109/135a)," *Acta musicologica*, 33 (1961), 169–192, with facsimiles of three of the pages (between pp. 176 and 177).

39. In addition to the work of Blaschitz and Einstein, mention should be made of Erich Hertzmann, "Mozart's Creative Process," *The Musical Quarterly*, 43 (1957), 187–200, reprinted in *The Creative World of Mozart*, ed. Paul Henry Lang (New York, 1963), pp. 17–30.

40. Otto Biba, "Grundzüge des Konzertswesens in Wien zu Mozarts Zeit," *Mozart-Jahrbuch 1978/79* (Kassel, 1979), pp. 132–143.

41. Alfred Einstein, "Mozart's Handwriting and the Creative Process," *Papers Read at the International Congress of Musicology Held at New York, September 11th to 16th, 1939* (New York, 1944), p. 149.

42. The removal of blank leaves from autograph scores may often have been due to the caprice of their owners, custodians, or binders. The autograph of *La clemenza di Tito*, for instance, still contains several blank leaves; that of *Die Zauberflöte* has hardly any.

43. Walter Gerstenberg, "Zum Autograph des Klavierkonzertes KV. 503 (C-Dur): Anmerkung zu Mozarts Schaffensweise," *Mozart-Jahrbuch 1953* (Salzburg, 1954), pp. 38–46.

44. The reproduction of the first page of the autograph in NMA V/15/7, p. xii, is not clear enough to show the changes at the beginnings of the staves, but it can be seen that mm. 9–14 in the "clarinets" are written at pitch. Besides being entered on fol. 26r, the clarinets' version of mm. 9–18 and 62–66 is also written out on a leaf containing cadenzas for the second and third movements of K.414 (Berlin, Staatsbibliothek Preussischer Kulturbesitz).

45. Personal communication from Wolfgang Plath.

46. The examples that I have cited are all taken from the Vienna years. But instances can also be found from an earlier period. Plath (pp. 145, 147–148) has drawn attention to a difference in handwriting between the opening measures of the symphony K.129 (dated "May 1772"), and their sequel, as well as between the Kyrie and start of the Gloria in the Mass K.167 (dated "June 1773") and the rest of that score. He suggests that in both cases Mozart laid the work aside and resumed it only after some time had elapsed. This idea is fully borne out by the paper-types, for in both cases the start of the score is on an earlier paper than its continuation.

47. See also some remarks by Dietrich Berke in his preface to NMA VIII/21, p. xiv.

12. The Dates of Mozart's *Missa brevis* K.258 and *Missa longa* K.262(246a)

1. This is the vertical distance from the top line of the top staff to the bottom line of the bottom staff on a page. When a batch of paper is ruled me-

chanically (as is the case with all the music paper to be discussed here), the total span (TS) remains almost constant and can sometimes be used to identify it. Other features of the staff-ruling, as we shall see, can also help in identifying the paper-type.

2. The most important exception is a paper that he bought in Italy early in 1770; it is found in the first three movements of the string quartet K.80(73f), written at Lodi on 15 March, in the "Contradanza" K.123(73g), written at Rome about 14 April, and probably also in the two minuets K.61g. The watermarks shows the letters PA in a circle, surmounted by a trefoil, and with the letters BMo (= Bergamo) under it; the TS is 144.5–145 mm. The same paper was used by Leopold Mozart for copying the Miserere K.85(73s), dated "Bologna 1770," and for transcriptions of some works by Ernst Eberlin (Köchel⁶, Anh. A 82, 83, 84, 85). Of three further papers in *Klein-Querformat* scores—those of the minuet K.122 (73t), the fragmentary tenor aria K.71, and the seven minuets K.61b—the first two were almost certainly bought in Italy in the spring of 1770; the third, however, is dated "26 January 1769" and is probably a "Salzburg" paper.

3. One obvious exception is provided by the 10-staff papers that Mozart purchased at the time of his stay in Salzburg from July to October 1783. Some of these were used for writing down the extra wind parts to the Mass in C Minor, K.427(417a), and others for sketches and drafts of *L'oca del Cairo*, K.422.

4. See Ernst Hess, preface to miniature score of K.219 published by Bärenreiter (TP no. 20), p. 3, note 9.

5. Plath, "Schriftchronologie," pp. 166–167.

6. The original date on the autograph of K.207 may have been "1773." (Personal communication from Dr. Plath.) See NMA V/14/1, p. xi.

7. See NMA IV/11/4, p. x.

8. According to Walter Senn's Kritischer Bericht to K.194 (186h), NMA I/1/1/2, p. b/30, a "springende Raubkatze (Tiger oder Panther)"; but a lion—of the kind found in many papers from Lombardy—seems more likely.

9. The date on K.204 has been crossed out, but it has been read as "li 5 d'agosto 1775" (see NMA IV/12/3, p. viii); the other two dates are intact.

10. For illustrations of similar watermarks depicting three bell-like hats, compare Georg Eineder, *The Ancient Paper-Mills of the Former Austro-Hungarian Empire and Their Watermarks*, Monumenta Chartae Papyraceae Historiam Illustrantia, VIII (Hilversum, 1960), Nos. 693, 697, 698.

11. See NMA VII/18, p. xiii, where Albert Dunning follows Carl Bär in connecting K.287 with the performance of an unidentified work for the Countess Lodron on 16 June 1777 (three days after the Countess's name-day). See Bär, "Die Lodronschen Nachtmusiken," *Mitteilungen der Internationalen Stiftung Mozarteum*, 10 (June 1961), 19–22.

12. Bauer-Deutsch, II, No. 439, p. 329; Anderson, No. 299a, p. 519.

13. The only exception known to me is a bifolium (Salzburg, St. Peter), with autograph cadenzas to K.175 (first two movements) and K.382, and two *Eingänge* for K.271. This was perhaps sent by Wolfgang from Vienna to his sister, Nannerl, in Salzburg on 15 February 1783; see Bauer-Deutsch, III, No. 728, p. 256 (Anderson, No. 481, p. 840). The paper-type of this bifolium is not among those discussed here; its watermark (top half of a sheet only) shows a brimmed hat under an ornamental baldachin (?), and a crown (?). The TS of the ten staves is 133 mm. See also the cadenzas to K.365(316a) copied by Leopold (with additions by Wolfgang) on Type II paper, and the cadenzas to K.413(387a) copied by Leopold on Type III paper.

14. The "S" is formed from three straight lines, resembling a "Z" in reverse.

15. André seems to have believed that it was the removal of the score of the mass K.220(196b) from the volume into which K.262, 257, 258, and 259 had also at one time been bound that resulted in the loss of the first leaf of K.262; for he supposed that the first measures of K.262 had been written on the last leaf of the K.220 score. But it would have been most uncharacteristic of Mozart to have begun a large-scale new work on the last leaf of a score that he had written earlier, and today we can see that the missing leaf of K.262, replaced by the copyist, had been the first leaf of a new gathering.

16. For recent reviews of the problematical date of K.262, and for an attempt to determine the occasion for which it was composed, see the remarks of Walter Senn in NMA I/1/1/2, pp. xvi—xvii, and (more fully) in his "Beiträge zur Mozartforschung," in *Acta Musicologica*, 48 (1976), 219—227. A service in the cathedral at Salzburg on 17 November 1776 at which Count Ignaz Joseph von Spaur was consecrated as coadjutor and administrator of the diocese of Brixen and also as titular bishop of Chrysopel is proposed there; but the fact that nearly all of the score is on Type I paper indicates that at any rate its date of composition was over a year earlier.

17. The foliation of the autograph in fact runs from 1 to 28, since two completely blank leaves at the end of the Credo were not foliated. The present discussion assumes a numbering of all thirty leaves.

18. The demonstration of this depends on matching small irregularities in the upper edges of the two bifolia. In favorable cases this can be done even when the leaves whose upper edges are to be matched are today in different locations. It is likely, for instance, that fols. 1—2 of K.499 match fols. 11—12 of K.497; that fols. 11—12 of K.499 match fols. 13—14 of K.497; and that fol. 29 of K.620 (the penultimate leaf of No. 1) matches fol. 1 of K.618. Many other examples could be given.

19. Wolfgang Plath, "Bemerkungen zu einem missdeuteten Skizzenblatt Mozarts," in *Festschrift Walter Gerstenberg zum 60. Geburtstag* (Wolfenbüttel and Zurich, 1964), pp. 143—150.

20. I fear I cannot follow Walter Senn in his view that the names of the

months on the scores of K.257, 258, and 259 are not authentic, being in the hand neither of Leopold nor of Wolfgang. (See NMA I/1/1/3, pp. viii–ix, and in greater detail, with enlarged photographs of the handwriting, the Kritischer Bericht to that volume, pp. c/6–7, c/27–8, and c/44–5.) In my opinion the months (and the composer's full names) on K.257 and 258 were written by Leopold; on K.259 the names were written by Leopold but the month, "Decembre," was possibly added by Wolfgang.

21. See the article by Wolfgang Plath cited above in note 5.

13. On the Composition of Mozart's *Così fan tutte*

1. For *Idomeneo* see, for instance, Daniel Heartz, "The Genesis of Mozart's 'Idomeneo,'" *Mozart-Jahrbuch 1967* (Salzburg, 1968), pp. 150–164; the same essay with minor alterations and with illustrations in *The Musical Quarterly*, 55 (1969), 1–19; and idem, "Raaff's Last Aria: A Mozartian Idyll in the Spirit of Hasse," *The Musical Quarterly*, 60 (1974), 517–543.

2. *Memorie di Lorenzo Da Ponte, da Ceneda*, 2d ed., vol. I, part II (New York, 1829), p. 111. The same author's earlier short tract in English, *An Extract from the Life of Lorenzo Da Ponte* (New York, 1819), likewise has almost nothing to say about the opera.

3. Fols. 88 and 89. This bifolium is of a rare paper-type, which otherwise has been found so far only in the autograph of *Die Zauberflöte*.

4. The D-major aria and its G-major replacement will be referred to here as No. 15a and No. 15b respectively.

5. See "*La clemenza di Tito* and Its Chronology," Chapter 4 above.

6. See, for instance, C. F. Pohl, *Joseph Haydn*, II (Leipzig, 1882), 123–124. Pohl cites her first name there as "Aloisia," but the two names were apparently interchangeable. Mozart's sister-in-law, Aloysia Lange (née Weber), sometimes signed herself "Louise Lange," as is shown by a letter of 1 November 1797, illustrated in Ursula Mauthe, "Briefe der 'Weberin' entdeckt," *Acta Mozartiana*, 29 (1982), 77.

7. This will be referred to here as "the unnumbered quintetto." Although most editions follow Breitkopf & Härtel's full score of 1810 in identifying it as "No. 9," Mozart called it merely "Recitativo," his own "No. 9" being the reprise of the soldiers' chorus, No. 8 (with the opening twenty-four measures for orchestra omitted). It is clear from the autograph that the quintetto originally had a string accompaniment only; the clarinets at the top of the score and the bassoons at the bottom were later additions.

8. The first critical edition of the opera was edited by Julius Rietz (1812–1877) and published by Breitkopf & Härtel, Leipzig, in 1871. The plates of this edition were later used for the opera in the *Gesamtausgabe* (1881); and the *Revisionsbericht* to the latter (1883) is based almost word for word on

Rietz's 1871 Foreword. References are given here to the more accessible *Gesamtausgabe* rather than to the 1871 edition.

9. One can extend the line of reasoning to cover No. 12, Despina's aria, as well. Since this recitative extends on to the top two staves of fol. 71r, it must have been written down *before* the aria, the score of which occupies staves 4–11 on this page (instead of being placed more centrally on staves 3–10, as it is on the subsequent pages).

10. The direction "attacca No. 16" at the end of No. 15a (called "No. 15") also suggests that the aria remained in the opera until it and the following terzetto had received their final numbering. By an oversight, its first line and a stage direction, "Revolgete a lui lo sguardo (*a Fiord.*)," were still retained in the later issue of the libretto (discussed below), after No. 15b had replaced it there.

11. No. 15a, also on Type I paper, was presumably not included in the bifoliation because it was being dropped.

12. Mozart was sensitive to the need for providing music to enable performers to enter or to leave the stage, and he sometimes wrote it at the very last minute: for example, the Priests' March at the beginning of Act II of *Die Zauberflöte*, a very late addition to the score, or the newly discovered Janissaries' March added to Act I of *Die Entführung*, for which see Gerhard Croll, "Ein Janitscharen-Marsch zur 'Entführung,'" *Mitteilungen der Internationalen Stiftung Mozarteum*, 28 (1980), 2–5, 31.

13. Something similar evidently happened at the end of Zerlina's aria "Vedrai, carino" in Act II of *Don Giovanni*. When completing the scoring of this aria, Mozart seems to have felt that the concluding orchestral measures, which probably consisted only of the material now found in mm. 85–92 on fol. 168v of the autograph, needed to be extended a little—perhaps to allow for the characters' exit and the scene change. This necessitated the insertion of a new leaf, fol. 169, which is Prague paper (unlike the rest of the aria) and therefore a late addition to the score. The elimination of a measure between the present mm. 84 and 85 probably happened at the same time.

14. In the autograph score of *Le nozze di Figaro* (Acts I–II, Berlin, Deutsche Staatsbibliothek; Acts III–IV, Kraków, Biblioteka Jagiellońska), there are similar cues for No. 13 (Susanna's "Venite, inginocchiatevi"), for No. 26 (Basilio's aria), and for the *recitativo accompagnato* before No. 29 (Susanna's "Deh vieni"). All these are written on the New Type of paper that Mozart adopted about halfway through his work on *Figaro:* see Chapter 10 above. In other words, they are among the later-written parts of that opera.

15. Otto Jahn, *W. A. Mozart,* IV (Leipzig, 1859), 490; *ibid.,* 5th ed., rev. Hermann Abert, II (Leipzig, 1921), 640.

16. *Le nozze di Figaro* is in four acts; none of its first three acts ends in the tonic.

17. Wolfgang Plath, "Mozartiana in Fulda und Frankfurt," *Mozart-Jahrbuch 1968/70* (Salzburg, 1970), pp. 333–386, with illustrations of the bifolium's first and last pages. The manuscript has been given the call mark Mus. Hs. 2350. Its first page includes the bizarre (and unique) spelling "Guilemo."

18. For its text, see NMA VIII/20/1/3 (1961), pp. 147–148.

19. It is the New Type adopted during the work on *Figaro;* see note 14.

20. See Chapter 11, page 139.

21. The sketches were first identified by Wolfgang Plath in 1964. For the leaf, see Plath's edition of the Fantasy in NMA, IX/27/2 (1982), pp. xxiv–xxv, and literature cited there.

22. See Chapter 4 above.

23. "Mozzart" is also found in the early (and incomplete) edition of the 1787 libretto (with Vienna, not Prague, on the title page as its place of publication), in the libretto for the 1788 Vienna revival, and on the playbill for that production.

24. Jahn (1859), IV, 488; ibid., 5th ed., rev. Abert, II, 639.

25. Wolfgang Hildesheimer, *Mozart* (Frankfurt am Main, 1977), pp. 300–301; ibid., trans. Marion Faber (New York, 1982), p. 290.

26. A note attached to it reads: "Eine Abkürzung zu Cosi fann tutte, um das Larghetto im 2n Finale zu ersparen, von Mozarts eigener Handschrift, für die kais: Hoftheater. / Sie ist in keine anderen Hände gekomen. / gefunden am 29 August 1804 / Fr. Treitschke."

27. In my own possession since 1961; formerly Hans Schneider, Tutzing (Catalogue 72, No. 1675).

28. The second-volume title pages of both H and S read: "La Scuola degli Amanti." And that was the original wording of H's first-volume title page, with "Cosi fan tutte / osia" and "Dramma giocoso / in due Atti . . . ," and so on, being added a little later.

29. This word, used in annotations in H, seems to imply a gathering made up of the bifolia from three sheets (that is, twelve leaves, the average size of the gatherings within H and S).

30. Two numbers bear the names of "Neumann" and "Mad. Fodor"; these were probably Friedrich Neumann, who appears to have sung Ferrando in the 1800s, and Mme Joséphine Mainvielle-Fodor, who sang Fiordiligi in the 1820s (a role that, for her, included Dorabella's aria No. 28). Several arias have been given a German text; and Fiordiligi's first aria (No. 14) carries the cue "e tradimento," which rightly belongs to her second (No. 25).

31. Figure 13.11 shows, at the top and the bottom of the score in measure 558 of H, a pair of Mozart's characteristic signs, used by him to show the place where a new passage or a correction should be inserted, or where the music should resume after an interruption. (Both signs here have been cropped by the binder.) Other examples of these Mozartian signs—stylized forms of

NB?—can be found: (1) before m. 545 in H, to mark the beginning of the cut; (2) on fols. 154v and 155r of the Act I autograph of *Così fan tutte*, to show where six measures with a repetition of the "magnet" music (mm. 385– 390), a last-minute addition to the score—it was not yet in the autograph when H was first copied—should be inserted; (3) on fols. 201v and 202v of the autograph of *Don Giovanni*, in the *recitativo accompagnato* preceding Donna Elvira's "Mi tradì" (written for the 1788 Vienna revival), to indicate where an alternative passage, devised to lead to the aria transposed down a semitone, could be accommodated; (4) on fol. 4v of the autograph of the string quartet K.575, at m. 190 of the first movement (four measures from the end), to show where a corrected version of the second violin part should be inserted; and (5) on fol. 3v of the autograph of the piano concerto K.595: see the illustration in NMA, V/15/8 (1960), p. xxxiv.

32. From this point of view it is regrettable that ternion 21 from Act I, which included Ferrando's aria No. 17, is missing from H; for the "tailoring" of the two cuts found in S and the other *Vervielfältigungen* may possibly have included interesting entries in Mozart's hand.

33. Curiously enough, one or two of the autograph's readings, preserved by H and S and by the first published full score, were overlooked or falsified in the *Gesamtausgabe*. The start of No. 18, the Act I finale, for instance, was marked "con sordini" by Mozart; and at the beginning of No. 16 Ferrando and Guilelmo laugh "smoderatamente," immoderately, not "moderamente" ("mit unterdrücktem Lachen"), moderately. At m. 76 of No. 14, "Come scoglio," H originally had the autograph's version of the first and second violin parts. But these were then changed in an unknown hand, as shown in Example 13.1; the new version is found throughout the *Vervielfältigungen*, indicating that the change was made at a very early date. The same is true of changes made in H to the first bassoon part of the same number, in mm. 16, 18, 67, 69, and 71. At first there were only quarter notes in these measures, as in the autograph; but the part was altered at a very early date—1790?—in order to double the trumpets. Could these changes have been authorized by Mozart, perhaps at a rehearsal? For even the entries made in H long after Mozart's death, referred to on pp. 206 and 208 above, do not appear to have resulted in any deliberate alteration of the notes that Mozart had written.

14. Mozart's Use of 10-Staff and 12-Staff Paper

1. Mozart's use of small-oblong-format paper in these years is examined in Chapter 12.

2. The transcription of Abel's symphony also has two systems of six staves.

3. See Walter Senn's observations in NMA I/1/1/1, pp. x–xi.

4. This autograph is today in the Mills College Library, Oakland, California.

5. Hanns Dennerlein, "Zur Problematik von Mozarts Kirchensonaten," *Mozart-Jahrbuch 1953* (Salzburg, 1954), pp. 95–111, esp. p. 103, n. 24; Plath, "Schriftchronologie," p. 153.

6. See Josef-Horst Lederer's remarks (1977) in NMA II/5/6, *Il sogno di Scipione*, Vorwort, pp. vii–ix.

7. Plath, "Schriftchronologie," pp. 136–137.

8. The watermark depicts a large Baden shield, the paper having been produced at Kandern in the margraviate of Baden. See Eugene K. Wolf and Jean K. Wolf, "A Newly Identified Complex of Manuscripts from Mannheim," *Journal of the American Musicological Society*, 27 (1974), 425.

9. This autograph is wrongly described in Köchel[6], p. 302, as being in *Klein-Querformat*, and as having ten staves, not twelve. Its first page is illustrated in NMA II/7/2, p. xxiv.

10. Mozart used 14-staff and 16-staff upright-format paper from the firm of Johannot at Annonay in several other works known to have been composed in Paris, including the "Paris" Symphony, K.297(300a), and the Piano Sonata in A Minor, K.310(300d).

11. In addition to oboes, horns, and the four strings, the Act II finale has seven solo voices. But it is only in a few measures that the singers have more than four different vocal lines, so that with a bit of ingenuity Mozart was able to fit all the parts onto ten staves.

12. See Ludwig Schiedermair, *W. A. Mozarts Handschrift in zeitlich geordneten Nachbildungen* (Leipzig, 1919), plate 22: reproduced in NMA V/15/1, p. xiv.

13. Although paper with any number of staves up to sixteen seems to have been readily obtainable in Vienna, Mozart's preference while living there in the last ten years of his life was almost exclusively for twelve staves. Only very exceptionally did he use paper with fourteen staves (K.469, cadenza to the *Schlusschor;* the songs K.472, 473, 474, 518), or with sixteen staves (K.441, "Das Bandel"; K.491, C-Minor Piano Concerto). Yet 16-staff paper was sometimes used by his pupil Thomas Attwood, and it was also the preference of Beethoven from the time of his arrival in Vienna in November 1792. The 10-staff paper in the autographs of the string quartets K.575 and 589 does not come into consideration here, since it was not machine-ruled but ruled twice with a 5-staff rastrum. It was probably acquired by Mozart in the course of his return journey from Berlin to Vienna at the end of May 1789: see Chapter 3 on the "Prussian" quartets.

14. For the dating of Köchel[6], Anh. A 12, see Chapter 6 on K.333(315c).

15. On the basis of the handwriting of this autograph, Plath has suggested a dating of "1782–84" (personal communication).

16. See NMA IX/27/2, Anhang Nos. 20 (K.153) and 13 (K.375h). The latter is there assigned the tentative date of "Wien, ca. 1782–83."

17. Bauer-Deutsch, III, No. 587, p. 103; Anderson, No. 397, p. 722.

18. Bauer-Deutsch, III, Nos. 728, 731, pp. 257, 259; Anderson, Nos. 481, 483, pp. 840, 842.

19. Georges de Saint-Foix, *Wolfgang Amédée Mozart: sa vie musicale et son œuvre,* III (Paris, 1936), 108, 92, and 110.

20. Plath, "Schriftchronologie," p. 171.

21. Ibid., p. 173.

22. See Chapter 6.

23. Cadenzas Nos. 15 and 17 of K.624(626a), 1. Teil, in the numbering of Köchel[6].

24. I am most grateful to the owner of the particella, Professor Otto Winkler, for enabling me to examine it in Munich.

25. Köchel[6] is not always a reliable guide to the number of staves in an autograph score. In addition to this error and the one mentioned in note 9, the Kyrie fragment K.166g (Anh. 19) has ten staves, not twelve; and the cadenza to the first movement of the B-flat Piano Concerto K.450—K.624(626a), 1. Teil, No. 43—has twelve staves, not ten.

26. Like the Mannheim paper referred to in note 8, this is paper from Kandern in Baden; it was made by the firm of Nicolaus Heusler. See Wolf and Wolf (1974), p. 427.

15. Notes on the Genesis of Mozart's "Ein musikalischer Spass," K.522

1. Bauer-Deutsch, I, 271 (No. 135, 30 July 1768); II, 296 (No. 429, Leopold, 23 February 1778), and 318 (No. 435, 7 March 1778).

2. From Moses Mendelssohn, *Phaedon oder über die Unsterblichkeit der Seele* (Berlin and Stettin, 1767). There was a copy in Mozart's *Nachlass:* see Eibl, VI, 351; and Wolfgang Hildesheimer, *Mozart* (Frankfurt am Main, 1977), pp. 20–23—English translation (New York, 1982), pp. 192–193.

3. See Christoph Wolff in NMA V/15/3, p. ix; and Neal Zaslaw in *The Musical Times,* 119 (1978), 68.

4. Heinz Wolfgang Hamaan, "Eine unbekannte Familien-Reminiszenz in Mozarts Serenade KV 522 ('Ein musikalischer Spass')," *Die Musikforschung,* 13 (1960), 180–182.

5. See Hans-Günter Klein, ed., *Wolfgang Amadeus Mozart: Autographe und Abschriften,* Staatsbibliothek Preussischer Kulturbesitz, Kataloge der Musikabteilung, herausgegeben von Rudolf Elvers, Erste Reihe: Handschriften, Band 6, *Katalog* (Berlin, 1982), pp. 86–87.

6. In the first-violin part the first movement is in brown ink. So is most of the following minuet; the end of the minuet, the trio, and the first ten measures of the slow movement (to the end of the second quarter note) are also in brown ink of a slightly yellower kind. The rest of the slow movement (from the trill in measure 10) is in a very gray or slate-colored ink.

7. NMA VII/18—*Divertimenti für 5–7 Streich- und Blasinstrumente* (1976), ed. Albert Dunning, p. xv.

8. London, British Library, Add. MS 58437, fols. 4–5, 13, 14 (= NMA X/30/1, pp. 5–8, 23–24, 25–26: probably August–September 1785). Attwood almost always used leaves of music paper with the cut edge (and the watermark) at the bottom; Mozart almost without exception wrote on such paper with the cut edge (and the watermark) at the top. The leaves among the Attwood papers in Add. MS 58437 that have the cut edge at the top are in practically every instance Mozart's own contributions: exercises prepared for Attwood to complete, or Mozart's own improved or corrected versions of passages in Attwood's compositions.

9. British Library, Add. MS 58437, fols. 120, 125 (= NMA X/30/1, pp. 223–224, 233–234).

10. For the watermark of K.525, see the Kritischer Bericht to NMA IV/12/6, p. f/15. For the rastrology, see the facsimile of the autograph (Kassel, 1955).

11. For the musical text, see NMA VII/18, Anhang 3, p. 266.

12. Franz Giegling, "Eine Skizze zum 'Musikalischen Spass' KV 522," *Mitteilungen der Internationalen Stiftung Mozarteum,* 8 (December 1959), 2–3; also in *Die Musikforschung,* 13 (1960), 179–180.

13. British Library, Add. MS 58437, fol. 85v (= NMA X/30/1, p. 163); the date should probably be *14* August 1786.

14. Daniel Heartz, "Thomas Attwood's Lessons in Composition with Mozart," *Proceedings of the Royal Musical Association,* 100 (1973–74), 181.

16. Mozart's D-Major Horn Concerto

1. The surviving autograph scores are located today as follows. K.412 (first movement and rondo draft): Kraków, Biblioteka Jagiellońska. K.417 (most of first movement, also the rondo, but none of the slow movement): *ibid.* K.447: London, British Library, Stefan Zweig Collection. K.495 (six leaves only, from the second and third movements): New York, Pierpont Morgan Library. K.370b, divided into small portions and dispersed as follows: Berlin, Deutsche Staatsbibliothek; Salzburg, Mozarteum; Paris, Bibliothèque Nationale; Salzburg, Museum Carolino Augusteum; Prague, Museum české hudby; and Seattle, Dr. Eric Offenbacher. K.371: New York, Pierpont Morgan Library. K.494a: Berlin, Deutsche Staatsbibliothek.

2. Since the music extends to the very end of the verso of a leaf, it is possible that some more of K.494a was written but has not survived.

3. The combination of the watermark, a common one, with a total staff-span of 186+ mm. is found elsewhere only in the autographs of works assignable to the early summer of 1781: the violin sonatas K.376(374d) and 377(374e), and the variations for violin and piano on "La Bergère Célimène," K.359(374a).

4. Georges de Saint-Foix, *Wolfgang Amédée Mozart: sa vie musicale et son œuvre*, IV (Paris, 1939), 386.

5. It is true that K.571 was entered by Mozart in his Verzeichnüss under the date of 21 February 1789. But that was the complete orchestral version; the string-trio versions of Mozart's dances were often composed a long time earlier.

6. For instance, paper with the same watermark and rastrology is found in the song "Das Veilchen," K.476, and in the two opening duettini of *Le nozze di Figaro*, K.492. But there are occasional examples from the year 1784 as well.

7. For a well-documented account of his life, see Karl Maria Pisarowitz, "Mozarts Schnorrer Leutgeb," *Mitteilungen der Internationalen Stiftung Mozarteum*, vol. 18 (1970), Heft 3/4, pp. 21–26.

8. In the London periodical *The Harmonicon*, 2 (1824), 41–42, there is an article consisting of extracts from a letter written from Frankfurt am Main by one "I.R.S.," describing a visit to Johann Anton André's collection of Mozart manuscripts at nearby Offenbach. "I. R. S." is no doubt Johann Reinhold Schultz, on whom see my article "J. R. Schultz and His Visit to Beethoven," *The Musical Times*, 113 (1972), 450–451. The article in *The Harmonicon* includes the following: "I saw a very curious MS., a concerto for the horn, with this droll superscription. 'Mozart has compassion on that silly fool, Leitgeber, and writes the fellow a concerto for the horn.' He has given this player, with whom he seems to have been on a very intimate footing, a great many other ludicrous epithets, which, however, do not bear translating. — The manuscript of this concerto has all the colours of the rainbow; and in some very difficult passages, written in blue ink, he has added queries like these: 'What do you say to that, Master Leitgeber?' As it is not in score, we could not judge the merit of the composition."

It would seem that Schultz, whose descriptions are not necessarily very accurate, was shown some autograph material for both K.417 and K.495 which he conflated in his letter. None of the leaves of K.495 extant today has the "very difficult passages" in blue ink with the query, "What do you say to that, Master Leitgeb(er)?"

9. This evidently escaped the attention of Saint-Foix, who suggested (IV, 386) that K.447 was written for the horn player Giovanni Punto.

10. Otto Jahn, *W. A. Mozart*, III (Leipzig, 1858), 293 and 294, n. 44; Köchel¹, pp. 333, 407–408.

11. See the manuscript copy made for Otto Jahn of J. A. André's thematic catalogue of Mozart's works composed before February 1784: London, British Library, Add. MS 32412, fol. 46v. Köchel¹ also states (p. 333) that the date of " 1782" added to the autograph is in André's hand.

12. Jahn, III, 294, n. 44. He may have taken the date of 1791 from Aloys Fuchs's authentication; see below, note 17.

13. Köchel¹, pp. 407–408.

14. See Emanuel Winternitz, "Gnagflow Trazom: An Essay on Mozart's Script, Pastimes, and Nonsense Letters," *Journal of the American Musicological Society,* 11 (1958), 200–216.

15. Dmitri Kolbin, "Ulybki Motsarta," *Sovetskaia muzyka,* February 1966, pp. 35–40; idem, "Ein wiedergefundenes Mozart-Autograph," *Mozart-Jahrbuch 1967* (Salzburg, 1968), pp. 193–204.

16. Wolfgang Plath, "Zur Echtheitsfrage bei Mozart," *Mozart-Jahrbuch 1971/72* (Salzburg, 1972), pp. 19–36, esp. pp. 26–27.

17. "Rondo aus D ♯ / (fürs obligate Waldhorn) / mit / Begleitung des Orchesters / componirt / für Herrn Leutgeb von / Wolfgang Amade Mozart / Original=Handschriftliche Partitur / des Componisten / (d.̩º 6. April 1791.)"

18. Hans Pizka, *Das Horn bei Mozart* (Kirchheim bei München, 1980).

19. See, for example, Friedrich Blume, "The Concertos: (1) Their Sources," in H. C. Robbins Landon and Donald Mitchell, eds., *The Mozart Companion* (London, 1956), p. 206.

20. This paper is the New Type used by Mozart in the autograph of *Le nozze di Figaro,* and discussed in Chapter 10.

21. The watermark of this paper-type is depicted in Figure 13.1b (see Chapter 13).

22. Although Plath excluded Süssmayr from consideration in 1973, he later changed his opinion: see his short article "Noch ein Requiem-Brief," *Acta Mozartiana,* 28, No. 4 (November 1981), 96–101, esp. n. 20. References to my own conclusions will be found in *The New Grove Dictionary of Music and Musicians,* ed. Stanley Sadie (London, 1980), XII, 707, and in somewhat greater detail in the *Bericht über die Mitarbeitertagung in Kassel, 29.-30. Mai 1981* (n.p.: Neue Mozart-Ausgabe, 1984), p. 54.

23. London, British Library, Add. MS 32181, fols. 115–126 and 127–130.

24. See also Figure 16.5, an *Ave verum corpus* apparently written by Süssmayr at Baden on 9 June 1792, perhaps in memory of the motet that Mozart had composed there almost exactly a year earlier (K.618, "Baaden, li 17 di giunnio 1791").

25. Except, that is, for the parts for oboes and bassoons, which Mozart would no doubt have added on a separate leaf if he had completed the movement.

26. See P. Engelbert Grau, "Ein bislang übersehener Instrumentalwitz von W. A. Mozart," *Acta Mozartiana,* 8, No. 1 (1961), 8–10.

27. Reginald Morley-Pegge, "Leutgeb, Joseph," *The New Grove,* X, 699.

28. Pisarowitz, p. 26. Further research might well throw light on Leutgeb's later years, though it seems probable that he shared his name with at least one other person. For instance, a Viennese street directory of 1795 (Johann Karl Schuender, *Verzeichniss der in der k.k. Haupt- und Residenz-Stadt Wien befindlichen numerirten Häuser, derselben wahrhaften Eigenthümer und Schilder*), lists a "Joseph Leutgeb" not only at Alt-Lerchenfelder No. 32, the

house that the horn player bought in February 1779 and where he died thirty-two years later, but also at Nos. 383 and 393 in the Wieden suburb. And a trade directory of 1806 (*Vollständiges Auskunftsbuch oder einzig richtiger Wegweiser in der kaiserl. auch kaiserl. königl. Haupt- und Residenz-Stadt Wien*) identifies the Joseph Leutgeb at Wieden No. 383 as a *Landkutscher*. In view of the extent of Leutgeb's indebtedness at his death in 1811, it seems unlikely that the horn player could have owned these houses in the Wieden.

Writing to Johann Anton André on 31 May 1800, Constanze Mozart describes Leutgeb as living in the outermost suburb ("in der äussersten Vorstadt"). And in the same letter she mentions that he has promised to give her a manuscript copy of the horn rondo with the comic superscription ("Rondo fürs horn mit scherzhafter Ueberschrift"); this is likely to have been a copy either of Mozart's fragment or of Süssmayr's completion of the D-major rondo. (See Bauer-Deutsch, IV, pp. 356 and 357.)

17. The Rondo for Piano and Orchestra, K.386

1. For the contract, see Bauer-Deutsch, IV, pp. 281–285 (= No. 1262).

2. Published with a title page stating that it was "Rondo (Posthumous) by W. A. Mozart, Arranged from the Original Score (in the Authors own hand writing) by The Editor," and appearing as No. 14 of "Chefs D'Oeuvre de Mozart, A New & Correct Edition of the Piano Forte Works (with & without acc.ᵗˢ) of this Celebrated Composer, Edited by Cipriani Potter . . . London, Published by Coventry & Hollier, 71, Dean Street, Soho."

3. This was a thematic catalogue of Mozart's manuscripts dating from the years 1764 to 1784, compiled by Johann Anton André and arranged in what was thought to be their chronological order. It was intended to complement Mozart's own thematic catalogue of his works from 9 February 1784 to 15 November 1791 (his Verzeichnüss), of which André had published a transcription earlier. The original of André's manuscript catalogue has not survived, but a transcription of it made for Otto Jahn is in the British Library, Add. MS 32412, fols. 2–53. The entry relating to K.386 is on fols. 9v and 10r.

4. *Rondo für Klavier und Orchester, K.V. 386*, Rekonstruirt und herausgeben von Alfred Einstein (Vienna: Universal-Edition, 1936).

5. *Konzert-Rondo, A-Dur, KV 386*, Rekonstruirt und herausgegeben von Paul Badura-Skoda und Charles Mackerras (Mainz: Schott, 1962).

6. NMA V/15/8, pp. 173–187.

7. Mozart's spelling of this word not only in the French way but with an "x" at the end is found within several of his autographs: e.g., K.169, K.269(261a), K.365(316a), K.374, K.498, and K.575. In K.298 he even wrote "Rondieaoux."

8. The identity of this person, referred to by Wolfgang Plath and others working on Mozart's manuscripts today as the "graue Schreiber," has not yet been determined.

9. Bauer-Deutsch, IV, p. 322 (= No. 1285, lines 131–132).

10. Bauer-Deutsch, IV, p. 357 (= No. 1299, lines 177–180).

11. The latter passage was identified as a reference to K.386 by C. B. Oldman in the extracts from Constanze Mozart's letters to J . A. Andrè that he contributed to Emily Anderson, ed., *The Letters of Mozart and His Family* (London, 1938), III, 1481, n. 3.

12. In *Festschrift Otto Erich Deutsch zum 80. Geburtstag am 5. September 1963*, herausgegeben von Walter Gerstenberg, Jan LaRue, und Wolfgang Rehm (Kassel, 1963): Cecil B. Oldman, "Cipriani Potter's Edition of Mozart's Pianoforte Works," pp. 120–127, and Wolfgang Rehm, "Miscellanea Mozartiana II: 1. 'A Catalogue of Musical Manuscripts,'" pp. 140–151.

13. Nos. 14, 15, 16, and 17 of Potter's Edition were announced by Coventry & Hollier in *The Musical World* on 8 February 1838.

14. A note by Sterndale Bennett attached to the autograph's first leaf begins: "The first page of a <u>Rondeau</u> (in Score) <u>in Mozarts own handwriting,</u> recently published by Coventry & Hollier and purchased of Andrè in Offenbach, near Frankfurt . . ."

15. *Stray Notes on Mozart and His Music*. Privately printed by R. & R. Clark, Ltd., Edinburgh, 1910. The preface is signed with the initials "W.W.F." The quotation is from p. 8.

16. The date of this incident is likely to have been in the early 1870s; by that time it would appear that Sterndale Bennett had given away everything apart from these two fragments.

17. The leaves were not foliated by Mozart; nor apparently did he even number the gatherings, as he did in the autograph of K.414 (see below).

18. One or two features in Potter's ending puzzled those who edited the work, but they were taken to be merely defects in his piano reduction. Einstein, for instance, noted that m. 238 appeared to be a condensed version of mm. 123–124, so he expanded it to form two measures. And Badura-Skoda and Mackerras expressed some doubts about the piano version of mm. 230–235 and 247–249.

19. Measure 171 in the autograph is not free from problems. Mozart first wrote "col B" on the violoncello staff, but then replaced it by four notes similar to those of the first violin. But instead of writing a tenor clef before them, which would make them an octave below the first violin's notes, he wrote a viola clef, making them only a sixth below. It seems clear that this was merely a slip of his pen.

20. "Die Instrumentierung bedarf nur noch einige Ergänzungen."

21. Alfred Einstein, *Mozart: His Character, His Work* (New York, 1945), p. 299. Presumably he was referring to the resemblances between m. 8 of

K.386 and m. 8 of K.414, and between mm. 55–56 of K.386 and mm. 58–59 (or 80–81) of K.414.

22. Type A, 188.5–189 mm.; Type B, 186.5 mm.; Type C, 188.5–189.5 mm.; Type D, 185.5–186 mm.; and Type E, 182.5–183 mm.

23. Bauer-Deutsch, III, pp. 245–246 (= No. 715, lines 8–13).

24. For a discussion of the date of these leaves, see above, p. 153.

25. The discarded bifolium was later used by Mozart for drafting a passage for string quartet in E major, and for writing out part of a string-quartet version (in C minor) of J. S. Bach's fugue in B-flat minor from Book II of Das Wohltemperirte Clavier. It was found by Professor Gerhard Croll among the Archduke Rudolph's papers at Kroměříž (Kremsier): Státní Zámek, A 4526. See Croll, "Eine neuentdeckte Bach-Fuge für Streichquartett von Mozart," Österreichische Musikzeitschrift (Sonderheft: October 1966), pp. 12–18.

26. The recto of the added leaf had already been used by Mozart for writing out a "solution" of a canon from Giovanni Battista Martini's Storia della musica, I, 25.

27. C. M. Girdlestone, Mozart et ses Concertos pour Piano (Paris, 1939), I, 156; Mozart's Piano Concertos (London, 1948), p. 144.

18. Some Problems in the Text of Le nozze di Figaro: Did Mozart Have a Hand in Them?

1. An up-to-date bibliography will be found in Rudolph Angermüller, Figaro (Munich, 1986), pp. 140–153. Some of the publications most relevant to the matters that I shall be discussing here are the following: Siegfried Anheisser, "Die unbekannte Urfassung von Mozarts Figaro," Zeitschrift für Musikwissenschaft, 15 (1933), 301–317; Ludwig Finscher, ed., Le nozze di Figaro, NMA II/5/16, 2 parts (Kassel, 1973), with the Vorwort in the first part; Karl-Heinz Köhler, "Mozarts Kompositionsweise—Beobachtungen am Figaro-Autograph," Mozart-Jahrbuch 1967 (Salzburg, 1968), pp. 31–45; Karl-Heinz Köhler, "Figaro-Miscellen: einige dramaturgische Mitteilungen zur Quellensituation," Mozart-Jahrbuch 1968/70 (Salzburg, 1970), pp. 119–131; Charles Mackerras, "What Mozart Really Meant," Opera, 16 (1965), 240–246; Michael and Christopher Raeburn, "Mozart Manuscripts in Florence," Music & Letters, 40 (1959), 334–340; Stefan Strasser, "Susanna und die Gräfin," Zeitschrift für Musikwissenschaft, 10 (1928), 208–216. See also Chapter 10 above.

2. Some aspects of this Abschrift are examined by Strasser, by Anheisser, and by Köhler (1970).

3. Dénes Bartha and László Somfai, Haydn als Opernkapellmeister (Budapest and Mainz, 1960), pp. 366–368, and p. 157 (the bill).

4. This Abschrift was apparently first discovered by Edward J. Dent; it is discussed in much detail by Anheisser.

5. A few unusual features of this score are described by Michael and Christopher Raeburn.

6. See Hans-Günter Klein, ed., *Wolfgang Amadeus Mozart: Autographe und Abschriften,* Staatsbibliothek Preussischer Kulturbesitz, Kataloge der Musikabteilung, herausgegeben von Rudolf Elvers, Erste Reihe: Handschriften, Band 6, *Katalog* (Berlin, 1982), pp. 172–173.

7. Bauer-Deutsch, IV, No. 1022; Anderson, No. 544.

8. The word turns up occasionally in the relations between Beethoven and his copyists in the 1820s. But at one time Beethoven apparently did not know its meaning. In a note of about June 1823 to Anton Schindler he wrote: "Here are the copies of the Gloria [of the *Missa Solemnis*]. The ternions are quite new instruments to me." See Emily Anderson, *The Letters of Beethoven* (London, 1961), vol. III, No. 1195.

9. New York Public Library (Library of the Performing Arts), Drexel 5933 and 5934; Vienna, Nationalbibliothek, Mus. Hs. 16566.

10. In the autograph this has fifty-four measures, but in some *Abschriften* and editions, including the 1879 one in the AMA, it has been cut to forty-four measures. The cuts were even marked in the autograph by someone. (The AMA, which included the fifty-four-measure version in an Anhang, claimed that the cuts were probably made by Mozart.)

11. Köhler (1970), pp. 126–131.

12. *Ibid.,* pp. 120, 126; Strasser, pp. 211–212.

13. It is also to be found among the old leaves (from the 1780s) in Act II of the Vienna Nationalbibliothek's *Abschrift,* O.A. 295.

14. This is a rare paper-type, found almost nowhere else except in the last number of Act I, "Non più andrai," and in the G-Minor Piano Quartet, K.478, the autograph of which is dated "li 16 d'Ottobre 1785."

15. This is the New Type described in Chapter 10.

16. These are reproduced in transcriptions in NMA II/5/16, Part II, pp. 641 and 628.

17. Fols. 1–4 = pp. 167–174, four leaves from the same sheet; and fols. 9–12 = pp. 219–226, four leaves from the same sheet. Fol. 5 = pp. 183–184, and fols. 6–7 = pp. 197–200; these three are from the same sheet, which suggests that the missing fol. 8 was the missing pp. 217–218, the fourth leaf of the sheet, with a watermark depicting the upper half of the letters PS.

18. See, for instance, Otto Jahn, *W. A. Mozart,* IV (Leipzig, 1859), 229, n. 30; Strasser, pp. 208–216; Anheisser, pp. 305–310; Mackerras, pp. 241–243; and Köhler (1970), pp. 123–125. There are several other places in which this problem is examined.

19. The Donaueschingen *Abschrift,* discussed below.

20. The autograph's version of the terzetto appears to have been first printed by Rudolf Gerber in his Eulenburg edition of the 1920s; today this version is readily accessible in Ludwig Finscher's NMA edition of 1973.

21. The suggestion has been made that the role of the Countess was origi-

nally intended for Nancy Storace, and that Mozart started to write her part with that in mind.

22. In the version of mm. 97–146 that appears to follow the autograph, there are only a couple of passages that deviate strikingly from it: these are mm. 104–109 and 133–140. Yet there are lots of smaller divergences, several of which correspond to the conventional version.

23. In the conventional version the Countess's only note in m. 69 is d'', not f''. In m. 102 Susanna's last note is an eighth note (preceded by an eighth-note rest), not a quarter note; and in m. 111 she begins not with a quarter-note g'' followed by a quarter-note c'', but with a dotted eighth-note g'' followed by a sixteenth-note c'' and a quarter-note c''. Several further deviations of this kind from the autograph's text (are they "refinements" of it?) are to be found in almost every *Abschrift*.

24. Alfred Einstein, "Eine unbekannte Arie der Marcelline," *Zeitschrift für Musikwissenschaft*, 13 (1931), 200–205.

25. Berlin, Staatsbibliothek Preussischer Kulturbesitz, Mus. ms. 15150/14.

26. See Georg Goerlipp, "Die Fürstenbergische Papiermühle an der Gauchach bei Döggingen, 1751–1802," in *Fürstenberger Waldbote* (1960), No. 6, pp. 14–20, published by the F. F. Forstdirektion, Donaueschingen. The curious version of the terzetto, No. 14, in the Donaueschingen *Abschrift* has just been mentioned; surprisingly enough, the 1787 performance parts for Susanna and the Countess do not follow it, but have instead the conventional version of this number, giving Susanna most of the upper notes. But in the Act II finale they give the Countess the higher part, as in that *Abschrift*.

27. *Memorie di Lorenzo Da Ponte, da Ceneda*, 2nd ed., vol. I, part II (New York, 1829), pp. 81–84; Eng. trans. by Elizabeth Abbott, *Memoirs of Lorenzo Da Ponte* (New York, 1967), pp. 159–161; see also Sheila Hodges, *Lorenzo Da Ponte: The Life and Times of Mozart's Librettist* (London, 1985), pp. 67–68.

28. Da Ponte says "the second act": this is obviously a slip on his part.

29. Budapest, Országos Széchényi Könyvtár, Ms. mus. OK-11/b-5.

30. Bartha and Somfai, p. 367.

31. Bauer-Deutsch, IV, No. 1110; Anderson, No. 570.

32. NMA, II/5/16, Part II, p. 165.

33. Not only are both these leaves of the same paper-type, with the same TS, but their watermark quadrants and mold are the right ones for a bifolium. It is true that no page numbers "83" and "84" are visible today on the Mozarteum leaf—but they could well have been erased.

34. Many scores were evidently made by teams of copyists, no doubt employed by a copying house; each copyist would write out several of the ternions from which a score was made up. Reference has often been made to the productions from the copying houses of Laurent Lausch and of Wenzel Sukowaty, both in Vienna; they may even have employed some of the same copyists.

Acknowledgments

The original versions of the essays and lectures in this volume were presented as follows:

Chapter 1. "New Dating Methods: Watermarks and Paper-Studies," a talk given at Kassel on 30 May 1981, and subsequently printed in the NMA's *Bericht über die Mitarbeitertagung in Kassel, 29.–30. Mai 1981* (1984).

Chapter 2. "Redating Mozart: Some Stylistic and Biographical Implications," a talk given at the American Musicological Society meeting at Louisville on 28 October 1983.

Chapter 3. "New light on Mozart's 'Prussian' Quartets," *The Musical Times,* 116 (1975), 126–130.

Chapter 4. "*La clemenza di Tito* and its chronology," *The Musical Times,* 156 (1975), 221–225, 227.

Chapter 5. "A Reconstruction of Nannerl Mozart's Music Book (Notenbuch)," *Music & Letters,* 60 (1979), 389–400.

Chapter 6. "The Date of Mozart's Piano Sonata in B flat, KV 333/315c: the 'Linz' Sonata?" in *Musik—Edition—Interpretation: Gedenkschrift Günter Henle,* ed. M. Bente (Munich: G. Henle Verlag, 1980), pp. 447–454.

Chapter 7. "Mozart's 'Haydn' Quartets: The Contribution of Paper-Studies," in *The String Quartets of Haydn, Mozart, and Beethoven: Studies of the Autograph Manuscripts,* Isham Library Papers III, ed. Christoph Wolff (Cambridge, Mass., 1980), pp. 179–190.

Chapter 8. "The Origins of Mozart's 'Hunt' Quartet, K.458," in *Music and Bibliography: Essays in Honour of Alec Hyatt King,* ed. Oliver Neighbour (London, 1980), pp. 132–148.

Chapter 9. "The Two Slow Movements of Mozart's 'Paris' Symphony K.297," *The Musical Times*, 122 (1981), 17–21.

Chapter 10. "*Le nozze di Figaro:* Lessons from the autograph score," *The Musical Times*, 122 (1981), 456–461.

Chapter 11. "The Mozart Fragments in the Mozarteum, Salzburg: A Preliminary Study of Their Chronology and Their Significance," *Journal of the American Musicological Society*, 34 (1981), 471–510.

Chapter 12. "The Dates of Mozart's Missa brevis KV 258 and Missa longa KV 262(246a): An Investigation into his 'Klein-Querformat' Papers," in *Bachiana et alia musicologica: Festschrift Alfred Dürr zum 65. Geburtstag*, ed. Wolfgang Rehm (Kassel: Bärenreiter-Verlag, 1983), pp. 328–339.

Chapter 13. "Notes on the Composition of Mozart's *Così fan tutte*," *Journal of the American Musicological Society*, 37 (1984), 356–401.

Chapter 14. "Mozart's Use of 10-Stave and 12-Stave Paper," in *Festschrift Albi Rosenthal*, ed. Rudolf Elvers (Tutzing: Hans Schneider Verlag, 1984), pp. 277–289.

Chapter 15. "Notes on the Genesis of Mozart's 'Ein musikalischer Spass,' KV 522," in *Festschrift Rudolf Elvers zum 65. Geburtstag*, ed. Ernst Herttrich and Hans Schneider (Tutzing: Hans Schneider Verlag, 1985), pp. 505–518.

Chapter 16. "Mozart's D-Major Horn Concerto: Questions of Date and of Authenticity," in *Studies in Musical Sources and Style: Essays in Honor of Jan LaRue*, ed. Edward H. Roesner and Eugene K. Wolf (Madison, Wisconsin: A-R Editions, 1987).

Chapter 17. This essay is printed here for the first time.

Chapter 18. "Some Problems in the Text of *Le nozze di Figaro:* Did Mozart Have a Hand in Them?" *Journal of the Royal Musical Association*, 112 (1987), 99–131.

For their kindness in granting permission to reproduce the illustrations of manuscripts or printed material within their collections, I wish to express my thanks to a number of institutions and individuals who have supplied me with photographs. I am grateful to the courtesy of the following:

The Newberry Library, Chicago (Figure 2.2)

The Library of Congress, Washington, D.C.: Music Division (Figures 10.1, 18.1a, 18.9)

Biblioteca Estense (Autografoteca Campori), Modena (Figure 10.2)

Internationale Stiftung Mozarteum, Salzburg (Figure 11.1)

Biblioteka Jagiellońska, Kraków (Figures 11.2–4, 13.2, 13.4–5, 14.1, 16.6, 17.1, 17.5, 18.17)

Österreichische Nationalbibliothek, Vienna: Musiksammlung (Figures 13.3, 13.10–15, 18.2)

Deutsche Staatsbibliothek, Berlin/DDR: Musikabteilung (Figures 13.7–9, 18.6)

Institute for Theater, Music, and Cinematography, Leningrad (Figures 16.3–4)

The British Library, London (Figures 16.1–2, 17.6–11, 18.3–4, 18.15–16)

Országos Széchényi Könyvtár, Budapest: Music Division (Figures 16.5, 18.7–8, 18.10)

Fürstlich Fürstenbergische Hofbibliothek, Donaueschingen (Figure 18.1c)

Conservatorio di Musica "Luigi Cherubini," Florence (Figures 18.11–14)

Museum české hudby, Prague (Figure 18.1b)

Collection of William H. Scheide, Princeton, N.J. (Figure 2.1)

Private collection, New York (Figure 18.5)

General Index

Index of Archival Institutions
and Their Holdings

Page numbers in italics indicate illustrations.

Index of Mozart's Compositions

Page numbers in italics indicate illustrations.

Köchel[6] Anhang A (copies of other composers' music made by the Mozarts)

Köchel⁶ Anhang C (dubious and incorrectly ascribed compositions)